Treasure of Ambedkar Series 07

# HISTORY OF INDIAN CURRENCY AND BANKING

Treasure of Ambedkar Series 07

# HISTORY OF INDIAN CURRENCY AND BANKING

Dr B.R. Ambedkar

KALPAZ

Treasure of Ambedkar Series 07

**HISTORY OF INDIAN CURRENCY AND BANKING**

ISBN: 978-93-5128-266-2

First Published 1947
Reprint **2017**, in India by
Kalpaz Publications
C-30, Satyawati Nagar,
Delhi – 110052
E-mail: kalpaz@hotmail.com
Ph.: 9212142040

*Printed at:* G. Print Process, Delhi

# CONTENTS

## PREFACE TO THE SECOND IMPRESSION

THE PROBLEM OF THE RUPEE was first published in 1923. Ever since its publication it has had a great demand : so great that within a year or two the book went out of print. The demand for the book has continued, but unfortunately I could not bring out a second edition of the book for the reason that my change-over from economics to law and politics left me no time to undertake such a task. I have, therefore, devised another plan: it is to bring out an up-to-date edition of the History of Indian Currency and Banking in two volumes, of which *The Problem of the Rupee* forms volume one. Volume two will contain the History of Indian Currency and Banking from 1923 onwards. What is therefore issued to the public now is a mere reprint of *The Problem of the Rupee* under a different name. I am glad to say that some of my friends who are engaged in the field of teaching economics have assured me that nothing has been said or written since 1923 in the field of Indian Currency which calls for any alteration in the text of *The Problem of the Rupee* as it stood in 1923. I hope this reprint will satisfy the public partially if not wholly. I can give them an assurance that they will not have to wait long for volume two. I am determined to bring it out with the least possible delay.

B. R. AMBEDKAR.

Rajagraha,
Bombay,
7-5-1947.

# PREFACE TO THE FIRST EDITION

In the following pages I have attempted an exposition of the events leading to the establishment of the exchange standard and an examination of its theoretical basis.

In endeavouring to treat the historical side of the matter, I have carefully avoided repeating what has already been said by others. For instance, in treating of the actual working of the exchange standard, I have contented myself with a general treatment just sufficiently detailed to enable the reader to follow the criticism I have offered. If more details are desired they are given in all their amplitude in other treatises. To have reproduced them would have been a work of supererogation; besides it would have only obscured the general trend of my argument. But in other respects, I have been obliged to take a wider historical sweep than has been done by other writers. The existing treatises on Indian currency do not give any idea, at least an adequate idea, of the circumstances which led to the reforms of 1893. I think that a treatment of the early history is quite essential to furnish the reader with a perspective in order to enable him to judge for himself the issues involved in the currency crisis and also of the solutions offered. In view of this, I have gone into that most neglected period of Indian currency extending from 1800 to 1893. Not only have other writers begun abruptly the story of the exchange standard, but they have popularized the notion that the exchange standard is the standard originally contemplated by the Government of India. I find that this is a gross error. Indeed, the most interesting point about Indian currency is the way in which the gold standard came to be transformed into a gold exchange standard. Some old, but by now forgotten, facts had therefore, to be recounted to expose this error.

On the theoretical side, there is no book but that of Professor Keynes which makes any attempt to examine its scientific basis. But the conclusions he has arrived at are in sharp conflict with those of mine. Our differences extend to almost every proposition he has advanced in favour of the exchange standard. This difference proceeds from the fundamental fact, which seems to be quite overlooked by Professor Keynes, that nothing will stabilize the rupee unless we stabilize its general purchasing power. That the exchange standard does not do. That standard concerns itself only with symptoms and does not go to the disease : indeed, on my showing, if anything, it aggravates the disease.

When I come to the remedy, I again find myself in conflict with the majority of those who like myself are opposed to the exchange standard. It is said that the best way to stabilize the rupee is to provide for effective convertibility into gold. I do not deny that this is one way of doing it. But, I think, a far better way would be to have an inconvertible rupee with a fixed limit of issue. Indeed, if I had any say in the matter, I would propose that the Government of India should melt the rupees, sell them as bullion and use the proceeds for revenue purposes and fill the void by an inconvertible paper. But that may be too radical a proposal, and I do not therefore press for it, although I regard it as essentially sound. In any case, the vital point is to close the Mints, not merely to the public, as they have been, but to the Government as well. Once that is done, I venture to say that the Indian currency, based on gold as legal tender with a rupee currency fixed in issue, will conform to the principles embodied in the English currency system.

It will be noticed that I do not propose to go back to the recommendations of the Fowler Committee. All those, who have regretted the transformation of the Indian currency from a gold standard to a gold exchange standard, have held that everything would have been all right if the Government had carried out *in toto* the recommendations of that Committee. I do not share that view. On the other hand, I find that the Indian currency underwent that transformation *because* the Government carried out those recommendations. While some people regard that Report as classical for its wisdom, I regard it as classical for its nonsense. For I find that it was this Committee which, while recommending a gold standard, also recommended and thereby perpetuated the folly of the Herschell Committee, that Government should coin rupees on its own account according to that most naive of currency principles, the requirements of the public, without realizing that the latter recommendation was destructive of the former. Indeed, as I argue, the principles of the Fowler Committee must be given up, if we are to place the Indian currency on a stable basis.

I am conscious of the somewhat lengthy discussions on currency principles into which I have entered in treating the subject. My justification of this procedure is twofold. First of all, as I have differed so widely from other writers on Indian currency, I have deemed it necessary to substantiate my view-point, even at the cost of being charged with over-elaboration. But it is my second justification, which affords me a greater excuse. It consists in the fact that I have written primarily for the benefit of the Indian public, and as their grasp of currency principles does not seem to be as good as one would wish it to be, an over-statement, it will be agreed, is better than an under-statement of the argument on which I have based my conclusions.

Up to 1913, the Gold Exchange Standard was not the avowed goal of the Government of India in the matter of Indian Currency, and although the Chamberlain Commission appointed in that year had reported in favour of its continuance, the Government of India had promised not to carry its recommendations into practice till the war was over and an opportunity had been given to the public to criticize them. When, however, the Exchange Standard was shaken to its foundations during the late war, the Government of India went back on its word and restricted, notwithstanding repeated protests, the terms of reference to the Smith Committee to recommending such measures as were calculated to ensure the stability of the Exchange Standard, as though that standard had been accepted as the last word in the matter of Indian Currency. Now that the measures of the Smith Committee have not ensured the stability of the Exchange Standard, it is given to understand that the Government, as well as the public, desire to place the Indian Currency System on a sounder footing. My object in publishing this study at this juncture is to suggest a basis for the consummation of this purpose.

I cannot conclude this preface without acknowledging my deep sense of gratitude to my teacher, Prof. Edwin Cannan, of the University of London (School of Economics). His sympathy towards me and his keen interest in my undertaking have placed me under obligations which I can never repay. I feel happy to be able to say that this work has undergone close supervision at his hands, and although he is in no way responsible for the views I have expressed, I can say that his severe examination of my theoretic discussions has saved me from many an error. To Professor Wadia, of Wilson College, I am thankful for cheerfully undertaking the dry task of correcting the proofs.

## FOREWORD

### By Professor Edwin Cannan

I am glad that Mr. Ambedkar has given me the opportunity of saying a few words about his book.

As he is aware, I disagree with a good deal of his criticism. In 1893, I was one of the few economists, who believed that the rupee could be kept at a fixed ratio with gold by the method then proposed, and I did not fall away from the faith when some years elapsed without the desired fruit appearing (see *Economic Review*, July 1898, pp. 400—403). I do not share Mr. Ambedkar's hostility to the system, nor accept most of his arguments against it and its advocates. But he hits some nails very squarely on the head, and even when I have thought him quite wrong, I have found a stimulating freshness in his views and reasons. An old teacher like myself learns to tolerate the vagaries of originality, even when they resist " severe examination " such as that of which Mr. Ambedkar speaks.

In his practical conclusion, I am inclined to think, he is right. The single advantage, offered to a country by the adoption of the gold-exchange system instead of the simple gold standard, is that it is cheaper, in the sense of requiring a little less value in the shape of metallic currency than the gold standard. But all that can be saved in this way is a trifling amount, almost infinitesimal, beside the advantage of having a currency more difficult for administrators and legislators to tamper with. The recent experience both of belligerents and neutrals certainly shows that the simple gold standard, as we understood it before the war, is not fool-proof, but it is far nearer being fool-proof and knave-proof than the gold-exchange standard. The percentage of administrators and legislators who understand the gold standard is painfully small, but it is and is likely to remain ten or twenty times as great as the percentage which understands the gold-exchange system. The possibility of a gold-exchange system being perverted to suit some corrupt purpose is very considerably greater than the possibility of the simple gold standard being so perverted.

The plan for the adoption of which Mr. Ambedkar pleads, namely that all further enlargement of the rupee issue should be permanently prohibited, and that the mints should be open at a fixed price to importers or other sellers of gold, so that in course of time India would have, in addition to the fixed stock of rupees, a currency of meltable and exportable gold coins, follows European precedents. In eighteenth-century England the gold standard introduced itself because the legislature allowed the ratio to remain unfavourable to the coinage of silver: in nineteenth-century France and other countries it came in because the legislatures definitely closed the mints to silver, when the ratio was favourable to the coinage of silver. The continuance of a mass of full legal tender silver coins beside the gold would be nothing novel in principle, as the same thing, though on a somewhat smaller scale, took place in France, Germany, and the United States.

It is alleged sometimes that India does not want gold coins. I feel considerable difficulty in believing that gold coins of suitable size would not be convenient in a country with the climate and other circumstances of India. The allegation is suspiciously like the old allegation that the "Englishman prefers gold coins to paper," which had no other foundation than the fact that the law prohibited the issue of notes for less than £5 in England and Wales, while in Scotland, Ireland, and almost all other English-speaking countries, notes for £1 or less were allowed and circulated freely. It seems much more likely that silver owes its position in India to the decision, which the Company made before the system of standard gold and token silver was accidentally evolved in 1816 in England, and long before it was understood, and that the position has been maintained, not because Indians dislike gold, but because Europeans like it so well that they cannot bear to part with any of it.

This reluctance to allow gold to go to the East is not only despicable from an ethical point of view. It is also contrary to the economic interest not only of the world at large, but even of the countries, which had a gold standard before the war and have it still or expect soon to restore it. In the immediate future, gold is not a commodity, the use of which it is desirable for these countries either to restrict or to economize. From the closing years of last century it has been produced in quantities much too large to enable it to retain its purchasing power and thus be a stable standard of value, unless it can constantly be finding existing holders willing to hold larger stocks, or fresh holders to hold new stocks of it. Before the war, the accumulation of hoards by various central banks in Europe took off a large part of the new supplies and prevented the actual rise of general prices being anything like what it would otherwise have been, though it was serious enough. Since the war, the Federal Reserve Board, supported by all Americans who do not wish to see a rise of prices, has taken on the new "White Man's Burden" of absorbing the products of the gold mines, but just as the United States failed to keep up the value of silver by purchasing it, so she will eventually fail to keep up the value of gold. In spite of the opinion of some high authorities, it is not at all likely that a renewed demand for gold reserves by the central banks of Europe will come to her assistance. Experience must gradually be teaching even the densest of financiers that the value of paper currencies is not kept up by stories of "cover" or "backing" locked up in cellars, but by due limitation of the supply of the paper. With proper limitation, enforced by absolute convertibility into gold coin which may be freely melted or exported, it has been proved by theory and experience that small holdings of gold are perfectly sufficient to meet all internal and international demands. There is really more chance of a great demand from individuals than from the banks. It is conceivable that the people of some of the countries, which have reduced their paper currency to a laughing stock, may refuse all paper and insist on having gold coins. But it seems more probable that they will be pleased enough to get better paper than they have recently been accustomed to, and will not ask for hard coin with sufficient insistence to get it. On the whole, it seems fairly certain that the demand of Europe and European-colonized lands for gold will be less rather than greater than before the war, and that it will increase very slowly or not at all.

Thus, on the whole, there is reason to fear a fall in the value of gold and a rise of general prices rather than the contrary.

*One obvious remedy would be to restrict the production of* gold by international agreement, thus conserving the world's resources in mineral for future generations. Another is to set up an international commission to issue an international paper currency so regulated in amount as to preserve an approximately stable value. Excellent suggestions for the professor's classroom, but not, at present at any rate nor probably for some considerable period of time, practical politics.

A much more practical way out of the difficulty is to be found in the introduction of gold currency into the East. If the East will take a large part of the production of gold in the coming years, it will tide us over the period which must elapse before the most prolific of the existing sources are worked out. After that we may be able to carry on without change or we may have reached the possibility of some better arrangement.

This argument will not appeal to those who can think of nothing but the extra profits which can be acquired during a rise of prices, but I hope it will to those who have some feeling for the great majority of the population, who suffer from these extra and wholly unearned profits being extracted from them. Stability is best in the long run for the community.

EDWIN CANNAN.

# CHAPTER I

## FROM A DOUBLE STANDARD TO A SILVER STANDARD.

Trade is an important apparatus in a society, based on private property and pursuit of individual gain; without it, it would be difficult for its members to distribute the specialized products of their labour. Surely a lottery or an administrative device would be incompatible with its nature. Indeed, if it is to preserve its character, the only mode for the necessary distribution of the products of separate industry is that of private trading. But a trading society is unavoidably a pecuniary society, a society which of necessity carries on its transactions in terms of money. In fact, the distribution is not primarily an exchange of products against products, but products against money. In such a society, money therefore necessarily becomes the pivot on which everything revolves. With money as the focusing-point of all human efforts, interests, desires, and ambitions, a trading society is bound to function in a regime of price, where successes and failures are results of nice calculations of price-outlay as against price-product.

Economists have no doubt insisted that "there cannot be intrinsically a more significant thing than money," which at best is only "a great wheel by means of which every individual in society has his subsistence, conveniences and amusements regularly distributed to him in their proper proportions." Whether or not money values are the definitive terms of economic endeavour may well be open to discussion.* But this much is

---

* Cf W. C. Mitchell, "The Rationality of Economic Activity," *Journal of Political Economy*, 1910, Vol. XVIII, pp. 97 and 197; also "The Role of Money in Economic Theory," by the same, in the *American Economic Review* (Supplement), Vol. VI, No. 1, March 1916.

certain, that without the use of money this "distribution of subsistence, conveniences and amusements," far from being a matter of course, will be distressingly hampered, if not altogether suspended. How can this trading of products take place without money? The difficulties of barter have ever formed an unfailing theme with all economists, including those who have insisted that money is only a cloak. Money is not only necessary to facilitate trade by obviating the difficulties of barter, but is also necessary to sustain production by permitting specialization. For, who would care to specialize if he could not trade his products for those of others which he wanted? Trade is the handmaid of production, and where the former cannot flourish the latter must languish. It is therefore evident that if a trading society is not to be out of gear and is not to forego the measureless advantages of its automatic adjustments in the great give-and-take of specialized industry, it must provide itself with a sound system of money.*

At the close of the Moghul Empire, India, judged by the standards of the time, was economically an advanced country. Her trade was large, her banking institutions were well developed, and credit played an appreciable part in her transactions. But a medium of exchange and a common standard of value were among others the most supreme desiderata in the economy of the Indian people when they came, in the middle of the eighteenth century, under the sway of the British. Before the occurrence of this event, the money of India consisted of both gold and silver. Under the Hindu emperors the emphasis was laid on gold, while under the Mussalmans silver formed a large part of the circulating medium.† Since the time of Akbar, the founder of the economic system of the Moghul Empire in India, the units of currency had been the gold *mohur* and the silver *rupee*. Both coins, the mohur and the rupee, were identical in weight, i.e., 175 grs. troy‡ and were "supposed to have been coined without any alloy, or at least intended to be

* For the whole of this discussion, cf H J Davenport, *The Economics of Enterprise* (1913), Chapters II and III.

† Princep, J, *Useful Tables*, Calcutta, 1834, pp 15-16

‡ Robert Chalmers, *History of Colonial Currency*, 1893, pp. 336, 340

so."* But whether they constituted a single standard of value or not is a matter of some doubt. It is believed that the mohur and the rupee, which at the time were the common measure of value, circulated without any fixed ratio of exchange between them. The standard, therefore, was more of the nature of what Jevons called a parallel standard† than a double standard.‡ That this want of ratio could not have worked without some detriment in practice is obvious. But it must be noted that there existed an alleviating circumstance in the curious contrivance by which the mohur and the rupee, though unrelated to each other, bore a fixed ratio to the *dam*, the copper coin of the Empire.§ So that it is permissible to hold that, as a consequence of being fixed to the same thing, the two, the mohur and the rupee, circulated at a fixed ratio.

In Southern India, to which part the influence of the Moghuls had not extended, silver as a part of the currency system was quite unknown. The pagoda, the gold coin of the ancient Hindu kings, was the standard of value and also the medium of exchange, and continued to be so till the time of the East India Company.

The right of coinage, which the Moghuls always held as *Inter jura Majestatis*,¶ be it said to their credit, was exercised with

* Dr P. Kelly *The Universal Cambist*, 1811, p. 115

† *Money and Mechanism of Exchange* (1890), p 95

‡ Dr. P Kelly's view is that they circulated at their market ratio *(loc. cit.)* On the other hand, Sir R Temple says · "In ancient and mediaeval India the relative value of the coins of each metal was fixed by the State, and all were legal tender virtually without any formal limitation" ("General Monetary Practice in India," *Journal of the Institute of Bankers*, Vol II p 406) On another occasion he said: "The earliest Hindu currency was in gold with a single standard. The Mohammedans introduced silver, and in later times up to British rule there was a double standard, gold and silver" (*ibid.*, Vol. XV, p 9) In contrast to this it may be noted that the Preamble to Currency Regulation XXXV of 1793 and other Currency Regulations of early date make it a point to emphasize that under pre-British regime there was no fixed ratio between the mohur and the rupee

§ Cf. Prof. S. V. Venkateswara, on "Moghul Currency and Coinage" in the *Indian Journal of Ecomomics*, July, 1918, p 169; and F. Atkinson, *The Indian Currency Question* (1894), p. 1.

¶ According to the Mohammedan historian, Khafi Khan, it enraged the Emperor Aurangzeb when the East India Company in 1694 coined some rupees at Bombay "with the name of their impure king" (*Imperial Gazetteer of India*, Vol. IV, p. 515).

due sense of responsibility. Never did the Moghul Emperors stoop to debase their coinage. Making allowance for the imperfect technology of coinage, the coins issued from the various Mints, situated even in the most distant parts of their Empire*, did not materially deviate from the standard. The table below of the assays of the Moghul rupees shows how the coinage throughout the period of the Empire adhered to the standard weight of 175 grs. pure.†

| *Name of the Rupee* | *Weight in pure Grs.* | *Name of the Rupee.* | *Weight in pure Grs.* |
|---|---|---|---|
| Akbari of Lahore | 175.0 | Delhi Sonat | 175.0 |
| ,, of Agra | 174.0 | ,, Alamgir | 175.0 |
| Jehangiri of Agra | 174.6 | Old Surat | 174.0 |
| ,, of Allahabad | 173.6 | Murshedabad | 175.9 |
| ,, of Kandhar | 173.9 | Persian Rupee of 1745 | 174.5 |
| Shehajahani of Agra | 175.0 | Old Dacca | 173.3 |
| ,, of Ahamadabad | 174.2 | Muhamadshai | 170.0 |
| ,, of Delhi | 174.2 | Ahmadshai | 172.8 |
| ,, of Delhi | 175.0 | Shaha Alam (1772) | 175.8 |
| ,, of Lahore | 174.0 | | |

So long as the Empire retained unabated sway, there was advantage rather than danger in the plurality of Mints, for they were so many branches of a single department governed by a single authority. But with the disruption of the Moghul Empire into separate kingdoms these branches of the Imperial Mint located at different centres became independent factories for purposes of coinage. In the general scramble for independence which followed the fall of the Empire, the right to coinage, as

* It is stated in the *Imperial Gazetteer of India* (Vol. IV., p. 514), that in the early days of the Moghul rule, there was only one Mint—at Delhi—which struck the Imperial coins. The Emperor Sher Sha was the first to introduce a plurality of Mints for coniage purposes—a practice continued and extended by the later emperors until between the reigns of Akbar and Bahadur Shah II the Mints numbered about 200 From the *East India Moral and Material Progress Report* for 1872-73 it is clear that not every Mint was open to the coinage of all three metals, gold, silver and copper; but that some Mints coined only gold, others silver, and the rest copper, (*see* Report, pp. 11-12).

† Prinsep, J., op. cit., p. 18.

one of the most unmistakable insignia of sovereignty, became the right most cherished by the political adventurers of the time. It was also the last privilege to which the falling dynasties clung, and was also the first to which the adventurers rising to power aspired. The result was that the right, which was at one time so religiously exercised, came to be most wantonly abused. Everywhere the Mints were kept in full swing, and soon the country was filled with diverse coins which, while they proclaimed the incessant rise and fall of dynasties, also presented bewildering media of exchange. If these money-mongering sovereigns had kept up their issues to the original standard of the Moghul Emperors, the multiplicity of coins of the same denomination would not have been a matter of much concern. But they seemed to have held that as the money used by their subjects was made by them, they could do what they liked with their own, and proceeded to debase their coinage to the extent each chose without altering the denominations. Given the different degrees of debasement, the currency necessarily lost its primary quality of general and ready acceptability.

The evils consequent upon such a situation may well be imagined. When the contents of the coins belied the value indicated by their denomination they became mere merchandise, and there was no more a currency by tale to act as a ready means of exchange. The bullion value of each coin had to be ascertained before it could be accepted as a final discharge of obligations.* The opportunity for defrauding the poor and the ignorant thus provided could not have been less † than that

* It was this necessity for ascertaining the true bullion value of the debased coins which gave rise to that class of money-changers known as Shroffs, who specialized in the business of evaluating the coins at their proper discount from the standard purity by means of the dates and other characteristics engraved upon them.

† It is stated that Dr. Roxburgh, who was an eye-witness, was so much impressed by the sufferings of the poor owing to the bad state of the currency that he urged upon A Dalrymple, in a letter dated June 30, 1791, to give prominence to the evils by inserting a paper in his *Oriental Repertory* (2 vols , London, 1808), "on the current coin in circulation over the Company's Territories which might be productive of the most solid and lasting advantage to the Governing and the Governed " and added, " You may be able to correct the evil, by which you will certainly go to heaven, if the prayers of the poor avail, and I may get a step nearer paradise." *Observations on the Copper Coinage wanted in the Circars*, by A Dalrymple, London, 1794, p. 1

*known to have obtained in England before the great re-coinage of 1696.* This constant weighing, valuing, and assaying the bullion contents of coins was, however, only one aspect in which the evils of the situation made themselves felt. They also presented another formidable aspect. With the vanishing of the Empire there ceased to be such a thing as an Imperial legal tender current all through India. In its place there grew up local tenders, current only within the different principalities into which the Empire was broken up. Under such circumstances exchange was not liquidated by obtaining in return for wares the requisite bullion value from the coins tendered in payment. Traders had to be certain that the coins were also legal tender of their domicile. The Preamble to the Bengal Currency Regulation XXXV, of 1793, is illuminating on this point. It says :—

> "The principal districts in Bengal, Behar and Orissa, have each a distinct silver currency which are the standard measure of value in all transactions in the districts in which they respectively circulate.
>
> * * * * *
>
> "In consequence of the Ryots being required to pay their rent in a particular sort of rupee they of course demanded it from manufacturers in payment of their grain, or raw materials, whilst the manufacturers, actuated by similar principles with the Ryots, required the same species of rupee from the traders who came to purchase their cloth or their commodities.
>
> "The various sorts of old rupees, accordingly, soon became the established currency of particular districts, and as a necessary consequence the value of each rupee was enhanced in the district in which it was current, for being in demand for all transactions. As a further consequence, every sort of rupee brought into the district was rejected from being a different measure of value from that by which the inhabitants had become accustomed to estimate their property, or, if it was received, a discount was exacted upon it, equal to what the receiver would have been obliged to pay upon exchanging it at the house of a shroff for the rupee current in the district, or to allow discount upon passing it in payment to any other individual.
>
> * * * * *

> "From this rejection of the coin current in one district when tendered in payment in another, the merchants and traders, and the proprietors and cultivators of land in different parts of the country, are subjected in their commercial dealings with each other to the same losses by exchange, and all other inconveniences that would necessarily result were the several districts under separate and independent governments, each having a different coin."

Here was a situation where trade was reduced to barter, whether one looks upon barter as characterized by the absence of a common medium of exchange or by the presence of a plurality of the media of exchange ; for in any case, it is obvious that the want of a " double coincidence " must have been felt by people engaged in trade. One is likely to think that such could not have been the case as the medium was composed of metallic counters. But it is to be remembered that the circulating coins on India, by reason of the circumstance attendant upon the diversity in their fineness and legal tender, formed so many different species that an exchange against a particular species did not necessarily close the transaction ; the coin must, in certain circumstances, have been only an intermediate to be further bartered against another, and so on till the one of the requisite species was obtained. This is sufficient indication that society had sunk into a state of barter. If this alone was the flaw in the situation, it would have been only as bad as that of international trade under diversity of coinages. But it was further complicated by the fact that although the denomination of the coins was the same, their metallic contents differed considerably. Owing to this, one coin bore a discount or a premium in relation to another of the same name. In the absence of knowledge as to the amount of premium or discount, every one cared to receive a coin of the species known to him and current in his territory. On the whole, the obstacles to commerce arising from such a situation could not have been less than those emanating from the mandate of Lycurgus, who compelled the Lacedaemonians to use iron money in order that its weight might prevent them from overmuch trading. The situation, besides being irritating, was aggravated by the presence of an element of gall in it. Capital invested in providing a currency is a tax upon the productive resources of the community. Nevertheless, wrote James Wilson,* no one would question

* *Capital Currency and Banking*, 1847, p 15.

> "that the time and labour which are saved by the interposition of coin, as compared with a system of barter, form an ample remuneration for the portion of capital withdrawn from productive sources, to act as a single circulator of commodities, by rendering the remainder of the capital of the country so much the more productive."

What is, then, to be said of a monetary system which did not obviate the evil consequences of barter, although enormous capital was withdrawn from productive sources, to act as a single circulator of commodities ? Diseased money is worse than want of money. The latter at least saves the cost. But society must have money, and it must be good money, too. The task, therefore, of evolving good money out of bad money fell upon the shoulders of the English East India Company, who had in the meanwhile succeeded to the Empire of the Moghuls in India.

The lines of reform were first laid down by the Directors of the Company in their famous Despatch, dated April 25, 1806,* to the authorities administering their territories in India. In this historic document they observed :—

> "17. It is an opinion supported by the best authorities, and proved by experience, that coins of gold and silver cannot circulate as legal tenders of payment at fixed relative values . . . without loss; this loss is occasioned by the fluctuating value of the metals of which the coins are formed. A proportion between the gold and silver coin is fixed by law, according to the value of the metals, and it may be on the justest principles, but owing to the change of circumstances gold may become of greater value in relation to silver than at the time the proportion was fixed, it therefore becomes profitable to exchange silver or gold, so the coin of that metal is withdrawn from circulation; and if silver should increase in its value in relation to gold, the same circumstances would tend to reduce the quantity of silver coin in circulation. As it is impossible to prevent the fluctuation in the value of the metals, so it is also equally impracticable to prevent the consequences thereof on the coins made from these metals . . . . To adjust the relative values of gold and silver coin according to the fluctuations in the values of the metals would create continual difficulties, and the establishment of such a principle would of itself tend to perpetuate inconvenience and loss."

* H. of C. Return 127 of 1898.

They therefore declared themselves in favour of monometallism as the ideal for the Indian currency of the future, and prescribed :—

> "21. . that silver should be the universal money of account (in India), and that all accounts should be kept in the same denominations of rupees, annas and pice.
>
> The rupee was not, however, to be the same as that of the Moghul Emperors in weight and fineness. The proposal that "9. the new rupee be of the gross weight of—
>
> | | | |
> |---|---|---|
> | Troy grains | | 180 |
> | Deduct one-twelfth alloy | .. | 15 |
> | And contain of fine silver troy grs. | .. | 165" |

Such were the proposals put forth by the Court of Directors for the reform of Indian currency.

The choice of a rupee weighing 180 grs. troy and containing 165 grs. pure silver as the unit for the future currency system of India was a well-reasoned choice.

The primary reason for selecting this particular weight for the rupee seems to have been the desire to make it as little of a departure as possible from the existing practice. In their attempts to reduce to some kind of order the disorderly currencies bequeathed to them by the Moghuls by placing them on a bimetallic basis, the Governments of the three Presidencies had already made a great advance by selecting out of the innumerable coins then circulating in the country a species of gold and silver coin as the exclusive media of exchange for their respective territories. The weights and fineness of the coins selected as the principal units of currency, with other particulars, may be noted from the summary table on the next page.

To reduce these principal units of the different Presidencies to a single principal unit, the nearest and the least inconvenient magnitude of weight which would at the same time be an integral number was obviously 180 grs., for in no case did it differ from the weights of any of the prevailing units in any marked degree. Besides, it was believed that 180, or rather 179.5511, grs. was the standard weight of the rupee coin originally issued from the Moghul Mints, so that the adoption of it was really a resto-

TABLE I

PRINCIPAL UNITS OF CURRENCY

| Issued by the Government of | Territory in which it circulated. | Date and Authority of Issue | Silver Coins | | | Gold Coins. | | |
|---|---|---|---|---|---|---|---|---|
| | | | Name. | Gross Weight Troy Grs | Pure Contents Troy Grs | Name | Gorss Weight Troy Grs. | Pure Contents Troy Grs. |
| Bombay | Presidency | | Surat Rupee | 179.0 | 164.740 | Mohur | 179 | 164.740 |
| Madras | ,, | | Arcot ,, | 176.4 | 166.477 | Star Pagoda | 52.40 | 42.55 |
| Bengal | Bengal, Bihar and Orissa Cuttock | Regulations XXXV of 1793 XII of 1805 | Sicca Rupee (19th Sun) | 179.66 | 175.927 | Mohur | 190.804 | 189.40 |
| Bengal | Ceded Provinces Conquered Provinces | XLV of 1803 | Furrukabad Rupee (Lucknow Sicca of the 45th Sun) | 173 | 166.135 | — | — | — |
| Bengal | Benares Provinces | III of 1806 | Benares Rupee (Muchleedar) | 175 | 168.875 | — | — | — |

ration of the old unit and not the introduction of a new one.* Another advantage claimed in favour of a unit of 180 grs. was that such a unit of currency would again become what it had ceased to be, the unit of weight also. It was agreed† that the unit of weight in India had at all times previously been linked up with that of the principal coin, so that the *seer* and the *maund* weights were simply multiples of the rupee, which originally weighed 179.6 grs. troy. Now, if the weight of the principal coin to be established was to be different from 180 grs. troy, it was believed there would be an unhappy deviation from the ancient practice which made the weight of the coin the basis of other weights and measures. Besides, a unit of 180 grs. weight was not only suitable from this point of view, but had also in its favour the added convenience of assimilating the Indian with the English units of weight.‡

While these were the reasons in favour § of fixing the weight of the principal unit of currency at 180 grs. troy, the project of making it 165 grs. fine was not without its justification. The ruling consideration in selecting 165 grs. as the standard of fineness was, as in the matter of selecting the standard weight, to cause the least possible disturbance in existing arrangements. That this standard of fineness was not very different from those of the silver coins, recognized by the different Governments in India as the principal units of their currency, may be seen from the following comparative statement.

---

* Cf The Despatch, op. cit., para. 8.

† Cf para. 26-28 of the letter from James Prinsep to the Calcutta Mint Committee, printed in the Appendix to the Indian Tables by John Muller, Calcutta, 1836

‡ *Ibid.* para. 28 How the English and the Indian systems of weights were made to correspond to each other may be seen from the following :—

| *Indian* | | | | *English* | | |
|---|---|---|---|---|---|---|
| 8 ruttees | = | 1 massa | = | 15 | troy | grs |
| 12 massas | = | 1 tola (or sicca) | = | 180 | " | " |
| 80 tolas | = | 1 seer | = | 2½ | " | pounds |
| 40 seers | = | 1 maund (or mun) | = | 100 | " | " |

§ Attention may be drawn in this connection to the dissenting opinion of Captain Jervis on the project of 180 grs. troy as the unit of weight for the rupee Cf his most exhaustive treatise called *The Expediency and Facility of establishing the Metrological and Monetary Systems throughout India on a Scientific and Permanent Basis, grounded on an Analytical Review of the Weights, Measures and Coins of India . . .*, Bombay, 1836, pp. 49-64.

TABLE II

DEVIATIONS OF THE PROPOSED STANDARD OF FINENESS FROM THAT OF THE PRINCIPAL RECOGNIZED RUPEES

| Silver Coins recognized as Principal Units and their Fineness | | Standard Fineness of the Proposed Silver Rupee Troy Grs | More valuable than the Proposed Rupee | | Less valuable than the Proposed Rupee | |
|---|---|---|---|---|---|---|
| Name of the Coin | Its Pure Contents Troy Grs | | In Grs | By p c | In Grs | By p c |
| Surat Rupee | 164.74 | 165 | — | — | .26 | .157 |
| Arcot ,, | 166.477 | 165 | 1 477 | 887 | — | — |
| Sicca ,, | 175.927 | 165 | 10.927 | 6.211 | — | — |
| Farrukabad R | 166.135 | 165 | 1.135 | .683 | — | — |
| Benares Rupee | 169.251 | 165 | 4.251 | 2.511 | — | — |

It will thus be seen that, with the exception of the Sicca and the Benares rupees, the proposed standard of fineness agreed so closely with those of the other rupees that the interest of obtaining a complete uniformity without considerable dislocation overruled all possible objections to its adoption. Another consideration that seemed to have prevailed upon the Court of Directors in selecting 165 grs. as the standard of fineness was that, in conjunction with 180 grs. as the standard weight, the arrangement was calculated to make the rupee eleven-twelfths fine. To determine upon a particular fineness was too technical a matter for the Court of Directors. It was, however, the opinion of the British Committee on Mint and Coinage, appointed in 1803, that* "one-twelfth alloy and eleven-twelfths fine is by a variety of extensive experiments proved to be the best proportion, or at least as good as any which could have been chosen." This standard, so authoritatively upheld, the Court desired to incorporate in their new scheme of Indian currency. They therefore desired to make the rupee eleven-twelfths fine. But to do so was also to make the rupee 165 grs. pure—a content which they desired, from the point of view stated above, the rupee to possess.

Reviewing the preference of the Court of Directors for monometallism from the vantage-ground of latter-day events, one might be inclined to look upon it as a little too short-sighted.

* Cf. The despatch, op cit., par 9

At the time, however, the preference was well founded. One of the first measures, the three Presidencies, into which the country was divided for purposes of administration, had adopted on their assuming the government of the country, was to change the parallel standard of the Moghuls into a double standard by establishing a legal ratio of exchange between the mohur, the pagoda, and the rupee. But in none of the Presidencies was the experiment a complete success.

In Bengal * the Government, on June 2, 1766, determined upon the issue of a gold mohur weighing 179.66 grs. troy, and containing 149.92 grs, troy of pure metal, as legal tender at 14 Sicca rupees, to relieve the currency stringency caused largely by its own act of locking up the revenue collections in its treasuries. to the disadvantage of commerce. This was a legal ratio of 16.45 to 1, and as it widely deviated from the market ratio of 14.81 to 1, this attempt to secure a concurrent circulation of the two coins was foredoomed to failure. Owing to the drain of silver on Bengal from China, Madras, and Bombay, the currency stringency grew worse, so much so that another gold mohur was issued by the Government on March 20, 1769, weighing 190.773 grs. troy and containing 190.086 grs. pure gold with a value fixed at 16 Sicca rupees. This was a legal ratio of 14.81 to 1. But, as it was higher than the market ratio of the time both in India (14 to 1) and in Europe (14.61 to 1), this second effort to bring about a concurrent circulation fared no better than the first. So perplexing seemed to be the task of accurate rating that the Government reverted to monometallism by stopping the coinage of gold on December 3, 1788, and when the monetary stringency again compelled it to resume in 1790 the coinage of gold, it preferred to let the mohur and the rupee circulate at their market value without making any attempt to link them by a fixed ratio. It was not until 1793 that a third attempt was made to forge a double standard in Bengal. A new mohur was issued in that year, weighing 190.895 grs. troy and containing 189.4037 grs. of pure gold, and made legal tender

* F. C. Harrison, "The Past Action of the Indian Government with regard to Gold," in *Economic Journal*, Vol. III, p. 54 *et seq*. Also Minute by Sir John Shore, in Bengal Public Consultations, dated September 29, 1796.

at 16 Sicca rupees. This was a ratio of 14.86 to 1, but, as it *did not conform to the ratio then prevalent in the market, this third attempt to establish bimetallism in Bengal failed as did* those made in *1766* and *1769.*

The like endeavours of the Government of Madras* proved more futile than those of Bengal. The first attempt at bimetallism under the British in that Presidency was made in the year 1749, when 350 Arcot rupees were legally rated at 100 Star pagodas. As compared with the then market ratio this rating involved an under-valuation of the pagoda, the gold coin of the Presidency. The disappearance of the pagoda caused a monetary stringency, and the Government in December, 1750, was obliged to restore it to currency. This it did by adopting the twofold plan of causing an import of gold on Government account, so as to equalize the mint ratio to the market ratio, and of compelling the receipts and payments of Government treasuries to be exclusively in pagodas. The latter device proved of small value ; but the former by its magnitude was efficacious enough to ease the situation. Unluckily, the case was only temporary. Between 1756 and 1771 the market ratio of the rupee and the pagoda again underwent a considerable change. In 1756 it was 364 to 100, and in 1768 it was 370 to 100. It was not till after 1768 that the market ratio became equal to the legal ratio fixed in 1749 and remained steady for about twelve years. But the increased imports of silver, rendered necessary for the prosecution of the second Mysore war, once more disturbed the ratio, which at the close of the war stood at 400 Arcot rupees to 100 Star pagodas. After the end of the war, the Government of Madras made another attempt to bring about a concurrent circulation between the rupee and the pagoda. But instead of making the market ratio of 400 to 100 the legal ratio, it was led by the then increasing imports of gold into the Presidency to hope that the market ratio would in time rise to that legally established in 1749. In an expectant mood so induced it decided, in 1790, to anticipate the event by fixing the ratio first at 365 to 100. The result was bound to be different from that desired, for it was an under-valuation of the pagoda. But instead of rectifying the error, the Government

* H. Dodwell, "Substitution of Silver for Gold in South India," in the *Indian Journal of Economics*, January, 1921

proceeded to aggravate it by raising the ratio still further to 350 to 100 in 1797, with the effect that the pagoda entirely went out of circulation, and the final attempt at bimetallism thus ended in a miserable failure.

The Government of Bombay seemed better instructed in the mechanics of bimetallism, although that did not help it to overcome the practical difficulties of the system. On the first occasion when bimetallism was introduced in the Presidency,* the mohur and the rupee were rated at the ratio of 15.70 to 1. But at this ratio the mohur was found to be over-rated, and accordingly, in August, 1774, the Mint Master was directed to coin gold mohurs of the fineness of a Venetian and of the weight of the silver rupee. This change brought down the legal ratio to 14.83 to 1, very nearly, though not exactly, to the then prevailing market ratio of 15 to 1, and had nothing untoward happened, bimetallism would have had a greater success in Bombay than it actually had in the other two Presidencies. But this was not to be, for the situation was completely altered by the dishonesty of the Nawab of Surat, who allowed his rupees, which were of the same weight and fineness as the Bombay rupees, to be debased to the extent of 10, 12, and even 15 per cent. This act of debasement could not have had any disturbing effect on the bimetallic system prevalent in the Bombay Presidency, had it not been for the fact that the Nawab's (or Surat) rupees were by agreement admitted to circulation in the Company's territories at par with the Bombay rupees. As a result of their being legal tender the Surat rupees, once they were debased, not only drove out the Bombay rupees from circulation, but also the mohur, for as rated to the debased Surat rupees the ratio became unfavourable to gold, and the one chance for a successful bimetallic system vanished away. The question of fixing up a bimetallic ratio between the mohur and the rupee again cropped up when the Government of Bombay permitted the coinage of Surat rupees at its Mint. To have continued the coinage of the gold mohur according to the Regulation of 1774 was out of the question. One Bombay mohur contained 177.38 grs. of pure gold, and 15 Surat rupees of the standard of 1800 contained 247,110 grs.

* Report of Dr. Scott on the History of Coinage in the Bombay Presidency, with Appendices, Public Consultations (Bombay, dated January 27, 1801).

of silver. By this Regulation the proportion of silver to gold would have been $\frac{247.11,}{177\ 38,}$ i.e. 13.9 to 1. Here the mohur would have been much under-valued. It was therefore resolved to alter the standard of the mohur to that of the Surat rupee, so as to give a ratio of 14.9 to 1. But as the market ratio was inclined towards 15.5 to 1, the experiment was not altogether a success.

In the light of this experience before them, the Court of Directors of the East India Company did well in fixing upon a monometallic standard as the basis of the future currency system of India. The principal object of all currency regulations is that the different units of money should bear a fixed relation of value to one another. Without this fixity of value, the currency would be in a state of confusion, and no precaution would be too great against even a temporary disturbance of that fixity. Fixity of value between the various components of the currency is so essential a requisite in a well-regulated monetary system that we need hardly be surprised if the Court of Directors attached special importance to it, as they may well have done, particularly when they were engaged in the task of placing the currency on a sound and permanent footing. Nor can it be said that their choice of monometallism was ill-advised, for it must be admitted that a single standard better guarantees this fixity than does the double standard. Under the former it is spontaneous, under the latter it is forced.

These recommendations of the Court of Directors were left to the different Governments in India to be carried into effect at their discretion as to the time and manner of doing it. But it was some time before steps were taken in consonance with these orders, and even then, it was on the realization of those parts of the programme of the Court which pertained to the establishment of a uniform currency that the efforts of the different Governments were first concentrated.

The task of reducing the existing units of currency to that proposed by the Court was first accomplished in Madras. On January 7, 1818, the Government issued a Proclamation* by which its old units of currency—the Arcot rupee and the Star

* Cf. Fort St. George Public Depart. Consultations, No. 19, dated January 7, 1818.

pagoda—were superseded by new units, a gold rupee and a silver rupee, each weighing 180 grs. troy and containing 165 grs. of fine metal. Madras was followed by Bombay six years later by a Proclamation * of October 6, 1824, which declared a gold rupee and a silver rupee of the new Madras standard to be the only units of currency in that Presidency. The Government of Bengal had a much bigger problem to handle. It had three different principal units of silver currency to be reduced to the standard proposed by the Court. It commenced its work of reorganization by a system of elimination and alteration. In 1819, it discontinued† the coinage of the Benares rupee and substituted in its place the Furrukabad rupee, the weight and fineness of which were altered to 180.234 and 135.215 grs. troy respectively. Apparently this was a step away from the right direction. But even here, the purpose of uniformity, so far as fineness was concerned, was discernible, for it made the Furrukabad rupee, like the new Madras and Bombay rupees, eleven-twelfth fine. Having got rid of the Benares rupee, the next step was to assimilate the standard of the Furrukabad rupee to that of Madras and Bombay, as may be seen from the following table.

Thus, without abrogating the bimetallic system, substantial steps were taken in realizing the ideal unit proposed by the Court, as may be seen from the following table.

TABLE III

UNIFORMITY OF COINAGE AT THE END OF AD. 1833

| Issued by the Government of | Silver Coins. | | | Gold Coins | | | Legal Ratio. |
|---|---|---|---|---|---|---|---|
| | Denomination. | Weight | Fineness | Denomination | Weight | Fineness. | |
| Bengal | Sicca Rupee | 192 | 176 or $\frac{11}{12}$ | Mohur | 204 710 | 187.651 | 1 to 15 |
| Bengal | Furrukabad Rupee | 180 | 165 or $\frac{11}{12}$ | — | — | — | — |
| Bombay | Silver Rupee | 180 | 165 or $\frac{11}{12}$ | Gold Rupee | 180 | 165 or $\frac{11}{12}$ | 1 to 15 |
| Madras | Silver Rupee | 180 | 165 or $\frac{11}{12}$ | ,, ,, | 180 | 165 or $\frac{11}{12}$ | 1 to 15 |

* Cf. Bombay Financial Consultations, dated October 6, 1824.

† Bengal Regulation XI of 1819.

‡ Bengal Regulation VII of 1833.

Taking stock of the position as it was at the end of 1833, we find that with the exception of the Sicca rupee and the gold mohur of Bengal, that part of the scheme of the Directors which pertained to the uniformity of coinage was an accomplished fact. Nothing more remained to carry it to completion than to discontinue the Sicca rupee and to demonetize gold. At this point, however, arose a conflict between the Court of Directors and the three Governments in India. Considerable reluctance was shown to the demonetization of gold. The Government of Madras, which was the first to undertake the reform of its currency according to the plan of the Court, not only insisted upon continuing the coinage of gold along with that of the rupee,* but stoutly refused to deviate from the system of double legal tender at a fixed ratio prevalent in its territories,† notwithstanding the repeated remonstrances addressed by the Court‡. The Government of Bengal clung to the bimetallic standard with equal tenacity. Rather than demonetize the gold mohur, it took steps to alter its standard§ by reducing its pure contents¶ from 189.4037 to 187.651 troy grs., so as to re-establish a bimetallic system on the basis of the ratio adopted by Madras in 1818. So great was its adherence to the bimetallic standard that in 1833 it undertook to alter §§ the weight and fineness of the Sicca rupee to 196 grs. troy and 176 grs. fine, probably to rectify a likely divergence between the legal and the market ratios of the mohur to the rupee.‡‡

* The Court of Directors were willing to permit the coinage and circulation of gold *unlinked* to the rupee, for they had observed in their Despatch —

"16. Although we are fully satisfied of the propriety of the silver rupee being the principal measure of value and the money of account, yet we are by no means desirous of checking the circulation of gold, but of establishing a gold coin on a principle fitted for general use. This coin in our opinion should be called a gold rupee and be made of the same standard as the silver rupee."

† Cf Fort St George Public Consultations of August 19, 1817, particularly the letter of the Accountant-General entered thereon

‡ Cf. The Public Despatches to Madras dated March 6, 1810, July 10, 1811, and June 12, 1816

§ Preamble to the Bengal Regulation XIV of 1818

¶ It, however, increased its weight from 190 895 to 204 710 troy grs

§§ Bengal Regulation VII of 1833.

‡‡ It may be that this alteration was also intended to make the Sicca rupee eleven-twelfths fine.

But in another direction the Government in India wanted to go further than the Court desired. The Court thought a uniform currency (i.e. a currency composed of like but independent units) was all that India needed. Indeed, they had given the Governments to understand that they did not wish for more in the matter of simplification of currency and were perfectly willing to allow the Sicca and the mohur to remain as they were, unassimilated.* A uniform currency was no doubt a great advance on the order of things such as was left by the successors of the Moghuls. But that was not enough, and the needs of the situation demanded a common currency based on a single unit in place of a uniform currency. Under the system of uniform currency each Presidency coined its own money, and the money coined at the Mints of the other Presidencies was not legal tender in its territories except at the Mint. This monetary independence would not have been very harmful if there had existed also financial independence between the three Presidencies. As a matter of fact, although each Presidency had its own fiscal system, yet they depended upon one another for the finance of their deficits. There was a regular system of " supply " between them, and the surplus in one was being constantly drawn upon to meet the deficits in others. In the absence of a common currency this resource operation was considerably hampered. The difficulties caused by the absence of a common currency in the way of the " supply " operation made themselves felt in two different ways. Not being able to use as legal tender the money of other Presidencies, each was obliged to lock up, to the disadvantage of commerce, large working balances in order to be self-sufficient.† The very system which imposed

---

* Cf. Despatch to Bengal dated March 11, 1829.

† The Accountant-General of Bengal, in a letter to the Calcutta Mint Committee, dated November 21, 1823, wrote:—

"Para. 32. The amount of the balance must also necessarily depend upon the state of the currency If the Madras, Bombay, and Furrukabad rupees instead of differing in weight and intrinsic value were coined of one standard weight and value bearing one inscription and in no way differing, the surplus of one Presidency would at all times be available for the deficiency of another, without passing through the Mint, and the balance of India might be reduced in proporion to the increased availability of currency for the disbursements of the three Presidencies" (Bombay Financial Consultations, February 25, 1824).

the necessity of large balances also rendered relief from other Presidencies less efficacious. For the supply was of necessity in the form of the currency of the Presidency which granted it, and before it could be utilized it had to be re-coined into the currency of the needy Presidency. Besides the loss on re-coinage, such a system obviously involved inconvenience to merchants and embarassment to the Government.*

At the end of 1833, therefore, the position was that the Court desired to have a uniform currency with a single standard of silver, while the authorities in India wished for a common currency with a bimetallic standard. Notwithstanding these divergent views, the actual state of the currency might have continued as it was without any substantial alteration either way. But the year 1833 saw an important constitutional change in the administrative relations between the three Presidential Governments in India. In that year by an Act of Parliament † there was set up an Imperial system of administration with a centralization of all legislative and executive authority over the whole of India. This change in the administrative system, perforce, called forth a change in the prevailing monetary systems. It required local coinages to be replaced by Imperial coinage. In other words, it favoured the cause of a common currency as against that of a mere uniform currency. The authorities in India were not slow to realize the force of events. The Imperial Government set up by Parliament was not content to act the part of the Dewans or agents of the Moghuls, as the British had theretofore done, and did not like that coins should be issued in the name of the defunct Moghul emperors who had ceased to govern. It was anxious to throw off the false garb‡ and issue an Imperial coinage in its own name, which being common to the whole of India would convey its common sway. Accordingly,

* The evil of the system had already made itself felt in Bombay, where the Government had been obliged by a Proclamation dated April 9, 1824, to declare the Furrukabad rupee of 1819 standard as legal tender within its territories on a par with the Bombay rupee, in order to facilitate the supply operation from Bengal. Cf. Bombay Financial Consultations, dated April 14, 1824.

† 3 & 4 Will, IV, c, 85

‡ Cf. the sentiments of Tucker in his *Memorials of Indian Government* (ed. by Kaye), 1853, pp. 17-19.

an early opportunity was taken to give effect to this policy. By an Act of the Imperial Government (XVII of 1835) a common currency was introduced for the whole of India, as the sole legal tender. But the Imperial Government went beyond and, as if by way of concession to the Court—for the Court did most vehemently protest against this common currency in so far as it superseded the Sicca rupee *—legislated "*that no gold coin shall henceforward be a legal tender of payment in any of the territories of the East India Company.*" †

That an Imperial Administration should have been by force of necessity led to the establishment of a common currency for the whole of India is quite conceivable. But it is not clear why it should have abrogated the bimetallic system after having maintained it for so long. Indeed, when it is recalled how the authorities had previously set their faces against the destruction of the bimetallic system, and how careful they were not to allow their coinage reforms to disturb it any more violently than they could help, the provision of the Act demonetizing gold was a grim surprise. However, for the sudden *volte-face* displayed therein, the Currency Act (XVII of 1835) will ever remain momerable in the annals of the Indian history. It marked the culminating-point of a long and arduous process of monetary reform and placed India on a silver monometallic basis, with a rupee weighing 180 grs. troy and containing 165 grs. fine as the common currency and sole legal tender throughout the country.

No piece of British India legislation has led to a greater discontent in later years than this Act XVII of 1835. In so far as the Act abrogated the bimetallic system, it has been viewed with a surprising degree of equanimity. Not all its critics, however, are aware ‡ that what the Act primarily decreed was a substitution of bimetallism by monometallism. The commonly entertained view of the Act seems to be that it replaced a gold standard by a silver standard. But even if the truth were more generally known, it would not justify any hostile attitude towards

* Cf. their Financial Despatch to India, No. 9, dated July 27, 1836.

† Section 9 of Act XVII of 1835.

‡ To mention only one, cf. S. V Doraiswami, *Indian Currency*, Madras, 1915. *passim.*

the measure on that score. For, what would have been the consequences to India of the gold discoveries of California and Australia in the middle of the nineteenth century, if she had preserved her bimetallic system ? It is well known how this increase in the production of gold relatively to that of silver led to a divergence in the mint and the market ratios of the two metals after the year 1850. The under-valuation of silver, though not very great, was great enough to confront the bimetallic countries with a serious situation in which the silver currency, including the small change, was rapidly passing out of circulation. The United States * was obliged by the law of 1853 to reduce the standard of its small silver coins sufficiently to keep them, dollar for dollar, below their gold value in order to keep them in circulation. France, Belgium, Switzerland, and Italy, which had a uniform currency based on the bimetallic model of the French with reciprocal legal tender,† were faced with similar difficulties. Lest a separatist policy on the part of each nation,‡ to protect their

* Laughlin, J. L., *History of Bimetallism*, New York, 1886, pp. 79-83.

† The cultural influence of France had led the other countries of Latin origin to adopt the French monetary system. The political independence acquired by Belgium in 1831 was followed by a change in her monetary system. By the law of 1832, Belgium from a monetary point of view, became a satellite of France. By that law she adopted in its entirety the monetary system of France, and even went so far as to give the French gold pieces of 20 and 40 francs and to the French silver 5-franc pieces the power of legal tender in Belgium. In Switzerland, Art. 36 of the Constitution of 1848 had vested in the Federal Government the authority to coin money. The law of May 7, 1850, adopted the French monetary system for Switzerland : Art. 8 declared " that such foreign silver coins as were minted in sufficiently close proximity with the French system might be granted a legal status as regular media for the payment of debts in Switzerland." The various Italian States, prior to unification, had, like the Swiss Cantons, each its own currency. But with the desire for uniformity of coinage consequent upon unification, there arose a problem either of selecting one of the old systems or of adopting a new one which would be common to the whole country. Some form of a grateful memorial to France was uppermost in the minds of the Italians for the help the French gave in the matter of their independence, and the adoption of the French monetary system for Italy was deemed to serve the purpose. Fortunately, Sardinia already possessed the French system, and the law of August 24, 1862, extended it to the whole of Italy, with the lire as the unit, and also conferred legal-tender power on the coins of France, Belgium, and Switzerland. Cf. H. P. Willis, *History of the Latin Monetary Union*, Chicago, 1910, pp. 15, 27, 36 37.

‡ Switzerland was the first to reduce the amount of silver in her small coins in order to keep them in circulation. But these Swiss coins of reduced fineness crossed the national frontier and, as they were legal tender in other countries of Latin origin,

silver currency and particularly the small change, should disrupt the monetary harmony prevailing among them all, they were compelled to meet in a convention, dated November 20, 1865, which required the parties, since collectively called the Latin Union, to lower, in the order to maintain them in circulation, the silver pieces of 2 francs, 1 franc, 50 centimes, and 20 centimes from a standard of $\frac{900}{1000}$ fine to $\frac{835}{1000}$ and to make them subsidiary coins.* It is true that the Government of India also came in for trouble as a result of this disturbance in the relative value of gold and silver, but that trouble was due to its own silly act.† The currency law of 1835 had not closed the Mints to the free coinage of gold, probably because the seignorage on the coinage of gold was a source of revenue which the Government did not like to forego. But as gold was not legal tender, no gold was brought to the Mint for coinage, and the Government revenue from seignorage fell off. To avoid this loss of revenue, the Government began to take steps to encourage the coinage of gold. In the first place, it reduced the seignorage ‡ in 1837 from 2 per cent. to 1 per cent. But even this measure was not sufficient to induce people to bring gold to the Mint, and consequently the revenue from seignorage failed to increase. As a further step in the same direction, the Government issued a Proclamation on January 13, 1841, authorizing the officers in charge of public treasuries to receive the gold coins at the rate of 1 gold mohur equal to 15 silver rupees. For some time no gold was received, as at the rate prescribed by the Proclamation gold was undervalued.¶ But the Australian and Californian gold discoveries altered the situation entirely. The gold mohur, which was undervalued at Rs. 15, became overvalued, and the Government which was at one time eager to receive gold, was alarmed at its influx.

---

began to displace their dearer coins of similar denominations, which contained more silver but which passed current at the same nominal value. This brought forth a decree in France (April 14, 1864) which revoked the legal tender power to a concerted action on the part of all the Latin countries concerned .

* For more particulars of the Latin Union, cf Laughlin , op cit, pp 146-9

† Cf. H. of C. Return, East Indian (Coinage) 254 of 1860.

‡ *Ibid.*, p. 8.

¶ *Ibid.*, p. 10.

By adopting the course it did of declaring gold no longer legal tender, and yet undertaking to receive it in liquidation of Government demands, it laid itself under the disadvantage of being open to be embarrassed with a coin which was of no use and must ordinarily have been paid for above its value. Realizing its position, it left aside all considerations of augmenting revenue by increased coinage, and promptly issued on December 25, 1852, another Proclamation withdrawing that of 1841. Whether it would not have been better to have escaped the embarrassment by making gold general legal tender than depriving it of its partial legal-tender power is another matter. But, in so far as India was saved the trials and tribulations undergone by the bimetallic countries to preserve the silver part of their currency, the abrogation of bimetallism was by no means a small advantage. For, the measure had the virtue of fore-arming the country against changes which, though not seen at the time, soon made themselves felt.

The abrogation of bimetallism in India, accomplished by the Act of 1835, cannot therefore be made a ground for censure. But it is open to argument that a condemnation of bimetallism is not *per se* a justification of silver monometallism. If it was to be monometallism it might well have been gold monomentallism. In fact, the preference for silver monometallism is not a little odd when it is recalled that Lord Liverpool, the advocate of monometallism,* whose doctrines the Court had sought to apply to India, had prescribed gold monometallism for similar currency evils then prevalent in England. That the Court should have deviated from their guide in this particular has naturally excited a great deal of hostile comment as to the propriety of this grave departure.† At the outset any appeal to ulterior motives must be baseless, for Lord Liverpool was not a "gold bug," nor was the Court composed of "silver men." As a matter of fact, neither of them at all considered the question from the standpoint as to which was a better standard of value, gold or silver. Indeed, in so far as that was at all a consideration worth atttending to, the

* The author of *A Treatise on the Coinage of the Realm* was anticipated by Sir John Shore, the Governor of Bengal, in his Minute, op. cit., par 55

† Cf. H M Dunning, *Indian Currency*, 1898, *passim*; also S V Doraiswami, op cit., *passim*.

choice of the Court, according to the opinion of the time, was undoubtedly a better one than that of Lord Liverpool. Not only were all the theorists, such as Locke, Harris, and Petty, in favour of silver as the standard of value, but the practice of the whole world was also in favour of silver. No doubt, England had placed herself on a gold basis in 1816. But that Act, far from closing the English Mint to the free coinage of silver, left it to be opened by a Royal Proclamation.* The Proclamation, it is true, was never issued, but it is not to be supposed that therefore Englishmen of the time had regarded the question of the standard as a settled issue. The crisis of 1825 showed that the gold standard furnished too narrow a basis for the English currency system to work smoothly, and, in the expert opinion of the time,† the gold standard, far from being the cause of England's commercial superiority, was rather a hindrance to her prosperity, as it cut her off from the rest of the world, which was mostly on a silver basis. Even the British statesmen of the time had no decided preference for the gold standard. In 1826, Huskisson actually proposed that Government should issue silver certificates of full legal tender.‡ Even as late as 1844 the question of the standard was far from being settled, for we find Peel, in his Memorandum § to the Cabinet, discussing the possibility of abandoning the gold standard in favour of the silver or a bimetallic standard without any compunction or predilection one way or the other. The difficulties of fiscal isolation were evidently not so insuperable as to compel a change of the standard, but they were great enough to force Peel to introduce his famous proviso embodying the Huskisson plan in part in the Bank Charter Act of 1844, permitting the issue of notes against silver to the extent of one-fourth of the total issues.¶ Indeed, so great was the universal faith in the stability of silver that Holland changed in 1847 from what was practically

---

* Cf. Dana Horton, *The Silver Pound*, 1887, p. 161

† Cf. the evidence of A. Baring (afterwards Lord Ashburton) before the Committee for Coin (1828), H. of C. Return 31 of 1830.

‡ *See* his Memorandum to the Cabinet printed by Gibbs, *A Colloquy on Currency* (1894), Appendix, p xlvii

§ For which, *see* Andreades, *History of the Bank of England*, Supplement I.

¶ For the original purpose of this defunct proviso, *see* Peel's Speech on the Bank Charter Act, dated May 20, 1844, Hansard, Vol LXXIV, pp 1334-35

*a gold monometallism* to silver monometallism because her statesmen believed that*

> "it had proved disastrous to the commercial and industrial interests of Holland to have a monetary system identical with that of England, whose financial revulsions, after its adoption of the gold standard, had been more frequent and more severe than in any other country, and whose injurious effects were felt in Holland scarcely less than in England. They maintained that the adoption of the silver standard would prevent England from disturbing the internal trade of Holland by draining off its money during such revulsions, and would secure immunity from evils which did not originate in and for which Holland was not responsible." †

But stability was not the ground on which either the Court or Lord Liverpool made their choice of a standard metal to rest. If that had been the case, both probably would have selected silver. As it was, the difference in the choice of the two parties was only superficial. Indeed, the Court differed from Lord Liverpool, not because of any ulterior motives, but because they were both agreed on a fundamental proposition that not stability but popular preference should be the deciding factor in the choice of a standard metal. Their differences proceeded logically from the agreement. For, on analysing the composition of the currency it was found that in England it was largely composed of gold and in India it was largely composed of silver. Granting their common premise, it is easy to account why gold was selected for England by Lord Liverpool and silver for India by the Court. Whether the actual composition of the currency is an evidence of popular preference cannot, of course, be so dogmatically asserted as was done by the Court and Lord Liverpool. So far as England is concerned, the interpretation of Lord Liverpool has been questioned by the great economist David Ricardo. In his *High Price of Bullion*, Ricardo wrote:—

> "For many reasons given by Lord Liverpool, it appears proved beyond dispute that gold coin has been for near a century the principal measure of value; but this is, I think, to be attri-

* In theory Holland had adopted bimetallism in 1816 But the legal ratio of 15.873 to 1 had undervalued silver so much that it had made gold the chief circulating medium of Holland

† *Report of the U. S. Silver Commission of* 1876, p 68

> *buted to the inaccurate determination of the mint proportions. Gold has been valued too high; no silver can therefore remain in circulation which is of its standard weight. If a new regulation were to take place, and silver be valued too high gold would then disappear, and silver become the standard money."* *

And it is possible that mint proportions rather than popular preference† could have equally well accounted for the preponderance of silver in India.‡

Whether any other criterion besides popular preference could have led the Court to adopt gold monometallism is a moot question. Suffice it to say that the adoption of silver monometallism, though well supported at the time when the Act was passed, soon after proved to be a measure quite inadequate to the needs of the country. It is noteworthy that just about this time great changes were taking place in the economy of the Indian people. Such a one was a change from kind economy to cash economy. Among the chief causes contributory to this transformation the first place must be given to the British system of revenue and finance. Its effects in shifting Indian society on to a cash nexus have not been sufficiently realized,§ although they have been very real. Under the native rulers most payments were in kind. The standing military force kept and regularly paid by the Government was small. The bulk of the troops consisted of a kind of militia furnished by Jageerdars and other landlords, and the troops or retainers of these feudatories were in great measure maintained on the grain, forage, and other supplies furnished by the districts in which they were located. The hereditary revenue and police officers were gene-

* *Works*, p 271

† Mr. Dodwell, in his otherwise excellent article, op. cit., seems to convey that silver was substituted for gold in Southern India as a result of the natural preference of the people for the former metal. So eager is he in meeting the contentions of writers like Mr Doraiswami that he fails to see how his own facts controvert his own thesis.

‡ The total coinage of India from 1800 to 1835 was, according to Mr. F. C. Harrison's estimate in the *Calcutta Review*, July, 1892:—

| | |
|---|---|
| Gold | 3,845,000 ounces |
| Silver | 3,781,250,000 ounces |

N.B.—In the case of silver, rupees are converted into ounces for comparison.

§ Cf. the article "The Silver Question as regards India," in the *Bombay Quarterly Review*, April, 1857.

rally paid by grants of land on tenure of service. Wages of farm servants and labourers were in their turn distributed in grain. Most of its officers being paid in kind, the State collected very little of its taxes in cash. The innovations made by the British in this rude revenue and fiscal system were of the most sweeping character. As territory after territory passed under the sway of the British, the first step taken was to substitute in place of the rural militia of the feudatories a regularly constituted and a well-disciplined standing army located at different military stations, paid in cash ; in civil employ, as in military, the former revenue and police officers with their followers, who paid themselves by perquisites and other indirect gains received in kind, were replaced by a host of revenue collectors and magistrates with their extensive staff, all paid in current coin. The payments to the army, police, and other officials were not the only payments which the British Government had placed on a money basis. Besides these charges, there were others which were quite unknown to the native Governments, such as the "Home Charges" and "Interest on Public Debt," all on a cash basis. The State, having undertaken to pay in cash, was compelled to realize all its taxes in cash, and as each citizen was bound to pay in cash, he in his turn stipulated to receive nothing but cash, so that the entire structure of the society underwent a complete transformation.

Another important change that took place in the economy of the Indian people about this time was the enormous increase of trade. For a considerable period, the British tariff policy and the navigation laws had put a virtual check on the expansion of Indian trade. England compelled India to receive her cotton and other manufactures at nearly nominal (2½ per cent.) duties, while at the same time she prohibited the entry of such Indian goods as competed with hers within her territories by prohibitory duties ranging from 50 to 500 per cent. Not only was no reciprocity shown by England to India, but she made a discrimination in favour of her colonies in the case of such goods as competed with theirs. A great agitation was carried on against this unfair treatment,* and finally Sir Robert Peel admitted Indian produce

* Cf Debates at the East India House on Duties affecting Indian Commerce, vide the *Asiatic Journal and Monthly Register for British and Foreign India China Australia* (London, New Series, Vol XXXVII, January, and Vol XXXVIII, May, 1842).

to the low duties levied by the reformed tariff of 1842. The repeal of the navigation laws gave further impetus to the expansion of Indian commerce. Along with this, the demand for Indian produce had also been growing. The Crimean War of 1854 cut off the Russian supplies, the place of which was taken by Indian produce, and the failure of the silk crop in 1853 throughout Europe led to the demand for Asiatic, including Indian, silks.

The effect of these two changes on the currency situation is obvious. Both called forth an increased demand for cash. But cash was the one thing most difficult to obtain. India does not produce precious metals in any considerable quantity. She has had to depend upon her trade for obtaining them. Since the advent of the European Powers, however, the country was not able to draw enough for the precious metals. Owing to the prohibitions on the export of precious metals then prevalent in Europe,* one avenue for obtaining them was closed. But there was little chance of obtaining precious metals from Europe, even in the absence of such prohibition ; indeed, precious metals did not flow to India when such prohibitions were withdrawn.† The reason of the check to the inflow of precious metals was well pointed out by Mr. Petrie in his Minute of November, 1799, to the Madras Committee of Reform.‡ According to Mr. Petrie, the Europeans before they acquired their territorial possessions

> "purchased the manufactures of India with the metals of Europe: but they were henceforward to make these purchases with gold and silver of India, the revenues supplied the place of foreign bullion and paid the native the price of his industry with his own money. At first this revolution in the principles of commerce was but little felt, but when opulent and extensive dominions were acquired by the English, when the success of war and commercial rivalship had given them so decided a superiority over the other European nations as to engross the whole of the

* For the history of those imposed by England, cf Ruding, *Annals of Coinage*, 3rd ed Vol I, pp 353-4, 372, 376, 386-7; Thomas Violet, *An Appeal to Caesar*, London, 1660, p. 26.

† The following figures of the export of precious metals to India from England are interesting:—

| | | |
|---|---|---|
| 1652-1703 | £1,131,653 | (from Mr. Petrie's Minute) |
| 1747-1795 | £1,519,654 | " " |

‡ For the proceedings of the Committee, see India Office Records, "*Home Miscellaneous*" Series, vol 456

> commerce of the East, when a revenue amounting to millions per annum was to be remitted to Europe in the manufactures of *the East, then were the effects of this revolution severely felt in every part of India. Deprived of so copious a stream, the river rapidly retired from its banks and ceased to fertilize the adjacent fields with overflowing water."*

The only way open, when the prohibitions were withdrawn to obtain precious metals, was to send more goods than this amount of tribute, so that the balance might bring them in. This became possible when Peel admitted Indian goods to low tariff, and the country was for the first time able to draw in a sufficient quantity of precious metals to sustain her growing needs. But this ease in the supply of precious metals to serve as currency was short-lived. The difficulties after 1850, however, were not due to any hindrance in the way of India's obtaining the precious metals. Far from being hindered, the export and import of precious metals was entirely free, and India's ability to procure them was equally great. Neither were the difficulties due to any want of precious metals ; for, as a matter of fact, the increase in the precious metals after 1850 was far from being small. The difficulty was of India's own making, and was due to her not having based her currency on that precious metal, which it was easy to obtain. The Act of 1835 had placed India on an exclusive silver basis. But, unfortunately, it so happened that after 1850, though the total production of the precious metals had increased, that of silver had not kept pace with the needs of the world, a greater part of which was then on a silver basis, so that as a result of her currency law India found herself in an embarrasing position of an expanding trade with a contracting currency, as is shown on the opposite page.

On the face of it, it seems that there need have been no monetary stringency. The import of silver was large, and so was the coinage of it. Why then should there have been any stringency at all ? The answer to this question is not far to seek. If the amount of silver coined had been retained in circulation it is possible that the stringency could not have arisen. India has long been notoriously the sink of the precious metals. But in interpreting this phenomenon, it is necessary to bear in mind the caution given by Mr. Cassels that

## TABLE IV
### Trade and Currency*

| Years. | Merchandise. | | Treasure. Net Imports of | | Total Coinage of | | Excess (+) or Defect (—) of Coinage on Net Imports of | | Annual Production (in £,00,000 omitted) of | |
|---|---|---|---|---|---|---|---|---|---|---|
| | Imports. £ | Exports. £ | Silver. £ | Gold £ | Silver £ | Gold. £ | Silver. £ | Gold. £ | Gold. | Silver. |
| 1850–51 | 11,558,789 | 18,164,150 | 2,117,225 | 1,153,294 | 3,557,906 | 123,717 | +1,440,681 | —1 029,577 | 8,9 | 7.8 |
| 1851–52 | 12,240,490 | 19,879,406 | 2,865 357 | 1,267,613 | 5,170,014 | 62,553 | +2,304,657 | —1,205,060 | 15,5 | 8,0 |
| 1852–53 | 10,170,863 | 20,464,633 | 3,605,024 | 1,172,301 | 5,902,648 | Nil | +2,297,624 | —1,172,301 | 36,6 | 8,1 |
| 1853–54 | 11,122,659 | 19,295,139 | 2,305,744 | 1,061,443 | 5,888,217 | 145,679 | +3,582,373 | — 915,764 | 31,1 | 28,1 |
| 1854–55 | 12,742,671 | 18,927,222 | 29,600 | 731,490 | 1,890,055 | 2,676 | +1,860,455 | — 728,814 | 25,5 | 8,1 |
| 1855–56 | 13,943,494 | 23,038,259 | 8,194,375 | 2,506,245 | 7,322,871 | 167,863 | + 871,504 | —2,338,382 | 27,0 | 8,1 |
| 1856–57 | 14,194,587 | 25,338,451 | 11,073,247 | 2,091,314 | 11,220,014 | 128,302 | + 146,767 | —1,962,912 | 29,5 | 8,2 |
| 1857–58 | 15,277,629 | 27,456,036 | 12,218,948 | 2,783,073 | 12,655,308 | 43,783 | + 436,360 | —2,739,290 | 26,7 | 8,1 |
| 1858–59 | 21,728,579 | 29,862,871 | 7,728,342 | 4,426,453 | 6,641,548 | 132,273 | +1,086,794 | —4,294,180 | 24,9 | 8,1 |
| 1859–60 | 24,265,140 | 27,960,203 | 11,147,563 | 4,284,234 | 10,753,068 | 64 307 | — 394,495 | —4,219,927 | 25,0 | 8,2 |

*Prepared from figures given in Palgrave's "Memorandum on Currency and Standard of Value," Appendix B to *Third Report of the Royal Commission on Depression of Trade and Industry.* C4797 of 1886. Figures for the production of gold and silver, which are for calendar years, are added from the "*Silver Quotation and the Gold Quotation,*" by R. Barclay

> "its silver coinage has not only had to satisfy the requirements of commerce as the medium of exchange, but it has to supply a sufficiency of material to the silversmith and the jeweller. The Mint has been pitted against the smelting-pot, and the coin produced by so much patience and skill by the one has been rapidly reduced into bangles by the other."*

Now it will be seen from the figures given that all the import of silver was coined and used up for currency purposes. Very little or nothing was left over for the industrial and social consumption of the people. That being the case, it is obvious that a large part of the coined silver must have been abstracted from monetary to non-monetary purposes. The hidden source of this monetary stringency thus becomes evident. To men of the time it was as clear as daylight that it was the rate of absorption of currency from monetary to non-monetary purposes that was responsible as to why (to quote from the same authority)

> "notwithstanding such large importations the demand for money has so far exceeded        that serious embarrassment has ensued and business has almost come to a stand from the scarcity of circulating medium. As fast as rupees have been coined they have been taken into the interior and have there disappeared from circulation, either in the Indian substitute for stocking-foot or in the smelting-pot into bangles."†

The one way open was to have caused such additional imports of silver as would have sufficed both for the monetary as well as the non-monetary needs of the country. But the imports of silver were probably already at their highest. For, as was argued by Mr. Cassels,

> "the annual production of silver of the whole world does not exceed ten million sterling. During the last few years, therefore, India alone has annually taken, and to a great extent absorbed, more of the metal than has been produced by the whole world. It is clear that this cannot long continue without producing serious embarrassment. Either the European markets will be unable or unwilling to supply us, or the value of silver will rise to an extravagant extent. Under such circumstances it is not difficult

* Minute on Gold Currency for India, dated December 8, 1863, in the *Report of the Bombay Chamber of Commerce*, 1863-64 App I, p 189

† Minute on Gold Currency for India, dated December 1, 1863 Report, op cit p. 184

> to foresee that the present crisis must continually recur, and the commerce in this country must be periodically, if not permanently, crippled by the scarcity of the circulating medium."*

Had there been any credit media the contraction of currency might not have been felt as severely as it was. But there was no credit money worth the name. The Government issued interest-bearing Treasury notes, which formed a part of the circulating medium of the country. But, apart from being insignificant in amount,† these Treasury notes had

> "proved a failure, owing, firstly, to the condition that they would not be received in payment of revenue for twelve months; secondly, they would be paid off or received only where issued, so that as the issues were confined to Calcutta, Madras and Bombay, their use and employment for purposes of circulation were limited to those cities . . . and lastly, because their amounts were too large and their period of running at interest too short."‡

Nor was banking so widely developed as to satisfy the currency needs of commerce. The chief hindrance to its growth was the attitude of the Court. Being itself a commercial body largely dealing in exchange, the Court was averse to the development of banking institutions lest they should prove rivals. As this traditional policy of hostility continued even after the Court had ceased to be a body of merchant princes, banks did not grow with the growth of trade. Indeed, as late as 1856 banks in India numbered few and their issues were small, as shown in the table on opposite page.

The insufficiency of silver and the want of credit currency caused such an embarrassment to trade that there grew up a

---

* Report, op cit p 189

† Amount of Indian Treasury notes outstanding:—

| | |
|---|---|
| On April 30, 1850 | £804,988 |
| " " " 1851 | 802,036 |
| " " " 1852 | 770,301 |
| " " " 1853 | 850,432 |
| " " " 1854 | 850,627 |
| " " " 1855 | 889,875 |
| " " " 1856 | 967,711 |

Extracted from Table No 2 of the Return relating to East India Revenues, etc, Parliamentary Paper 201, VIII, 1858

‡*How to meet the Financial Difficulties of India*, by A C B, London, 1859, p 13. This is in many ways a most remarkable pamphlet, which suggested many of the later reforms in Indian currency and banking.

TABLE V

BANKS IN INDIA*

| Name of the Bank. | Year of Establishment | Head Offices. | Branches and Agencies. | Capital. Subscribed. £ | Capital. Paidup. £ | Notes in Circulation. £ | Specie in Coffers. £ | Bills under Discount. £ |
|---|---|---|---|---|---|---|---|---|
| Bank of Bengal | 1809 | Calcutta | | 1,070,000 | 1,070,000 | 1,714,771 | 851,964 | 125,251 |
| Bank of Madras | 1843 | Madras | | 300,000 | 300,000 | 123,719 | 139,960 | 59,871 |
| Bank of Bombay | 1840 | Bombay | | 522,000 | 522,000 | 571,089 | 240,073 | 195,836 |
| Oriental Bank | 1851 | | | 1,215,000 | 1,215,000 | 199,279 | 1,146,529 | 2,918,399 |
| Agra and U. P. | 1833 | Calcutta | Agra, Madras, Lahore, Canton and London | 700,000 | 700,000 | — | 74,362 | — |
| N. W. Bank | 1844 | " | Bombay, Simla, Mussowri and Agra Agencies in Delhi and Cawnpore | 220,560 | 220,000 | — | — | — |
| London & Eastern Bank | 1854 | | | 250,000 | — | 325,000 | — | — |
| Commercial Bank | 1854 | Bombay | Agents in London, Calcutta, Canton, & Shanghai | 1,000,000 | 456,000 | — | — | — |
| Delhi Bank | 1844 | Delhi | Agents in London, Calcutta, Bombay and Madras | — | 180,000 | — | — | — |
| Simla Bank | 1844 | | | — | 63,850 | — | — | — |
| Dacca Bank | 1846 | | | 30,000 | — | — | — | — |
| Mercantile Bank | | Bombay | London, Calcutta, Colombo, Kandy, Canton and Shanghai. | 500,000 | 328,826 | 777,156 | 77,239 | 109,547 |
| India, China and Australian Bank | | | | had not | commenced | business | | |

*R. M. Martin, *The Indian Empire*, Vol. I, p 565. N B.—The table in original does not specify dates, but internal evidence shows that it is about 1856.

change in the attitude toward the Currency Act of 1835, and people for once, began to ask whether, although it was well to have changed from bimetallism to monometallism, it would not have been better to have preferred gold monometallism to silver monometallism. As more and more of gold was imported and coined, the stronger grew the demand for giving it a legal status in the existing system of Indian currency.* All were agreed on the principle of a gold currency: whatever difference there was, was confined to the method of its adoption. The introduction of gold on a bimetallic basis was out of the question, for the Govenment refused to make what it deemed to be the "hopeless attempt" to fix the value of gold and silver and compel their acceptance at that value.† The projects which the Government was willing to consider‡ were : (1) to introduce the "sovereign" or some other gold coin and to let it circulate at its market price from day to day as measured in silver; (2) to issue a new gold coin, bearing the exact value of a given number of rupees, and make it a legal tender for a limited period, when it might be readjusted and again valued, and made a legal tender for a similar period at the new rate; (3) to introduce the English sovereign as a legal tender for Rs. 10, but limited in legal tender to the amount of Rs. 20 or two sovereigns; or (4) to substitute a gold standard for the silver standard.

Of these projects, the first three were evidently unsafe as currency expedients. Fixity of value between the various components of the currency is an essential requisite in a well-regulated monetary system. Each coin must define a fixed value, in terms of the others realizable by the most untutored intellect. When it ceases to do so, it becomes a mere commodity, the value of which fluctuates with the fluctuations of the market. This criterion ruled out the first two projects. To have introduced a coin as money, the value of which could not be vouched for—as would have been the case under the first project—from one day to

* The matter was first broached by the native shroffs and merchants of Calcutta in April, 1859, in a letter to the President of the Bengal Chamber of Commerce Both agreed to urge upon the Government the necessity of a gold currency in India Cf *Papers relating to the Introduction of a Gold Currency in India*, Calcutta, 1866, pp 1-3

† *Ibid* , p 6

‡ Cf Minute by the Rt Hon James Wilson, dated December 25, 1859, *Ibid* p 23

another, apart from the trouble of computing and ascertaining the fluctuations, would have been a source of such embarrassment that the Government, it must be said, acted wisely in not adopting it. There was no saving grace in the second project to recommend its adoption in preference to the first. If it had been adopted the result would have been that during the period when a rate remained fixed, gold would have been forced into circulation supposing that its market value was lower, and at the end of the year, if it was known that the rate would be revised and the value of the coin be reduced in conformity with the fall of gold, a general struggle to get rid of the overrated gold coin and shift the inevitable loss to the shoulders of others would have certainly ensued. The third was a somewhat strange proposal. It is possible with a low-priced metal to strike coins of less than full value for the purposes of small payments and limit their tender. But this is not possible with a high-priced metal, the *raison d'etre* of which is to facilitate large transactions. The objections to the plan could hardly be concealed. So long as gold was undervalued, it would not circulate at all. But once it became overvalued owing to changes in the market ratio, the rupee would go out of circulation, and shopkeepers and traders would remain possessed of a coin which would be of no use in liquidating large transactions.

The only project free from these faults was the adoption of a gold standard, with silver as a subsidiary currency. The strongest argument, the Government could advance against this demand was that "in a country where all obligations have been contracted to be paid in silver, to make a law by which they could forcibly be paid in anything else would simply be to defraud the creditor for the advantage of the debtor, and to break public faith."* However sound the argument might have been, it was hopelessly inadequate to meet the growing demand to place the Indian currency on an expanding basis. Indeed, it cannot be said that the Government was really serious in its opposition to a gold currency. For the strength of its position, it relied not so much on the soundness of its arguments against gold, but on its discovery that a better solution than a gold currency existed at hand.

*Ibid., p. 26.

If what was wanted was a supplement to the existing currency, then the remedy proposed by the Government was unassailable. Gold would have been uneconomical and inconvenient. Silver backed by paper would make the currency economical, convenient, and expansive. Indeed, the advantages were so much in favour of the official alternative that this first attempt against the silver standard resulted not in the establishment of a gold standard, but in the introduction of a Government paper currency to supplement the existing silver standard.

None the less, the desire for a gold standard on the part of the people was too great to be altogether ignored, though the demand for it was supposed to have been met by the alternative measure. The paper currency, as originally conceived by Mr. Wilson, was a complete counterblast to the gold agitation. But his successor, Mr. Laing, differed from him in what he regarded as the "barbarous" exclusion of gold from Indian currency. He therefore introduced two important provisos in the original Bill, when the task of carrying it through fell upon him, owing to the untimely death of Mr. Wilson. One was to raise the lowest denomination of notes from Rs. 5 to Rs. 20. The other was

> " to authorize the Governor-General in Council from time to time to direct by order to be published in the Gazettes of Calcutta, Madras and Bombay, that notes to an extent not exceeding one-fourth of the total amount of issues represented by coin and bullion . . . . be issued in exchange for gold coin . . . or bullion computed at rates to be fixed by such order "

The Act, which afterwards embodied the Bill, adopted the second proviso *in toto*, and the first after being modified so as to fix Rs. 10 as the lowest denomination of notes to be issued. Although its general tenor is clear, the immediate aim of the second proviso does not become quite clear from a perusal of the official papers. The Select Committee on the Paper Currency Bill seems to have held that the proviso was innocuous, if not good. It thought

> "that on special occasions and in particular transactions it might be a great advantage to the mercantile community to know that gold could be made available as money at a fixed rate. If, on the other hand, at the rate fixed gold did not enter into circulation it would prove that silver, with a secure and convertible

> paper currency, gave perfect confidence and answered all the wants of the trade and of the community, and the enactment would remain a dead letter and be perfectly harmless."

But there is no doubt that Mr. Laing looked upon it as an easy means of making a transition to the gold standard. In his Minute on Currency and Banking, dated May 7, 1862, he wrote:

> "The object of this proviso was simply to leave the door open for cautious and tentative experiments with regard to the future use of gold. The importation of gold already exists and is increasing, and the metal is much appreciated by the native population as generally to command a premium Thus, after a time, if the use of gold becomes more general, and its value more fixed, some further step might be taken."

And such seems to have been the impression of the Secretary of State at the time, for he undrstood the force of the recommendation in favour of issuing notes against gold was that it would "effectively contribute to the introduction of a gold currency in India.*

But whether conceived as a relief to the mercantile community or as an avenue for introducing a gold currency the proviso was not put into effect. The Secretary of State objected† to any action being taken with regard thereto. In the meantime the paper currency did not prove the panacea, it was avowed to be. The extent it reached and the economy it effected were comparatively insignificant.

TABLE VI

EXTENT AND ECONOMY OF PAPER CURRENCY

| Presidencies. | Bullion. | Coin. | Government Securities. | Value of Notes in Circulation |
|---|---|---|---|---|
| Calcutta on Oct. 31, 1863 . . | — | 1,84,55,922 | 1,10,44,078 | 2,95,00,000 |
| Madras on Oct. 31, 1863 . . | — | 73,00,000 | — | 73,00,000 |
| Bombay on Jan. 4, 1864 . . | 1,17,00,000 | 1,19,00,000 | — | 2,36,00,000 |
| Total . . | 1,17,00,000 | 3,76,55,922 | 1,10,44,078 | 6,04,00,000 |

* Par. 59 of the Secretary of State's Despatch, No. 158, dated September 16, 1862.
† *See* par 64 of his Despatch, *supra*.

As was pointed out by Mr. Cassels* the currency notes, after three years, had been taken only to the extent of about 6 per cent. of the whole metallic currency, which was then estimated by Mr. Wilson to be £100,000,000 in sterling, and that they had actually fulfilled their primary object of releasing the reproductive capital of the country only to the extent of a million sterling or 1 per cent. of the whole. Owing to the demand for Indian cotton in the Liverpool market to take the place of American cotton, the export of which was stopped during the Civil War, the growing foreign trade assumed enormous proportions. And as the paper currency gave no relief, the entire stress fell upon silver. The production of silver, however, was not increasing much faster than it did previously, and its absorption by India had not slackened. The inadequacy of a currency medium therefore continued to be felt as acutely as before, notwithstanding the introduction of a paper currency. Not only was gold imported in large quantities, but was employed for monetary purposes, although it was not legal tender. The fact was brought to the notice of the Government of India by the Bombay Chamber of Commerce† in a memorial praying for the introduction of a gold currency in India, in which it was pointed out

> "that there is an increasing tendency to the creation of a gold ingot currency, by the natives of this country, as a rude remedy for the defects of the existing silver one,"

and

> "that gold bars, stamped with the mark of Bombay banks, are for this purpose circulated in several parts of the country."

This led to an agitation for requiring the Government to give effect to the proviso in the Paper Currency Act,‡ and the movement assumed such dimensions that it forced the hands of the

---

* Cf his letter to the Government of Bombay, dated January 1, 1864 *Vide* Papers, etc , on the Introduction of Gold in India, pp 51-69

†*Report of the Bombay Chamber of Commerce*, 1863-64, App. I, p 206.

‡ This time the Government was memorialized by all the Chambers of Commerce —Bengal, Bombay, and Madras Action was also urged by the Bombay Association and the Manchester Chamber of Commerce But the movement derived its greatest strength from the support of the Government of Bombay, particularly by Sir William Mansfield's famous Minute on Gold Currency for India

# TABLE VII*

## TRADE AND CURRENCY

| Years. | Merchandise | | Treasure: Net Imports of | | Total Coinage of | | Excess (+) or Defect (—) of Coinage on Net Imports of | | Annual Production (in £, 00,000 omitted of) | |
|---|---|---|---|---|---|---|---|---|---|---|
| | Imports £ | Exports £ | Silver £ | Gold £ | Silver £ | Gold £ | Silver £ | Gold £ | Gold | Silver. |
| 1860–61 | 23,493,716 | 32,970,605 | 5,328,009 | 4 232,569 | 5,297,150 | 65,038 | — 30,859 | —4,167,531 | 23,9 | 8,2 |
| 1861–62 | 22,320,432 | 36,317,042 | 9,036,456 | 5,184,425 | 7,470,030 | 58,667 | —1,616,426 | —5,125,758 | 22,8 | 8,5 |
| 1862–63 | 22,632,384 | 47,859,645 | 12,550 155 | 6,848,156 | 9,355,405 | 130,666 | —3,194,750 | —6,717,490 | 21,6 | 9,0 |
| 1863–64 | 27,145,590 | 65,625,449 | 12,796 717 | 8,898 306 | 11,556,720 | 54,354 | —1,239,997 | —8,843,952 | 21,4 | 9,8 |
| 1864–65 | 28,150,923 | 68 027,016 | 10,078,798 | 9 839,964 | 10,911,322 | 95,672 | + 832,524 | —9,744,292 | 22,6 | 10,3 |
| 1865–66 | 29,599,228 | 65,491,123 | 18,668,673 | 5,724,476 | 14,639,353 | 17,665 | —4,029,320 | —5,706,811 | 24,0 | 10,4 |
| 1866–67 | 29,038,715 | 41,859,994 | 6,963 073 | 3,842,328 | 6,183,113 | 27,725 | — 779,960 | —3,814,603 | 24,2 | 10,1 |
| 1867–68 | 35,705,783 | 50,874,056 | 5,593,961 | 4,609 466 | 4,385,080 | 21,534 | —1,208,881 | —4,587,932 | 22,8 | 10,8 |
| 1868–69 | 35,990,142 | 53 062,165 | 8,601,022 | 5,159,352 | 4,269,305 | 25,156 | —4,331,717 | —5,134,196 | 22,0 | 10,0 |
| 1869–70 | 32,927,520 | 52,471,376 | 7,320,337 | 5,592,016 | 7,510,480 | 78,510 | + 190,143 | —5,513,506 | 21,2 | 9,5 |

* Sources same as those used in the case of Table IV

Government. On this occasion, the plan for effecting the change *was boldly conceived. Sir Charles Trevelyan saw through the weak point of the proviso on which the Government was called* upon to act. *He argued that the currency notes were payable only in the current coin of the country, which in India was the* silver rupee, and to hold a portion of the reserve gold which could not be tendered in payment of the notes was seriously to endanger their convertibility in times of political distrust or commercial panic.* He therefore ventured beyond the scope of the agitation, and pronounced that instead of allowing gold a back-door entry into the currency system it ought to be made the standard of value in India. He did not agree with Mr. Wilson that the substitution of gold for the silver standard would be "to break faith with the creditor." Nor was he much deterred by the fact that before the silver currency could be reduced to a subsidiary position, the introduction of gold in India would give rise to a double standard for the time being; for he argued that "all nations must pass through a transition stage of a double standard before they arrive at a single standard." Accordingly he proposed that (1) sovereigns and half-sovereigns of British or Australian standard should be legal tender in India, at the rate of one sovereign for Rs. 10. and that (2) Government currency notes should be exchangeable either for rupees or sovereigns at the rate of one sovereign for Rs. 10, but that they should not be exchangeable for bullion.

His proposals were accepted by the Government of India and were communicated to the Secretary of State† for his sanction. But the Secretary of State, impatient and intolerant of any deviation from a monometallic system, whittled down the whole project with scant courtesy. His reply‡ is a grotesque piece of reasoning and terribly shallow. He was unwilling to allow the measure,

* Cf. his Minute dated June, 20 1864 *Vide* Papers, etc., on Gold in India p 147 *et seq* He was even opposed to holding silver *bullion* in the paper currency reserve, for this involved on the Currency Department the obligation to get the silver coined, which was a matter of time, having regard to the limited capacity of the Indian Mints at the time, while the notes issued were payable *in coin on demand* There was a run on the Paper Currency Department, which found itself short of coin

† Cf Government of India's Despatch, No 89, dated Simla, July 14, 1864

‡ Financial Despatch from the Secretary of State, No 224, dated September 26, 1864

because he felt satisfied that the rate of Rs. 10 to a sovereign underrated the sovereign too much to permit its circulation. Here he was on solid ground. The cost of producing a sovereign at a Mint in India was estimated* at the time to be Rs. 10-4-8; while the cost of importing it to Calcutta from England was estimated at Rs. 10-4-10, and from Australia at Rs. 10-2-9. Whichever was the proper rate, it was certain that sovereigns could not circulate at the rate of Rs. 10 to 1. It was a pity that Sir Charles Trevelyan did not propose a higher ratio† so as to make the circulation of the sovereign an assured event. But the Secretary of State would have been averse to the measure just the same, even if the ratio had been favourable to the sovereign. To the Secretary of State, the measure, based as it was on an unfavourable ratio, was useless. But if based on a favourable ratio it was none the less pernicious, for, it portended the possibility of what he considered as the most vicious system of double standard, however temporary it might have been. The mere contingency of giving rise to a bimetallic system was enough to frighten the Secretary of State into opposition to the whole measure, for he refused to admit that "it may be for the public advantage to pass through a period of double standard in order to change the basis of the currency from silver to gold."

The only concession that the Secretary of State was willing to make was to permit "that gold coin should be received into public treasuries at a rate to be fixed by Government and publicly announced by Proclamation" without making it a general legal tender in India. It will be recalled that this was a revival of that foolish measure which was abandoned in 1852 for having embarrassed the Government. To offer to receive coin which you cannot pay back is to court trouble, and it was to obviate the too-well-known danger inherent in the project that this more com-

* Cf. Letter from the Hon. Claud Brown to the Hon. Sir C. E. Trevelyan, dated Calcutta, May 28, 1864. *Vide* Papers, etc., on Gold, p. 265.

† The reason why he prefered the ratio of 10 to 1 was that that was the prevalent market ratio in India. His argument was that "the sovereign must be rated for circulation in India, not with reference to its English, but to its Indian price estimated in silver." Probably he was unwilling to overrate the sovereign because of his fear that "the existing Indian currency would be rapidly revolutionized and creditors would receive much less than their due." Cf. his Minute dated November 23, 1864. *Vide* Papers, etc. on Gold in India.

plete measure was proposed. But the currency stringency was so great that the Government of India, rather than obstinately cling to their view, consented to avail themselves of the suggestion of the Secretary of State, and issued a Government Notification in November, 1864, which proclaimed that

> "sovereigns and half-sovereigns coined at any authorized Royal Mint in England or Australia of current weight, shall until further notice be received in all the Treasuries of British India and its dependencies in payment of sums due to Government, as the equivalent of 10 and 5 Rs. respectively; and that such sovereigns and half-sovereigns shall, whenever available at any Government Treasury, be paid at the same rates to any person willing to receive them in payment of claims against the Government."

The real par, however, was somewhat above Rs. 10 to the sovereign,* and the notification was therefore inoperative. The currency situation, on the other hand, continued to be as acute as ever, and the Government of India was again moved in 1866 by the Bengal Chamber of Commerce to take steps to make the circulation of gold effective. This time the Chamber insisted on the institution of a Commission of Inquiry "as to the expediency of introducing gold into the monetary system of India." But the Government of India held† that "instead of a gold a paper currency has been introduced, in the expectation that it would prove a more convenient and acceptable circulating medium than either of the precious metals," and consequently "it must be shown that paper has not proved and is not likely to prove a circulating medium adequate to the wants and suitable to the habits of the country, before an endeavour is made to introduce gold in supersession of, or in addition to, paper." A commission was therefore appointed to inquire into the "operation of the existing currency arrangements which were established under Act XIX of 1861," and to report as to "what may be the advantage, as based on expediency, of the introduction of the legal tender of gold into India, in addition to that of silver." After an exhaustive investigation, the Commission came to the conclusion‡ that owing

* Cf. Appendix A to the Minute by Sir William Mansfield on Gold Currency for India, H. of C. Return 79 of 1865.

† Resolution in the Financial Department, dated February 3, 1866, in the *Fort William Gazette* of the same date, under Notification No. 592.

‡ For the Report of the Commission, *see* H. of C. Return 148 of 1868.

to several causes the paper currency had failed to establish itself among the circulating media of the country, but that gold was finding a larger place in the transactions of the people. The Commission ended by urging upon the Government "to cause a legal tender of gold to be a part of the currency arrangements of India." Now it was the turn of the Government to give effect to the recommendation. But, curiously enough, it did not go to the extent of adopting the recommendation of the Commission which it had itself appointed. Instead of making gold legal tender, as advised by the Commission, the only action the Government took was to issue another Notification on October 28, 1868, which simply altered the rate of the sovereign to Rs. 10-8, without doing anything further to avoid the evil consequence attendant upon that one-sided measure. Fortunately for the Government, even this correction of the rate did not induce any flow of gold into the circulation of the country. The currency troubles had by then subsided, and as no new pressure was exerted upon the Government, this proved the last of two abortive attempts the Government made to introduce gold into India.

For the time being, the problem was solved by the natural course of events. But, as subsequent events showed, the change to a gold standard would have been better for India* and would have been welcomed† in the interests of Europe, which was then suffering from high prices due to the superfluity of gold. At this particular juncture, the Government of India was really at the crossing of ways, and could have averted the misfortunes that were to befall it and its people if it had sided with the forces of change and replaced the silver standard by a gold standard, as it could most easily have done. That those in charge of Indian affairs should have thrown the weight of their authority against the change was no dishonest act deserving of reproach,‡ but it does furnish one more illustration of those disastrous human ways, which often lead people to regard the situation in which they

* It is true Prof J E Cairnes was against the introduction of a gold standard in India; but later he withdrew his objections Cf his *Essays in Political Economy* (London, 1873, pp 88-90)

‡ Cf J R McCulloch, *Dictionary of Commerce*, Ed 1869, p 1131

‡ Mr H B Russell says that they retained the silver standard because they profited by it on their remittances Cf his *International Monetary Conferences*, 1898, p 32

live as most secure, just when it is most precarious. So secure did they feel about the currency situation that in 1870, when the Mint Law came to be revised and consolidated, they were content, as though nothing had happened or was likely to happen, to allow the silver standard of 1835 to continue pure and unsullied by any admixture of gold.*

Alas! those, who then said† that they were not called upon to take more than a "juridical" view of the Indian currency question, knew very little what was in store for them.

---

* The original Mint and Coinage Bill contained clauses embodying the notification of 1868, compelling the Government to receive sovereigns at Public Treasuries Cf *Gazette of India*, Part V, dated July 23, 1870 But such was the degree of indifferences shown that they were afterwards dropped by the Select Committee, which preferred to leave the matter to the discretion of the Executive

† Cf the speech of the Hon Mr Stephen on September 6, 1870, introducing the Coinage and Mint Bill Vide *Supreme Legislative Council Proceedings* (abbreviated into *S L.C.P* ), Vol IX, p 398

## CHAPTER II

# THE SILVER STANDARD AND THE DISLOCATION OF ITS PARITY

It is clear how the evolutionary process with respect to the Indian currency culminated in the establishment of a silver standard and how the agitation for a gold currency ended in the silver standard being supplemented by a paper currency. Before proceeding to inquire into the working of such a mixed system, it would be useful to review briefly the nature of its framework.

The metallic part of it was regulated by Act XXIII of 1870. The coins authorized and legalized thereunder were as shown on p. 47.

The Act made no innovations either in regard to the number of coins issued by the Mints or their legal-tender powers. Identical though it was with the earlier enactments in the matter of coins,* its juridical provisions were designed to perfect the monetary law of the country as had never been done before. The former Acts which it repealed were very sparing in their recognition of the principle of mint "remedy" or "toleration," as it is called. The point has been largely deemed to be one of mere mint technique. That is so; but it is not without its monetary significance. When the precious metals were current by weight the question of a mint toleration could not possibly have arisen, for

---

* This may be seen from the following :—

(*a*) *Gold Coins.* (i), (ii), and (iii) were authorized by Section VII of Act XVII of 1835. Only (iv) was an addition made by this Consolidating Act of 1870.

(*b*) *Silver Coins.* (i), (ii), and (iii) were authorized by Section I of Act XVII of 1835. This Act had also authorized the issue of a silver coin called "Double Rupee," but this was discontinued by Section II of Act XIII of 1862, which substituted in its place the silver coin No. iv.

(*c*) *Copper Coins.* (i), (ii), and (iv) were first authorized by Section I of Act XXI of 1835, which, however, restricted their circulation to the Presidency of Bengal. They were afterwards universalized for the whole of India by Act XXII of 1844. Coin No. (iii) was first introduced by Section II of Act XI of 1854.

TABLE VIII

| Denomination of Coins issued by the Mint. | Gross Wt. Troy Grs. | Remedy in Weight. | Fineness. Troy Grs | Remedy in Fineness. | Legal-tender Power. |
|---|---|---|---|---|---|
| I. *Gold Coins* (*a*) | | | | | |
| (i) Mohur | 180 | $\frac{2}{1000}$ths | 165 | $\frac{2}{1000}$ths | Not Legal Tender at all. |
| (ii) Third of a Mohur | 60 | ,, | 65 | ,, | |
| (iii) Two-thirds of a Mohur | 120 | ,, | 110 | ,, | |
| (iv) Double Mohur | 360 | ,, | 330 | ,, | |
| II. *Silver Coins* (*b*) | | | | | |
| (i) Rupee | 180 | $\frac{5}{1000}$ths | 165 | $\frac{2}{1000}$ths | Unlimited Legal Tender. |
| (ii) Half-rupee | 90 | ,, | 82·5 | ,, | |
| (iii) Quarter-rupee | 45 | $\frac{7}{1000}$ths | 41·25 | $\frac{3}{1000}$ths | Legal Tender for Fractions of a Rupee only. |
| (iv) Eighth of a Rupee | 22.5 | $\frac{10}{1000}$ths | 20·625 | ,, | |
| III. *Copper Coins* (*c*) | | | | | |
| (i) Pice | 100 | $\frac{1}{40}$ths | — | — | Legal Tender for $\frac{1}{64}$th part of a Rupee. |
| (ii) Double Pice | 200 | ,, | — | — | Legal Tender for $\frac{1}{32}$nd part of a Rupee. |
| (iii) Half-pice. | 50 | ,, | — | — | Legal Tender for $\frac{1}{128}$th part of a Rupee. |
| (iv) Pie | 33·3 | ,, | — | — | Legal Tender for $\frac{1}{192}$nd part of a Rupee. |

it was open to every one to ascertain the same by weighing the value of his return. But since the invention of coinage, when currency came to be by tale, every one has trusted that the coins contained the value they were certified to contain. The actual value of the coin cannot, however, always be in exact agreement with its certified value. Such differences are bound to exist, and even with all the improvements in the art of coinage it would be difficult to avoid them. What matters is the extent of the deviation from the true mint standard. The mint laws of all countries, therefore, contain provisions which declare that coins shall not be legal tender at their certified value if they err from their legal standard beyond a certain margin. Indeed to make coins legal tender without prescribing a limit to their toleration is to open a way to fraud. In so far as the Act laid down a limit of toleration to the coins it authorized to be issued from the Mint, it was a salutary measure. It is to be regretted, however, that the Act instituted no machinery with which to ascertain that the coinage conformed to the law.* Another important improvement made by the Act was the recognition of the principle of free coinage. The principle, though it has not received the attention it deserves, is the very basis of a sound currency in that it has an important bearing on the cardinal question of the quantity of currency necessary for the transactions of the community. Two ways may be said to be open by which this quantity can be regulated. One way is to close the Mint and to leave it to the discretion of the Government to manipulate the currency to suit the needs. The other is to keep the Mint open and to leave it to the self-interest of individuals to determine the amount of currency they require. In the absence of unfailing tests to guide the exercise of discretion necessary in the case of closed Mints, the principle of open Mints has been agreed upon

* This machinery is provided in England by what is known as the "Trial of the Pyx." For a history of this institution and the way it functions, cf. H. of C. Return 203 of 1866 During the time of the East India Company the maintenance of the standard purity of the Indian coins always formed a most anxious concern of the Court of Directors. The coins of Indian mintage were regularly required to be sent over to England, where they were tested at a special Trial of the Pyx and the verdict reported back for the future guidance of the Mint Masters in India. Cf. H. of C. Return 14 of 1849. Since the winding-up of the Company there is no machinery to bring the Mint Masters to book.

as the superior of the two plans. When every individual can obtain coin for bullion and convert coin into bullion, as would be the case under open Mints, the quantity is automatically regulated. If the increasing demands of commerce require a large amount of circulating medium, it is for the interest of the community to divert a larger quantity of its capital for this purpose; if, on the contrary, the state of trade is such as to require less, a portion of the coin is withdrawn, and applied as any other commodity for purposes other than those of currency. Because the Act of 1870 expressly recognised the principle of open Mint, it is not to be supposed that the Mints were closed before that date. As a matter of fact they were open to the free coinage of both gold and silver, although the latter alone was legal tender. But, strange as it may seem, none of the earlier Acts contained a word as to the obligation of the Mint Master to coin *all* the metal presented to him—a condition which is of the essence of the open mint system. The provisions of the Act on this point are unmistakable. It required:—

> "Section 19. Subject to the Mint-rules for the time being in force, the Mint Master shall receive all gold and silver bullion and coin brought to the Mint:
>
> "Provided that such bullion and coin be fit for coinage:
>
> "Provided also that the quantity so bought at one time by one person is not less, in case of gold, than fifty tolas, and, in the case of silver, than one thousand tolas.
>
> "Section 20. A duty shall be levied at the rate of one rupee per cent. at the Mint on the produce of all gold bullion and on all gold coin brought for coinage to the Mint in accordance with the said Mint-rules.
>
> "Section 21 . All silver bullion or coin brought for coinage to the Mint, in accordance with the said Mint-rules, shall be subject to a duty at the rate of 2 per cent. on the produce of such from the return to be made to the proprietor.
>
> "Section 22. A charge of one-fourth per mille on gold bullion and coin, and of one per mille on silver bullion and coin, shall also be levied for melting or cutting such bullion and coin so as to render the same fit for receipt into the Mint.
>
> Section 23. All gold and silver bullion and coin brought to the Mint for coinage, and which is inferior to the standard

fineness prescribed by this Act, or which, from brittleness or other cause, is unfit for coinage, shall, in case it is refined, be subject, in addition to the duty and charge aforesaid, to such charge on account of the loss and expense of refining as the Governor-General in Council prescribes in this behalf.

"Section 24. The Mint Master, on the delivery of gold or silver bullion or coin into the Mint for coinage, shall grant to the proprietor a receipt which shall entitle him to a certificate from the Assay Master for the net produce of such bullion or coin payable at the General Treasury.

"Section 25. For all gold bullion and coin, in respect of which the Assay Master has granted a certificate, payment shall be made, as nearly as may be, in gold coins coined under this Act or Act No. XVII of 1835; and the balance (if any) due to the proprietor shall be paid in silver, or in silver and copper, coins, in British India."

In the matter of paper currency the Government, it is to be noted, did not proceed upon the principle of freedom of issue, which then obtained in the country. There prevails the erroneous view that before the introduction of the Government paper currency the right of note issue was confined to the three Presidency banks of India. As a matter of fact there existed in India what is called the free banking system, in which every bank was at liberty to issue its notes. It is true that notes of the Presidency banks enjoyed a status slightly superior to that enjoyed by the notes of other banks in that they were received by the Government to some extent in payment of revenue*—a privilege for which the Presidency banks had to submit to a stringent legislative control on their business,† from which other banks whose

* Cf. F. C. Harrison, *Economic Journal*, 1891, Vol. I, p. 726.

† The reasons for such control are to be found in the peculiar relationship that subsisted between the Government and the Presidency banks. Prior to 1862, as a safeguard against their insolvency, the Presidency Bank Charters restricted the kind of business in which they were to engage themselves. Put very briefly, the principal restrictions imposed prohibited the banks from conducting foreign-exchange business, from borrowing or receiving deposits payable out of India, and from lending for a longer period than six months, or upon mortgage, or on the security of immovable property, or upon promissory notes bearing less than two independent names, or upon goods unless the goods or title to them were deposited with the banks as security. The Government held shares in the banks and appointed a part of the Directorate. In 1862, when the right of note issue was withdrawn, these statutory limitations on the

issues were not so priviliged were immune. But this disadvantage was not sufficient to discourage other banks from indulging in the right of issue which was left open to them by law. However, this freedom of issue does not seem to have been exercised by any of the banks on any very large scale, not even by the Presidency Banks,* and was taken away from all in 1861,† when there was established a national issue for the whole of India entrusted to the management of a Government Department called the Department of Paper Currency. But if private interest was not allowed to play the same part in determining the quantity of paper currency as was the case with regard to metallic currency, neither was any discretion left to the Government Department in the regulation of the paper currency. The Department of Paper Currency had no more discretion in the matter of paper currency than the Mint Master had in the matter of metallic currency.

The Department's duty was confined by law‡ to the issue of notes in exchange for the amount thereof: (1) in current silver

business of the banks were greatly relaxed, though the Government power of control remained unchanged But the banks having in some cases abused their liberty, nearly all the old restrictions of the earlier period were reimposed in 1876 by the Presidency Banks Act, Government, however, abandoning direct interference in the management, ceasing to appoint official directors, and disposing of its shares in the banks. Some of these limitations have been incorporated in Act XLVII of 1920, which amalgamated the three Presidency banks into the Imperial Bank of India. Banks other than Presidency banks have been entirely immune from any legislative control whatsoever, except in so far as they are made amenable to the provisions of the Indian Companies Act Cf. in this connection Minutes by Sir Henry Maine, No. 47, and the accompanying note by W Stokes. The control of these banks is one of the important problems of banking legislation in India.

* It should, however, be noted that in 1860 the circulation of notes of the three Presidency banks was larger than their current accounts, as is evident from the following.—

| *Name of the Bank.* | *Accounts current* | *Notes in circulation* |
|---|---|---|
| Bank of Bengal | £1,254,875 | £1,283,946 |
| „ Bombay | 438,459 | 765,234 |
| „ Madras | 161,959 | 192,291 |

(*Bankers' Magazine*, April, 1893, p. 547)

† For a summary of the controversy *re.* Bank issue *v.* Government issue, see *Report of the Bombay Chamber of Commerce for* 1859-60. Appendix L, pp. 284-318

‡ Sect IV of Act XIX of 1861.

coin of the Government of India; (2) in standard silver bullion or foreign silver coin computed according to standard at the rate of 979 rupees per 1,000 tolas of standard silver fit for coinage; (3) in other notes of the Government of India, payable to bearer on demand of other amounts issued within the same circle; and (4) in gold coin of the Government of India, or for foreign gold coin or bullion, computed at such ratio and according to such rules and conditions as may be fixed by the Governor-General, provided that the notes issued against gold did not exceed one-fourth of the total amount of issues represented by coin and bullion. The whole of this amount was required by law to be retained as a reserve for the payment of notes issued with the exception of a fixed amount which was invested in Government securities, the interest thereon being the only source of profit to the Government. The limit to the sum to be so invested was governed "by the lowest amount to be estimated to which, according to all reasonable experience, the paper currency might be expected to fall."* Estimating on this basis, the limit to the investment portion was fixed at 4 crores in 1861,† at 6 crores in 1871,‡ and at 8 crores in 1890.§ But notwithstanding the growing increase in the investment portion, never was the fiduciary issue based thereon so great¶ as to abrogate the essential principle of the Indian Paper Currency Law, the object of which was to so regulate the volume of paper currency that it should always preserve its value by contracting and expanding in the same manner and to the same extent as its metallic counterpart.

* Cf. Sir Richard Temple's speech introducing the Paper Currency Bill, dated March 25, 1870 *Supreme Legislative Council proceedings*, Vol. IX, pp. 151-52.

† Act XIX, Sec. X. ‡ Act III, Sec. 16. §Act XV, Sec. I.

¶ The following table shows the distribution of the paper currency reserve at three different periods:

| Period. | Note Circulation. | Composition of the Reserve. | | | | Percentage of each Component of the Reserve to the Total Circulation. | | |
|---|---|---|---|---|---|---|---|---|
| | | Silver. | Gold | Securities. | Total. | Silver. | Gold. | Securities. |
| 1862-1871 | 7 63 | 4.80 | 0.03 | 2 80 | 7.63 | 63 | — | 37 |
| 1872-1881. | 11 82 | 5 98 | — | 5.84 | 11.82 | 51 | — | 49 |
| 1882-1891. | 15.74 | 9.64 | — | 6.10 | 15 74 | 61 | — | 39 |

Such was the organisation of the mixed currency that existed in India before it underwent a profound change during the closing years of the nineteenth century. Though of a mixed character, the paper portion formed a comparatively small part of the total. The principal reasons why the paper currency did not assume a large proportion are to be found in the organization of the paper currency itself.* One such reason was that the lowest denomination of the notes was too large to displace the metallic currency. By the law of 1861 the denomination of notes ranged upwards from Rs. 10 as the lowest to Rs. 20, 50, 100, 500, and 1,000. In a country where the average range of transactions did not exceed R. 1 and were as low as 1 anna or even lower, it is impossible to expect that paper currency could, to any great extent, figure in the dealings of the people. Even Rs. 5 notes, the issue of which was first sanctioned in the year 1871,† were not low enough to penetrate into the economic life of the people. The other impediment to the increase of paper currency was the difficulty of encashing notes. One of the infelicitous incidents of the paper currency in India consisted in the fact that they were made legal tender everywhere within a circle, but encashable only at the office of issue. For such a peculiar organization of the paper currency in India, what was largely responsible was the prevalence of internal exchange‡ in the country. It raised a serious problem for the Government to cope with. If notes were to be made universally encashable it was feared that merchants, instead of using

* For a clear and concise sketch of the organization of the paper currency in India, *see* the Note of the Government of India in the Report of the U.S. Director of the Mint, Washington, 1894, pp. 231-33.

† Sec. 3 of Act III.

‡ It may be pointed out that although the Presidency banks had ceased to issue notes, yet under the agreements made with the Government in virtue of Act XXIV of 1861 the banks were employed by the Government "for superintending, managing and becoming agents for the issue, payment and exchange of promissory notes of the Government of India, and for carrying on the business of an agency of issue" on a remuneration of ¾ per cent. per annum "on the daily average amount of Government currency notes outstanding and in circulation through the agency of the bank." In the conflict that ensued between the Government of India and the Secretary of State because it believed that it would help the extension and popularization of the notes as to the propriety of thus employing the banks, the former was in favour of the plan, while the latter disliked the arrangement because it seemed to him to compromise the principle of complete separation between the business of issue and the business of

notes as currency, might use them as remittance on different centres to avoid internal exchange, and the Government be obliged to move funds between different centres to and fro, lest it should have to suspend cash payments. To undertake resource operations on such a vast scale between such distant centres when facilities for quick transport were so few, was obviously impossible,* and the Government therefore decided to curtail the encashment facilities of notes it issued. For the purposes of the paper currency, the Government divided the country into a number of circles of issue, and each currency circle was further subdivided into sub-circles,† and the notes issued bore on their face the name of the circle or sub-circle from which they originated. Notes issued from any agency of issue situated in the territory comprised within a circle of issue were not legal tender in the territory of any other currency circle, nor were they encashable outside their own circle. Nay more, the notes issued from sub-circles subject to the same chief circle were legal tender in one another's territory, but were not encashable except at their office of issue or at the issue office of their chief circle. The sub-circle notes could thus be cashed at two places, but the notes of the issue office of the chief circle, though legal tender in the entire territory covered by it, were encashable nowhere except at its own counter, not even at any of its own sub-circles.‡ This want of universal encashability, though it saved the Government from the possibility of embarrassment, proved so great a hindrance to the popu-

banking. Neither of the two, however, grasped the fact that the profit on remittances on different centres owing to the prevalence of internal exchange was so great that the commission allowed to the banks was an insufficient inducement to cause them to promote the circulation of notes by providing facilities at their branches for the free encashment of them. So high was the internal exchange, and so reluctant seemed the banks to popularize the notes, that Government finally dischraged them from being their agents for paper cursency from January 2, 1866. *See* House of Commons Return, East Indian (Paper Money) 215 of 1862.

* Cf. the speech of the Hon. Mr. Laing on the Paper Currency Bill dated February 16, 1861, *S.L.C.P.*, Vol. VII, pp. 73-74

† Each sub-circle had within it a number of agencies of issue; but the agencies were centres not of encashment but only of issue.

‡ For the inconveniences of the "circle" system and the various measures contemplated by Government to facilitate the encashment of notes, see *Report of the Bombay Chamber of Commerce for* 1868-69, Appendix, pp. 309-16.

larity of the notes that it may be doubted whether the paper currency could have made a progress greater than it did even if the lowest denomination of the notes had been lower than it actually was.

It must, however, be borne in mind that it was not the intention of the Indian Legislature to make the Indian currency as economical* as was desired by the Executive Government. The Legislature was no doubt appealed to by the original author of the paper currency to turn India into a new Peru, where as much currency could be had with as little cost,† but the Legislature showed a rather prudent reserve on the matter of aiding the consummation of such a policy. As the centres of encashment were so few, and the area included within each so large as to separate the furthest point in a circle by a distance of about 700 miles from the centre of encashment of the circle, it viewed with dread the authorizing of notes of smaller denomination which the poor could not refuse and yet could not cash.‡ Besides the hardship involved in the want of encashability in the notes, the Legislature feared they would prove a "fugitive treasure" in the hands of the Indian peasant. Not being able to preserve them from rain and ants, he might have had to pay a heavy discount to be rid of the notes he could have been forced to accept.§ So opposed was the Legislature to the economizing clauses of the Paper Currency Bill as contrived to drive out metallic currency that it gave the Government an option to choose between legal-tender notes but of higher denomination and lower-denomination notes but of no

* Cf. the whole speech of the Hon. Mr. Sconce dated September 22, 1860, *S L C P*, Vol. p. 1143 *et seq.*

† Cf. the speech of Mr. Wilson, the originator of paper currency in India, dated March 3, 1860, where he says: "In short, to abstract so much coin from the mere mechanical purpose of the circulation, supplying its place with convertible paper, would be exactly the same in effect as if suddenly, in the centre of the Maidan, a rich silver mine had been discovered which produced silver at little or no cost." *Supreme Legislative Council Proceedings*, Vol. VI, p. 250.

‡ Cf. the speeches of the Hon. Mr. Forbes, dated July 13, 1861, *S.L C.P.* 1154

§ Cf. the speech of the Hon. Mr. Forbes, dated July 13, 1861. *Supreme Legislative Council Proceedings*, Vol. VII, p. 768.

legal-tender power.* And as the Government chose to have legal-tender notes, the Legislature in its turn insisted on their being of higher denomination. At first it adhered to notes of Rs. 20 as the lowest denomination, though it later on yielded to bring it down to 10, which was the lowest limit it could tolerate in 1861. Not till ten years after that, did the Legislature consent to the issue of Rs. 5 notes, and that, too, only when the Government had promised to give extra legal facilities for their encashment.† On the whole, the desire of the Indian Legislature was to make the Indian currency safer, rather than economical, and such it undoubtedly was.

How did the currency system thus constituted work? Stability of value is one of the prime requisites of a good currency system. But if we judge the Indian currency from this point of view, we find that there existed such variations in its value that it is difficult to escape the conclusion that the system was a failure.

Taking the rate of discount as an evidence of the adequacy of currency for internal commerce, it was the opinion of such a high financial authority as Mr. Van Den Berg that the unexpected contortions and sudden transitions in the Indian money market were unparalleled in the annals of any other money market in any other part of the world.‡ India is pre-eminently a country subject to seasonal swings.§ Mid-summer is naturally a period of diminished activity, while autumn brings renewed vigour in all activities of social and economic life. Not production alone is affected by seasons. On the side of consumption, Indian social life is also subject to seasonal variations. There are marriage season, holiday seasons and holy seasons. Even distribution has assumed in India quite a seasonal character. The practice of paying rents, wages, dividends, and settling accounts at stated intervals has been gaining ground as a result of

* Cf the speech of the Hon Mr. Scone, September 22, 1880, *S L C P*, Vol. VI p. 1151.

† For such extra facilities, and measures adopted to materialize them, cf. the interesting speech of the Hon Sir Richard Temple on the Paper Currency Bill dated January 13, 1871, *S L C P*, Vol X. pp. 22-25.

‡ *The Money Market and Paper Currency of British India*, Batavia, 1884, p. 3.

§ It should be noted that the slack and the busy seasons are not uniformly dis-

contact with Western economic organization. All these generate a kind of rhythm in the social demand for money, rising at certain periods of the year and falling at others. Having regard to the seasonal character of the economic and social life, the fluctuations caused by the discount rate soaring high during busy months when it should have been low enough to liquidate the transactions, and falling low during slack months when it should have been high enough to prevent the market from being demoralized, are unavoidable. But what made the contortions of the Indian money market so obnoxious was the circumstance that the seasonal fluctuations in the discount rate were so abnormal.*

The explanation for such a market phenomenon is to be sought in the irregularity of the money supply of the country. In

tributed over the whole surface of the country. The distribution is roughly as follows —

| Months | Eastern India | | Western India Bombay and Karachee | Nothern India | | Southern India Madras |
|---|---|---|---|---|---|---|
| | Rangoon | Calcutta | | Cawnpore | Lahore | |
| Busy<br>Slack | 3 Months<br>9 ,, | 4 Months<br>8 ,, | 6 months<br>6 ,, | 6 months<br>6 ,, | 9 months<br>3 ,, | 6 months<br>6 ,, |
| Jan. | Busy | Slack | Busy | Slack | Busy | Slack |
| Feb | ,, | ,, | ,, | Busy | ,, | Busy |
| March | ,, | ,, | ,, | ,, | ,, | ,, |
| April | Slack | ,, | ,, | ,, | ,, | ,, |
| May | ,, | ,, | Slack | Slack | ,, | ,, |
| June | ,, | ,, | ,, | ,, | ,, | ,, |
| July | ,, | ,, | ,, | ,, | Slack | ,, |
| Aug | ,, | Busy | ,, | ,, | ,, | Slack |
| Sept | ,, | ,, | ,, | Busy | ,, | ,, |
| Oct | ,, | ,, | ,, | ,, | Busy | ,, |
| Nov | ,, | ,, | Busy | ,, | ,, | ,, |
| Dec | ,, | Slack | ,, | Slack | ,, | ,, |
| Busy | Jan to March | Aug to Nov | Nov. to April | Feb to April | April to June | Feb to July |
| Slack | April to Dec | Dec to July | May to Oct | May to Aug | July to Sept | April to Dec |
| Busy | — | — | — | Sept. to Nov | Oct to March | — |
| Slack | — | — | — | Dec to Jan | | — |

* The rate of discount of the Bank of Bengal for private paper running thirty

order that money may be had at a uniform price, its supply should be regulated according to the variations in the demand for it. It is well to recognize that the demand for money is never fixed. But it will avail nothing until it is realized that the changes in the demand for money which take place from year to year with the growth of population, trade, etc., belong essentially to a different category from the fluctuations in the demand for money which occur within the course of a year owing to seasonal influences. In any well-regulated currency it is necessary to distinguish these two categories of changes in monetary demand, the one requiring steadiness and expansibility and the other elasticity. On a comparative view it seems more than plausible that a metallic money is as especially adapted to furnish this element of steadiness and stability as paper money is to furnish that of elasticity. Indeed, so appropriate seem to be their respective functions that it has been insisted * that in an ideal system, these two forms of money cannot interchange their functions without making the currency burdensome or dangerous. The proof of the soundness of this view, it may be said, is found in the fact that, excluding the small transactions which take place by direct barter, the purchasing medium of any commercially advanced country is always a compound of money and credit.

On the face of it, the Indian currency is also a compound of money and credit, and as such it may be supposed that it contained provisions for expansibility as well as elasticity. But when we come to analyse it we find that it makes no provision whatever for elasticity. Far from allowing the credit part of it to expand and contract with the seasonal demands, the Paper Currency Act

---

days and after was altered—

| | | | | | | | | |
|---|---|---|---|---|---|---|---|---|
| In 1876 | 16 | times, with | 6½ | per cent. as minimum | and | 13½ | per cent. | as maximum. |
| „ 1877 | 21 | „ | „ 7½ | „ | „ „ | 14½ | „ | „ |
| „ 1878 | 10 | „ | „ 5½ | „ | „ „ | 11½ | „ | „ |
| „ 1879 | 15 | „ | „ 6½ | „ | „ „ | 11½ | „ | „ |
| „ 1880 | 8 | „ | „ 5½ | „ | „ „ | 9½ | „ | „ |
| „ 1881 | 9 | „ | „ 5½ | „ | „ „ | 10½ | „ | „ |
| „ 1882 | 9 | „ | „ 6½ | „ | „ „ | 12½ | „ | „ |
| „ 1883 | 14 | „ | „ 7½ | „ | „ „ | 10½ | „ | „ |

*(Van Den Berg, loc. cit.)*

*Cf. Prof. R. P. Falkner in *A Discussion of the Interrogatories of the Monetary Commission of the Indianapolis Convention*, 1898, Publications of the University of Pennsylvania in Political Economy and Public Law, No. 13, pp. 25-26.

placed a rigid limit upon the volume of its issue regardless of any changes in the volume of the demand. Here, then, is to be found one of the causes for the "convulsions" in the discount rates prevalent in the Indian money market. As was pointed out by Mr. Van Den Berg :—

> "The paper currency established by the Indian legislator fully answers the purpose, so far as business requires an easier means of exchange than gold or silver coin ; but no connection whatever exists between the issue of the fiduciary currency and the wants of the public to have their bills or other commodities converted into a current medium of exchange . . . and this is the sole cause of the unexpected convulsions and sudden transitions in the money market so utterly detrimental to business to which the British Indian trade is constantly exposed." *

It may, however, be objected that such a view is only superficial. The Indian Paper Currency Act is a replica of the English Bank Act of 1844 in all its essentials. Like the English Bank Act, it set a definite limit to the fiduciary issue of notes. Like it, it separated the Issue Business from the Banking Business,† and if it made the banks in India mere banks of discount, it is because it copied the Bank Charter Act, which deprived banks in England, including the Bank of England, from being banks of issue. And yet, it cannot be said that the English money market is affected by such "convulsions and sudden transitions" as has been the case with the Indian money market. On the other hand, it was the considered opinion of Jevons‡ that "the Bank of England and bankers generally have just the same latitude in increasing or diminishing their advances

* Op. cit., p. 7.

† The Indian Paper Currency Act carried the principle of separation further than did the English Bank Charter Act. It not only prevented the Issue Department being conducted under the aegis of a Banking Department, but also disallowed the two being housed under the same roof. Such an ideal of separation was held out by Sir Charles Wood during the debate on the Bank Charter Act. Cf. *Hansard Parliamentary Debates*, Vol. LXXIV, p. 1363. Though he was then disappointed he did not fail to realize his ideal when he became the Secretary of State for India.

‡ Cf. his Essay on the "Frequent Autumnal Pressure in the Money Market and the Action of the Bank of England," *Investigations in Currency and Finance* (ed. Foxwell), 1884, p. 179. Italics by Jevons. There is, however, an apparent misprint in the original, which at the close of the quotation reads "as they would have under a restricted system."

now (i.e. under the Act of 1884) as they would have under a [n un] restricted system"; for, as he elsewhere argued, if the limitation on fiduciary issue is arbitrary, and if people want more money, "it is always open to them to use metallic money instead. The limitation is imposed not upon money itself, but upon the representative part."* What, then, is the reason that the Indian Paper Currency Act should produce the evils which its English prototype did not? *A priori* there need be no such convulsions in a money market subject to such law. The Act, by limiting the issue of notes, did seem to leave no choice but to use metallic money even for seasonal demand. This would be true if notes were the only form in which credit could be used. As a matter of fact, this is not so. Credit could take the form of a promise to pay, issued by a bank, as well as it could take the form of an order on the bank to pay, without making any difference to the social economy of the people who used them. Consequently, if under the provisions of the Act banks are restricted from issuing promises to pay, it does not follow that the only way open to them is a resort "to use metallic money instead," for they are equally free to consent to honour as many orders to pay as they like. Indeed, the success or failure of the Act depends upon which of the two alternatives the banks adopt. It is obvious that those who will submit to the ruling of the Act and resort to metallic money will have to bear the "convulsions," and those who will circumvent the Act by utilizing other forms of credit will escape them. The chief reason, then, why the Act has worked so well in England and so badly in India, is due to the fact that, whereas English banks have succeeded in implanting the order or cheque system of using credit in place of the note system, Indian banks have unfortunately failed. That they should have failed was however, inevitable. A cheque system presupposes a literate population, and a banking system which conducts its business in the vernacular of the people. Neither of these two conditions obtains in India. The population is mostly illiterate, and even were it otherwise it could not have availed itself of the cheque system, because Indian banks refuse to conduct their business in any other medium but English. Besides, the growth of the

* *Money and the Mechanism of Exchange*, Kegan Paul, London, 1890, p. 225.

cheque system presupposes a widespread network of banks, a condition which is far from being fulfilled in India. In the absence of banking, a cheque is the worst instrument that could be handled. If not presented within a certain time, a cheque may become stale and valueless, and is therefore inferior to a note as a store of wealth. In such circumstances as these, it is no wonder that in India cheques did not come into being on a sufficiently large scale to amend the inelasticity of the notes.

But even if Indian banks had succeeded in making use of credit in a form other than that of notes, they could not have eased the money market to the same extent as the English banks have been able to do. One of the incidents of banking consists in the liability of banks to pay cash on demand. If all their deposits were received in cash this liability would involve no risk. As a matter of fact, a large part of their deposits consists of bills which they make it their business to undertake to pay in cash. One of the first things, therefore, that a banker has to look to is the proportion which his cash deposits bear to his credit deposits. Now, this proportion may be adversely affected either by an increase in his credit deposits or by diminution in his cash deposits. In either case his ability to pay cash is *pro tanto* weakened by lowering the ratio of his total cash to his total liabilities. Against an undue expansion of credit a banker may effectually guard himself. But, notwithstanding the development of the cheque system, there is always lurking the possibility of withdrawal of some cash at some time or other. A banker must, therefore, provide by keeping on hand a certain minimum reserve. How large should be the reserve depends upon what the possibilities for the withdrawal of cash are. The point is that to the extent of the reserve the power of the bank to grant credit is curtailed. If the reserve of the bank is already at the minimum it must stop discounting or must strengthen its position by recovering the cash withdrawn from its coffers. Now, it is obvious that if the amount of money withdrawn is kept in the current of business where the banks can get at it, they of course can strengthen their position again immediately, and not only always keep themselves well away from the danger line of minimum reserve, but be always prepared to meet the needs of the money market. What was the position of the Indian banks from this point of view? Owing to the absence of a cheque system the possibilities for the withdrawal of cash are great, and the reserve was required to be large in consequence thereof. A large part of their funds being thus held for a reserve, their resources for discounting were small. But there was a further weakening of their position as lenders by reason of the fact that the cash withdrawn did not speedily return to them. The result was that the Indian banks were obliged to curtail their discounts to a far greater extent than were the English banks, in order to preserve a due proportion between their cash and their credits. The absence of branch banking was an important desideratum in this regard. But, even if there were branch banks, the money withdrawn could not have returned, for it was not left in the current channels of business. It was locked up in Government treasuries, whose operations were independent of the banking transactions of the country. Of course, there could be nothing inherently wrong in the maintenance by a Government of an Independent Treasury, and if its operations were to have a resultant connection with the operations of the business community no harm need arise. But the operations of the Indian Treasury ran counter to the needs of business. It locked up when it should have released its hoards, and released its hoards when it should have locked them up.

The causes that "convulsed" the Indian money market had therefore been the inelasticity of the credit media and the working of the Independent Treasury System in so far as they were the prime factors affecting the money supply of the country (*see* Chart I). The evil effects of such convulsions of the discount rate can hardly be exaggerated.* In an economy in which almost every business man must rely, at certain seasons, if not all the year round, on borrowed capital, the margin of profit may be wiped out by a sudden rise or augmented by a sudden fall in the rate of discount leading to under-trading or over-trading. Such fluctuations increase business risks, lead to higher business expenses and a greater cost to the consumer. They bring about swings in prices, promote speculation, and prepare for panics.

* For American experience, cf. E. W. Kemmerer, "Seasonal Variations in the New York Money Market," in *The American Economic Review*, March, 1911.

## CHART I

### Discount Rates in India

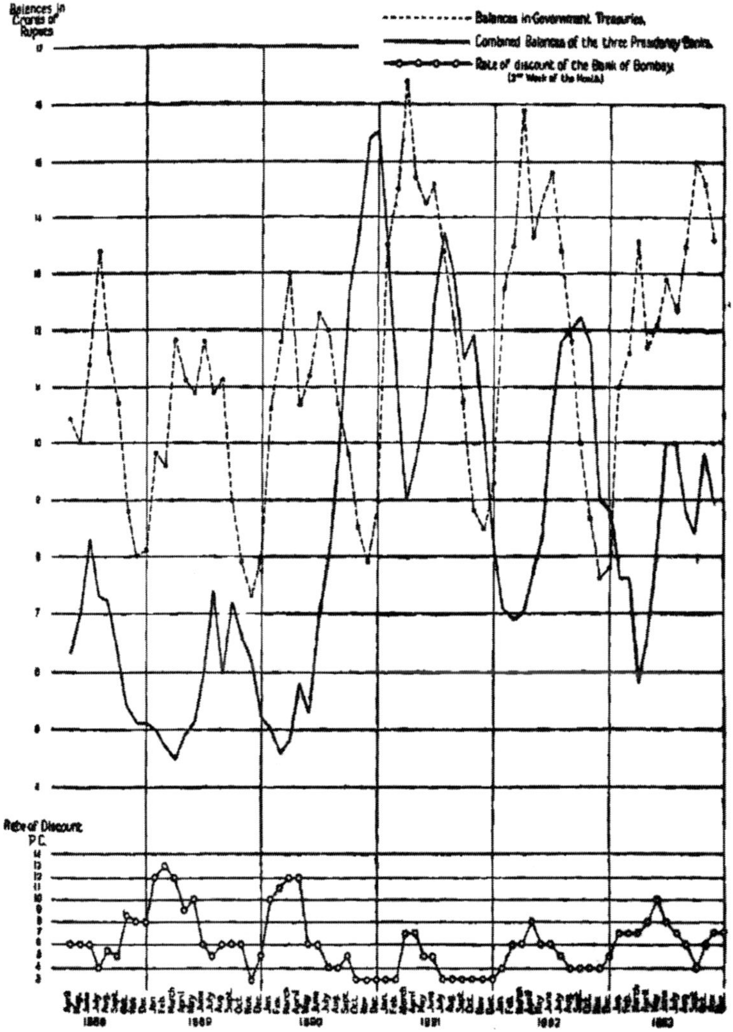

Evils such as these would have in any other country compelled the authorities to take proper steps to deal with them. But it is a curious fact that in India no serious attempts were made to alleviate the sufferings they inflicted upon the trading community. A reform of the paper currency or the abolition of the Independent Treasury System would have eased the situation, though a reform of both would have been better. The general community, however, was not desirous for a change of the paper currency,* but was anxious for the abolition of the Independent Treasury. The Government, on the other hand, refused to do away with its Independent Treasury System,† and repudiated

---

* Cf. *India in* 1880, by Sir Richard Temple, p. 469; Sir Charles Wood's *Administration of Indian Affairs*, p. 89; also *The Indian Statesman*, January 15 (1884).

† It should, however, be noted that between 1862 and 1876, at some centres comprising the head offices and branch offices of the Presidency banks, the Independent Treasury System was suspended. By way of compensation for the loss of their right of note issue, the Presidency banks were given certain concession by the Government under agreements entered into in accordance with Act XXIV of 1861. Among the concessions one was the use by the banks of Government balances. The first agreement, that of 1862, conceded to the banks the following privileges in regard to the Government balances: (1) The unrestricted use for banking purposes "of all moneys and balances which but for the agreement would have been received or held at the General Treasury" up to the limit of 70 lakhs in the case of the Bank of Bengal, 40 lakhs in the case of the Bank of Bombay, and 15 lakhs in the case of the Bank of Madras. (2) The option of setting aside the excess over these sums in a separate strong room for production when demanded, or of investing it in Government paper or other authorized securities, the power of investment being subject to the condition that the banks should be "at all times answerable and accountable to Government for the surplus cash balance for the time being." (3) The right to interest from Government on the difference between the actual balance and 50 lakhs in the case of the Bank of Bengal, 30 lakhs in the case of the Bank of Bombay, and 10 lakhs in the case of the Bank of Madras, whenever the balances at these banks fell below these minima. (4) Permission to the banks to use the Government balances at their branches on similar terms, suitable limits being fixed in each case, as in the head office agreements.

A year after the agreements were executed, difficulties arose with the Bank of Bengal, which had locked up the funds to such an extent that it was unable to meet the demands of the Government on the public balances it held. Negotiations were therefore opened in 1863 for the revision of the agreements, and the revised agreements came into force on January 2, 1866. They contained the following provisions regarding the public balances: (1) Undertaking by Government to maintain in the hands of the banks at their head offices an "average cash balance" of 70 lakhs at the Bank of Bengal, 40 lakhs at the Bank of Bombay, and 25 lakhs at the Bank of Madras, "so far as the same may conveniently be done." (2) Permission to the banks

even its moral obligation to help the business community on the somewhat pedantic plea that in locking up currency it did not lock up capital.* Nor is it possible to say, since it was not called upon to enunciate a policy, how far it would have gone to modify the Paper Currency Act so as to relieve the situation. Before, however, this controversy could end in a satisfactory solution for imparting to the currency system that element of elasticity which it needed, there developed another and a greater evil, which affected its metallic counterpart in a degree sufficient to destroy its most vital element of steadiness and stability of value, which it was its virtue to furnish. So enormous did the evil grow, and so pervasive were its effects, that it absorbed all attention to the exclusion of everything else.

What fixity of value between the different units of its currency is to the internal transactions of a country, a par of exchange is to its internal transactions. A par of exchange between any two countries expresses the relative exchange values of their respective currencies in terms of each other. It is obvious from

---

to use the whole balances for the time being deposited with them for banking purposes. (3) The right to interest from Government when the Government balance at the head offices of the Bank of Bengal, Bank of Bombay, and Bank of Madras fell below the minimma of 45 lakhs, 25 lakhs, and 20 lakhs respectively. (4) Permission to employ "the whole of the balances (at branches) however large for the time being" for banking purposes, subject to the condition that each branch should "at all times be ready to meet the drafts of the Government" to the extent of the Government balances at the branch.

These revised agreements were to remain in force till March, 1, 1874. In 1874 the question of the revision of the charters of the Presidency banks was under consideration, and it was the aim of the Government to continue to the banks the right to use the whole Government balances. Just at this time (1874) difficulties occurred with the Bank of Bombay and the Government could not draw upon their balances. This led to a reconsideration of the policy of merging the Government balances with the bank balances and leaving them in the custody of the banks. After a somewhat lengthy discussion the Government of India reverted to the system of Independent Treasury by instituting what were called Reserve Treasuries at the headquarters of the Presidencies which held the Government balances previously held by the Presidency banks. For a history of this episode *see* House of Commons Returns 109 and 505 of 1864; also J. B. Brunyate, *An Account of the Presidency Banks*, Chap. VII.

* In the despatch of May 6, 1875, sanctioning the re-establishment of the Independent Treasury System, the banks were admonished by the Secretary of State thus: "Capital supplied by Government, and not representing the savings of the community,

this that the par of exchange between any two countries will be stable if they employ the same metal functioning as their standard money, freely convertible into and exportable as bullion, for in that case they would have as a measure of value a common medium, the value of which could not differ, given freedom of commerce, in the two countries by more than the cost of its transhipment, i.e., within specie points. On the other hand, there can be no fixed par of exchange between two countries, having different metals as their currency standards of value. In that case, their exchange is governed by the relative values of gold and silver, and must necessarily fluctuate with changes in their value relation. The limit to the exchange fluctuations between them will be as wide or as narrow as the limit to fluctuations in the relative values of the two metals may happen to be. When, therefore, two countries such as England and India are separated by differences in their metallic standards, theoretically there could be no possibility for a stable par of exchange between them. But, as a matter of fact, notwithstanding the difference in their metallic standards, the rate of exchange between England and

---

is a resource on whose permanence no reliance can be placed, and which therefore tends to lead traders into dangerous commitments. It gives ease for a time, and produces prosperity which is at the mercy of an accident. A political exigency suddenly withdraws the adventitious resources, and the commerce which trusted to it finds itself pledged beyond what its own resources can make good." Under the arrangements of 1876 leading to the establishment of the Reserve Treasuries, the Government agreed as before to pay interest to the banks when their balances at the banks fell below certain minima. The Government entered into no formal undertaking as regards maxima, and gave the banks to understand "that the Government will ordinarily not leave with the headquarters of the banks, otherwise than temporarily, more than the following sums: Bank of Bengal 100 lakhs, Bank of Madras 30 lakhs, and Bank of Bombay 50 lakhs. But this condition will not be inserted in the contract, which will impose no obligation upon the Government to leave any balances whatever with the banks . . . The Government will not undertake to give to the banks the exclusive custody of all the public balances where the Government banks with the banks." The question of the amount of balances which the Government would have with the banks in the ordinary course being thus settled, the only way left open to give help to the banks to meet seasonal demands was to grant loans to the Presidency banks for its balances held in the Reserve Treasuries. After 1900 it agreed to make such loans of a limited amount at the bank rate. Up to 1913 only six loans were made, which shows that the terms of such loans were rather onerous. The Chamberlain Commission of 1913 recommended loans rather than the abolition of the In-

India seldom deviated* from the normal† rate of 1*s.* 10½*d.* for R. 1. So steady was the rate up to 1873 that few people were conscious of the fact that the two countries had different currency standards. After 1873, however, the rupee-sterling exchange suddenly broke loose from this normal parity, and the dislocation it caused was so great and so disorderly (Chart II) that no one knew where it would stop.

The rupee-sterling exchange was in reality a reflection of the gold-silver exchange. When, therefore, it is said that the rupee-sterling before 1873 was stable at 1*s.* 10½*d.*, it merely meant that the gold-silver exchange before 1873 was stable at the ratio of 1 to 15½ ; and that the rupee-sterling exchange was dislocated after 1873 meant that the gold-silver exchange lost its old moorings. The question which therefore arises is why was the ratio of exchange between gold and silver disturbed after 1873, as it never was before that year? Two factors have been appealed to as affording a sufficient explanation of what then appeared as a strange phenomenon. One was the demonetization of silver as the standard money medium by the principal countries of the world. This movement in favour of demonetization of silver was

---

dependent Treasury system. The war, however, hastened the course of events. It proved the necessity of co-operation between the Presidency banks and the Government, and also the need of a large and powerful Banking Institution. This was accomplished by the amalgamation of the Presidency banks into an Imperial Bank of India (Act XLVII of 1920), with the inauguration of which the Independent Treasury system is again in the process of abolition. For a history of episodes of the Independent Treasury after 1876, *see* Appendices to the *Interim Report of the Chamberlain Commission*, Vol. I, Cd. 7070 of 1913, Nos. I and II.

* It appears, however, from the chart that the rupee-sterling exchange before 1873 was not quite stable. But the fluctuations in it are to be attributed to quite a different set of factors. It should be noted that the rates of exchange used for reducing the Indian moneys into sterling during the time of the East India Company had been various : moreover, they had so little relation to the intrinsic value of the coins exchanged that the actual rates officially given were far from the actual market rates. As having a bearing on this interesting subject, consult H. of C. Sessional Papers 735 II of 1931-32 ; Appendix No. 20, *Correspondence, etc., relating to the rates of exchange at which the currencies of India are converted into sterling* ; also Tucker, H. St. George, *Remarks on the Plans of Finance*, 1821, *passim*, and *Memorials of Indian Government*, 1853, by the same, pp. 382-85.

† Normal only if 15½ to 1 be taken as the normal ratio between gold and silver, which was the case for nearly seventy years.

## CHART II

### Fall of the Rupee-Sterling Exchange

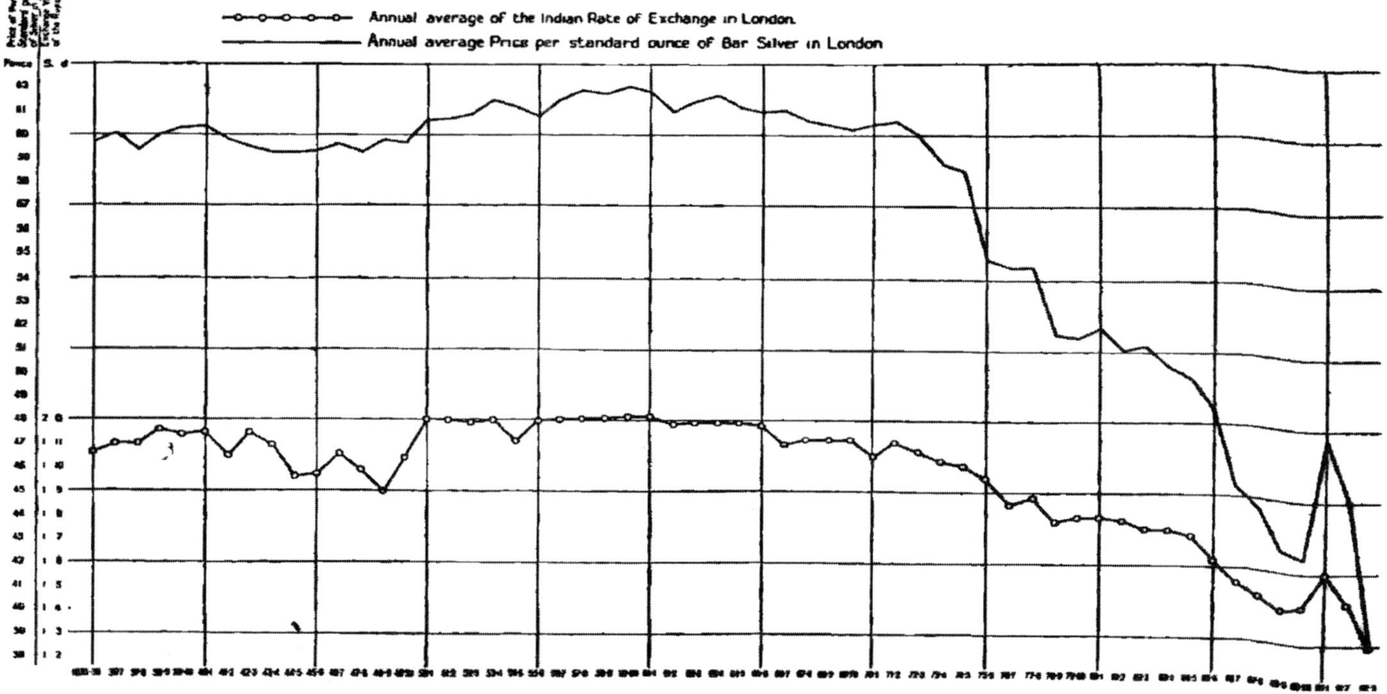

the outcome of an innocent agitation for uniformity of weights, measures, and coinages. In so far as the agitation was aimed at such uniformity, it was in every way beneficial. But it also exemplifies how the pursuit of good sometimes leaves behind a legacy of evils. At the Great Exhibition held in London in 1851 the great difficulty of comparing the different exhibits, owing to the differences of weights, measures, and coinages as between the countries of their origin and other countries, was amply demonstrated to the representatives of the different nations assembled at that exhibition.* The question of international uniformity in weights, measures, and coins was discussed by the various scientific assemblies gathered at this exhibition, and although nothing tangible came out of it, the question was not allowed to be dropped : it was taken up at the Brussels International Statistical Congress held two years after. Opinion had so far advanced that the next Statistical Congress, held at Paris, issued a declaration, which was confirmed by the Vienna Statistical Congress of 1859, strongly urging the necessity of bringing about the desired uniformity in the weights, measures, and coinages of different countries.† Encouraged by the action of England, which had made in 1862 the metric system of weights and measures optional, the 1863 International Statistical Congress of Berlin resolved to invite the different Governments "to send to a special Congress delegates authorized to consider and report what should be the relative weights in the . . . . gold and silver coins, and to arrange the details by which the monetary systems of the different countries might be fixed, upon a single unit decimally subdivided." ‡ The significance of this Congress can hardly be overlooked. It made a departure. At the former Congresses the question debated was largely one of uniformity in weights and measures. But at this Congress "that phase of it was subordinated to uniform coinage and was well-nigh laid aside." § Though the resolution was a departure, it should not have been fraught with serious consequences if the reform had been confined to the

* *Report of the Royal Commission on International Coinage*, 1868, p. v.

† Cf Russell, H B, *International Monetary Conferences*, 1898, pp. 18-25.

‡ Quoted by Russell, op. cit., p. 25.

§ Russell, loc. cit.

question of uniformity of coinage. But there occurred a circumstance which extended its application to the question of currency. When this agitation for uniform coinage grew apace, the French *quite naturally wished that their coinage system, which had already been extended over the area comprised by the Latin Union,* should be taken as a model to be copied by other countries outside the Union in the interest of uniformity. With this end in view the French Government approached the British Government of the time, but was told in reply that the British Government could not consider the suggestion until France adopted the single gold standard.* Far from being taken aback, the French Government, then so anxious to cultivate the goodwill of England, proved so complacent that it felt no compunction in conceding to the British the pre-requisite it demanded, and indeed went so far out of the way, when the Conference met in Paris in 1867, that it actually manoeuvred † the Assembly into passing a resolution "that for uniform international coinage it was necessary that gold alone should be the principal currency of the world." So much importance was attached to the question of uniformity of coinage that those who passed the resolution seemed not to have noticed what sacrifice they were called upon to make for its achievement. Perhaps it would be more correct to say that they did not know that they were affecting by their decision the currency system of the world. All they thought they were doing at the time was to promote uniformity of coinage and nothing more.‡ But whatever the extenuating circumstances, the result was disastrous, for when the resolution came to be acted upon by the different countries assembled, the real end of the Conference, namely uniformity of coinage, was completely lost sight of, and the proposed means eventually became the virtual end.

The ball once set rolling, the work of demonetizing silver began to grow apace. First in the field was Germany. Having vanquished France in the war of 1870, she utilized the war in-

* Cf evidence of Prof Foxwell, Q 23,876, Royal Commission on Agricultural Depression in England, 1892.

† For which cf Russell, op., p. 46

‡ An honourable exception must be made in the case of Dr Mees, the representative of Holland, who drew attention to the harm likely to result from this resolution.

demnity in the reform of her chaotic currency* by hastening to adopt a gold currency for the United Empire of Germany. The law *of December 4, 1871, authorized the change, with the mark as the unit of currency. Silver was demonitized* by this enactment; but the existing silver coins continued to be legal tender though their further coinage was stopped, along with the new gold coins at the legal ratio of 15 to½ to 1. This full legal-tender power of the silver coins was taken away from them by the law of June, 9, 1873, which reduced them to the position of a subsidiary currency.† This policy was immediately copied by other countries of Germanic culture.‡ In 1872 Norway, Sweden, and Denmark formed a Scandinavian Monetary Union, analogous to the Latin Monetary Union, by which they agreed to demonetize silver as was done by Germany. This treaty, which established a gold standard and reduced the existing silver currency to a subsidiary status, was ratified by Sweden and Denmark in 1873 and by Norway in 1875. Holland also followed the same course. Till 1872 she had a pure silver standard. In that year she closed her Mint to the free coinage of silver, although the old silver money continued to be legal tender to any amount. In 1875 she went a step further and opened her Mints to the free coinage of gold Her policy differed from that of the Germanic countries in that she only suspended the free coinage of silver, while the latter had demonetized it. Even the Latin Union was unable to resist this tide against silver. As a consequence of this exclusion of silver, the Latin Union, enlarged as it was by additional members, naturally desired to take precautionary measures against being flooded by the influx of this depreciated silver. Nor was this fear unfounded, for the silver tendered for coinage at the Belgian Mint in 1873 was three times greater than what was tendered in 1871. Rather than be embarrassed, Belgium, by the law of December 8, 1873, suspended the free coinage of her silver five-franc pieces. This action of Belgium forced the hands of the other members

* For a history of the movement for the unification of German currency prior to 1870, cf. H. P. Willis, "The Vienna Monetary Treaty of 1857," in the *Journal of Political Economy*, Vol IV, p 187 *ett seq*.

† For the text of the Laws, *see* Appendix to *History of Bimetallism*, by Prof J. L. Laughlin, New York, 1886.

‡ Cf. *Report of the Committee on the Depreciation of Silver*, 1876, p. xxix

of the Union to adopt similar measures. The delegates of the Union met in Paris in January, 1874, and

> "agreed to a treaty supplementary to that originally framed in 1865, and determined on withdrawing from individuals the full power of free coinage by limiting to a moderate sum the silver five-franc pieces which should be coined by each State of the Union during the year 1874.*

The respective quotas fixed for 1874 were slightly increased in 1875, but were reduced in 1876.† But the actual coinage did not even reach these small quotas. So greatly was the Union perturbed by the silver situation that during 1877 the coinage of silver five-franc pieces was, with the exception of Italy,‡ entirely suspended. This action was, however, only a preliminary to the Treaty of November 5, 1878, by which the Latin Union agreed to close its Mints to the free coinage of silver till further action. Though at first *sine die*, the closure proved in the end perpetual.‡‡ Simultaneously with the precautionary measures of the Latin Union, Russia suspended, in 1876, the free coinage of silver except to such an amount as was necessary for the purposes of her trade with China,§ and the Imperial Decree of November 22, 1878, directed that all customs duties above 5 roubles and 15 copecks should be payable in gold.¶ Austria in like manner suspended the free coinage of silver in 1879.**

---

* Laughlin, op cit, p 155

† The quotas fixed at the Conferences for the several members of the Union were :— *In Millions of Francs*

| | 1874. | 1875. | 1876. |
|---|---|---|---|
| France | 60 | 75 | 54 |
| Belgium | 12 | 50 | 36 |
| Italy | 40 | 15 | 10 |
| Switzerland | 8 | 10 | 7 |
| Greece | — | — | 3 |
| | 120 | 150 | 110 |

In 1874 Italy was allotted an extra 20 million francs. *Ibid.*, p 155

‡ She was allowed to coin 10 millions of them.

‡ *Ibid.*, p. 158.

§ *Report of the Directors of the Mint*, Washington, 1893, p. 23

¶ Cf. P. Willis, "Monetary Reform in Russia," in the *Journal of Political Economy*, Vol. V, p. 291.

** Cf. F. Wieser, "Resumption of Specie Payment in Austria-Hungary," in *Journal of Political Economy*, Vol. I, pp. 380-7.

On the other side of the Atlantic, an important event had taken place in the United States. In 1870 that Governmen resolved to consolidate the Mint laws, which had not been revised since 1837, in a comprehensive statute. Since the legislation of 1853, the silver dollar was the only coin which the United States Mints coined freely. But in the new consolidated Mint Statute of 1873, the silver dollar was deleted from the list of coins to be issued from the Mint, so that it virtually amounted to suspension of the free coinage of silver in the United States.* The silver dollars previously coined continued to circulate as full legal tender, but that power was taken away by the law of June, 1874, which declared that "the silver coins of the United States shall be a legal tender at their nominal value for any amount not exceeding five dollars in any one payment."

The other factor appealed to in explanation of the dislocation of the relative values of gold and silver was the great increase in the production of silver as compared to gold.

TABLE IX

RELATIVE PRODUCTION OF GOLD AND SILVER

(OUNCES)

| Period | Total Production. | | Annual Average Production | | Index Number for Average Annual Production. | |
|---|---|---|---|---|---|---|
| | Gold | Silver | Gold. | Silver | Gold. | Silver. |
| 1493-1600 | 24,266,820 | 734,125,960 | 224,693 | 6,797,463 | 100 | 100 |
| 1601-1700 | 29,330,445 | 1,197,073,100 | 293,304 | 11,970,731 | 130·5 | 176·1 |
| 1701-1800 | 61,088,215 | 1,833,672,035 | 610,882 | 18,336,720 | 271·8 | 269·7 |
| 1801-1840 | 20,488,552 | 801,155,495 | 512,217 | 20 028,887 | 227·9 | 293·1 |
| 1841-1870 | 143,186,224 | 931,091,326 | 4,772,876 | 31,038,378 | 2,124·1 | 456·6 |
| 1871-1890 | 106,950,802 | 1,715,039,955 | 5,347,545 | 85,751,998 | 2,375 4 | 1,261·5 |

* This measure was the subject of a strange controversy The gold men argued that it was deliberately adopted, while the silver men decried it as a surreptitious act due to a "combination of rascally contrivance and rascally connivance" Prof. Laughlin has well cleared the mystery surrounding this Act He shows by reference to debates in Congress on the legislation of 1853 that Congress knew that by refusing to alter the ratio between gold and silver it was placing the country on a gold standard. Too much consideration, he thinks, has been wasted on the Act of 1873, which merely took legal notice of the consequences of the Act of 1853 Cf. his *History of Bimetallism*, pp. 80 and 93-95.

The history of the production of the precious metals in modern times begins from the year 1493, a date which marks the discovery of the American continent. Reviewing the results of the production from 1493 to 1893, a period in all of 400 years, we find that during the first hundred years the production of gold and silver rises at a uniform rate of progression. Assuming the annual average production of each during the first century (1493-1600) in the modern history of their production to be 100, it will be seen that in the next century (1601-1700 the index number for the production of gold rises to 130 and that of silver to 176. This rate of progression is also kept up in the succeeding century (1700-1800), during which the figure for both gold and silver approximates to 270, and continues without much disturbance up to 1840, when the respective index numbers stood at 228 for gold and 293 for silver. From this point onwards, the relative production of the two metals underwent a complete revolution. During the next thirty years (1841-70) the production of gold reached unprecedented heights, while that of silver lagged behind, relatively speaking. The index number for silver production advanced only to 450, but that for gold went up to 2,124. This revolution was followed by a counter-revolution, as a result of which the position as it stood at the end of 1870 was well-nigh reversed. The production of gold received a sudden check, and though it had increased enormously between 1840-70 it remained stationary between 1870-93. On the other hand, the production of silver, which was steady between 1841-70, increased threefold between 1870-93, so that the index number for its average annual production during the latter period stood at 1,260.

In the controversy which arose over the reasons, which brought about this dislocation and decline in the value of silver in terms of gold, there were parties to whom one of these two factors was a sufficient cause. One side argued that had suspension or demonetization of silver not taken place, its value could never have fallen. This position was vehemently challenged by the other side, which believed in the over-supply of silver as the primary cause of its depreciation. Now, was the argument from relative over-supply sufficient to account for the fall in the gold value of silver? On the face of it, the explanation has the plausibility of a simple proposition. It is one of the elementary theorems of political economy that the value of a thing varies inversely with its supply, and if the supply of silver had largely increased, what could be more natural than that its value in terms of gold should fall? The following were the relevant facts which formed the basis of the argument :—

### TABLE X

GOLD AND SILVER *

RELATIVE PRODUCTION AND RELATIVE VALUE

| Period. | Ratio of Production (by Weight) of Gold to Silver. As 1 Grain to: | Ratio of Value of Gold to Silver. As 1 Grain to | Index Number for the Ratio of Production. | Index Number for the Ratio of Value. | Correlation between Relative Production and Relative Value. | |
|---|---|---|---|---|---|---|
| | | | | | Relative Production of Silver. Falls— Rises+ | Relative Value of Silver Falls— Rises+ |
| 1681-1700 | 31.8 | 14.95 | 100 | 100 | — | — |
| 1701-1720 | 27.7 | 15.21 | 87 | 101.7 | - 13 | - 1.7 |
| 1721-1740 | 22.6 | 15.10 | 71 | 101 | - 29 | - 1.0 |
| 1741-1760 | 21.7 | 14.70 | 67 | 98.3 | - 33 | + 1.7 |
| 1761-1780 | 31.5 | 14.40 | 99 | 96.3 | - 1 | + 3.7 |
| 1781-1800 | 49.4 | 15.08 | 155.6 | 100.8 | +55.6 | - .8 |
| 1801-1810 | 50.3 | 15.67 | 158.0 | 104.8 | +58.0 | - 4.8 |
| 1811-1820 | 47.2 | 15.68 | 148.0 | 104.9 | +48.0 | - 4.9 |
| 1821-1830 | 32.4 | 15.82 | 101.9 | 105.8 | + 1.9 | - 5.8 |
| 1831-1840 | 29.4 | 15.77 | 92.4 | 105.4 | - 7.6 | - 5.4 |
| 1841-1850 | 14.2 | 15.81 | 44.6 | 105.8 | - 55.4 | - 5.8 |
| 1851-1855 | 4.4 | 15.45 | 13.8 | 103.3 | - 86.2 | - 3.3 |
| 1856-1860 | 4.5 | 15.28 | 14.0 | 102.2 | - 86.0 | - 2.2 |
| 1861-1865 | 5.9 | 15.42 | 18.55 | 103.1 | - 81.5 | - 3.1 |
| 1866-1870 | 6.9 | 15.52 | 21.7 | 103.8 | - 78.3 | - 3.8 |
| 1871-1875 | 11.3 | 16.10 | 35.5 | 107.6 | - 64.5 | - 7.6 |
| 1876-1880 | 13.2 | 17.79 | 41.5 | 119.0 | - 58.5 | - 19.0 |
| 1881-1886 | 17.3 | 18.81 | 54.4 | 125.8 | - 45.6 | - 25.8 |
| 1886-1890 | 19.9 | 20.98 | 62.6 | 140.3 | - 37.4 | - 40.3 |
| 1891-1885 | 20.0 | 26.75 | 62.9 | 178.9 | - 37.1 | - 78.9 |

The facts thus presented led to two conclusions. The first is that the supposed enormous increase in the relative production of

* The table is based on figures of M. de Foville of the French Mint, as given by Mr. F. B. Forbes in *The Bimetallist* of July, 1897, pp. 125-28.

silver was an assumption which had no foundation in reality. On the contrary, a glance at the figures for relative production discloses the curious fact that since the beginning of the eighteenth century silver, instead of rising, has been falling in proportion. With the exception of the first quarter of the nineteenth century, silver had formed, throughout the two centuries covered by the table, a *diminishing proportion* as compared with *gold.** Indeed, never was the proportion of silver so low as it was in the latter half of the nineteenth century, and even when after 1873 it began to grow it did not reach half the magnitude it had reached in the beginning of the eighteenth century. The second conclusion which these facts were claimed to sustain was that the value of silver in terms of gold did not move in sympathy with its supply relative to that of gold. According to theory, the value of silver should have been rising because the relative volume of its production had been diminishing. On the other hand, a closer examination of the figures of relative values and relative productions, as given in the foregoing table, instead of showing any close correlation (*see* Chart III) between them, pointed to the contrary. Instead of supply and value being inverse in proportion, it showed that as its supply was falling there was also a fall in its value. Such being the facts of history, it was contended that they gave no support to those who rested their case on over-supply rather than on demonetization as a sufficient explanation for the depreciation of silver.

Apart from such minor points, the issue was considerably narrowed by the peculiarity of the events of the twenty years preceding and following the year 1873† Compare, it was said, the period commencing with 1848 and ending with the year 1870 with the period following 1870, and there emerges the arresting fact that these two periods, though they have been the opposite of each

* In view of this, it is a matter of some surprise that such an eminent economist as Prof. W. Lexis should have ceased to be bimetallist on the ground that the enormous increase of silver militated against the establishment of a permanently high ratio with gold. Cf. his essay on "The Present Monetary Situation," in the *Economic Studies of the American Economic Association*, 1896, Vol. I, No. 4, pp. 273-77. The habit of measuring the production of silver in terms of value is no doubt largely responsible for this quite unfounded notion.

† Cf. H. S. Foxwell, "Bimetallism: Its Meaning and Aims," in *The (Oxford) Economic Review* (1893), Vol. III. p. 302.

# CHART III

## Relative Values and Relative Production of Gold and Silver

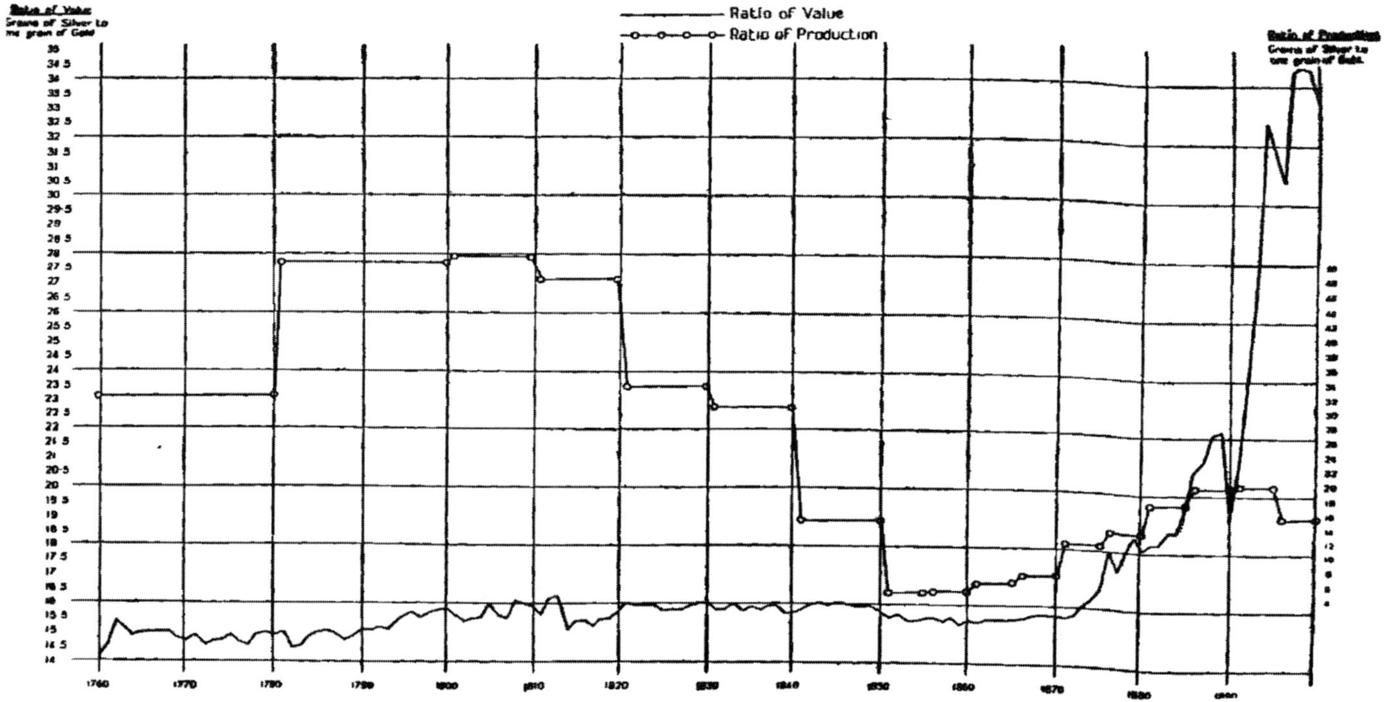

other with reference to the relative values of the two metals, were alike with reference to the changes in their relative supply. The period between 1870 and 1893 on the side of relative production was marked by the preponderance of silver. The period between 1848 and 1870 is an exact parallel to the above period with respect to changes in the relative supply of the two precious metals, only in this case it was gold that had increased in volume. Now, if it is over-supply that governed the value relations of the two metals in the second period (1870-93) the same should be true of their value relations in the first period (1848-70). Was there, then, a disturbance in the relative values of the two metals in the first period anything like what took place in the second period? It was insisted that the disturbance in the ratios of production of the two metals in the first period was enormously greater than that which occurred in the second period. Indeed, comparatively speaking, the disturbance in the second period was nothing to speak of. And yet their relative value during the first period was well-nigh constant at the ratio of 1 to 15½, while in the second it fluctuated between 16.10 and 26.75. Those, who argued that the value of silver fell after 1873 because of its over-supply, were thus faced with the problem as to why the value of gold did not fall when its supply had become so abundant before 1873. The whole controversy was therefore centred into the question as to what could have made this difference in the two situations? If the colossal increase in the production of gold in the first period did not raise the value of silver by more than 2 per cent., how was it that a comparatively insignificant rise in the relative production of silver in the second period led to such an enormous rise in the price of gold? What was the controlling influence present in the one case which was absent in the other? Those who held that it was demonetization of silver that was responsible for its depreciation argued that, though alike in every way, the two periods differed in one important particular. What distinguished them was the fact that in the former it was a common practice to define the standard money of a country as a certain quantity of gold *or* a certain quantity of silver. Prior to 1803 the two metals were rated differently in different countries,* but since that date the

* For these ratios, *see* Appendix, Table B, to *A Colloquy on Currency*, by H. H. Gibbs.

rating of 1 to 15½ became more uniform, with the result that the monetary standard throughout that period was either 1 gr. of gold *or* 15½ grs. of silver. On the other hand, during the second period, the "*or*" which characterized the first period was deleted by the silver-demonetizing and suspending decrees. In other words, the first period was characterized by the prevalence of bimetallism under which the two metals could be used interchangeably at a fixed given ratio. In the second period they could not be so used owing to the fact that the fixed ratio necessary for interchange had been abrogated. Now, could the existence or non-existence of a fixed ratio be said to be such a powerful influence as to make the whole difference that set the two periods in such marked contrast? That this was the factor which made the whole difference was the view of the bimetallists. It was said that, by virtue of the monetary system prevalent during the first period, gold and silver were rendered substitutes and were regarded as "one commodity of two different strengths." So related, the conditions of supply had no effect upon their ratio of exchange, as would have been the case in respect of a commodity without a substitute. In the case of commodities which are substitutes, the relative scarcity of one can give it no greater value in terms of the other than that defined by their ratio of exchange, because by reason of the freedom of substitution the scarcity can be made good by the abundance of the other. On the other hand, the relative abundance of one cannot depreciate its value in terms of the other below the ratio of exchange, because its superfluity can be absorbed by the void created in consequence of a paucity of the other. So long as they remain substitutes with a fixed ratio of substitution, nothing originating in demand or supply could disturb their ratio. The two being one commodity, whatever changes take place in the demand or supply of either system beyond the needs of commerce express themselves in the price level exactly as though one of them alone was the money medium; but their ratio of exchange will be preserved intact in any case.

In support of this was cited the authority of Jevons, who said* :

* *Theory of Political Economy*, 4th ed., 1911, pp. 134-36.

"Whenever different commodities are thus applicable to the same purposes their conditions of demand and exchange are not independent. Their mutual ratio of exchange cannot vary much for it will be closely defined by the ratio of their utilities. Beef and mutton differ so slightly that people eat them almost indifferently. But the wholesale price of mutton, on an average, exceeds that of beef in the ratio of 9 to 8, and we must therefore conclude that people generally esteem mutton more than beef in this proportion, otherwise they would not buy the dear meat.... So long as the equation of utility holds true, the ratio of exchange between mutton and beef will not diverge from that of 8 to 9. If the supply of beef falls off people will not pay a higher price for it, but will eat more mutton; and if the supply of mutton falls off, they will eat more beef.... We must, in fact, treat beef and mutton as one commodity of two different strengths—just as gold at 18 carats and gold at 20 carats are hardly considered as two but rather as one commodity, of which twenty parts of one are equivalent to eighteen of the other.

"It is upon this principle that we must explain, in harmony with Cairnes' views, the extraordinary permanence of the ratio of exchange of gold and silver, which from the commencement of the eighteenth century up to recent years never diverged much from 15 to 1. That this fixedness of ratio did not depend entirely upon the amount or cost of production is proved by the very slight effect of the Australian and Californian gold discoveries, which never raised the gold price of silver more than about 4 2/3 per cent., and failed to have more than a permanent effect of 1½ per cent. This permanence of relative values may have been partially due to the fact that gold and silver can be employed for exactly the same purposes, but that the superior brilliancy of gold occasions it to be preferred, unless it be about 15 or 15½ times as costly as silver. Much more probably, however, the explanation of the fact is to be found in the fixed ratio of 15½ to 1, according to which these metals are exchanged in the currency of France and some other continental countries. The French Currency Law of the year XI established an artificial * equation—

$$\text{Utility of gold} = 15\tfrac{1}{2} \times \text{utility of silver}$$

and it is probably not without some reason that Wolowski and

* It is this artificiality of the bimetallic system which unfortunately befogs the minds of some people and prejudices those of others. Some do not understand why the price determination of two commodities used as money should be so different from the price determination of any other two commodities as to be governed by a ratio fixed by law. Others are puzzled as to why, if gold and silver are a pair of substitutes, should they require a legal ratio while other pairs of substitutes circulate without a legal ratio, merely on the basis of the ratio of their utility. These difficulties are well explained away by Prof. Fisher thus:

other recent French economists attributed to this law of replacement an important effect in preventing disturbance in the relations of gold and silver."

But granting that before 1873 the ratio was preserved owing to the compensatory action of the bimetallic law, can it be said that it would have been maintained after 1873 if the law had not been suspended? To give an uncompromising affirmative as the bimetallists did is to suppose that bimetallism can work under all conditions. As a matter of fact, though it is workable under certain conditions it is not workable under other conditions. These conditions are well described by Prof. Fisher.* The question under bimetallism is whether the market ratio between gold and silver bullion will always be the same as the legal ratio between gold and silver coins freely minted and possessing unlimited legal-tender power. Now supposing the supply of silver

". . . two forms of money differ from a random pair of commodities in being substitutes. Two substitutes proper are regarded by the consumer as a single commodity. Thus lumping together of the two commodities reduces the number of demand conditions, but does not introduce any indeterminateness into the problem because the missing conditions are at once supplied by a *fixed ratio of substitution*. Thus if ten pounds of cane sugar serve the same purpose as eleven pounds of beet-root sugar, their fixed ratio of substitution is ten to eleven. . . . In these cases the fixed ratio is based on the relative capacities of the two commodities to fill a common need, and is quite antecedent to their prices. . . . The substitution ratio is fixed by nature, and in turn fixes the price ratio.

"In the single case of money, however, there is no fixed ratio of substitution. . . . We have here to deal not with relative sweetening power, nor relative nourishing power, nor with any other capacity to satisfy wants—no capacity inherent in the metals and independent of their prices. We have instead to deal only with relative *purchasing* power. We do not reckon a utility in the metal itself, but in the commodities it will buy. We assign their respective desirabilities or utilities to the sugars. . . . before we know their prices, but we must inquire the relative circulating value of gold and silver before we can know at what ratio we ourselves prize them. To us the ratio of substitution is incidentally the price ratio. The case of the two forms of money is unique. They are substitutes, but have no natural ratio of substitution, dependent on consumers' preferences.

"The foregoing considerations. . . are overlooked by those who imagine that a fixed legal ratio is merely superimposed upon a system of supply and demand already determinate, and who seek to prove thereby that such a ratio is foredoomed to failure . . .the . . analogy. . . .is unsound . . Gold and silver . . are not completely analogous even to two substitutes because for two forms of money there is no consumers' natural ratio of substitution. There seems, therefore, room for an artificial ratio. . . ."
—*Purchasing Power of Money*, 1911, pp. 376-77.

* *Elementary Principles of Economics*, 1912, pp. 228-29. In the illustrations given by Prof. Fisher he appears, although he does not mean it, to make the success or failure

bullion has increased relatively to that of gold bullion, the result will obviously be a divergence in the mint and the market ratio. Will the compensatory action of the bimetallic law restore the equilibrium? It may succeed in doing it or it may not. If the increase in the supply of silver bullion and the decrease in that of gold bullion are such that a decrease in that of silver caused by its inflow into the currency and an increase in that of gold caused by its outflow from currency can restore them to their old levels as bullion, bimetallism would succeed ; in other words, the market ratio of the two bullions would tend to return to the mint ratio. But if the increase in the supply of silver bullion and the decrease in that of gold is such that the outflow of silver bullion into currency reduces the level of the silver bullion to the old level, but the outflow of gold bullion from currency does not suffice to raise the level of the gold bullion to the old level, or if the outflow of gold from currency raises the level of the gold bullion to the old level, but the inflow of silver into currency does not result in the reduction of the level of silver bullion to its old level, bimetallism must fail ; in other words, the market ratio of the two bullions will remain diverted from the mint ratio legally established between their coins.

Under which of these two possibilities could the circumstances arising after 1873 have fallen? That is a question about which no one can say anything definitely. Even Jevons, who admitted the success of the bimetallic law in the earlier period, was not very sanguine about its success in the latter period. It was he who observed*

of bimetallism hang upon the question whether or not the two metals are maintained in circulation. For in the illustration which he gives to show the failure of bimetallism—Fig. 14 (b)—his film *f* shows gold to be entirely thrown out of circulation ; while in the illustration he gives to show the success of bimetallism—Fig. 15 (b)—his film *f* shows gold to be only partially thrown out of circulation. But there seems to be no reason to suppose that there cannot be a third possibility, namely, that while the position of the film is *f* is as in Fig. 14 (b) the level of the gold bullion and silver bullion may be as in Fig. 15 (b)—a possibility in which bimetallism succeeds although one of the two metals is entirely pushed out of circulation. For the success of bimetallism it is not necessary that both the metals should remain in circulation. Its success depends upon whether or not the compensatory action succeeds in restoring the relative values of the two bullions to that legally established between the two coins. If it succeeds in achieving that, the ratio would be preserved even if the compensatory action drives one metal entirely out of circulation.

* *Investigations*, etc. (ed. Foxwell), p. 317.

> *"that the question of bimetallism is one which does not admit of any precise and simple answer. It is essentially an indeterminate* problem. It involves several variable quantities and many constant quantities, the latter being either inaccurately known or, in many cases, altogether unknown. . . ."

Nonetheless, it is certain that the divergence between the mint ratio and the market ratio under a bimetallic system must be smaller than may be the case where there is no bimetallic system. Whenever the market ratio diverges from the mint ratio the compensatory action under the bimetallic law tends to restore the equilibrium, and even where it fails in restoring it, it does succeed in abridging the gulf between the two ratios. That being the case, it is safe to argue that had there been no demonetization of silver after 1873 the ratio between gold and silver would have probably been preserved as it was during the monetary disturbances of the earlier period. At any rate, this much is certain, that the market ratio between the two metals could not have diverged from the mint ratio to the extent it actually did.*

It is therefore a sad commentary on the monetary legislation of the seventies that if it did not actually help to create, for no purpose, a problem unknown before, it certainly helped to make worse a bad situation. Prior to 1870, not all countries had a common currency. There were India and countries of Western Europe which were exclusively on a silver basis, and others, like England and Portugal, which were exclusively on a gold basis, and yet none of them felt the want of a common standard of value in their mutual dealings. So long as there existed the fixed-ratio system in France and the Latin Union the problem was really provided for, for under it the two metals behaved as one and thereby furnished a common standard, although all countries did not use the same metal as their standard money. It was therefore a matter of comparative indifference to most countries which metal they used so long as there was some one country which used either at a certain defined ratio. With the destruction of this fixed ratio what was thus a matter of comparative indifference became a matter of supreme concern. Every country which had before enjoyed the benefits of a common international standard without having a common currency was faced with

* Fisher, *Purchasing Power of Money*, 1911, pp. 134-35.

*a crisis in which the choice lay between sacrificing its currency to securing a common standard or hugging its currency and foregoing the benefits of a common standard.* That exigencies of a common standard ultimately led to its accomplishment was as it should have been, but it was not a fact before a great deal of harm and some heavy burdens had brought home to people what the want of it really meant to them.

## CHAPTER III

## THE SILVER STANDARD AND THE EVILS OF ITS INSTABILITY

The economic consequences of this rupture of the par of exchange were of the most far-reaching character. It divided the commercial world into two sharply defined groups, one using gold and the other using silver as their standard money. When so much gold was always equal to so much silver, as was the case previous to 1873, it mattered very little, for the purposes of international transactions, whether a country was on a gold or on a silver standard; nor did it make any difference in which of the two currencies its obligations were stipulated and realized. But when, owing to the dislocation of the fixed par, it was not possible to define how much silver was equal to how much gold from year to year or even from month to month, this precision of value, the very soul of pecuniary exchange, gave place to the uncertainties of gambling. Of course, all countries were not drawn into this vortex of perplexities in the same degree and to the same extent, yet it was impossible for any country which participated in international commerce to escape from being dragged into it. This was true of India as it was of no other country. She was a silver-standard country intimately bound to a gold-standard country, so that her economic and financial life was at the mercy of blind forces operating upon the relative values of gold and silver which governed the rupee-sterling exchange.

The fall increased the burden of those who were under an obligation to make gold payments. Amongst such, the most heavily charged was the Government of India. Owing to the exigencies of its political constitution, that Government has been under the necessity of making certain payments in England to meet: (1) interest on debt and on the stock of the guaranteed railway companies; (2) expenses on account of the European troops maintained in India; (3) pensions and non-effective allowances payable in England; (4) cost of the home administration*;

*Since the Reform Act of 1920 that part of this cost which was "political" has been placed upon the British Estimates.

and (5) stores purchased in England for use or consumption in India. England being a gold-standard country, these payments were necessarily gold payments. But the revenues of the Government of India out of which these payments were met were received in silver, which was the sole legal-tender money of the country. It is evident that even if the gold payments were a fixed quantity their burden must increase *pari passu* with the fall in the gold value of silver. But the gold payments were not a fixed quantity. They have ever been on the increase, so that the rupee cost of the gold payments grew both by reason of the growth in their magnitude, and also by reason of the contraction of the medium, i.e. the appreciation of gold, in which they were payable. How greatly this double levy diminished the revenues of India, the figures in Table XI give a convincing testimony.

TABLE XI

INCREASE IN THE RUPEE COST OF GOLD PAYMENTS*

| Financial Year | Average Rate of Exchange for the Year | | Total Excess of Rupees needed to provide for the net Sterling Payments of the Year over those required to meet the Sterling Payments of 1874-75 | Amount of this Excess due to | |
|---|---|---|---|---|---|
| | | | | (1) Fall in the Rate of Exchange over that of 1874-75 | (2) Increase in gold payments over those of the Year 1874-75. |
| | s. | d. | R | R | R |
| 1875-76 | 1 | 9.626 | 86,97,980 | 41,13,723 | 45,84,257 |
| 1876-77 | 1 | 8.508 | 3,15,06,824 | 1,44,68,234 | 1,70,38,590 |
| 1877-78 | 1 | 8.791 | 1,30,05,481 | 1,14,58,670 | 1,15,46,811 |
| 1878-79 | 1 | 7.794 | 1,85,23,170 | 1,04,16,718 | 81,06,452 |
| 1879-80 | 1 | 7.961 | 39,23,570 | 1,65,37,394 | - 1,26,13,824 |
| 1880-81 | 1 | 7.956 | 3,12,11,981 | 1,92,82,582 | 1,19,29,399 |
| 1881-82 | 1 | 7.895 | 3,18,19,685 | 1,98,76,786 | - 1,19,42,899 |
| 1882-83 | 1 | 7.525 | 62,50,518 | 1,86,35,246 | 2,48,85,764 |
| 1883-84 | 1 | 7.536 | 3,44,16,685 | 2,33,46,040 | 1,10,70,645 |
| 1884-85 | 1 | 7.308 | 1,96,25,981 | 2,48,03,423 | 51,77,442 |
| 1885-86 | 1 | 6.254 | 1,82,11,346 | 2,54,95,337 | - 4,37,06,683 |
| 1886-87 | 1 | 5.441 | 4,69,16,788 | 4,46,68,299 | 22,48,489 |
| 1887-88 | 1 | 4.898 | 4,63,13,161 | 4,96,60,537 | - 33,47,376 |
| 1888-89 | 1 | 4.379 | 9,00,38,166 | 6,59,71,998 | 2,40,66,168 |
| 1889-90 | 1 | 4.566 | 7,75,96,889 | 6,06,98,370 | 1,68,98,519 |
| 1890-91 | 1 | 6.090 | 9,06,11,857 | 4,65,48,302 | 4,40,63,555 |
| 1891-92 | 1 | 4.733 | 10,44,44,529 | 6,54,52,999 | 3,89,91,530 |

* Compiled from figures in Appendix II, p. 270, of the Indian Currency Committee of 1893.

The effect of such a growing burden on the finance of the Government may well be imagined ; the condition of the Government, embarrassing at first, later became quite desperate under this continuously increasing burden. It enforced a policy of high taxation and rigid economy in the finances of the Government. Analysing the resource side of the Indian Budgets from the year 1872-73, we find that there was hardly any year which did not expire without making an addition to the existing imposts of the country. In 1872-73, there commenced the levy of what were called Provincial Rates. The fiscal year 1875-76 witnessed the addition of R. 1 per gallon in the excise duty on spirits. In 1877-78 the Pass Duty on Malwa opium was raised from Rs. 600 to Rs. 650 per chest. An addition of a Licence Tax and Local Rates was made in the year 1878-79, and an increase of Rs. 50 per chest took place in the Malwa Opium Duty in the following year. With the help of these imposts the Government expected to place its finances on an adequate basis. By the end of 1882, it felt quite secure and even went so far as to remit some of the taxes, which it did by lowering the customs duties and the Patwari Cess in the North-Western Provinces. But the rapid pace in the fall of the exchange soon showed that a resort to further taxation was necessary to make up for the increased cost of the sterling payments. To the existing burdens, therefore, was added in 1886 an Income Tax, a duty of 5 per cent. on imported and also on non-illuminating petroleum. The Salt Duty was raised in 1888 in India from Rs. 2 to Rs. 2½, and in Burma from 3 annas to R. 1 per maund. The Patwari Cess of the North-Western Provinces, repealed in 1882, was re-imposed in 1888. The rates of duty on imported spirit and the excise duties on spirits were not only raised in 1890, but were afterwards added to in every province. An excise duty on malt liquor was levied in 1893, and another on salted fish at the rate of 6 annas per maund. The yield of the taxes and duties levied from 1882-83 was* as follows :—

| Sources. | 1882-83. | 1892-93. |
|---|---|---|
| | Rs. | Rs. |
| Salt | 5,67,50,000 | 8,14,90,000 |
| Excise | 3,47,50,000 | 4,97,90,000 |
| Customs | 1,08,90,000 | 1,41,80,000 |
| Assessed Taxes | 48,40,000 | 1,63,60,000 |

* *Report of the Indian Currency Committee*, 1893, App. II, p. 263.

All this additional burden was due to the enhanced cost of meeting the gold payments, and "would not have been necessary but for the fall in the exchange."*

Along with this increase of resources the Government of India also exercised the virtue of economy in the cost of administration. For the first time in its history, the Government turned to the alternative of employing the comparatively cheaper agency of the natives of the country in place of the imported Englishmen. Prior to 1870, the scope of effecting economy along this line was very limited. By the Civil Service Reforms of 1853† the way was cleared for the appointment of Indians to the posts reserved by the Statute of 1793‡ for the members of the covenanted Civil Service. But this reform did not conduce to any economy in the cost of the administration, because the Indian members carried the same high scale of salaries as did the English members of the Civil Service. It was when the Statute of 1870 (33 Vic. c. 3) was passed permitting the appointment by nomination of non-covenanted Indians to places reserved for the covenanted Civil Service on a lower scale of salary, that a real scope for economy presented itself to the Government of India. Hard pressed, the Government of India availed itself of the possibilities for economy held out by this statute. So great was the need for economy and so powerful was the interest of the Government in reducing its expenditure that it proceeded, notwithstanding increased demands for efficient administration, to substitute the less expensive agency of non-covenanted civilians in place of the more expensive agency of the covenanted civilians. The scale on which this substitution was effected was by no means small, for we find that between 1874 and 1889 the strength of the covenanted service recruited in England was reduced by more than 22 per cent., and was further expected to be reduced by about 12 per cent., by the employment of uncovenanted Indians to the posts usually reserved for covenanted civilians.§ Besides substituting a cheap for a dear agency in the administration, the Government also sought

* J. E. O'Conor, *Report of the Indian Currency Committee*, 1898, App. II, p. 182.

† Cf. *Report of the Public Service Commission*, C. 5327 of 1887.

‡ This provision of the Act has been re-enacted by the Act of 1861.

§ Cf. evidence of Mr. Jenkins, Q. 12. Mit. of Evid. of the Select Committee on East India (Civil Servants), H. of C. 327 of 1890.

to obtain relief by applying the pruning knife to the rank growth in departmental extravagances.* Even with such heroic efforts to increase the revenue and reduce the expenditure the finances of the Government throughout the period of the falling exchange were never in a flourishing state, as is shown in Table XII.

Much more regrettable was the inability of the Government, owing to its financial difficulties, to find money for useful public works. The welfare of the Indian people depends upon turning to best account the resources which the country possesses. But the people have had very little of the necessary spirit of enterprise in them. The task, therefore, has fallen upon the Government of India to provide the country with the two prime requisites of a sustained economic life, namely a system of transport and a network of irrigation. With this object in view the Government had inaugurated a policy of developing what were called "Extraordinary Public Works," financed by capital borrowings. For such borrowings India, as was to be expected, hardly offered any market, the people being too poor and their savings too scanty to furnish a modicum of the required capital outlay. Like all Governments of poor peoples, the Government of India had therefore to turn to wealthier countries that had surplus capital to lend. All these countries unfortunately happened to be on the gold standard. As long as it was possible to say that so much gold was equal to so much silver, the English investor was indifferent whether the securities of the Government of India were rupee securities or sterling securities. But the fall in the gold value of silver was also a fall in the gold value of the rupee securities, and what was once a secure investment ceased to be so any more. This placed the Government in a difficult position in the matter of financing its extraordinary public works. Figures in Table XIII are worth study.

The English investor would not invest in the rupee securities. An important customer for the Indian rupee securities was thus lost. The response of the Indian money market was inadequate. To issue sterling securities was the only alternative to enable the Government to tap a bigger and a more constant reservoir for the

‡ Cf. *Calcutta Civil Finance Committee's Report*, 1886; also *The Report of the Civil Finance Commissioner* (1887), who completed the work of the Committee after it was dissolved.

TABLE XII

REVENUE AND EXPENDITURE OF THE GOVERNMENT OF INDIA

| Year. | Average Rate of Exchange. | In India. Net Revenue | In India. Net Expenditure excluding Exchange | In India. Surplus Revenue. | In England. Net Sterling Revenue | In England. Exchange. | Final Result. Surplus (+) or Deficit (—) |
|---|---|---|---|---|---|---|---|
| | d. | R. | R. | | £ | R. | R. |
| 1874-75 . | 22.156 | 39,564,216 | 25,897,098 | 13,667,118 | 12,562,101 | 1,045,239 | 59,778 |
| 1875-76 . | 21.626 | 40,053,419 | 24,541,923 | 15,511,496 | 12,544,813 | 1,377,428 | 1,589,255 |
| 1876-77 . | 20.508 | 38,253,366 | 25,355,285 | 12,898,081 | 13,229,646 | 2,252,611 | −2 ,584,176 |
| 1877-78 . | 20.791 | 39,275,489 | 27,658,021 | 11,617,468 | 13,756,478 | 2,123,030 | − 4,262,040 |
| 1878-79 . | 19.794 | 44,415,139 | 25,778,928 | 18,636,211 | 13,610,211 | 2,891,902 | 2,134,098 |
| 1879-80 . | 19.961 | 45,258,197 | 29,384,030 | 15,874,167 | 14,223,891 | 2,878,169 | − 1,227,893 |
| 1880-81 . | 19.956 | 44,691,119 | 34,880,434 | 9,810,085 | 11,177,231 | 2,264,848 | − 3,031,394 |
| 1881-82 . | 19.895 | 45,471,887 | 27,717,249 | 17,754,638 | 11,737,688 | 2,421,499 | 3,595,451 |
| 1882-83 . | 19.525 | 42,526,173 | 25,500,437 | 17,025,736 | 13,299,976 | 3,050,923 | 674,837 |
| 1883-84 . | 19.536 | 43,591,273 | 23,566,381 | 20,024,892 | 14,770,257 | 3,375,158 | 1,879,477 |
| 1884-85 . | 19.308 | 41,585,347 | 24,763,779 | 16,821,568 | 13,844,028 | 3,363,986 | − 386,446 |
| 1885-86 . | 18.254 | 42,635,953 | 27,352,132 | 15,283,821 | 13,755,659 | 4,329,888 | − 2,801,726 |
| 1886-87 . | 17.441 | 44,804,774 | 25,124,335 | 19,680,439 | 14,172,298 | 5,329,714 | 178,427 |
| 1887-88 . | 16.898 | 45,424,150 | 25,968,025 | 19,456,125 | 15,128,018 | 6,356,939 | − 2,028,832 |
| 1888-89 . | 16.379 | 46,558,354 | 25,051,147 | 21,507,207 | 14,652,590 | 6,817,599 | 37,018 |
| 1889-90 . | 16.566 | 50,005,810 | 26,367,855 | 23,637,955 | 14,513,155 | 6,512,767 | 2,612,033 |
| 1890-91 . | 18.090 | 49,403,819 | 25,579,727 | 23,824,092 | 15,176,866 | 4,959,055 | 3,688,171 |
| 1891-92 . | 16.733 | 50,023,142 | 27,013,618 | 23,009,524 | 15,716,780 | 6,825,909 | 467,525 |

drawing of capital to India; but as it was bound to increase the burden of the gold payments, which it was the strongest interest of the Government to reduce, the resort to the London money market, unavoidable as it became, was somewhat restrained,* with the result that the expansion of extraordinary public works did not proceed at a pace demanded by the needs of the country. The effects of this financial derangement, consequent on the fall of the exchange, were not confined to the Government of India. They were immediately felt by the municipalities and other local bodies who were dependent upon the Government for financial aid. So long as the cash balances were overflowing in the Treasury of the Government, "one of the most useful ways" to employ them was found in lending a portion of them to these local institutions. As they had just then been inaugurated under the local self-government policy of Lord Ripon's regime, and were looked upon only as an experiment, their taxing and borrowing powers were rigidly limited. Consequently, this financial aid from the Central Government by way of temporary advances was a resource of inestimable value to them. When, however, the cash balances of the Central Government began to diminish owing to the continued losses by exchange, these facilities were severely curtailed,† so that the very vitality of these institutions was threatened just at the moment when they needed all help to foster their growth and strengthen their foundations.

Addressing the Secretary of State, the Government of India, in a despatch of February 2, 1886, observed ‡:—

> "10. We do not hesitate to repeat that the facts set forth in the preceding paragraphs are, from the point of Indian interests, intolerable; and the evils which we have enumerated do not exhaust the catalogue. Uncertainty regarding the future of silver discourages the investment of capital in India, and we find it impossible to borrow in silver except at an excessive cost.

* During the period of falling exchange the distribution of the debt of India was as follows:—

| | Sterling Debt. | Rupee Debt. |
|---|---|---|
| End of 1873-74 . . . | 41,117,617 | 66,41,72,900 |
| End of 1898-99 . | 124,268,605 | 1,12,65,04,340 |

*Indian Currency Committee* (1898), Appendix II p 179.

† Cf. *Financial Statement*, 1876-77, p. 94.

‡ See C. 4868 of 1886, p. 8.

TABLE XIII

PRICE MOVEMENTS OF RUPEE AND STERLING SECURITIES OF THE GOVERNMENT OF INDIA*

| Year. | Rates of Exchange | | Price of 4 per cent Rupee Paper | | | | Price of Sterling India Stock | | | | | |
|---|---|---|---|---|---|---|---|---|---|---|---|---|
| | | | In Calcutta | | In London | | 4 per cent. | | 3½ per cent | | 3 per cent. | |
| | Highest | Lowest | Highest | Lowest | Highest | Lowest | Highest | Lowest. | Highest. | Lowest. | Highest. | Lowest. |
| | d. | d | | | | | | | | | | |
| 1873 | 22 7/8 | 21 5/8 | 105 | 101 7/8 | 97 | 94 1/2 | 106 1/2 | 101 1/4 | | | | |
| 1874 | 23 1/8 | 21 3/4 | 104 1/2 | 99 1/2 | 98 | 94 1/2 | 103 3/4 | 101 | | | | |
| 1875 | 22 3/16 | 21 1/4 | 102 7/8 | 101 3/4 | 94 | 91 | 106 1/4 | 103 1/4 | | | | |
| 1876 | 22 3/8 | 18 1/2 | 101 7/8 | 98 3/4 | 89 3/4 | 78 | 105 7/8 | 101 7/8 | | | | |
| 1877 | 22 1/4 | 20 9/16 | 98 7/8 | 93 1/4 | 88 1/2 | 81 | 104 5/8 | 102 1/4 | | | | |
| 1878 | 21 | 18 3/4 | 96 7/8 | 93 1/2 | 82 1/2 | 75 3/8 | 104 5/8 | 99 | | | | |
| 1879 | 20 5/8 | 18 5/8 | 94 7/8 | 91 1/4 | 80 | 77 1/4 | 105 5/8 | 100 7/8 | | | | |
| 1880 | 20 3/8 | 19 3/4 | 100 | 92 15/16 | 81 3/8 | 77 3/4 | 105 5/8 | 102 1/8 | | | | |
| 1881 | 20 1/16 | 19 1/2 | 104 5/8 | 100 | 86 | 81 1/2 | 106 3/8 | 103 7/8 | 103 7/8 | 100 3/4 | | |
| 1882 | 20 5/16 | 19 1/16 | 102 1/16 | 95 5/8 | 85 | 81 | 105 1/8 | 102 7/8 | 101 7/8 | 99 3/4 | | |
| 1883 | 19 9/16 | 19 3/16 | 101 1/8 | 97 9/16 | 82 | 79 3/4 | 104 5/8 | 102 [illegible]/16 | 103 1/8 | 101 3/8 | | |
| 1884 | 19 3/4 | 18 15/16 | 100 3/8 | 95 9/16 | 81 3/4 | 78 1/4 | 104 3/8 | 101 5/8 | 107 1/8 | 101 3/4 | 96 1/4 | 91 3/4 |
| 1885 | 19 3/16 | 17 21/32 | 98 [illegible]/16 | 92 1/4 | 77 1/2 | 73 1/4 | 103 1/16 | 98 3/4 | 102 3/4 | 97 1/2 | 91 1/2 | 85 3/4 |
| 1886 | 18 | 16 1/8 | 97 3/4 | 97 3/16 | 73 | 66 1/4 | 103 1/8 | 101 1/4 | 102 3/4 | 99 3/4 | 90 1/8 | 86 3/8 |
| 1887 | 18 3/16 | 15 5/8 | 99 3/16 | 95 5/16 | 71 11/16 | 67 7/8 | 102 3/4 | 100 1/2 | 103 1/4 | 100 1/4 | 92 3/4 | 95 3/8 |
| 1888 | 17 1/8 | 16 | 100 1/16 | 97 3/4 | 69 3/8 | 66 1/4 | 102 7/8 | 100 1/2 | 107 1/4 | 104 5/8 | 98 | 95 |
| 1889 | 16 15/16 | 16 | 100 3/8 | 97 11/16 | 69 1/8 | 66 3/8 | | | 109 1/2 | 106 7/8 | 101 1/8 | 99 |
| 1890 | 20 19/32 | 16 7/8 | 103 7/8 | 96 13/16 | 87 1/4 | 68 3/4 | | | 108 1/2 | 105 1/4 | 100 3/4 | 95 1/4 |
| 1891 | 18 1/4 | 16 5/8 | 107 13/16 | 104 1/16 | 80 3/4 | 74 1/4 | | | 109 1/2 | 105 | 99 | 94 1/2 |
| 1892 | 16 11/16 | 14 5/8 | 108 15/16 | 103 13/16 | 74 1/2 | 62 | | | 109 1/2 | 106 1/4 | 98 1/2 | 94 7/8 |

* Appendix II to the *Report of the Indian Currency Committee* of 1893, p 272. These prices differ slightly from those given in Appendix IV to the First Report of the Gold and Silver Commission, 1886, and also from those in the Statistics of British India (First Issue) for 1906-07, Part IV, (a) Finance Tables 7 and 8 of the division called Prices

"On the other hand, the Frontier and Famine Railways which we propose to construct, and the Coast and Frontier defences which we have planned, are imperatively required and cannot be postponed indefinitely.

"We are forced, therefore, either to increase our sterling liabilities, to which course there are so many objections, or to do without the railways required for the commercial development of the country, and its protection against invasion and the effects of famine.

"11. Nor can the difficulties which local bodies experience in borrowing in India be overlooked. The Municipalities of Bombay and Calcutta require large sums for sanitary improvements, but the high rate of interest which they must pay for silver loans operates to deter them from undertaking expensive works, and we need hardly remind your Lordship that it has quite recently been found necessary for Government to undertake to lend the money required for the construction of docks at Calcutta and Bombay, and that when the Port Commissioners of Calcutta attempted to raise a loan of 75 lakhs of rupees in September, 1885, guaranteed by the Government of India, the total amount of tenders was only Rs. 40,200, and no portion of this insignificant amount was offered at par. . . . ."

The importation of capital on private account was hampered for similar reasons, to the great detriment of the country. It was urged on all hands, and was even recommended by a Royal Commission,* that one avenue of escape from the ravages of recurring famines, to which India so pitifully succumbed at such frequent intervals, was the diversification of her industries. To be of any permanent benefit, such diversified industrial life could be based on a capitalistic basis alone. But that depended upon the flow of capital into the country as freely as the needs of the country required. As matters then stood, the English investor, the largest purveyor of capital, looked upon the investment of capital in India as a risky proposition. It was feared that once the capital was spread out in a silver country every fall in the price of silver would not only make the return uncertain when drawn in gold, but would also reduce the capital value of his investment in terms of

*Cf. *The Report of the Famine Commission of* 1880, Part II, C. 2735 of 1880, pp. 175-76.

gold, which was naturally the unit in which he measured all his returns and his outlays. This check to the free inflow of capital was undoubtedly the most serious evil arising out of the rupture of the par of exchange.

Another group of people, who suffered from the fall of exchange because of their obligation to make gold payments, was composed of the European members of the Civil Service in India. Like the Government to which they belonged, they received their salaries in silver, but had to make gold remittances in support of their families, who were often left behind in England. Before 1873, when the price of silver in terms of gold was fixed, this circumstance was of no moment to them. But as the rupee began to fall the face of the situation was completely altered. With every fall in the value of silver they had to pay more rupees out of their fixed salaries to obtain the same amount of gold. Some relief was no doubt given to them in the matter of their remittances. The Civil Servants were permitted, at a sacrifice to the Government, to make their remittances at what was called the Official Rate of Exchange.* It is true the difference between the market rate and the official rate was not very considerable. None the less, it was appreciable enough for the Civil Servants to have gained by 2½ per cent. on the average of the years 1862-90 † at the cost of the Government. The Military Servants obtained a similar relief to a greater degree, but in a different way. Their salary was fixed in sterling, though payable in rupees. It is true the Royal Warrant which fixed their salary also fixed the rate of exchange between the sterling and the rupee for that purpose. But as it invariably happened that the rate of exchange fixed by the Warrant was higher than the market rate, the Military

* As was explained by Mr. Waterfield before the Select Committee on East India (Civil Servants), H. C. Return 327 of 1890, Q. 1905-17, it was first instituted in 1824 and was arrived at as follows : In December of each year a calculation was made at the India Office of the cost of sending a rupee to India, based on the market price of silver in London, and of the cost of bringing a rupee from India, based on the price of bills on London in Calcutta. A mean between the two was struck and taken as the adjusting rate for the coming official year between the India Office and the British Treasury in regard to such transactions or payments undertaken by one Government as the agent of the other. It was fixed anew for each and formed a fair average rate, although it was sometimes above and sometimes below the market rate of exchange.

† *Ibid.*, Q. 1925-26.

Servants were compensated to the extent of the difference at the cost of the Indian Exchequer.* This relief was, comparatively speaking, no relief to them. The official or the warrant rates of exchange, though better than the market rates of exchange, were much lower than the rate at which they were used to make their remittances before 1873. Their burden, like that of the Government, grew with the fall of silver, and as their burden increased their attitude became alarmist. Many were the memorialists who demanded from the Government adequate compensation for their losses on exchange.† The Government was warned ‡ that

> "the ignorant folk who think India would be benefited by lowering present salaries are seemingly unable to comprehend that such a step would render existence on this reduced pay simply impossible, and that recourse would of necessity be had to other methods of raising money."

Such, no doubt, was the case in the earlier days of the East India Company, when the Civil Servants fattened on pickings because their pay was small,§ and it was to put a stop to their extortions that their salaries were raised to what appears an extraordinary level. That such former instances of extortions should have been held out as monitions showed too well how discontented the Civil Service was owing to its losses through exchange.

Quite a different effect the fall had on the trade and industry of the country. It was in a flourishing state as compared with the affairs of the Government or with the trade and industry of a gold-standard country like England. Throughout the period of falling silver there was said to be a progressive decline relatively to population in the employment afforded by various trades and industries in England. The textile manufactures and the iron and coal trade were depressed as well as the other important trades,

* Cf F. S. 1887-8, pp. 39-40. This cost was as follows:

| | | | |
|---|---|---|---|
| 1874-75 | Rs. 6,40,000 | 1885-86 | Rs. 4,00,000 |
| 1884-85 | Rs. 18,43,000 | 1886-87 | Rs. 5,15,000 |

† Cf. *Report of the Indian Currency Committee*, 1893, App. I, pp. 185-90 and p. 202, for memorials of the European Civil Servants.

‡ Cf. Col. Hughes-Hallett, M.P., *The Depreciation of the Rupee: its Effect on the Anglo-Indian Official—the Wrong and the Remedy*, London, 1887, p. 14.

§ The connection between the rapacious conduct of the early European Civil Servants and the smallness of their salaries was well brought out by Clive in his speech dated March 30, 1772, during the course of the debate in the House of Commons on the East India Judicature Bill, *Hansard*, Vol. XVII, pp. 334-39.

including the hardware manufactures of Birmingham and Sheffield, the sugar-refining of Greenock, Liverpool, and London, the manufactures of earthenware, glass, leather, paper, and a multitude of minor industries.* The depression in English agriculture was so widespread that the Commissioners of 1892 were "unable to point to any part of the country in which [the effects of the depression] can be said to be entirely absent," and this notwithstanding the fact that the seasons since 1882 "were on the whole satisfactory from an agricultural point of view."† Just the reverse was the case with Indian trade and industry. The foreign trade of the country, which had bounced up during the American Civil War, showed greater buoyancy after 1870, and continued to grow throughout the period of the falling exchange at a rapid pace. During the short space of twenty years the total imports and exports of the country more than doubled in their magnitude, as is shown by Table XIV.

Not only had the trade of India been increasing, but the nature of her industries was also at the same time undergoing a profound change. Prior to 1870, India and England were, so to say, non-competing groups. Owing to the protectionist policy of

TABLE XIV

IMPORTS AND EXPORTS (BOTH MERCHANDIZE AND TREASURE)*

| Year. | Exports. R. | Imports. R. | Year. | Exports. R | Imports. R. |
|---|---|---|---|---|---|
| 1870-71 | 57,556,951 | 39,913,942 | 1881-82 | 83,068,198 | 60,436,155 |
| 1871-72 | 64,685,376 | 43,665,663 | 1882-83 | 84,527,182 | 65,548,868 |
| 1872-73 | 56,548,842 | 36,431,210 | 1883-84 | 89,186,397 | 68,157,311 |
| 1873-74 | 56,910,081 | 39,612,362 | 1884-85 | 85,225,922 | 69,591,269 |
| 1874-75 | 57,984,549 | 44,363,160 | 1885-86 | 84,989,502 | 71,133,666 |
| 1875-76 | 60,291,731 | 44,192,378 | 1886-87 | 90,190,633 | 72,830,670 |
| 1876-77 | 65,043,789 | 48,876,751 | 1887-88 | 92,148,279 | 78,830,468 |
| 1877-78 | 67,433,324 | 58,819,644 | 1888-89 | 98,833,879 | 83,285,427 |
| 1878-79 | 64,919,741 | 44,857,343 | 1889-90 | 105,366,720 | 86,656,990 |
| 1879-80 | 69,247,511 | 52,821,398 | 1890-91 | 102,350,526 | 93,909,856 |
| 1880-81 | 76,021,043 | 62,104,984 | 1891-92 | 111,460,278 | 84,155,045 |

* From Appendix II (Nos. 1 and 2) to the *Report of the Indian Currency Committee* of 1898.

* Report by Dunraven, Farrer, Muntz, and Lubbock in the *Final Report of the Royal Commission on Depression of Trade and Industry, par.*, 54, C. 4893.

† *Final Report of the Royal Commission on Agricultural Depression in England*, C. 8540 of 1897, par. 28.

TABLE XV. NATURE OF INDIAN AND BRITISH EXPORTS.*

| | Distribution of *Indian* Exports exclusive of Treasure. | | | | | Distribution of *English* Exports exclusive of Treasure. | | | | |
|---|---|---|---|---|---|---|---|---|---|---|
| | Manufactured Articles | Raw Materials | Food Articles | Unclassified Articles | Total | Manufactured Articles | Raw Materials | Food Articles | Unclassified Articles. | Total. |
| 1857 | 11 | 34 | 22 | 23 | 100 | 90.9 | 4 | 4.9 | .2 | 100 |
| 1858 | 6 | 35 | 26 | 33 | 100 | 91.4 | 3.4 | 5.1 | .1 | 100 |
| 1859 | 6.5 | 40 | 15.5 | 38 | 100 | 91.5 | 3.8 | 4.6 | .1 | 100 |
| 1860 | 5.7 | 43.6 | 17.7 | 33 | 100 | 91.9 | 3.6 | 4 4 | .3 | 100 |
| 1861 | 5.8 | 46.5 | 15.3 | 32.4 | 100 | 90.4 | 4.8 | 4.8 | — | 100 |
| 1862 | 5 | 52 | 16 | 27 | 100 | 90.3 | 4 | 4.8 | .9 | 100 |
| 1863 | 3.7 | 58.7 | 10.6 | 27 | 100 | 91.0 | 4 | 4 | 1.0 | 100 |
| 1864 | 4 | 69.2 | 9.3 | 17.5 | 100 | 92.5 | 3.7 | 3.7 | .1 | 100 |
| 1865 | 3.5 | 68 | 12 | 16.6 | 100 | 92.1 | 3 6 | 3.6 | .7 | 100 |
| 1866 | 4.2 | 67.2 | 10.3 | 18.3 | 100 | 92 | 3.7 | 3.7 | .4 | 100 |
| 1867 | 4 | 58 | 11 | 27 | 100 | 92.2 | 3.8 | 3.7 | .3 | 100 |
| 1868 | 4 | 58.5 | 11.5 | 26 | 100 | 92 | 4.4 | 3.4 | .2 | 100 |
| 1869 | 4.8 | 60.5 | 14 | 20.7 | 100 | 92 | 4.2 | 3.1 | .7 | 100 |
| 1870 | 4.4 | 63.6 | 9 | 23 | 100 | 91 | 4 | 4 | 1.0 | 100 |
| 1871 | 3.7 | 65.3 | 11 | 20 | 100 | 90 | 4.4 | 4.9 | .7 | 100 |
| 1872 | 3.3 | 61.4 | 13.4 | 21.8 | 100 | 91.2 | 5.4 | 3.5 | .9 | 100 |

* The figures for India are calculated from the *Statistical Abstract for British India, Second Number* (1857-1866), Table No. 34, and the Eighth Number (1864-1873), Table No 24 Figures for England are taken from Appendix C (Statement 6) to the *First Report of the Royal Commission of the Depression of Trade and Industry*, 1885, with this alteration—that the separate figures in the original under "Manufactured" and "Partially Manufactured" are here grouped under "Manufactured." The "Unclassified Articles" under Indian Exports are for the most part "Jewellery"

TABLE XVI

CHANGES IN INDUSTRIAL PURSUITS OF INDIA†

| Years. | Imports. | | Exports. | |
|---|---|---|---|---|
| | Manufactured | Raw. | Manufactured | Raw. |
| | Rs. | Rs | Rs | Rs |
| 1879 . . | 25,98,65,827 | 13,75,55,837 | 5,27,80,340 | 59,67,27,991 |
| 1892 . . | 36,22,31,872 | 26,38,18,431 | 16,42,47,566 | 85,52,09,499 |
| Percentage of increase | | | | |
| Total . . | 39 | 91 | 211 | 43 |
| Annual . | 2.8 | 6.5 | 15 | 3 |

the Navigation Laws, and owing also to the substitution of man by machinery in the field of production, India had become exclusively an agricultural and a raw-material-producing country, while England had transformed herself into a country which devoted all her energy and her resources to the manufacturing of raw materials imported from abroad into finished goods. How marked was the contrast in the industrial pursuits in the two countries is well revealed by the analysis of their respective exports on opposite page.

After 1870, the distribution of their industrial pursuits was greatly altered, and India once again began to assume the role of a manufacturing country. Analysing the figures for Indian imports and exports for the twenty years succeeding 1870, (*see Table below*) we find that the progress in the direction of manufactures formed one of the most significant features of the period.

This change in the industrial evolution was marked by the growth of two principal manufactures. One of them was the manufacture of cotton. The cotton industry was one of the oldest industries of India, but during 100 years between 1750 and 1850 it had fallen into a complete state of decrepitude. Attempts were made to resuscitate the industry on a capitalistic basis in the sixties of the nineteenth century and soon showed signs of rapid advance. The story of its progress is graphically illustrated in the following summary in Table XVII :—

† From Ranade's *Essays on Indian Economics*, p. 104.

## TABLE XVII

*The Development of Indian Cotton Trade and Industry*

| | Growth of Trade (Average Annual Quantities in each Quinquennium). | | | | |
|---|---|---|---|---|---|
| | 1870-71 to 1874-75 | 1875-76 to 1879-80 | 1880-81 to 1884-85 | 1885-86 to 1889-90 | 1890-91 to 1894-95 |
| Imports of raw cotton—thousands of cwts | 23 | 52 | 51 | 74 | 89 |
| Exports of raw cotton—thousands of cwts | 5,236 | 3,988 | 5,477 | 5,330 | 4,660 |
| Imports of twist and yarn | 33.55 | 33.55 | 44.34 | 49 09 | 44·79 |
| | Growth of Industry (at end of each fifth year). | | | | |
| Number of mills | 48 | 58 | 81 | 114 | 143 |
| ,, ,, spindles—000 omitted | 1,000 | 1,471 | 2,037 | 2,935 | 3,712 |
| Number of looms—000 omitted | 10 | 13 | 16 | 22 | 34 |
| Number of persons employed | — | 39,537 | 61,836 | 99,224 | — |

Another industry which figured largely in this expansion of Indian manufactures was jute. Unlike the cotton industry of India, the jute industry was of a comparatively recent origin. Its growth, different from that of the cotton industry, was fostered by the application of European capital, European management, and European skill, and it soon took as deep roots as the cotton industry and flourished as well as the latter did, if not better. Its history was one of continued progress as will be seen from Table XVIII.

This increasing trend towards manufactures was not without its indirect effects on the course of Indian agriculture. Prior to 1870 the Indian farmer, it may be said, had no commercial outlook. He cultivated not so much for profit as for individual self-sufficiency. After 1870 farming tended to become a business and crops came more and more to be determined by the course of market prices than by the household needs of the farmer. This is well illustrated by figures in Table XIX.

Such was the contrast in the economic conditions prevalent in the two countries. This peculiar phenomenon of a silver-standard country steadily progressing, and a gold-standard country tending to a standstill, exercised the minds of many of its

TABLE XVIII

DEVELOPMENT OF JUTE INDUSTRY AND TRADE

| Growth of Trade. | Average Annual of each Quinquennium. | | | | |
|---|---|---|---|---|---|
| | 1870-71 to 1874-75 | 1875-76 to 1879-80 | 1880-81 to 1884-85 | 1885-86 to 1889-90 | 1890-91 to 1894-95 |
| Exports— | | | | | |
| Raw, million cwt. | 5.72 | 5.58 | 7.81 | 9.31 | 10.54 |
| Gunny bags, millions | 6 44 | 35 96 | 60 32 | 79 98 | 120.74 |
| Cloth, million yds | — | 4.71 | 6.44 | 19.79 | 54.20 |
| *Growth of Industry.* | | | | | |
| Number of— | | | | | |
| Mills | — | 21 | 21 | 24 | 26 |
| Looms, 000 omitted | — | 5.5 | 5.5 | 7 | 8.3 |
| Spindles, 000 omitted | — | 88 | 88 | 138.4 | 172.4 |
| Persons employed, in thousands | — | 38.8 | 38 8 | 52.7 | 64.3 |

observers. The chief cause was said to be the inability of the English manufacturers to hold out in international competition. This inability to compete with the European rivals was attributed to the prevalence of protective tariffs and subsidies which formed an essential part of the industrial and commercial code of the European countries. Nothing of the kind then existed in India, where trade was as free and industry as unprotected as any could have been, and yet the Lancashire cotton-spinner, the Dundee jute manufacturer and the English wheat-grower complained that they could not compete with their rivals in India. The cause, in

TABLE XIX

GROWTH OF AGRICULTURAL EXPORTS OF INDIA

| | 1868-69 | 1873-74 | 1877-78 | 1882-83 | 1887-88 | 1891-92 |
|---|---|---|---|---|---|---|
| Wheat | 100 | 637.41 | 2,313 47 | 5,152 36 | 4,914 37 | 11,001.44 |
| Opium | 100 | 118.38 | 123.83 | 122.47 | 120.20 | 116.82 |
| Seeds | 100 | 111.26 | 305.87 | 239.97 | 403.60 | 480.99 |
| Rice | 100 | 131.66 | 119.84 | 203.28 | 185.55 | 220.36 |
| Indigo | 100 | 116.91 | 121.57 | 142.17 | 140.76 | 126.33 |
| Tea | 100 | 169 35 | 293.17 | 507.25 | 775.09 | 1,075.75 |
| Coffee | 100 | 86.04 | 89.98 | 85.31 | 64.59 | 74.11 |

this case, was supposed to be the falling exchange.* So much were some people impressed by this view that even the extension of the Indian trade to the Far East was attributed to this cause. Already, it was alleged, the dislocation of the par of exchange between gold and silver had produced a kind of segregation of gold-using countries and silver-using countries to the exclusion of each other. In a transaction between two countries using the same metal as standard it was said the element of uncertainty arising from the use of two metals varying in terms of each other was eliminated. Trade between two such countries could be carried on with less risk and less inconvenience than between two countries using different standards, as in the latter case the uncertainty entered into every transaction and added to the expense of the machinery by which trade was carried on. That the Indian trade should have been deflected to other quarters † where, owing to the existence of a common standard the situation trade had to deal with was immune from uncertainties, was readily admitted. But it was contended that there was no reason why, as a part of the segregation of commerce, it should have been possible for the Indian manufacturer to oust his English rival from the Eastern markets to the extent he was able to do (*see* Table XX, p. 101).

The causes which effected such trade disturbances formed the subject of a heated controversy.‡ The point in dispute was whether the changes in international trade, such as they were, were attributable to the monetary disturbances of the time. Those who held to the affirmative explained their position by arguing that the falling exchange gave a bounty to the Indian producer and imposed a penalty on the English producer. The existence of this bounty, which was said to be responsible for the shifting of the position of established competitors in the field of international commerce, was based on a simple calculation. It was said that if the gold value of silver fell the Indian exporter got more rupees for his produce and was therefore better off, while by reason of

* Cf. *The Final Report of the Royal Commission on Gold and Silver* Part I, paras. 99-101, for a summary of the argument.

†The distribution of Indian trade during this period was as shown on the page 99 footnote.

‡ *See* the evidence and memoranda by Profs. Marshall and Nicholson before the Royal Commission on Gold and Silver (1886); also Prof. Lexis, "The Agio on Gold and International Trade," in the *Economic Journal*, Vol. V, 1895.

## TABLE XX

### Exports of Cotton Goods to Eastern Markets

| Years. | Yarn, lbs., 000 omitted. | | Piece-goods, yds., 000 omitted. | |
|---|---|---|---|---|
| | From India. | From U.K. | From India. | From U.K. |
| 1877 . . | 7,927 | 33,086 | 15,544 | 394,489 |
| 1878 . . | 15,600 | 36,467 | 17,545 | 382,330 |
| 1879 . . | 21,332 | 38,951 | 22,517 | 523,921 |
| 1880 . . | 25,862 | 46,426 | 25,800 | 509,099 |
| 1881 . . | 26,901 | 47,479 | 30,424 | 587,177 |
| 1882 . . | 30,786 | 34,370 | 29,911 | 454,948 |
| 1883 . . | 45,378 | 33,499 | 41,534 | 415,956 |
| 1884 . . | 49,877 | 38,856 | 55,565 | 439,937 |
| 1885 . . | 65,897 | 33,061 | 47,909 | 562,339 |
| 1886 . . | 78,242 | 26,924 | 51,578 | 490,451 |
| 1887 . . | 91,804 | 35,354 | 53,406 | 618,146 |
| 1888 . . | 113,451 | 44,643 | 69,486 | 652,404 |
| 1889 . . | 128,907 | 35,720 | 70,265 | 557,004 |
| 1890 . . | 141,950 | 37,869 | 59,496 | 633,606 |
| 1891 . . | 169,253 | 27,971 | 67,666 | 595,258 |

### Distribution of Indian Trade.

Annual Average for each Quinquennium in Millions of Rupees

| Countries. | 1875-76 to 1879-80 | | | 1880-81 to 1884-85 | | |
|---|---|---|---|---|---|---|
| | Imports. | Exports. | Total. | Imports. | Exports. | Total. |
| United Kingdom . | 323.68 | 278.15 | 601.83 | 434.45 | 344.22 | 778.67 |
| China . . . | 14.05 | 132.27 | 146.32 | 19.23 | 134.94 | 154.17 |
| Japan . . . | .02 | .33 | .35 | .19 | 2.09 | 2.28 |
| Ceylon . . . | 5.74 | 22.97 | 28.71 | 5.35 | 16.37 | 21.72 |
| Straits Settlements . | 10.83 | 26.11 | 36.94 | 15.88 | 33.65 | 49.53 |

Annual Average for each Quinquennium in Millions of Rupees

| Countries. | 1885-86 to 1889-90 | | | 1890-91 to 1894-95 | | |
|---|---|---|---|---|---|---|
| | Imports. | Exports. | Total. | Imports. | Exports. | Total. |
| United Kingdom . | 510.47 | 360.59 | 871.06 | 526.24 | 338.40 | 864.64 |
| China . . . | 21.64 | 134.54 | 156.18 | 28.69 | 133.30 | 161.90 |
| Japan . . . | .25 | 7.27 | 7.52 | 1.51 | 14.44 | 15.95 |
| Ceylon . . . | 5.86 | 20.56 | 26.42 | 6.42 | 31.18 | 37.60 |
| Straits Settlements . | 20.09 | 42.54 | 62.63 | 23.32 | 52.56 | 75.88 |

the same fact the English producer got fewer sovereigns and was therefore worse off. Put in this naive form, the argument that the falling exchange gave a bounty to the Indian exporters and imposed a penalty on the English exporters had all the finality of a rule of arithmetic. Indeed, so axiomatic was the formula regarded by its authors that some important inferences as to its bearing on the trade and industrial situation of the time were drawn from it. One such inference was that it stimulated exports from and hindered imports into the silver-using countries. The second inference was that the fall of exchange exposed some English producers more than others to competition from their rivals in silver-using countries. Now, can such results be said to follow from the fall of exchange? If we go behind the bald statement of a fall of exchange and inquire as to what determined the gold price of silver the above inferences appear quite untenable. That the ratio between gold and silver was simply the inverse of the ratio between gold prices and silver prices must be taken to be an unquestionable proposition. If therefore the gold price of silver was falling it was a counterpart of the more general phenomenon of the fall of the English prices which were measured in gold, and the rise of the Indian prices which were measured in silver. Given such an interpretation of the event of the falling exchange, it is difficult to understand how it can help to increase exports and diminish imports. International trade is governed by the relative advantages which one country has over another, and the terms on which it is carried on are regulated by the comparative cost of articles that enter into it. It is, therefore, obvious that there cannot be a change in the real terms of trade between countries except as a result of changes in the comparative cost of these goods. Given a fall in gold prices *all round*, accompanied by a rise in silver prices *all round*, there was hardly anything in the monetary disturbance that could be said to have enabled India to increase her exportation of anything except by diminishing her exportation or increasing her importation of something else. From the same view of the question of the falling exchange it follows that such a monetary disturbance could not depress one trade more than another. If the falling or rising exchange was simply an expression of the level of *general* prices, then the producers of all articles were equally affected. There was no reason why the cotton trade or the wheat trade should have been more affected by the fall of exchange than the cutlery trade.

Not only was there nothing in the exchange disturbance to disestablish existing trade relations in general or in respect of particular commodities, but there was nothing in it to cause benefit to the Indian producer and injury to the English producer. Given the fact that the exchange was a ratio of the two price-levels, it is difficult to see in what sense the English producer, who got fewer sovereigns but of high purchasing power, was worse off than the Indian producer, who got more rupees but of low purchasing power. The analogy of Prof. Marshall was very apt. To suppose that a fall of exchange resulted in a loss to the former and a gain to the latter was to suppose that, if a man was in the cabin of a ship only ten feet high, his head would be broken if the ship sank down twelve feet into a trough. The fallacy consisted in isolating the man from the ship when, as a matter of fact, the same force, acting upon the ship and the passenger at one and the same time, produced like movements in both. In like manner, the same force acted upon the Indian producer and the English producer together, for the change in the exchange was itself a part of the more sweeping change in the general price-levels of the two countries. Thus stated, the position of the English and Indian producer was equally good or equally bad, and the only difference was that the former used fewer counters and the latter a larger number in their respective dealings.

A bounty to the Indian producer and a penalty to the English producer, it is obvious, could have arisen only if the fall of silver in England in terms of gold was greater than the fall of silver in terms of commodities in India. In that case the Indian producer would have obtained a clear benefit by exchanging his wares for silver in England and thus securing a medium which had a greater command over goods and services in India. But *a priori* there could be no justification for such an assumption. There was no reason why gold price of silver should have fallen at a different rate from the gold price of commodities in general, or that there should have been a great difference between the silver prices in England and in India. Statistics show that such *a priori* assumptions were not groundless. (See Table XXI).

## TABLE XXI. MOVEMENTS OF PRICES, WAGES AND SILVER BETWEEN INDIA AND ENGLAND*

| Net Imports of Silver into India. | | Index No for Gold Price of Silver | Years | Index No for Silver Prices of Commodities in India | Index No for Wages in India | Index No for Gold Prices of Commodities in England. | Index No. for Wages in England |
|---|---|---|---|---|---|---|---|
| Years | Amount Rs | | | | | | |
| (1) | (2) | (3) | 4) | (5) | (6) | (7) | (8) |
| 1871-72 | 6,587,296 | 99 7 | 1871 | 100 | — | 100 | 100 |
| 1872-73 | 739,244 | 99 2 | 1872 | 105 | — | 109 | 105.8 |
| 1873-74 | 2,530,824 | 97 4 | 1873 | 107 | 100 | 111 | 112 |
| 1874-75 | 4,674,791 | 95 8 | 1874 | 116 | 101 | 102 | 113 |
| 1875-76 | 1,640,445 | 93 3 | 1875 | 103 | 97 | 96 | 111.6 |
| 1876 77 | 7,286,188 | 86 4 | 1876 | 107 | 98 | 95 | 110 |
| 1877 78 | 14,732,194 | 90 2 | 1877 | 138 | 97 | 94 | 109.8 |
| 1878-79 | 4,057 377 | 86 4 | 1878 | 148 | 99 | 87 | 107 |
| 1879-80 | 7 976,063 | 84 2 | 1879 | 135 | 100 | 83 | 105.8 |
| 1880-81 | 3,923,612 | 85 9 | 1880 | 117 | 99 | 88 | 106.5 |
| 1881-82 | 5,381,410 | 85 0 | 1881 | 106 | 99 | 85 | 106.5 |
| 1882-83 | 7,541,427 | 84 9 | 1882 | 105 | 100 | 84 | 106.5 |
| 1883-84 | 6,433,886 | 83 1 | 1883 | 106 | 102 | 82 | 108 |
| 1884-85 | 7,319,581 | 83 3 | 1884 | 114 | 101 | 76 | 109 |
| 1885-86 | 11,627,028 | 79 9 | 1885 | 113 | 106 | 72 | 108 |
| 1886 87 | 7,191,743 | 74 6 | 1886 | 110 | 105 | 69 | 107 |
| 1887-88 | 9,319,421 | 73 3 | 1887 | 111 | 114 | 68 | 108 |
| 1888 89 | 9,327,529 | 70 4 | 1888 | 119 | 112 | 70 | 109.8 |
| 1889-90 | 11,002,078 | 70 2 | 1889 | 125 | 112 | 72 | 113 |
| 1890-91 | 14,211,408 | 78 4 | 1890 | 125 | 113 | 72 | 118 |
| 1891-92 | 9,165 684 | 74 3 | 1891 | 128 | 118 | 72 | 118 |
| 1892-93 | 12,893,499 | 65 5 | 1892 | 141 | 110 | 68 | 117.4 |
| 1893-94 | 13,759,273 | 58 5 | 1893 | 138 | 119 | 68 | 117.4 |

* Col (2) is from Appendix II, Table No 2 of the I C C of 1898 Cols (3), (5), (6), and (7) are from Atkinson's "Silver Prices in India," in the *Journal of the Statistical Society* March, 1897 Col. (8) is based on the figures given by W. T. Layton in his *Introduction to the Study of Prices* (1912), Table I, Col 1, p 150, re scaled to 1871 as 100.

It is obvious that if silver was falling faster than commodities, *and if silver prices in India were lower than silver prices in* England, we should have found it evidenced by an inflow of silver from England to India. What were the facts? Not only was there no extraordinary flow of silver to India, but the imports of silver during 1871-93 were much smaller than in the twenty years previous to that period.* This is as complete a demonstration as could be had of the fact that the silver prices in India were the same as they were outside, and consequently the Indian producer had very little chance of a bounty on his trade.

Although such must be said to be the *a priori* view of the question, the Indian producer was convinced that his prosperity was due to the bounty he received. Holding such a position he was naturally opposed to any reform of the Indian currency, for the falling exchange which the Government regarded a curse he considered a boon. But however plausible was the view of the Indian producer, much sympathy would not have been felt for it had it not been coupled with a notion, most commonly held, that the bounty arose from the *export trade*, so that it became an article of popular faith that the fall of exchange was a source of gain to the *nation as a whole*. Now was it true that the bounty arose from the export trade? If it were so, then every fall of exchange ought to give a bounty. But supposing that the depreciation of silver had taken place in India *before* it had taken place in Europe could the fall of exchange thus brought about have given a bounty to the Indian exporter? As was explained above, the Indian exporter stood a chance of getting a bounty only if with the silver he obtained for his produce he was able to buy more goods and services in India. To put the same in simpler language, his bounty was the difference between the price of his product and the price of his outlay. Bearing this in mind, we can confidently assert that in the supposed case of depreciation of silver having taken place in India first, such a fall in the Indian exchange would have been accompanied by a penalty instead of a bounty on his trade. In that case, the exporter from India would have found that though the Indian exchange, i.e. the gold price of silver, had

* Cf. figures for imports of silver in Chap. I. It will, however, be noted how closely the flow of silver into India between 1872 and 1893 followed the fall in gold price of silver.

fallen, yet the ratio which gold prices in England bore to silver prices in India had fallen more, i.e. the price he received for his product was smaller than the outlay he had incurred. It is not quite established whether silver had fallen in Europe before it had fallen in India.* But even if that were so the possibility of a penalty through the fall of exchange proves that the bounty, if there was any, was not a bounty on the export trade as such, but was an outcome of the disharmony between the general level of prices and the prices of particular goods and services within the country, and *would have existed* even if the country had no export *trade.*

Thus the bounty was but an incident of the general depreciation of the currency. Its existence was felt because prices of *all* goods and services in India did not move in the same uniform manner. It is well known that at any one time prices of certain commodities will be rising, while the general price level is falling. On the other hand, certain goods will decline in price at the same time that the general price-level is rising. But such opposite movements are rare. What most often happens is that prices of some goods and services, though they move in the same direction, do not move at the same pace as the general price level. It is notorious that when general prices fall wages and other fixed incomes, which form the largest item in the total outlay of every employer, do not fall in the same proportion; and when general prices rise they do not rise as fast as general prices, but generally lag behind. And this was just what was happening in a silver-standard country like India and a gold-standard country like England during the period of 1873-93 (*see* Chart IV). Prices had fallen in England, but wages had not fallen to the same extent. Prices had risen in India, but wages had not risen to the same extent. The English manufacturer was penalized, if at all, not by any act on the part of his Indian rival, but by reason of the wages of the former's employees having remained the same, although the price of his products had fallen. The Indian producer got a bounty, if any, not because he had an English rival to feed upon, but because he did not have to pay higher wages, although the price of his product had risen.

---

* *See infra*, Chap. IV.

## CHART IV

### Prices and Wages in India and England, 1873-93

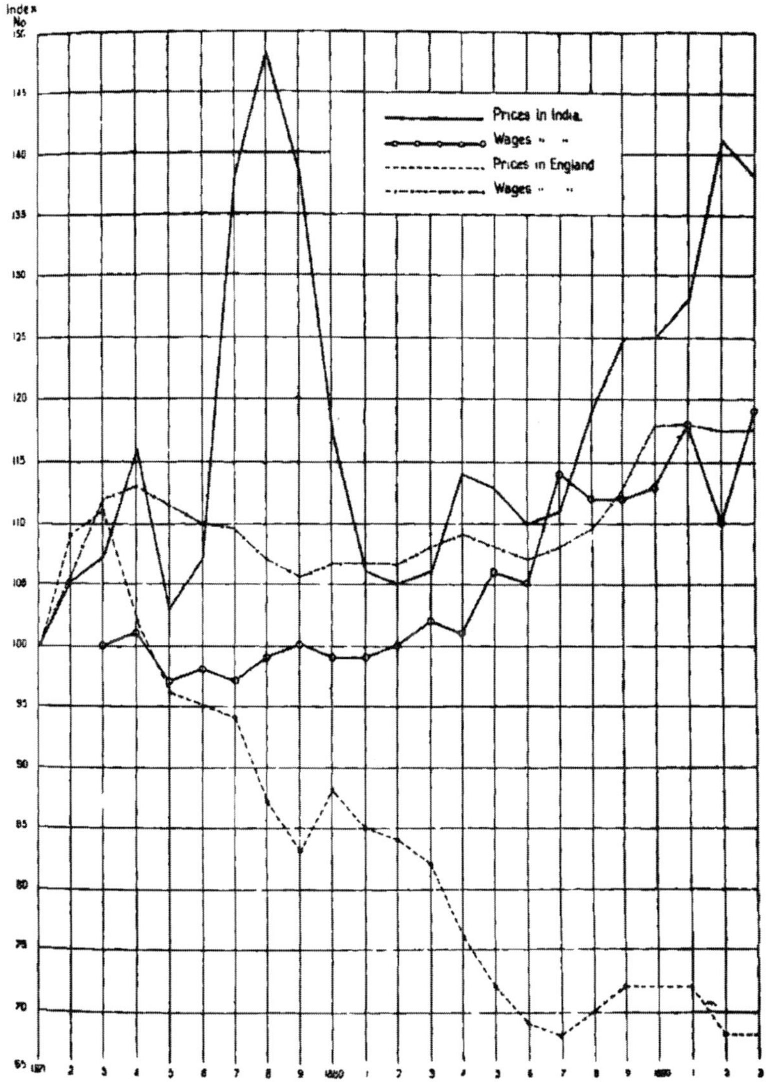

The conclusion, therefore, is that the falling exchange could not have disturbed established trade relations or displaced the commodities that entered into international trade. The utmost that could be attributed to it is its incidence in economic incentive. But in so far as it supplied a motive force or took away the incentive, it did so by bringing about changes in the social distribution of wealth. In the case of England, where prices were falling, it was the employer who suffered; in the case of India, where prices were rising, it was the wage-earner who suffered. In both cases there was an injustice done to a part of the community and an easy case for the reform of currency was made out. The need for a currency reform was recognized in England; but in India many people seemed averse to it. To some the stability of the silver standard had made a powerful appeal, for they failed to find any evidence of Indian prices having risen above the level of 1873. To others the bounty of the falling exchange was too great a boon to be easily given away by stabilizing the exchange. The falsity of both the views is patent. Prices in India did rise and that, too, considerably. Bounty perhaps there was, but it was a penalty on the wage-earner. Thus viewed, the need for the reform of Indian currency was far more urgent than could have been said of the English currency. From a purely psychological point of view there is probably much to choose between rising prices and falling prices. But from the point of view of their incidence on the distribution of wealth, very little can be said in favour of a standard which changes in its value and which becomes the *via media* of transferring wealth from the relatively poor to the relatively rich. Scrope said: "Without stability of value money is a fraud." Surely, having regard to the magnitude of the interests affected, depreciated money must be regarded as a greater fraud. That being so, the prosperity of Indian trade and industry, far from being evidence of a sound currency, was sustained by reason of the fact that the currency was a diseased currency. The fall of exchange, in so far as it was a gain, registered a loss to a large section of the Indian people with fixed incomes who suffered from the instability of the silver standard equally with the Government and its European officers.

So much for the fall of silver. But the financial difficulties and social injustices it caused did not sum up the evil effects produced by it. Far more disturbing than the fall were the fluctuations which accompanied the fall (*see* Chart V).

The fluctuations greatly aggravated the embarrassment of the Government of India caused by the fall in the exchange value of the rupee. In the opinion of the Hon. Mr. Baring (afterwards Lord Cromer),*

> "It is not the fact that the value of the rupee is, comparatively speaking, low that causes inconvenience. It would be possible, although it might be exceedingly troublesome, to adjust the Indian fiscal system to a rupee of any value. What causes inconvenience alike to Government and to trade is that the value of the rupee is unstable. It is impossible to state accurately in Indian currency what the annual liabilities of the Government of India are. These liabilities have to be calculated afresh every year according to the variations which take place in the relative value of gold and silver, and a calculation which will hold good for even one year is exceedingly difficult to make."

Owing to such fluctuations, no rate could be assumed in the Budget which was likely to turn out to be the true market rate. As matters stood, the rate realized on an average during a particular year differed so widely from the Budget rate that the finances of the Government became, to employ the phraseology of a finance minister, a "veritable gamble." How greatly the annual Budget must have been deranged by the sudden and unprovided-for changes in the rupee cost of the sterling payments Table XXII on page 107 may help to give some idea.

If Government finance was subjected to such uncertainties as a result of exchange fluctuations, private trade also became more or less a matter of speculation. Fluctuations in exchange are, of course, a common incident of international trade. But if they are not to produce discontinuity in trade and industry there must be definite limits to such fluctuations. If the limits are ascertainable, trade would be reasonably certain in its calculation, and speculation in exchange would be limited within the known limits of deviations from an established par. Where, on the other hand, the limits are unknown, all calculations of trade are frustrated and speculation in exchange takes the place of legitimate trading. Now, it is obvious that fluctuations in the exchange between two

* *Financial Statement*, 1883-84, p. 26.

CHART V

MONTHLY FLUCTUATIONS OF THE RUPEE-STERLING EXCHANGE

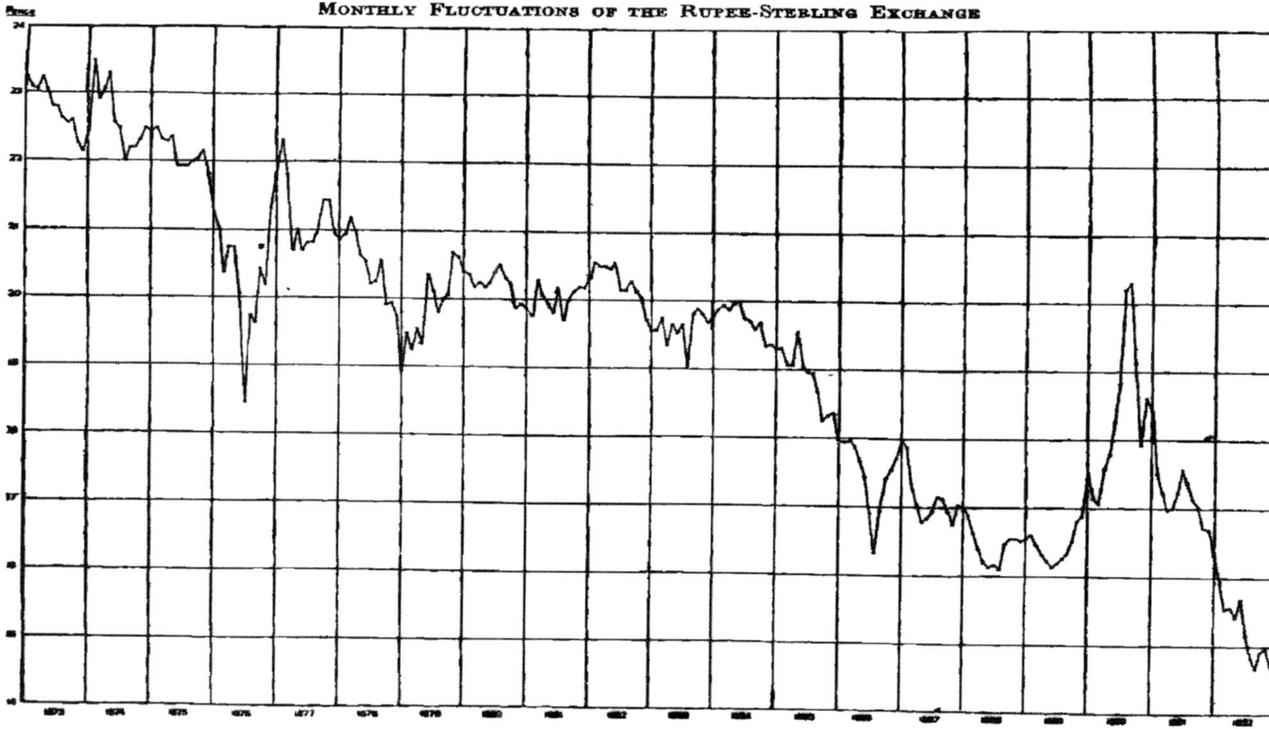

# TABLE XXII

## Fluctuations of Exchange and Fluctuations in the Rupee Cost of Gold Payments*

| Financial Year. | Estimated Rate of Exchange on which the Budget of the Year was framed. | Rate of Exchange actually realized on the Average during the Year. | Changes in the Rupee Cost of Sterling Payments consequent upon Changes between the Estimated and the Realized Rates of Exchange. | |
|---|---|---|---|---|
| | | | Increase. | Decrease. |
| | s. d. | s d. | Rs. | Rs. |
| 1874-75 | 1 10.375 | 1 10.156 | 15,91,764 | — |
| 1875-76 | 1 9.875 | 1 9.626 | 19,57,917 | — |
| 1876-77 | 1 8.5 | 1 8.508 | — | 76,736 |
| 1877-78 | 1 9.23 | 1 8.791 | 38,43,050 | — |
| 1878-79 | 1 8.4 | 1 7.794 | 56,87,129 | — |
| 1879-80 | 1 7 | 1 7.961 | — | 84,40,737 |
| 1880-81 | 1 8 | 1 7.956 | 4,24,722 | — |
| 1881-82 | 1 8 | 1 7.895 | 10,17,482 | — |
| 1882-83 | 1 8 | 1 7.525 | 37,46,890 | — |
| 1883-84 | 1 7.5 | 1 7.536 | — | 3,62,902 |
| 1884-85 | 1 7.5 | 1 7.308 | 18,97,307 | — |
| 1885-86 | 1 7 | 1 6.254 | 56,82,638 | — |
| 1886-87 | 1 6 | 1 5.441 | 65,17,721 | — |
| 1887-88 | 1 5.5 | 1 4.898 | 71,90,097 | — |
| 1888-89 | 1 4.9 | 1 4.379 | 77,98,400 | — |
| 1889-90 | 1 4.38 | 1 4.566 | — | 27,31,892 |
| 1890-91 | 1 4.552 | 1 6.09 | — | 2,35,51,744 |
| 1891-92 | 1 5.25 | 1 4.733 | 80,09,366 | — |

* Compiled from figures given in the *Final Report of the Gold and Silver Commission*, p. 40, and in App. II, p. 270, to the *Report of the Indian Currency Committee*, 1893.

countries will be limited in extent if the two countries have the same standard of value. Where there is no such common standard of value the limits, though they exist, are too indefinite to be of much practical use. The rupture of the fixed par of exchange, having destroyed a common standard of value between gold and silver countries, removed the limits on the exchange fluctuations between such countries. As a result of such variations in the value of the standard measure, trade advanced by "rushes and pauses," and speculation became feverishly active.*

That progress of trade depends on stability is a truism which seldom comes home until it is denied in fact. It is difficult to appreciate its importance to healthy enterprise when govenment is stable, credit is secure, and conditions are uniform. And yet so great is the handicap of instability that everywhere business men have been led by a variety of devices to produce stability in domains enveloped by uncertainty. Everywhere there have grown up business barometers forewarning business men of impending changes and so enabling them to forearm against them by timely changes in their operations. The whole of insurance business is aimed at giving stability to economic life. The necessity which compelled all regularly established Governments to maintain standard measures by which the true proportion between things as to their quantities might be ascertained and dealings in them regulated with certainty was motivated by the same purpose. The meticulous precision with which every civilized country defines its standard measures, and the large machinery it maintains to preserve them from deviation, are only evidences of the great importance that an economic society must continue to attach to the matter of providing precision of expression and assurance of fulfilment with regard to the contracts entered into by its members in their individual or corporate capacities.

Important as are the standard measures of a community, its measures of a community, its measure of value is by far the most important of them all.* The measures of weight, extension, or volume enter only into particular transactions. If the pound, the

* Evid. Indian Currency Committee, 1898, Q. 6,290, 9,808-10.

* Cf. Harris, *An Essay upon Money and Coins* (reprinted by J. R. McCulloch in his volume of *Scarce Tracts on Money*, Part I, Chap. II, par. 21; Part II, Chap. II, pars. 11, 13, and 20).

bushel, or the yard were altered the evils would be comparatively restricted in scope. But the measure of value is all-pervading.

> "There is no contract," Peel declared, † "public or private, no engagement national or individual, which is unaffected by it. The enterprises of commerce, the profits of trade, the arrangements made in all domestic relations of society, the wages, of labour, pecuniary transactions of the highest amount and of the lowest, the payment of national debt, the provision for national expenditure, the command which the coin of the smallest denomination has over the necessaries of life, are all affected"

by changes in the measure of value. This is because every contract, though ultimately a contract in goods, is primarily a contract in value. It is, therefore, not enough to maintain constancy in the measures of weight, capacity, or volume. A contract as one of goods may remain exact to the measure stipulated, but may nevertheless be vitiated as a contract in values by reason of changes in the measure of values. The necessity of preserving stability in its measure of value falls on the shoulders of every Government of an orderly society. But its importance grows beyond disputes as society advances from status to contract. The conservation of the contractual basis of society then becomes tantamount to the conservation of an invariable measure of value.

The work of reconstituting a common measure of value in some form or other, which those misguided legislators of the seventies helped to destroy, it was found, could not be long delayed with impunity. The consequences that followed in the wake of that legislation, as recounted before, were too severe to allow the situation to remain unrectified. That efforts for reconstruction should have been launched before much mischief was done only shows that a world linked by ties of trade will insist, if it can, that its currency systems must be laid on a common gauge.

---

† Cf. his speech dated May 6, 1844, delivered during the Commons debates on the Bank Charter Act. Hansard, Vol. XXXIV, p. 720.

## CHAPTER IV

# TOWARDS A GOLD STANDARD

The establishment of stable monetary conditions was naturally enough dependent upon the restoration of a common standard of value. Plain as was the aim, its accomplishment was by no means an easy matter. Two ways seemed at first to be open for carrying it out in practice. One was to adopt a common metal as currency, and since all important countries of the world had gone over to the gold standard it meant the silver-standard countries should abandon their standard in favour of gold. The other was to let the gold and silver standard countries keep to their currencies and to establish between them a fixed ratio of exchange so as to make the two metals into a common standard of value.

The history of the agitation for the reform of the Indian currency is a history of these two movements. The movement for the introduction of a gold standard was, however, the first to occupy the field. The failure of the notification of 1868 may be said to have marked the failure of a policy, but the movement for a gold currency in India started in the sixties was not altogether stamped out of the country. That the movement still had life in it is shown by the fact that it was revived four years later by Sir R. Temple, when he became the Finance Minister of India, in a memorandum* dated May 15, 1872. The important particular in which he differed from his predecessors consisted in the fact that while they all aimed to make the British sovereign the principal unit of the gold currency in India, he desired to give that place to the Indian gold coin, the "mohur." Why his predecessors did not do the same when the problem of correctly rating the sovereign was said to have baffled them so much is a little surprising when it is recalled that the Indian Mints had been

* Printed as Appendix I, No. 12, to the *Report of the Indian Currency Committee of 1898*.

since long past issuing the "mohur," which, as it was possible to rate it correctly, could as well have been made the principal unit of the gold currency in India. That they did not can only be explained on the assumption that they were anxious to kill two birds with one stone. The adoption of the sovereign, besides supporting a gold currency in India, was also calculated to promote the movement of international uniformity of coinage then in vogue. The utility of the "mohur" was in this respect comparatively inferior to that of the sovereign. But when Sir Richard Temple came upon the scene the prospect of some universal coin being internationally adopted seemed to be fast vanishing. At all events the Report of the English Commission on International Coinage, presided over by Lord Halifax, had pronounced adversely as to any change in the standard of the English sovereign. Untrammelled by any considerations for such a wider issue, Sir R. Temple was free to recommend the adoption of the "mohur" as the unit of currency in place of the sovereign.*

> "We have," he wrote, "gold pieces representing fifteen, ten and five rupees respectively; and believed to represent these several sums very correctly, as regards the relative value of gold and silver . . . that . . . we should take the first opportunity to declare the gold coins legal tender to unlimited amount; that gold pieces should continue to bear the fixed relation to the rupee; that for a time it might be necessary to permit the rupee to remain legal tender to an unlimited amount, which would involve temporarily the difficulty of a double standard; that the transition period of double standard should be as short as possible, silver being reduced to a token coinage, and being made legal tender up to a small amount only; and that gold should be ultimately the one legal standard."

He proposed the ratio of 10 rupees for 120 grs. of standard i.e. 110 grs. of fine gold, † but he did not share the temerity of Sir Charles Trevelyan. ‡ So intent was he on the project of a gold

* Nevertheless, he said, "I would not object to make the sovereign a legal tender for 10 rupees and 4 annas. But, the sovereign being worth 10 rupees and a fraction over, there might be some slight trouble of calculation in changing it for silver, and this would be a drawback in respect of the use of the sovereign as currency in India. And if this objection were urged, I would not press for the sovereign being declared legal tender. But we should continue, under any circumstances, to receive the sovereign in our Treasuries at the present rating."

† This was a ratio of 15 : 1, which was a slight undervaluation of gold.

‡ *Supra*, Chap. I.

currency that he was prepared to alter the ratio so as to make it *favourable to gold.* The question of ratio, he observed, was one which

> "the Government of India ought to be able to determine. These are questions which have been determined by every nation that has adopted a gold currency. No doubt it is a difficult and important problem, but it cannot be insoluble, and it ought to be solved."

Such in outline was the first proposal for a gold currency. It was projected before the fall in the value of silver had commenced, and was therefore more a culmination of the past policy than a remedy against the ensuing depreciation of silver. In that consisted, probably, the chief strength of the proposal. It was in good time to avoid the cost of hauling up the currency which later on proved so very deterrent and caused the defeat of so many other projects. Besides, it cannot be said that at the time the memorandum was presented the Government was not warned of the impending crisis; for the wave of demonetizing silver had already commenced two years before.* But, for some reason not known to the public, no action was taken on the proposal.

The second plan for the introduction of a gold currency was that of Colonel J. T. Smith, the able Mint Master of India. His plan was avowedly a remedy for the falling exchange.† The plan was set forth in the first essay in the brochure, *Silver and the Indian Exchanges,*‡ and may be described in his own words as follows:—

> "6. Although it cannot be denied that the difficulty of effecting this object of restoring the Indian exchange to its nor-

* Lord Northbrook, who was the Viceroy of India when this proposal was made, in his evidence before the I.C.C. of 1898, Q. 8,447, suggested that the reason for his not adopting it then was that "that was a time when gold was appreciating, and it was impossible to do." This is, of course, historically untrue except on the hypothesis that the proposal came for consideration long after it was submitted.

† He had previously taken part in the agitation for the introduction of a gold standard in India during the sixties with the sovereign as the unit. But that was as an advocate of the movement for uniformity of international coinage. Cf. his *Remarks on a Gold Currency for India and Proposal of Measures for the Introduction of the British Sovereign*, etc., etc., London, 1868.

‡ London, Effingham Wilson, 1876.

mal condition is much greater now than it would have been some years ago, owing to the decline which has already taken place, yet there seems to be sufficient ground for belief that, even now, if decided measures were adopted, it would not be too late to restore the currency to its former value for home (India) payments; and that, too, without any shock or disturbance; the principal step being that of putting a stop to the coinage of silver on private account, at the same time taking measures to discourage the importation, or at the least the circulation, of foreign-made, silver coins, and opening the Mints for the receipt of gold bullion for coinage.

"7. To explain how this would operate, I must observe that

"8. . . . the internal trade of the Empire of India has increased and is increasing ...............

"9. Whatever may be the cause, the internal trade of India has, ever since the beginning of this century, required constant and steady additions to her currency, averaging during the last thirty-eight years upwards of five millions of pounds sterling per annum in value. Besides this, the returns show that the balance of imports over exports of gold bullion, during the same period, exceeded an average of two and a half millions sterling annually, having been, during the last twenty years, more than four millions per annum.

"10. Such being the case, it appears to be a necessary consequence that, if the supply of rupees were put a stop to, the remainder must increase in local value, as compared with commodities, till they resumed the position which they held on a par with gold, at the rate of 10 rupees to a sovereign, for the fifteen years previous to 1870.

"11. After that point had been attained, it would be the interest of merchants to take gold into the Indian Mints for coinage; and they would do so, indeed, before the attainment of this improvement of the exchanges, owing to the premium or 'batta' which would at first be obtained for the gold coins.

"12. By this means gold would gradually be brought into India; and, as it has been shown that an addition to the circulating medium of at least five million sterling per annum is necessary, and no more silver coins being admitted (into the currency), it will slowly accumulate there ........

"13. The proposal therefore is that, after due notice, the coinage of silver on behalf of private individuals and advances upon silver bullion should be suspended; that part of the Act 23 of 1870, which makes it incumbent on the Government to receive and coin it, being repealed; the Government retaining in their own hands the power of replenishing the silver currency whenever they may deem it expedient. That gold bullion should be received by the Government at the mint rate of 38 rupees 14 annas per standard ounce, and coined into sovereigns and half-sovereigns (representing 38 rupees 15 annas), or ten or five rupee-pieces of the same value, which should be declared legal tender, but not demandable, the present silver rupees continuing to be legal tender, as before."*

At the time the Smith plan was presented, the fall of silver had made itself felt so that a considerable support in favour of the plan was forthcoming. The support of the trading community was embodied in the resolution, dated July 15, 1876, of the Bengal Chamber of Commerce, which urged "that it was expedient, in view of any ultimate measures that the Government may adopt, that Clause 19 of Act XXIII of 1870, making it obligatory on the Mints in India to receive all silver tendered for coinage, and also Section II, Clause (*b*) of Act III of 1871, making it obligatory on the Currency Department to issue notes against silver bullion sent in, be temporarily suspended, at the discretion of Government, and that during each such suspension or till further notice it be not lawful to import coined rupees from any foreign port." A similar feeling was voiced by the Calcutta Trades Association. By this time the fall of exchange had also commenced to tell upon the finances of the Government of India, so much so that Sir William Muir, in his Financial Statement for 1876-77, was led to observe:—

"The sudden depreciation of silver and the consequent enhancement of charge to the Government of India in laying down yearly the sum required in England of about fifteen millions sterling, without doubt cast a grave shadow on the future. In truth, it may be said that the danger, from whatever point of view considered, is the gravest which has yet threatened the finances of India. War, famine, and drought have often inflicted losses on the Exchequer far greater than the charge which threatens us in the present year. But such calamities pass away; the loss is limited; and when it has been provided for the finances are again on sure and stable ground. This is not the case with the present cause of anxiety. Its immediate effects are serious

* This was calculated to make the rupee-sterling exchange 2*s*. gold. The average rupee-sterling exchange in 1876 was about 1s. 9.645d. This would have placed a small premium on gold which would have no doubt soon disappeared owing to the appreciation of the rupee consequent upon the stoppage of its coinage.

> enough.. ....But that which adds significance to it is that the end cannot be seen; the future is involved in uncertainty.' *

In the face of such a situation nothing would have been more natural than to expect the Government precipitating into some kind of action to save itself, if not others, from an impending calamity. Far from taking immediate steps, the Government not only failed to take any initiative, but showed, when pressed by the Bengal Chamber of Commerce to act upon the foregoing resolution, a surprising degree of academic somnolence only to be expected from an uninterested spectator. No doubt the proposal of the Bengal Chamber was defective in that it did not suggest the opening of the Indian Mints to the coinage of gold. The Government of India was sharp enough to fasten upon this defect. It made plain to the Chamber that if it had proposed the free coinage of gold

> "such a recommendation would not have been open to the objections that appear fatal, *in limine*, to the adoption of the resolution actually adopted . . . viz. to close the Mints temporarily to the free coinage of the one metal into legal-tender money, without simultaneously opening them to the free coinage of the other into legal-tender money."

Did it, then, adopt the proposal of Colonel Smith, which contained such a recommendation? Not at all! Why did it not, then, adopt a remedy to which it saw no objections? The reason was that it had arrived at a different diagnosis of the causes of the monetary disturbances. To the Government the possibilities of explaining "the disturbance in the equilibrium of the precious metals" seemed to be many and varied. † (1) The value of gold being unchanged, the value of silver had fallen; (2) the value of silver being unchanged, the value of gold had risen; (3) the value of gold had risen, and the value of silver had fallen; (4) the value of both metals had risen, but the value of gold more than that of silver; (5) the value of both metals had fallen, but the value of silver more than that of gold. In the midst of such possibilities, marked more by pedantry than logic, the Government warned the currency reformers that

* P. 93.

† Cf. The Resolution of the Government of India relating to the Depreciation in the Value of Silver, dated September 22, 1876, par. 6, Commons Paper 449 of 1893.

> "the character of the remedies indicated, if the disturbance is found to be due to a rise in the value of gold, will obviously differ from what would be suitable in the case of a fall in the value of silver."*

Out of these possibilities what seemed to it to be proven was that "*gold had risen in value since March, 1872,*" † and therefore if any reform was to be effected it should fall upon the gold-standard countries to undertake it. Situated as the Government of India then was, it could have suffered itself without incurring much blame to be hurried into some kind of currency reform that promised to bring relief. To have refused to allow the exigencies of a crisis to rule its decisions on such a momentous issue as the reform of currency, need not imply a spirit of obstinacy. On the other hand, it bespeaks a spirit of caution which no reader of that illuminating despatch of October 13, 1876, conveying to the Secretary of State its decision to wait and watch, can fail to admire. But it is hardly possible to speak in a similar commendatory manner of the underlying attitude of the Government of India. Whether it is possible to hold that gold had appreciated but that silver had not depreciated may be left for logician to decide upon. But for a silver-standard country to refuse to undertake the reform of her currency system on the plea that it was gold that had appreciated was no doubt a tactical error. In military matters there is probably such a thing as depending on a position; but in currency matters there cannot be such a thing. The reason is that in the former strength sometimes lies in the weakness of the other. But in the case of the latter the weakness of one becomes the weakness of all. There can be no doubt, therefore, that the Government, in discarding its responsibility to do the needful in the matter, committed the same kind of mistake as a man who, in the words of Prof. Nicholson, "should suppose that the ship cannot sink because there is no leak in the particular cabin in which he happens to sleep."

That the attitude of inaction was unwise was soon brought home to the Government of India. Within a short space of two years it was obliged to reconsider the position taken in 1876. In

---

* *Ibid.* † *Ibid.*, par. 16.

‡ *Money and Monetary Problems*, 1895,, p. 90.

a despatch dated November 9, 1878,* the Government of India observed:—

"5. It was to have been expected that a subject so encompassed with difficulties should not receive any early settlement, and it was probably the wisest, as it was certainly the most natural course, to allow further time to elapse before attempting any final solution of the grave problem it involved. The improvement that took place in the value of silver in the year 1877 favoured this policy in action; and it is only now, when a fresh fall has brought down the rupee to a value hardly greater than that which it had in July, 1876, that the serious nature of the risk which our existing currency law entails on us is once more forced on our attention by its practical effects on the Home remittances.

* * *

"21. The uncertainty that has now for some years prevailed with reference to the value of silver, and the consequent disturbances in the exchange, have . . . been causes of continued financial difficulty to the Government . . . . and it is not possible to doubt that similar results must have been produced by these disturbances in the trade transactions of the country, or that investments of foreign capital in India, either for trading or other purposes, must have been very seriously interfered with by their influence.

"23. Such we hold to be a true statement of the present difficulties and prospective risks of maintaining the existing Currency Law, and we feel assured that they have not been in any way overstated. It remains for us to inquire whether any practical remedy could be devised that should not be open to serious objections, or the risks attending the adoption of which should not be so great as to prohibit it. We feel most fully the heavy responsibility that will rest on us in dealing with the currency of India; but it is plain that the responsibility for doing nothing is no less great. Whether the law is left as it is, or whether it is changed, the result will be equally due to our action, and we cannot, if we would, avoid facing this grave question.

"24. To obtain fixity of exchange by the adoption of a gold standard, and the substitution of a gold for a silver currency through the direct action of Government, has, we think, been conclusively shown to be impracticable by the despatch of the Government of India of October last, and this plan therefore calls for no further notice. The increase in the weight of the rupee, also noticed in that despatch, is equally undeserving of attention, as in fact, it would give no security for the future, and would entail a heavy charge without accomplishing the essential point to be aimed at. There remains the simpler, and first proposed suggestion, the limitation of the coinage of silver, which, though

* P.P., C. 4868, of 1886, p. 18.

rejected in 1876 by the Government of India . . . appears to us to call now for a closer examination.

"25. This suggestion in its main features is, that the Coinage Act shall be so far modified as to withdraw the free right of the public to take silver bullion to the Mint for coinage, and either to suspend it entirely in future, or limit it for a time.

"26. It is obviously an essential part of any such scheme, if it is to have the effect of fixing the exchange value of the rupee, that the power of obtaining that coin in future shall be regulated in some manner by a gold payment, and that the relation between sterling and rupee currency shall thus be fixed irrespective of the fluctuations in the relative value of the metals of which the coins are formed.

"27. It is not, on the other hand, an essential part of such a plan that any particular relation of value should be thus fixed at two shillings . . . or at any smaller or larger proportion. All that is necessary is that the rate, being once fixed, shall remain for the future unchanged.

* * *

"33. Probably the most important question is . . . whether or not it is practicable to maintain a silver coinage as the principal element in our currency, with a very limited gold coinage, or without a legal-tender gold coinage at all. The Government of India, in its despatch of 1876, expressed an opinion adverse to the possibility of maintaining such a system. . . . On a full reconsideration of this point, we are led to take the opposite view, and to think that such a system would be perfectly practicable and would lead to no material difficulty. It is true that there is no country in which such a condition of things actually exists. But those countries, and there are many of them, in which an inconvertible paper currency exists or has existed, give proof that the far greater anomaly of a currency devoid of any intrinsic value whatever is capable of performing the work of a metallic currency satisfactorily, and of maintaining its local exchange value, so long as an excessive issue is only guarded against.

* * *

"37. (Such) instances (as the British shilling and the French five franc piece) seem to show that neither in the way of surreptitious coinage, nor of discredit from depreciation of intrinsic value, is it probable that there would be any serious difficulty in keeping the rupee in circulation at its present weight, at a nominal value of two shillings, with a gold standard and a partial gold coinage.

* * *

"46. We are thus led to the general conclusion that it will be practicable, without present injury to the community as a whole, or risk of future difficulties, to adopt a gold standard, while retaining the present silver currency of India, and that we may thereby in the future fully protect ourselves from the very real and serious dangers impending over us so long as the present system is maintained. We consequently desire to recommend to Her Majesty's Government the adoption of such a change at the earliest moment possible, and we shall proceed to explain, in all necessary detail, the measures by which we advise that it should be effected.

* * *

"50. It has to be borne in mind that it is not the object of our action to force on India a gold currency, or to displace the silver currency, but rather to avoid such a result, or to check the tendency in that direction, so far as it can be done consistently with the adoption of the gold standard. We are consequently led to the conclusion that, while we give certain facilities for the introduction of gold coins into India, we should not yet go so far as to declare them a general legal tender; and that we should at the same time, make provision for the coining of silver, without limit as to quantity, but on terms that will give no advantage to the introduction of silver in relation to gold.

"51. These objects we propose to attain as follows:—We first take power to receive British or British Indian gold coin in payment for any demands of the Government, at rates to be fixed from time to time by the Government, till the exchange has settled itself sufficiently to enable us to fix the rupee value in relation to the pound sterling, permanently at two shillings. Simultaneously with this, the seignorage on the coining of silver would be raised to such a rate as would virtually make the cost of a rupee, to persons importing bullion, equal in amount to the value given to the rupee in comparison with the gold coins above spoken of. We should thus obtain a self-acting system under which silver would be admitted for coinage, at the fixed gold rate, as the wants of the country required; while a certain limited scope would be given for the introduction and use of gold coin, so far as it was found convenient or profitable."

Such was the scheme outlined by the Government of India. The reason why it rejected the Smith plan, although it was simple, economical, and secure, was because it contemplated a demand by India on the world's dwindling stock of gold. Now, in the circumstances then existing, this was a fatal defect, and the powers-that-be had already decided that at all cost India must be kept out of what was called the "scramble for gold." Therefore, to have proposed an effective gold standard was to have courted defeat. A mild and diluted edition of a gold standard such as was proposed by the Government was all that stood any chance of success. But even this timid attempt did not fare well at the hands of the Committee* appointed jointly by the Secretary of State and the Chancellor of the Exchequer to examine and report upon the proposals. The members of the Committee were "unanimously of opinion that they cannot recommend them for the sanction of Her Majesty's Government."† The reasons which led to the rejection of the proposals we are not permitted to know. Although the Report of the Committee was made public, the proceedings have never seen the light of day. Indeed, there has been a most stern and obstinate refusal on the part of the officials to allow a peep into them. Why they should be regarded as confidential after a lapse of nearly half a century it is difficult to imagine. Enough, however, was revealed by Sir Robert Giffen, who was a member of this Committee, in evidence before the Indian Currency Committee of 1898‡ for us to know the contents of this closely guarded document. It seems that the Committee declared against the proposals because it thought they were calculated to make the Indian currency a "managed" currency. At the time when the Committee delivered its opinion the current prejudice was unanimously against such a system. All acknowledged writers on currency were pronounced opponents of an artificially regulated system.§ A naturally automatic currency was their ideal. In addition to being misled by this prejudice, the Committee felt convinced that the situation would soon ease itself by the natural working of economic forces without necessitating a reform of the Indian currency. This conviction on the part of the Committee was founded on the high authority of the late Mr. Walter Bagehot¶ that the disturbance could not but be temporary. His argument was that the depreciation would

* It was composed of Louis Mallet, Edward Stanhope, T. L. Seccombe, R. E. Welby, T. H. Farrer, R. Giffen, and A. J. Balfour.

† For Report of the Committee, *see* Commons Paper C. 4868 of 1886, p. 26.

‡ Q. 10,025-50.

§ So novel was the idea at the time that the United States Monetary Commission, 1876, was surprised when some of the witnesses expressed themselves in favour of regulating the principal metallic unit of account in the currency system of a country by Government agency. *See* 44 Congress 2nd Session Senate Document, No. 703 p. 47-48.

¶ Cf. his *Some Articles on the Depreciation of Silver, and on Topics connected with it*, London, 1877; pp. 10, 55, and 80; also his evidence before the Select Committee on the Depreciation of Silver, Lords Paper 178 of 1876, Q. 1,361-1,450.

encourage exports from India, and discourage imports, and the unfavourable balance of trade thus brought about would induce a flow of silver to India, tending to raise its price. He was also of opinion that increased demand for silver would also arise from outside India. He argued that the reduction of demand caused by the demonetization of silver by some countries would be more than compensated for by the adoption of silver by other countries then on a paper basis for their impending resumptions of specie payment.

Whatever might be said with regard to the Committee's preference of a natural to an artificial system of currency, there can be no doubt that in turning down the proposals of the Government, in the hope that silver would recover, it was grossly deceived. The basic assumptions on which the Committee was led to act failed to come true. To the surprise of everybody India refused to absorb this "white dirt." Indeed, it was one of the puzzles of the time to know why, if silver had fallen so much in Europe, it did not go to India in larger quantities. Many blamed the Secretary of State for the sale of his Council Bills.* These bills, it was said, presented an alternative mode of remittance so much better as to prevent the sending of silver to India, and thereby caused a diminution in the demand for it. That this was not a correct view is obvious.† Silver could not have gone to India more than it did even if Council Bills had been abolished. Council Bills must be regarded as ordinary trade bills drawn against services and commodities, and could not be said to have competed with the transmission of bullion in any special manner different to that attributable to the trade bills. The only bearing the Council Bills may be said to have had upon the issue in question lies in the fact that to the extent they figured in the transactions they prevented India from buying other commodities. But there was nothing to prevent her residual buying power left over after paying for the Council Bills from being utilized in the pur-

* This argument was prominently put forth in the *Report* (pp. xxx—xxxv) of the *Select Committee on the Depreciation of Silver.*, 1876; and also by Monometallic Members of the Gold and Silver Commission, 1886. Cf. pp. 77-79 of the final Report, Part II.

† Cf. evidence of Professor Marshall before the Gold and Silver Commission, 1886, Q. 10,164-76.

chase of silver in preference to other commodities. That this buying power would be used in purchasing silver because it was depreciated in Europe was theoretically an unsound assumption on the part of Mr. Bagehot. The deciding factor which could have caused such a diversion of this residual buying power to the purchase of silver was whether it was *appreciated in India.* Only on that condition could there have been a flow of it to India. But as matters then stood, it was the opinion of Prof. Pierson* that when the general depreciation of silver commenced all over the world, it had been forestalled in that part of the globe in which India lies. India was already glutted with silver. Under ordinnary circumstances India would have sent back a large portion of its silver to Europe. But the general depreciation prevented her from doing so; and now there were two opposing forces, one tending to produce an export of silver from India to Europe and the other tending to produce an export of silver from Europe to India; and, although the latter was the stronger of the two, the former was sufficiently powerful to prevent any considerable quantity of silver from being exported from Europe to India. If the Committee was deceived in one part of its assumptions, it was also disappointed in others. Far from resuming specie payments in terms of silver, as Mr. Bagehot expected the countries then on paper basis to do, they one and all demonetized silver to the great disappointment of all those who adhered to the policy of "wait and see."

The falsification by India and other countries of such anticipations led to a change in the angle of vision of most of the European countries who had theretofore shown no inclination to do anything by way of reducing the chaotic currencies to some kind of order. They were advised by eminent authorities not to hurry. Jevons said † :—

> "We only need a little patience and a little common sense to surmount the practical difficulties. Within the next few years good harvests in India will, in all probability, enable that country to buy up all our surplus silver, as it has been in the habit of doing, with rare exceptions, since the time of Pliny . . . In future years any amount of silver could be got rid of without loss, if it be sold gradually and cautiously."

* Cf. his reply to the Circular of the Gold and Silver Commission, 1886. Second Report, App. VII (1), p. 254.

† Op. cit., p. 354.

When, however, it was found that the waiting period would be more painful if not longer than what it pleased the proverbial peasant to undergo, in order to let the stream run dry so as to permit of his forbidding it without wetting his feet, there grew up an agitation in Europe to undertake the necessary reform to prevent the depreciation of silver.

Far from being sentimental, the agitation was real and derived its force from the evils which arose out of the existing currency conditions. The monetary condition of most of these countries was very unhealthy. Their schemes of an effective gold standard with silver as token currency were arrested in the midst of their progress. Germany, when she demonetized silver, had retained her silver thalers as full legal tender at the old ratio with gold, only to get time to be rid of them to the extent necessary to reduce them to a truly subsidiary position. But, before she could do so, her policy of demonetization had commenced to tell upon the value of silver, and the continued fall thereof compelled Germany to retain the thalers as legal tender at their old value, despite the fact that their metallic value was fast sinking. Precisely the same was the result of the action of the Latin Union on their system of currency. They had stopped their further coinage of the silver five-franc pieces; but they could do nothing with those that were already coined except to permit them to circulate at the old mint par, although the metallic par continued to change with changes in the market values of gold and silver. The United States was also involved in similar evils, although they arose from choice rather than from necessity. Yielding to an agitation of the silver men, it passed in 1878 a law called the Bland Allison Act, requiring the Secretary of the Treasury to purchase and coin each month not less than $2,000,000 and not more than $4,000,000 worth of silver bullion into standard silver dollars, which were to be full legal tender for all debts public and private, "except where otherwise expressly stipulated in the contract."* As the metallic value of these dollars fell with every fall, while their legal value remained as before, they became, like the thalers and the francs,

* *Report of the Monetary Commission of the Indianapolis Convention*, Chicago, 1898, pp. 138-145.

overvalued coins. It is clear* that when the stock of a country's currency is not equally good for all purposes it is relatively speaking in an unsatisfactory condition. Though good for internal purposes, these coins were useless for international payments. Besides making the whole currency system unstable and top-heavy, they could not be made to serve the purpose of banking reserves, which it is the *prime* function of a metallic currency to perform in modern times. The possibilities they opened for illicit coinage were immense. But what made their existence such a source of menace was the fact that a large proportion of the total metallic money of these countries was of this sort. The figures given by Ottomar Haupt in Table XXIII (see p. 125 prove sufficiently the difficulties that these countries had to face in regulating and controlling such a mass of token currency.

If a gold-standard country like England had escaped these difficulties it was only to meet others equally embarrassing. As has been pointed out before, the continued fall of prices, the reflex part of the appreciation of gold, had produced a depression in the trade and industry of the country never known before in its history. Apart from this, the monetary disturbances affected the yield on capital investment, the mainstay of so many of her people, by reducing the field for its employment. Said the American Commission:—

> "Within twenty years from 1877 to 1897, it could probably be correctly stated that the power of money to earn dividends was reduced to one-half, or in nearly that proportion. That reduction of the earning power of capital affected injuriously everybody who depended upon investments for a living. It affected also the profits and enterprises of the captains of industry and the kings of finance. In England and in France the price of Government securities rose to a point which made it no longer possible for the man of small means to invest in them and acquire an adequate support during his declining years."†

It is, of course, open to doubt whether the conclusion drawn is the right one. But the fact remains that owing to monetary dis-

* Cf. the speech of Prof. Pierson, Delegate of the Netherlands at the International Monetary Conference of 1881, *Report of the Delegates of the United States*, Cincinnati, 1881, pp. 77-84.

† Report on the Introduction of the Gold-exchange Standard into China and other Silver-using Countries by the Commission on International Exchange. 58th Congress, 2nd Session, House of Representatives Document, No. 144, Washington, 1903, p. 101.

TABLE XXIII

DISTRIBUTION OF THE STOCK OF MONEY IN DIFFERENT COUNTRIES *

| Countries. | | Monetary Circulation at the *beginning* of 1892. | | | | |
|---|---|---|---|---|---|---|
| | | Gold. | Silver. | Uncovered Notes. | Fractional Currency. | Billion Money. |
| Austria | fl. | 65,000,000 | 197,000,000 | 601,000,000 | 40,000,000 | 14,000,000 |
| England | £ | 118,000,000 | — | 10,000,000 | 26,000,000 | 1,900,000 |
| France | fr. | 3,900,000,000 | 3,200,000,000 | 572,000,000 | 280,000,000 | 280,000,000 |
| Germany | m. | 2,500,000,000 | 430,000,000 | 450,000,000 | 457,000,000 | 57,000,000 |
| Holland | fl. | 64,000,000 | 135,000,000 | 98,000,000 | 7,600,000 | 1,800,000 |
| Italy | li. | 485,000,000 | 81,000,000 | 847,000,000 | 150,000,000 | 75,000,000 |
| Russia | £ | 59,500,000 | — | 51,200,000 | 8,200,000 | 1,000,000 |
| Spain | pes. | 160,000,000 | 646,000,000 | 548,000,000 | 190,000,000 | 157,000,000 |
| U.S.A. | $ | 671,000,000 | 458,000,000 | 419,000,000 | 77,000,000 | 18,000,000 |

* The figures are as given by Ottomar Haupt (London · Effingham, Wilson & Co., 1892, p 160).

turbances the field for the investment of English capital had become considerably restricted. And, as a way of getting a living, capital investment was an important resource to the English people.

To mend such a situation there were convened one after another three International Monetary Conferences to establish a bimetallic par between gold and silver. The first International Monetary Conference was convened at Paris in the year 1878 at the invitation of the United States. The second met at the same place in 1881 at the joint call of France and the United States. The third and the last assembled by the wish of United States in Brussels during the year 1892.

From the gravity of the situation nothing could have been more natural than to expect these Conferences to fructify into an agreement upon the consummation of the project for which they were called into being. But, far from reaching any agreement, the deliberations of these Conferences proved to be entirely futile. Only the second Conference showed any sign of agreement. The first and the third marked a strong deviation in the opposite direction. The advance, if any, that was made, as a result of these deliberations, was summed up in the pious opinion that it was necessary to retain and enlarge the monetary use of silver. But so weak on the whole was the response that practice failed to testify as to the sincerity of this solemn declaration.

The reasons for the failure of these Conferences to reach a bimetallic agreement have not been properly understood. One cannot read the debates on bimetallism at these Conferences without observing that the opposing parties approached the subject with different objectives. To one the principal objective was the maintenance of a stable ratio of exchange between gold and silver irrespective of the question whether one or both remained in circulation; to the other it was the maintenance of the two metals in concurrent circulation. As a consequence of this difference in the lines of their approach an agreement on a bimetallic project became wellnigh impossible.

The workability of bimetallism in the sense of maintaining a stable ratio between gold and silver is necessarily an indefinite proposition. Nonetheless, it cannot be said, if the debates at these Conferences are taken as a guide, that the possibility of a successful bimetallic system in the stable-ratio sense of the term had been denied by the majority of economic theorists, or by the Governments who met at these Conferences. On the other hand, the Conference of 1881, the most important of the three, was remarkable for its confession regarding the workability of the system. All Governments, barring a few minor ones, were in favour of it. Even the British Government, in consenting to bring into operation the silver clause of the Bank Charter Act, must be said to have given its word of approval.

But what did bimetallism promise, as a piece of mechanism, to maintain the two metals in concurrent circulation? The bimetallists used to cite the example of France in support of the stability of the double standard. But was there a concurrent circulation of two metals in France under the bimetallic system? Far from it. For, although it was a virtue of the system that changes in the production of the two metals made no appreciable variations in the fixed ratio of exchange, yet the slightest of such as did occur were sufficient to effect the greatest revolution in the relative circulation of the two metals, as the following table clearly brings out:—

TABLE XXIV

MINTAGE OF GOLD AND SILVER IN FRANCE *

| Period. | Gold Million Francs | Silver Million Francs | Ratio of Value |
|---|---|---|---|
| 1803 to 1820 . | 868 | 1,091 | 1 : 15 58 |
| 1821 to 1847 . | 301 | 2,778 | 1 : 15.80 |
| 1848 to 1852 . | 448 | 543 | 1 : 15.67 |
| 1853 to 1856 . | 1,795 | 102 | 1 : 15.35 |
| 1857 to 1866 . | 3,516 | 55 | 1 . 15.33 |
| 1867 to 1873 . | 876 | 587 | 1 : 15.62 |

* Table submitted to the Paris International Monetary Conference of 1881 by M Pierson, Delegate for the Netherlands.

In mitigation of this, the bimetallists had nothing to offer. There were, no doubt, such schemes as the one proposed by Prof.

Marshall, consisting of paper based on a linked bar of gold and silver in certain fixed proportions,* having the object of converting this "either-metallism" into double-metallism. But such schemes apart, the free-mintage-cum-fixed-ratio plan of bimetallism gave no guarantee against alternation in the circulation. Indeed, under that plan the alternation is the very soul of the mechanism which keeps the ratio from being disturbed. The only thing the bimetallists could say in mitigation of this was that† the alternation in currency would confine itself to bank reserves and would not be extended to the pockets of the people. This was only an eyewash,‡ for how could the banks arrange their reserves except in conformity with the prejudices of the people? Even international agreement to use gold and silver at a fixed ratio was no guarantee that this concurrent circulation would be maintained. Stability of ratio did depend to a large extent upon an international agreement, for, although it could be maintained by the action of one nation, the deviations of the ratio in that case would probably be greater. But mere international agreement has no virtue of itself to prevent one metal driving out the other. To suppose that Gresham's Law is powerless under international agreement is a gross mistake. Gresham's Law is governed by the relative production of the two metals to the total currency needs of the movement. Supposing the production of one metal relatively to the other was so enormous as to more than suffice for the currency needs, how could international agreement prevent the former from driving the latter entirely out of circulation? On the other hand, international agreement, far from discouraging, would encourage the process.

In adopting bimetallism, therefore, the nations had to make a choice between a stable ratio and a concurrent circulation, for

* Cf. *Contemporary Review* for March, 1887. It is interesting to note that essentially the same plan was suggested 115 years before Prof Marshall by James Stewart when his advice was sought by the East India Company as to the method of reforming the then chaotic currency of Bengal. He refrained from pressing it upon the Company because he thought "mankind were not all philosophers." Cf. his *Principles of Money as applied to the Present State of the Coin of Bengal* (2nd Edition, 1772), pp. 8-11; cf. also William Ward, On Monetary Derangements, in a *Letter addressed to the Proprietors of Bank Stock*, London, 1840, p. 8.

† Cf. Prof. Foxwell, *Oxford Economic Review*, 1893, Vol. III, p. 297.

‡ Cf. the reply by Prof. Cannan, *ibid.*, p. 457.

there might arise a situation in which there was a stable ratio but no concurrent circulation of both the metals. If the Conferences broke down, it was not because they did not recognize the possibility, which was unanimously upheld by such an impartial tribunal as the Gold and Silver Commission of 1886, of a stable ratio being maintained under a bimetallic regime. They broke down because the bimetallic system did not guarantee the concurrent circulation of the two metals. However, it is certain the impossibility of concurrent circulation could not have been such a drawback if the immediate effect of bimetallism would have been a flow of gold into circulation. But as matters then stood the immediate effect would have been to bring silver into circulation. It was this more than anything else which scared away most of the nations from the adoption of the bimetallic system. Now, it is a curious thing that nations which had assembled together to bring about a stable ratio between gold and silver should have rejected a system which gave a promise of such a stability on the comparatively less significant ground that it had the effect of altering the composition of the circulation from gold to silver. But the fact must be recognized that at the time the question of reconstituting the bimetallic system was agitating the public mind, in most of the European countries gold and silver had ceased to be regarded as equally good for currency purposes. The superiority of gold to silver as a carrier of large value in small bulk was coming more and more to be appreciated in the latter part of the nineteenth century, and no plan of stabilization which did not provide for the unhindered circulation of gold was likely to meet with common approval. This prejudice was in no way confined to a gold-standard country like England. The closing of the Mints by the Latin Union is a proof positive of the change in the attitude of the bimetallic countries. As Jevons argued *:—

> "So long . . . as its operation resulted in substituting a beautiful coinage of napoleons, half-napoleons, and five-franc pieces in gold for the old heavy silver ecus, there was no complaint, and the French people admired the action of their compensatory system. But when [after 1873] it became evident that the heavy silver currency was coming back again . . . the matter assumed a different form."

So great was the prejudice in favour of gold that the interests of the chief Powers in the various Conferences, it may be

* *Money and Mechanism of Exchange*, 1890, p. 143.

truly said, waxed and waned with the changes in the volume of their gold reserves.* In 1878, the United States took the lead in calling the Conference because the working of the Bland Allison Act checked the inflow of gold necessary for its cash payments. Germany was indifferent because she had enough gold and was confident of selling off her demonetized silver without loss. In 1881 France and Germany showed more anxiety for reform because the former had lost all her gold and the latter was unable to palm off her silver. By 1892 none was so poorly supplied with gold as was the United States, largely as a result of a reckless policy which did her harm without doing good to anyone else, and she was therefore left alone to support the cause of silver.

Possessed as almost every Government was by this prejudice for gold, it was not an ineradicable prejudice. What the countries wanted was a lead from an influential nation. Throughout the debates at these Conferences one thing stood out very clearly. If England could have brought herself to adopt a bimetallic system, others, like sheep, would have followed suit. But she was too much wedded to her system to make a change, with the result that bimetallism, as a way out of the currency difficulties, became a dead project. The vanishing of the prospect of re-establishing the bimetallic system as a result of her obstinacy was a small matter to the European countries. They had virtually made gold, the international form of money, as the basis of their currency, and were therefore quite indifferent as to the issue ; but it was a terrible blow to the hopes of India. After the proposal of 1878 had been turned down, bimetallism was considered by the Government of India as the remedy, and its advent looked forward to for salvation. It is true that in the beginning of bimetallic discussions the attitude of the Indian Government was rather lukewarm. In a despatch dated June 10, 1881,† to the Secretary of State, it was revealed that the Government of the time was divided in its opinion regarding the merits of bimetallism. The Viceroy and another member of Council refused their support on the ground that bimetallism was unsound in principle,‡ and even the majority who thought differently on this aspect of the ques-

* Cf. *The Report of the Indian Delegation to the International Monetary Conference of* 1881, C. 3229 of 1882, p. 7 , also Russell, op. cit , pp. 374-5.

† P P C 3229 of 1882, p. 33 *et seq.* ‡ *Ibid.*, p. 37.

tion were not then prepared to go to the length of joining a bimetallic union, although they did not see any objection to doing so "if a sufficiently large number of other Governments were prepared to join" in it. With the growth of their financial difficulties, however, this slender faith in bimetallism considerably deepened, so much so that in 1886 the Government addressed to the Secretary of State a despatch* urging him to take the initiative in calling an International Monetary Conference to establish a stable ratio between gold and silver. So intense was its interest in the consummation of bimetallism that it did not hesitate to administer a sharp rebuke to the Treasury when they negatived its suggestion referred to them for consideration by the Secretary of State.† With such feelings of faith and hope the Government of India entered these international Conferences and watched their fortunes. But no Government could have been treated with such suspicion and injustice as was the Government of India. Its admission to the bimetallic union was desired by none of the Powers, not even by England.‡ It was treated as a villain whose advances were nothing but manoeuvres to pounce upon the already dwindling stock of gold. Not only was it planned to keep India out of the bimetallic union, but she was to be required to pledge herself not to take a mean advantage of the union after its efforts had succeeded in establishing a stable ratio by making gold legal tender. § All these guarantees the Government of India had offered in a pathetic faithfulness to the cause of bimetallism, on the success of which it had depended so much. Consequently, when the attempt failed, the disappointment caused to the Government of India almost broke its heart. It is not too severe to say that the part played by the British authorities in causing this disappointment was highly irresponsible—one might almost say wicked. They forced India against her declared wishes to keep to the silver standard, partly to trail her off from making any demand for gold, and partly to silence the criticisms of other

* Dated February 2, 1886, *see* C. 4868 of 1886, p. 5 *et seq.*

† Cf. the despatch of September 4, 1886, App. II to the *First Report of the Royal Commission on Gold and Silver*, 1886.

‡ Cf. the evidence before the Gold and Silver Commission of 1886 of Mr. S. Smith, Q. 4,825-30 ; also of Mr. Watney, Q. 9,427.

§ Cf. *The Report of the Indian Delegates*, p. 12.

nations that Britain was not taking her share in the matter of rehabilitating silver.* This was not the only advantage exacted from a country bound to obey. On the one hand it restrained the Government of India from taking any independent line of action in the matter of currency reform, and on the other such means as were calculated to make good the losses which arose from a depreciating currency were subjected to Parliamentary censure. The House of Commons was twice moved, once in 1877 and again in 1879, to resolve that the Government of India should lower its tariff, ostensibly in the interest of free trade, but really in the interests of relief to the depressed condition of Lancashire. The consequence was that the Government could not tap one important source of its revenue in times of its greatest adversity. The only adequate recompense, the British authorities could have made to a Government so completely paralysed by their dictations, and of whose interests they so loudly claimed to be the lawful trustees, was to have consented to join the bimetallic union, the consummation of which only waited upon their grace. But, as is well known, they did nothing of the kind, so that, after a period of enforced waiting and by no means unavoidable suffering, the Government of India, at the end of 1893, found itself just where it was at the beginning of 1878.

Like all common-sense people who pray and yet do not fail to keep their powder dry, this interval was utilized by the silver-ridden countries, with the exception of the United States, in strengthening their gold basis no less than in attending the deliberation of the Monetary Conferences on the amusing plans for extending the use of silver.† Mr. Goschen, at the Conference of 1878, had quite philosophically remarked that States feared to employ silver because of its depreciation, and the depreciation continued because the States feared to employ it. Now, if the first part of the diagnosis was correct, we should have found the States seriously engaged in the task of rehabilitating silver when

* Cf. the speech of Mr Goschen at the International Monetary Conference of 1878, Third Session. Report of the American Delegates, Senate Executive Document, No. 58, Forty-fifth Congress, Third Session, Washington, 1879, pp. 50-52.

† Cf. for the variety of plans suggested at the Conferences *The Report of the American Delegates to the International Monetary Conference of* 1892, Washington, 1893.

its price was propped up by the silver legislation of the United States. On the other hand, just so far as the monthly purchases of silver, under the Bland Allison Act of 1878, or the Sherman Act of 1890, held up the price of silver, not only did they not feel anxious to take steps to restore it to its former position, but they actually took advantage of the rise to discard it.* And it is not possible to blame them either, for with the prospect of a bimetallic union vanishing into thin air the accumulation of this dead weight would have only ended in a gratuitous embarrassment. India alone refused to profit by the squeeze, which the United States took vicariously for other nations, and allowed precious time to slip by, with the result that it was thrown back upon the same remedy, the adoption of which was negatived in 1878.

If it was to be a gold standard it would have been better if it had been done in 1878. The plan then outlined by the Government of India was no doubt too complicated and too flimsy to be practicable. But its rejection should not have altogether suspended the introduction of a gold standard. If it was to be one of an orthodox kind on the English pattern, it would have no doubt involved some cost to the Government in being obliged to sell at a reduced price a part of the silver stock of the country in order to give the rupee a subsidiary position and to fill the void by a gold currency. The cost of this conversion in 1878 would have been inconsiderable, for the fall of silver from its normal gold price was only 12½ per cent. On the other hand, if it was to be on such an unorthodox plan as that of Colonel Smith, it would have involved no cost at all to the Government† beyond that involved in the installation of new machinery for the coinage of gold at the Mint. But in 1893 both these processes of bringing about a gold standard seemed quite hopeless. The impossibility of the plan of conversion was quite out of the question. The fall in the value of silver in 1893 was nearly 35 per cent. Even the prospect of the Smith plan did not appear very bright owing to the enormous addition of rupees to the circulation of

* Cf. Russell, op. cit., p 410; also Prof. F. A. Walker, "The Free Coinage of Silver," in *The Journal of Political Economy* (Chicago), Vol. I, p. 174.

† So evident was this the case that the London *Times*, although it did not agree that any change was then urgently called for, yet observed in the leading article in its issue of October 25, 1876, p. 9, cl. 2: "The Governor-General in Council dismisses the suggestion of a gold standard on the ground that the present condition of affairs,

the country. If it had been adopted in 1878, all the subsequent additions to the currency would have been in gold, with the result that by 1893 the proportion of gold to silver would have been large enough to have endowed the whole currency system with the desired stability in relation to countries on a purely gold basis. In 1893 the mass of silver currency had grown to enormous proportions, so that it looked certain that it would take decades before the stoppage of silver coinage could make the rupee a stable and secure form of currency.

The plans showing a way out of an *impasse* such as this were legion. One was the issue of heavier rupees.* The second was to make silver limited legal tender and to authorize the Secretary of State to sell in London gold or silver Indian stock to the extent of his gold payments, to be liquidated by the Government of India by the issue of unlimited legal-tender notes called "bons."† The third was that England and India should, as between them, adopt a bimetallic standard on a new basis,‡ or to admit the rupee as full legal tender in the United Kingdom.§ The fourth was to regulate the opening and closing of Mints to coinage on the basis of deviations of actual exchange rates from the rate of exchange fixed at the opening of each year for the Council drafts of the Secretary of State. Under this scheme, so long as the actual rate did not exceed the fixed rate by less than 5 per cent., the free coinage of silver was to be suspended.¶ The fifth was to provide

bad as it is, does not call for so costly a remedy; but this involves a misconception of the proposal. The substitution of a gold for a silver currency in India would be a most extensive and costly operation, but to refuse to coin silver and to offer to coin gold for all comers would involve no cost beyond that of new machinery. If it was announced that after a certain day the coinage of silver was suspended, and that gold could be coined instead, for whoever might bring it, in coins that would be exchangeable for rupees at a fixed rate, there would be introduced into India the bimetallic system prevailing in France, and a change in the currency would be gradually introduced. At first no gold would be brought to be coined, but as the suspense of the coinage of silver operated to raise the value of the rupees in existence to the par value defined by the fixed rate of exchange of rupees and gold, gold would be more and more brought to the Mint, and would find its way into circulation. The process would be automatic and not costly, but it would be extremely slow, etc."

* By Aston and also by R. West, I. C. C., 1893. App. III, pp. 281 and 325.

† By Atkins, *ibid.*, p. 282.

‡ By Chapman, *ibid.*, p. 282.

§ By Woodhouse, *ibid.*, p. 33.

¶ By Graham, *ibid.*, p. 305.

that on the one hand the Secretary of State should fix a minimum rate for his drafts, and that the Government of India on the other should levy a duty on all imports of silver equal to the difference between the daily official quotations of bar silver in London and the price of silver corresponding to the rate fixed for the Council drafts.* The sixth was to introduce a bimetallic coin, to be called the Imperial florin or rupee, made of the value of 2*s.* and containing 4 per cent. weight in gold and the balance in silver.† The seventh was to establish independent gold and silver standards without any fixed ratio of exchange between them,‡ or with some slight inducement for the use of gold in transactions of larger denominations.§ Although the Government of India was not in agreement with these clever if not crazy plans of currency reforms, it agreed in the aim they had in view, namely, to place India on a gold basis without involving the actual use of gold in place of the existing rupees in circulation. With this aim in view it revived for adoption the more simple and more scientific plan of Colonel Smith. As a preliminary, the Government reverted to the policy of the resolution of the Bengal Chamber of Commerce, to the adoption of which it saw such "fatal objections" in 1876. In the despatch dated June 21, 1892, which contained the proposals, the Government of India asked for nothing more. In the words of their author¶ they proposed

> " that the Indian Mints should be closed to the unlimited coinage of silver, and *no further steps taken* until the effect of closing the Mints had been ascertained.
>
> "The ratio at which the change from silver to the gold standard should be made was subsequently to be settled and it was said that a ratio based on the average price of silver during a limited period before the Mints had been closed would probably be the safest and most equitable. When this ratio had been settled, the Mints were to be opened to the coinage of gold at that ratio, and gold coins were to be made legal tender to any amount."

These proposals were submitted for examination to a Departmental Committee, commonly known as the Herschell Com-

* By M. Schilizz, *ibid*, p. 319.

† By Stalkart, *ibid*, p 322, also a very similar one by Merington, *ibid*, p 316

‡ By Perry, *ibid*, p 323

§ By Claremonth Daniell, *ibid*, p 292.

¶ Sir David Barbour, *The Standard of Value*, 1912, pp. 202-3. Italics not in the original.

mittee. They were said to be defective in one important particular, and that was the absence of due recognition of the necessity of a gold reserve for the maintenance of the value of the rupee. Many people felt doubtful of the success of the proposals unless backed by an adequate gold reserve. But the Herschell Committee, after an extended investigation into the working of the currency systems of different countries, reported* :—

> "It is impossible . . . to review foreign systems of currency, without feeling that, however admirable may be the precautions of our own [English] currency system, other nations have adopted different systems which appear to have worked without difficulty, and enabled them to maintain for their respective currencies a gold standard and a substantial parity of exchange with the gold-using countries of the world"

with little or no gold. The Committee, therefore, was completely satisfied with the proposals of the Government of India, and not only sanctioned their adoption, † but added, by way of introducing a modification in them, that

> "The closing of the Mints against the free coinage of silver should be accompanied by an announcement that, though closed to the public, they will be used by the Government for the coinage of rupees in exchange for gold at a ratio to be then fixed, say 1*s*. 4*d*. per rupee, and that at the Government Treasuries gold will be received in satisfaction of public dues at the same ratio"‡

These recommendations were carried into effect on June 26, 1893, which forms as great a landmark in the history of Indian currency as did the year 1835. On that date were promulgated one legislative enactment and three executive notifications, together calculated to accomplish the object in view. The Act (VIII) of 1893 was only a repealing Act. It repealed :—

(i) The Indian Coinage Act, XXIII of 1870.

Sections 19 to 26 (both inclusive), requiring the Mint Masters to coin all silver brought to their Mints for coinage.§

---

* Report, par. 93.

† Report, par. 155.

‡ Report, par. 156.

§ These sections also contained provisions for the coinage of all gold brought to the Mints for the purpose by private persons. The quantity brought to the Mints was quite trifling, and the gold coins, i.e. the mohurs struck, were not legal tender. As

(ii) The Indian Paper Currency, 1882.*

(a) Section 11, Clause (b), requiring the Paper Currency Department to issue notes against silver coin made under the Portuguese Convention Act, 1881.†

(b) Section 11, Clause (d), requiring the Paper Currency Department to issue notes against silver bullion or foreign silver coin.‡

(c) Section 13. Only the proviso limiting the gold portion of the Paper Currency Reserve to one-fourth of the Total Reserve. §

These repeals by the Act were supplemented by an executive Notification No. 2663, announcing in conformity with the suggestion of the Herschell Committee that the Government Treasuries would receive sovereigns and half-sovereigns of current weight in payment of public dues at the rate of 15 rupees and 7 rupees 8 annas respectively.

Since gold was not made general legal tender by any of the above measures, it was feared that the Government might be embarrassed by the accumulation in its Treasuries of a stock money which it could not pay out in discharge of its obligations. To enable Government to rid the Treasuries of gold, should it accumulate in them to an inconvenient extent, there followed another Notification, No. 2664, requiring that the Currency Department should issue, on the requisition of the Controller-General, currency notes in exchange for gold coin or gold bullion, at the rate of one Government rupee for 7.53344 grs. troy of fine

---

they were to be superseded by sovereigns to be coined at the Mints upon their being subsequently thrown open to the free coinage of gold, it was thought undesirable that any more of these mohurs should be coined. Consequently, along with silver, Mints were also closed to gold.

* The repeal of these sections of the Act also called for the repeal of other sections depending upon them, such as sections 14 and 15 and alterations in Sections 21 and 28, to bring the whole Act in accord with the policy of a gold standard then inaugurated.

† The Convention had come to an end and the retention of the clause was therefore unnecessary.

‡ The retention of this clause would have been inconsistent with the closure of the Mints.

§ As gold was to be the future standard of India, this limitation was no longer necessary.

gold, or sovereigns or half-sovereigns at the rate of 15 rupees and 7 rupees 8 annas respectively.

To give effect to the second modification introduced by the Herschell Committee, there was issued a third Notification, No. 2662, to the effect that

> "The Governor-General in Council hereby announces that, until further orders, gold coins and gold bullion will be received by the Mint Masters of the Calcutta and Bombay Mints respectively, in exchange for Government rupees, at the rate of 7.53344 grs. troy of fine gold for one rupee on the following conditions :—
>
> (1) Such coins or bullion must be fit for coinage.
>
> (2) The quantity tendered at one time must not be less than 50 tolas.
>
> (3) A charge of one-fourth per mille will be made on all gold coin or bullion which is melted or cut so as to render the same fit for receipt into the Mint.
>
> (4) The Mint Master, on receipt of gold coin or bullion into the Mint, shall grant to the proprietor a receipt which shall entitle him to a certificate from the Mint and Assay Masters for the amount of the rupees to be given in exchange for such coin or bullion payable at the General (Reserve) Treasury, Calcutta or Bombay. Such certificates shall be payable at the General Treasury after such lapse of time from the issue thereof as the Comptroller-General may fix, from time to time."

Before the policy adumbrated by these measures was carried to completion there came up a move for the undoing of it. After the failure of the International Monetary Conference of 1892 the United States and France, two countries most heavily burdened with an overvalued stock of silver, opened negotiation with the British Government, asking the latter to agree to certain conditions on the grant of which they were to open their Mints to the free coinage of silver at the ratio of 15½ to 1. These conditions included :*

(1) Opening of the Indian Mints, which had been closed to the free coinage of silver, and an undertaking not to make gold legal tender in India.

(2) Placing one-fifth of the bullion in the Issue Department of the Bank of England in silver.

* Cf. Correspondence respecting the Proposals on Currency made by the Special Envoys from the United States, P.P.C. 8667 of 1897, p. 3.

(3) *(a)* Raising the legal-tender limit of silver in England to £10.

*(b)* Issuing the 20*s*. notes based on silver, which shall be legal tender.

*(c)* Retirement, gradual or otherwise, of the 10*s*. gold pieces, and substitution of paper based on silver.

(4) Agreement to coin annually a certain quantity of silver.

(5) Opening of English Mints to the coinage of rupees and for coinage of British dollars, which shall be full legal tender in Straits Settlements and other silver-standard Colonies, and tender in the United Kingdom to the limit of silver legal tender.

(6) Colonial action, and coinage of silver in Egypt.

(7) Something having the general scope of the Huskisson plan.

In these negotiations the Treasury again reverted to its old pose. It refused to discuss the conditions requiring a change in the British currency, but argued that the opening of the Indian Mints, if brought about, should be regarded as an adequate "contribution which could be made by the British Empire towards any international agreement with the object of securing" a stable monetary par of exchange between gold and silver,* and the representatives of the United States and France seemed to have concurred in that view. The negotiations, however, failed, because of the firm stand taken by the Government of India. The Government had suffered too long to be the scapegoat of the Treasury. Nor did it see any reason why it should be called upon to pull the chestnuts off the fire for the benefit of France and the United States. In a letter commenting upon the proposals, the Government of India observed† :—

> "The changes which are involved in the arrangements proposed to Her Majesty's Government are the following : France and the United States are to open their Mints to the free coinage of silver, continuing the free coinage of gold and the unlimited legal tender of coins of both metals, the ratio remaining unchanged

* Cf. letter dated October 16, 1897, to the Foreign Office, *ibid.*, p. 15.

† Despatch dated September 16, 1897, to the Secretary of State, *ibid.*, p. 9. Italics not in the original.

in France and being altered to the French ratio of 15½ to 1 in the United States. *India is to open her Mints to silver to keep them closed to gold, and to undertake not to make gold legal tender. France and the United States would thus be bimetallic; India would be monometallic (silver); whilst most of the other important countries of the world would be monometallic (gold).*

* * * * *

"The first result of the suggested measures, if they even temporarily succeed in their object, would be an immense disturbance of Indian trade and industry, by the sudden rise from about 16d. to about 23d. the rupee. Such a rise is enough to kill our export trade, for the time at least . . . such an arrangement as is proposed is an infinitely more serious question for India than for either of the other two countries, for it seems clear that practically the whole risk of disaster from failure would fall on India alone. What would happen in each of the three countries if the agreement broke down and came to an end? France possesses a large stock of gold, and the United States are at present in much the same situation as France, though the stock of that metal is not so large. It may be admitted that if no precautions were taken these gold reserves might disappear under the operation of the agreement, and in that case, if the experiment ultimately failed, the two countries concerned would suffer great loss. But it is inconceivable that precautions would not be taken, at all events, so soon as the danger of the depletion of the gold reserves manifested itself, and, therefore, it is probable that no particular change would take place in the monetary system of France or the United States, the only effect of the agreement being a coinage of silver which would terminate with the termination of the agreement. Thus the whole cost of the failure, if the experiment should fail, would be borne by India. Here the rupee would rise with great swiftness, it would keep steady for a time, and then, when the collapse came, it would fall headlong. What course could we then adopt to prevent the fluctuation of the exchange value of our standard of value with the fluctuations in the price of silver? We do not think that any remedy would be open to us, for if the Indian Mints were reopened to silver now, it would . . . be practically impossible for the Government of India to close them again, and even if they were closed it would only be after very large additions had been made to the amount of silver in circulation."

But soon after it had refused to be diverted from the goal it had placed before itself, namely the introduction of a gold standard, it was faced with a crucial problem in its existing monetary arrangements. The rupee stock, the addition to which was stopped since 1893 by the closure of the Mints, was large enough to meet the needs of the people for some considerable time. In the first few years after the closure, the rupee currency was not only abundant but was also redundant. Soon it ceased to be redundant, and indeed by the end of 1898 it became scarce, so much so that the discount rate in the Indian money market rose to 16 per cent., and continued at that pitch during the larger part of the year. Such was the outcry against what was called the policy of "starving" the currency, that the Government was obliged to pass an Act (No. II) of 1898 to permit currency notes issued in India against gold tendered in London to the Secretary of State. The Act was doubly easeful to the then starved condition of the Indian money market. By the measures adopted in 1893 gold was not general legal tender, so it could not be used when the rupee currency fell short of the needs of the time. The new Act, it is true, did not make gold general tender, but permitted it to be used on behalf of the general public* as a backing for the issue of currency notes which were general legal tender. The Act, however, could have required that gold be laid down *in India* before notes could be issued. But as the remittance of gold to India took some three or four weeks, it was feared† that the remedy might "prove too tardy to be effective" unless the interval was done away with by providing that gold with the Secretary of State in London was lawfully tantamount to gold with the Paper Currency Department in India for the purposes of note issue.

In doing this the Act only testified to the urgency of the situation. A sound currency system must be capable of expansion as well as contraction. The Government, by the closure of the Mints in 1893, had contracted the currency to the point of danger. In 1898 it was called upon to undertake measures to provide for its expansion. Now, there were two methods open to bring about this desired result. One was to keep the Mints closed and to permit additions to currency through the use of the gold by making the sovereign general legal tender. This was the plan

* By Notification No. 2664 of 1893, notes could be issued against gold only to the Comptroller-General.

† Cf. the speech of the Hon. Sir James Westland introducing the Bill, dated January 14, 1898.

proposed by the Government of India. In their despatch dated March 8, 1898,* they argued :—

> "Our present intention is rather to trust to the automatic operations of trade. The amount of coin required for the needs of commerce increases every year : and as we print no increase in the amount of silver coin, we may reasonably expect that the effect of the increasing demand for coin will raise exchange to a point at which gold will flow into the country, and remain in circulation. The position will thus become stronger and stronger as time goes on, but at the beginning at least, gold will not be in circulation in the country to more than the extent necessary to secure stability of exchange. The mass of the circulation will be a silver circulation, maintained at an appreciated value (just as it is at present), and we can be content to see gold coin remain little more than a margin, retained in circulation by the fact that its remittance out of the country could create a scarcity of coin which would have the effect of raising the exchange value of the silver rupee in such manner as to bring it back, or, at the very best, stop the outward current of remittance. We shall have attained a gold standard under conditions not dissimilar from those prevailing in France, though not a gold circulation in the English sense ; and this last may possibly not be necessary at all."

Besides expanding the currency through the use of gold, there was also another mode of effecting the same object. It was urged that this increase of currency might as well take place by Government coining rupees whenever there arose a need for additional currency. Though the Mints were closed, the Government, by Notification No. 2662, had undertaken to give rupees to anyone desiring to have them at the rate of 7.53344 grs. troy of fine gold per rupee.† The Government had only to give effect to that notification to augment the currency to any extent desired. Prominent in the advocacy of this plan of expanding the currency were Mr. Probyn and Mr. A. M. Lindsay. Both claimed that the plan of the Government of India was defective because, although it provided for the expansion of currency by making gold legal tender, it made the rupee entirely inconvertible, and thereby likely to defeat the policy of stabilizing its exchange value. On the other hand, they deemed their plans to be superior to that of the Government of India because they

* Cf. correspondence respecting the Proposals on Currency made by the Government of India, C. 8840 of 1898, p. 3.

† *See supra.*

recognized the obligation to provide for the conversion of the rupee currency on certain terms. Although the plans of both of them had contemplated some kind of convertibility, yet they materially differed in the particular mode in which conversion was to be effected. Mr. Probyn proposed*:—

> 1. That legislative effect should be given to the notification of 1893, under which the public can obtain rupees at the Indian Mints and Reserve Treasuries in exchange for gold, at the rate of 1s. 4d.
>
> 2. That the gold so received should be part of the paper currency reserve, and should be held either in the form of full legal-tender gold coins of the United Kingdom, or gold bars representing not less than Rs. 1,000 each.
>
> 3. That in order to give the rupee currency automatic power of contraction, Government should be empowered (though not required) so soon as the portion of the paper currency reserve has continuously for one year been less than that held in gold, to give gold in exchange for rupees or rupee notes at the rate of 1s. 4d., if presented for the purpose in quantities of Rs. 10,000.
>
> 4. That the existing Rs. 10,000 notes should be called in, and, in future, notes of Rs. 10,000, payable at the option of the holder either in gold or in silver rupees, should be issued in exchange for gold alone, gold in the form of bars being specially reserved to meet any such notes outstanding.

Mr. Lindsay, on the other hand, followed on lines quite different from those adopted by Mr. Probyn. He proposed† that the Government should offer to sell, without limit on the one hand, rupee drafts on India at the exchange of 16 1/16d. the rupee, and on the other hand, sterling drafts on London at the rate of exchange of 15¾d. the rupee. The funds necessary for the transactions were to be kept separate from the ordinary Government balances in "Gold Standard" Offices in London and in India.

---

* Cf. his *Indian Coinage and Currency*, Effingham Wilson, London, 1897, *passim*, particularly p. 121. Also the summary by Lindsay in the *Economic Journal*, Vol. VII, pp. 574-75.

† The earliest elaboration of his plan is to be found in his article in the *Calcutta Review* for October, 1878, under the title, "A Gold Standard without a Gold Coinage in England and India," and the latest, in his pamphlet called *Ricardo's Exchange Remedy*, Effingham Wilson, 1892. The plan was further developed in the newspaper *Pioneer* of Allahabad (India), dated January 6, 1898, full extracts from which are given in C. 8840 of 1898, p. 13.

The London Office was to be kept in funds to meet drafts drawn on it—

(1) by borrowing in gold to the extent of five or ten million sterling ;

(2) by the receipts realized by the sale of drafts on India ;

(3) by the receipts realized by the sale of silver bullion in rupee melted down;* and

(4) when necessary, by further gold borrowing.

The Indian Gold Standard Office was to be kept in funds to meet the drafts drawn on them—

(1) by the receipts realized by the sale of drafts on London ; and

(2) by the coinage when necessary of new rupees from bullion, purchased by the London Gold Standard Office and sent to India.

The principal point of difference between the scheme of currency advocated by the Government of India on the one hand and that put forth by Messrs. Probyn and Lindsay consisted in the fact that the former proposed to establish a gold standard *with* a gold currency , while the latter proposed to establish a gold standard *without* a gold currency.

To adjudicate upon the relative merits of a gold standard with a gold currency and a gold standard without a gold currency, the Secretary of State appointed another departmental Committee, under the chairmanship of Sir Henry Fowler. After taking a mass of important evidence, the Committee observed† :—

> "50. On this scheme [of Mr. Probyn] we remark that, while bullion may be regarded as the international medium of exchange, there is no precedent for its permanent adoption for purposes of internal currency ; nor does it accord with either European or Indian usage that the standard metal should not pass from hand to hand in the convenient form of current coin. No real support for such a scheme is to be drawn from the purely temporary provisions of 'Peel's Act' of 1819, whereby, for a limited period, the Bank of England, as a first step to the resump-

---

*Mr. Lindsay contemplated that when the demand for gold drafts on London became so great as to indicate the necessity, the volume of the rupee currency should be contracted by melting down the rupees and selling the silver for gold to be deposited in the London "Gold Standard" Office.

†Report of the Committee appointed to inquire into the Indian Currency, P. P. C. 9390 of 1899, p. 15.

tion of cash payments, was authorized to cash, in stamped gold bars, its notes, when presented in parcels of over £200. Little or no demand for gold bullion appears to have been made on the Bank itself in 1821.

* * *

"53. It is evident that the arguments which tell against the permanent adoption of Mr. Probyn's bullion scheme, and in favour of a gold currency for India, tell more strongly against Mr. Lindsay's ingenious scheme for what has been termed 'an exchange standard.' We have been impressed by the evidence of Lord Rothschild, Sir John Lubbock, Sir Samuel Montagu and others, that any system without a visible gold currency would be looked upon with distrust. In face of this expression of opinion, it is difficult to avoid the conclusion that the adoption of Lindsay's scheme would check that flow of capital to India upon which her economic future so greatly depends. We are not prepared to recommend Mr. Lindsay's scheme, or the analogous schemes proposed by the late Mr. Raphael and by Maior Darwin, for adoption as a permanent arrangement; and existing circumstances do not suggest the necessity for adopting any of these schemes as a provisional measure for fixing the sterling exchange."

The Committee preferred the scheme of the Government of India, and outlined a course of action to be adopted for placing it on a permanent footing, which may be stated in the Committee's own language as follows :—

"54. We are in favour of making the British sovereign a legal tender and a current coin in India. We also consider that, at the same time, the Indian Mints should be thrown open to the unrestricted coinage of gold on terms and conditions such as govern the three Australian branches of the Royal Mint. The result would be that, under identical conditions, the sovereign would be coined and would circulate both at home and in India. Looking forward, as we do, to the effective establishment in India of a gold standard and currency, based on the principles of the free inflow and outflow of gold, we recommend these measures for adoption."

These recommendations were accepted by the Secretary of State,* who decided that

"the policy of keeping the Indian Mints closed to the unrestricted coinage of silver shall be maintained,"

and called upon the Government of India as soon as it deemed expedient to

* *See* despatch dated July 25, 1899, No. 140 (Financial), C. 9421 of 1899.

> "take the necessary steps for making the British sovereign a legal tender and a current coin, and make preparations for the coinage of gold under the conditions suggested by the Committee."

The first recommendation of the Committee was given effect to by the Government passing an Act commonly called the Indian Coinage and Paper Currency Act (XXII) of 1899. That Act made the sovereign and half-sovereign legal tender throughout India at the rate of Rs. 15 and Rs. 7½ respectively, and authorized the issue of currency notes in exchange for them.

Along with placing the Indian currency on a gold basis, the Government was anxious to open a Mint for the free coinage of gold. But as the coin to be issued from the Mint was the English "sovereign" the Government of India was entirely in the hands of the British Treasury. According to the provisions of the English Coinage Act of 1870, it was necessary to issue a Royal Proclamation in order to constitute an Indian Mint a branch of the Royal Mint, a matter entirely dependent on the consent of the Treasury. It was the intention of the Government of India to announce the Proclamation simultaneously with the passing of the Act making the sovereign legal tender. Indeed it held back the legislation pending the arrival of the Proclamation,* and proceeded with it reluctantly when it was advised that there was likely to be "some further delay over the Proclamation owing to legal and technical questions." The objections raised by the Treasury, though merely technical, at first seemed to be quite insuperable,† and had it not been for the conciliatory attitude of the India Office the negotiations would have broken down. But the Treasury was not willing to give the project a chance. Just when a compromise was arrived at on the technical side of the question, the Treasury turned round and raised the question whether a Mint for gold coinage was at all necessary in India. The Treasury argued :—

> "While expressing their satisfaction that an agreement has now been reached, my Lords think it desirable, before practical steps are taken to carry out the scheme, to invite Lord George Hamilton to review the arguments originally advanced in favour

* Cf. the speech of the Hon. Mr. Dawkins on the Indian Coinage and Paper Currency Bill, dated September 8, 1899.

† Cf. H. of C. Return 495 of 1913, p. 14.

of the coinage of the sovereign in India, and to consider whether the course of events, in the two years which have elapsed since the proposal was made, has not tended to diminish their force, and to render such advantages as are likely to accrue from the establishment of a branch Mint wholly incommensurate with the expense to be incurred. . . . . The gold standard is now firmly established, and the public requires no proof of the intention of the Indian Government not to go back on their policy, which is beyond controversy. Sovereigns are readily attracted to India when required under existing conditions. . . . On the other hand the estimates of the Government of India of gold available for coinage in that country are less than was anticipated, nor is any considerable increase expected, at any rate for some time . . . .

The staff would have to be maintained in idleness for a large part of the year, at a considerable cost to the Indian Exchequer. . . . It is, of course, for Lord George Hamilton to decide whether, in spite of these objections, the scheme is to be proceeded with."

The India Office replied :—

"The establishment of a Mint for the coinage of gold in India is the clearest outward sign that can be given of the consummation of the new currency system ; and to abandon the proposal now must attract attention and provoke criticism and unrest. . . . His Lordship is not inclined to abandon the scheme at the stage which it has now reached."

The Treasury sent a trenchant rejoinder, in which it remarked :—

"Indian currency needs are provided from other sources, and there is no real demand for the local coinage of sovereigns. . . . . My Lords cannot believe that the position of the Gold Standard in India will be strengthened, or public confidence in the intention of the Government confirmed, by providing machines for obtaining gold coins. . . . The large measure of confidence already established is sufficiently indicated by the course of exchange since the Committee's Report and still more by the readiness with which gold has been shipped to India. . . ."

That the Treasury acted "in a spirit of scarcely veiled hostility to the whole proposal" is unmistakable. But it cannot be denied that the Treasury used arguments that were perfectly sound. It was inconsequential to the working of the gold standard whence the coined sovereigns came. So long as a Mint was open to the free coinage of sovereigns the Indian gold standard would have been complete irrespective of the location of the Mint. Indeed, to have obtained coined sovereigns from London would have not only sufficed, but would have been economical.

The anxiety displayed by the Government was not, however, on account of the want of a gold Mint. Indeed, so slight was its faith in the necessity of it that in view of the opposition of the Treasury it gracefully consented to drop the proposal. What troubled it most was the peculiar position of the rupee in the new system of currency. Throughout the despatch of the Government of India there ran a strain of regret that it could not see its way to demonetize the rupee and to assimilate the Indian currency to that prevailing in England. A general perusal of the despatch leaves the impression that though it recommended the assimilation of the Indian currency to that of France and the United States, it did so not because it thought that their systems furnished the best model, but because it believed that a better one was not within reach. Having regard to the accepted view of the French and the United States currency systems, it was natural that the Government of India did not feel very jubilant about its own. According to that view of the currency systems of these two countries, the pcsition of the five-franc piece and the silver dollar has always been presented as being very anomalous. Even so great an authority as Prof. Pierson was unable to assign them a place intelligible in the orthodox scheme of classifying different forms of money.* In a well-ordered system of gold standard of the orthodox type, gold is the only metal freely coined and the only one metal having full legal-tender power ; silver, though coined, is coined only on Government account in limited amounts, and being of less intrinsic value than its nominal value, is a limited legal tender. The former type of coins are called standard coins and the latter subsidiary coins, and the two together make up the ideal of a monometallic gold standard such as has been established in England since 1816. In a scheme of things like this, writers have found it difficult to fit in the dollar or the five-franc piece. Their peculiarity consists in the fact that although their intrinsic value is less than their nominal value they have been inconvertible and are also unlimited legal tender. It is owing to this anomaly that the title of gold standard has been refused to the American and French currency

* Cf. Principles of Economics, Vol. I, p. 569.

systems. Few can have confidence in what is called the limping standard,* in which it is said that somehow "the silver coin, though intrinsically of less value than the gold, hobbles along, maintained at equality by being coupled with its stronger associate."†

But was the French system of currency so very different from the English as to create doubt as to its stability? Whatever may have been the differences between the two systems a closer analysis shows that they are fundamentally identical. If we read together the French bimetallic law of 1803 and the Mint Suspension Decree of 1878 on the one hand, and on the other the provisions of the English Gold Standard Act of 1816, together with the Bank Charter Act of 1844, and compare, do we find any substantial difference between the French and English systems of currency? Prior to 1878 there was an unlimited issue in France of both gold and silver coins of unlimited legal tender. Prior to 1844 there was an unlimited issue in England of both gold sovereigns and Bank of England notes, both of unlimited legal tender. In 1844 England put a limit on the issue of bank notes, but did not deprive the issues of their legal-tender power.‡ In 1878 France did precisely the same thing as England did with her notes in 1844. By the decree of mint suspension, France virtually, though indirectly, put a limit on the silver five-franc coins without depriving them of their legal-tender power. If we regard the French five-franc coins as notes printed on silver, it is difficult to see what constitutes the difference between the two systems which leads economists to call one a gold standard and the other a limping standard. If the silver franc limps or hobbles along, so does the bank note, and the former can hobble better than the latter because of the two it has a comparatively greater intrinsic value. If, however, it is argued that the bank

* It was owing to this want of faith that Germany took away, by the law of October 1, 1907, the full legal-tender power from her silver thalers. In the United States the silver dollar is not legal tender if it is specifically excluded by the terms of a contract. Cf. A. C. Whitaker, *Foreign Exchange*, Appleton, New York, 1920, pp. 8 and 477.

† C. F. W. Taussig, *Principles*, 2nd ed., 1918, p. 280

‡The Bank of England notes were made legal tender by Lord Althorpe's Act of 1833.

note is convertible into gold, while the five-franc piece is not, the reply is that the comparison must be made with the fiduciary notes of the Bank of England. Those notes are practically inconvertible. For, at any given time, with the gold the Bank of England has in its Issue Department the fiduciary portion of the notes remains uncovered, and may, therefore, be regarded as inconvertible as the delimited issue of the five francs. But even if it is insisted that the fiduciary notes cannot be regarded as inconvertible as the five-franc pieces, it must be pointed out that the similarity of the two is not to be determined by considerations of convertibility or inconvertibility. The attribute of convertibility with which the fiduciary notes of the Bank of England are endowed is a superfluous attribute which in no way improves their position as compared with the five-franc pieces. What makes them indentical is the fact that they are both subjected to a fixed limit of issue. Thus viewed, the French limping standard and the English gold standard are nothing but two different illustrations of the "currency principle" in so far as a fixed limit of issue on a fiduciary currency is a cardinal feature of that principle.

Not only is the French monetary system identical with the English in its organization, but the design in both cases was identical. In the controversy which raged over the Bank Charter Act of 1844, the motives of Lord Overstone were not quite clearly grasped by his opponents of the banking school of thought. Lord Overstone was not very much interested in providing a method for preventing the depreciation of the note issue, as his opponents thought him to be. His supreme concern was to prevent gold disappearing from circulation. Starting from a chain of reasoning the solidity of which can hardly be said to be open to question, he came to the conclusion that gold would be driven out of circulation by an increase in the issue of notes. To keep gold in circulation the only remedy was to put a limit on the issue of notes, and this was the purpose of the Bank Charter Act of 1844. Now, precisely the same was the object of France in suspending the coinage of silver. As has already been pointed out, owing to the fall in the value of silver after 1873, gold was being rapidly driven out of circulation by the substitution of this depreciated metal. To prevent this result from assuming a vast proportion, the French adopted the same remedy as that of Lord Overstone, and through their suspension of silver coinage protected their gold from going out of circulation, which would have certainly been the case if no limit had been put on silver issues.

It would not, therefore, be amiss to argue that the plan contemplated by the Government of India, and approved of by the Fowler Committee in being similar to the French system, was based on the same principles as governed the English currency system, which, according to Jevons, were a "monument of sound financial legislation."

## CHAPTER V

# FROM A GOLD STANDARD TO A GOLD EXCHANGE STANDARD

For once it seemed that the problem of a depreciating rupee was satisfactorily solved. The anxieties and difficulties that extended over a long period of a quarter of a century could not but have been fully compensated by the adoption of a remedy like the one described in the last chapter. But by an unkind turn of events, the system originally contemplated failed to come into being. In its place there grew up a system of currency in India which was in every way the very reverse of it. Some thirteen years after legislative sanction had been given to the recommendations of the Fowler Committee, the Chamberlain Commission on Indian Finance and Currency reported that

> "in spite of the fact the Government adopted and intended to carry out the recommendations of the Committee of 1898, the Indian currency system to-day differs considerably from that contemplated by the Committee, whilst the mechanism for maintaining the exchange has some important features in common with the suggestions made to the Committee by Mr. A. M. Lindsay."*

It will be recalled† that in Mr. Lindsay's scheme Indian currency was to be entirely a rupee currency; the Government was to give rupees in every case in return for gold, and gold for rupees only in case of foreign remittances. The scheme was to be worked through the instrumentality of two offices, one located in London and the other located in India, the former to sell drafts on the latter when rupees where wanted and the latter to sell drafts on the former when gold was wanted. Surprisingly similar is the system prevailing in India to-day. Corresponding to Mr. Lindsay's proposals, which, be it noted, were rejected in 1898, the Government of India has built up two reserves, one of gold and the other of rupees, out of the cash balances, the paper

---

* Report, P. P. Cd. 7068 of 1913, p. 13.

† *See* Chap. IV, *supra*.

currency, and the gold-standard reserve. Each of these is, by the nature of the currency system, composite. The cash balances, which are fed from revenue receipts, gather in their net rupees as well as sovereigns, both being legal tender. Notes being issuable against both, the paper-currency reserve always contains sovereigns and rupees. Up to August, 1915, the gold-standard reserve was also held partly in gold and partly in rupees.* By a system of sorting, technically called "transfers," the Government secures the command over rupees and sovereigns necessary for discharging the obligations it has undertaken.† The location of these funds is also very much as designed by Mr. Lindsay. The cash balances, being the till-money of the Government, are necessarily distributed between the Government of India in India and the Secretary of State in London, the portion held by the latter being entirely in gold and that held by the former being in silver. The gold-standard reserve, like the cash balances, is not a statutory reserve. Consequently its location is perfectly within the competence of the Executive. That being so, it has been so arranged that the gold portion of the fund shall be held by the Secretary of State in London, and the rupee portion, so long as it was maintained, by the Government of India in India. The only reserve which did not easily lend itself to currency manipulation was the paper-currency reserve, for the reason that its disposition and location were governed by law. In that behalf, legal power has been taken to alter the location of the gold part of that reserve by making permanent the provision of the temporary Act II of 1898, which authorized the issue of notes in India against gold tendered to the Secretary of State in London. Thus the Secretary of State and the Government of India, under the new system of currency, hold two reserves, one of gold, mainly in the possession of the former and located in London, and the other of rupees, entirely in the possession of the latter and held in India. But the similarity of the existing system to that of Mr. Lindsay is not confined to the maintenance of these funds and their location. It extends even to the modes of operating these two funds. For,

* The rupee branch has been discontinued since that date, on the recommendation of the Chamberlain Commission.

† Besides, if the Government falls short of rupees, it has the legal power to convert the gold in the paper-currency reserve into rupees to replenish the stock.

as suggested by Mr. Lindsay, when rupees are wanted in India the Secretary of State sells what are called "Council Bills," encashable into rupees at the Government Treasuries in India, thereby providing the rupee currency in India. When gold is wanted the Government of India sells what are called "Reverse Councils" on the home Treasury in London, which are encashed by the Secretary of State, thereby providing gold for foreign remittances. The result of the sale of "Council Bills" and of the "Reserve Councils" on the two funds has been to transform the Indian currency from being a gold standard with a gold currency, as desired by the Fowler Committee, into what is called a gold standard without a gold currency, as wished for by Mr. Lindsay.

This system which has grown up in place of the system originally contemplated by the Government of India is called the gold-exchange standard. Whatever that designation may mean it was not the plan originally contemplated by the Government of India in 1898. How the departure came about we shall deal with in another place. Here it is enough to state—one may also say necessary, for many writers seem to have fallen into an error on this point—*that the Government did not start to establish a gold-exchange standard*. Rather it was contemplating the establishing of a true gold standard, which, however inadequately understood by the men who framed it, was in essential agreement with the principles governing the English Bank Charter Act of 1844.

What are we to say about the new system ? The Chamberlain Commission, while reporting that there was a departure from the ideal of a gold standard with a gold currency, observed*:—

> " But to state there has been this departure is by no means to condemn the action taken, or the system actually in force. "

Now why not ? Is not the system the same as that proposed by the Government in India in 1878 and condemned by the Committee of 1879 ? It is true the arguments urged against that plan by the Committee of 1879 were not of much weight.† Nonetheless the plan was essentially unsound.

* Report, par. 46

† *See supra*, Chap. IV.

The material point in the introduction of a gold standard must be said to be one of limitation on the volume of rupees, and it is from this point of view that we must judge the plan. But there was nothing in the plan of 1878 that could be said to have been calculated to bring that about. Far from putting any limitation on the volume of rupees, the plan had deliberately left the Mints open to the free coinage of silver. A matter of some interest in the plan was the projection of a system of seignorage so arranged so to make the bullion value of the rupee equal to the gold value given to it. But as a means of limiting the coinage of rupees it was futile. The mere levy of a seignorage cannot be regarded as sufficient in all circumstances to effect a limitation of coinage. Everything would have depended upon how closely the seignorage corresponded with the difference between the mint and market price of silver in terms of gold. If the seignorage fell short of the difference it would have given a direct impetus to increased coinage of rupees until their redundancy had driven them to a discount. In this respect the plan was a reproduction in a worse form of the English Gold Standard Act of 1816. Like the Government of India's plan of 1878, that Act, while purporting to introduce a gold standard, had authorized the opening of the Mint, which was closed, to the free coinage of silver with a seignorage charge. It is not generally recognized how stupid were the provisions of that Act,* the ideal of all orthodox gold monometallists, in so far as they contemplated the free coinage of silver. Fortunately for England the Royal Proclamation, compelling the Mint Master to coin all silver brought to the Mint, was never issued. Otherwise the working of the gold standard would have been considerably jeopardized.† The Act of 1816 had at least taken one precaution, and that was a limit on the legal-tender power of silver. In the scheme of the Government of India, not only free coinage of silver was permitted, but silver was conceded the right of full

*Cf., however, R. G. Hawtrey, *Currency and Credit*, 1919, pp. 302-3.

†Some witnesses before the Lords Committee on Cash payments, appointed in 1819, raised doubts whether, having regard to the silver clause of the Act of 1816, resumption of cash payments was worth while as a means of establishing a gold standard in England. Cf. particularly the evidence of Mr. Fletcher and also Mr. Mushet before the Committee.

legal tender. In so far, therefore, as the plan did not provide for controlling the volume of rupees it was subversive of the gold standard it had in view.

The only difference between this plan of 1878 and the system now in operation in India is that under the former the Mints were open to the public, while under the latter they are open to the Government alone. In other words, in the one case rupees were coined on behalf of the public, and in the other they are being coined on behalf of the Government. It is not to be supposed that the plan of closing the Mints to the public was not thought of by the Government in 1878. On the other hand, the Government of India had then considered the feasibility of taking over into its hands the coinage of rupees, and had rejected it on some very excellent grounds. In their despatch outlining the scheme the Government of the day observed :—

> "48. The first point to be guarded in attempting to carry out the proposed change, is to provide for complete freedom for any expansion of the currency which the trade requirements of the country demand. This, we think, could not be properly secured if the Mints were wholly closed for the coining of silver for the public. If this measure were adopted, the responsibility for supplying the silver demand would be thrown on the Government, and in the present position of the market for gold and silver bullion in India it would not be possible to accept such a duty.
>
> "49. What might at first sight appear the simplest, and therefore the best way of allowing for the expansion of the Indian silver currency with a gold standard, would be for the Government to undertake to give silver coin in exchange for gold coin to all comers, at the rates fixed by the new system, and to open the Mints for the coinage of gold, while they were closed for silver. But in the absence of any supply of silver in India from which to obtain the necessary material for coinage, such an obligation could not be accepted, without involving the Government in complicated transactions in the purchase and storing of bullion which it would be very inexpedient to enter on."

With these reasons, interesting in so far as they were prophetic of the scandals connected with the recent silver purchases by the India Office,* we are not directly concerned. What is of importance is whether this difference in the mode of issue makes

* *See* P.P. 400 of 1912.

any vital difference to the question of an effective limit on the volume of rupees. Now, there is a great deal of confused thinking as to the precise virtue of the closing of the Mints to the private coinage of silver. It was generally believed, the closing of the Mints having given a monopoly to the Government in the matter of issuing rupees, that this monopoly would somehow sustain the value of the rupees in terms of gold by preventing their over-issue. The closing of the Mints, it must be admitted, has given the Government the position of a monopolist. But how a monopoly prevents an over-issue is not easy to grasp. The closing of the Mints to the free coinage of silver is the same as depriving banks of the liberty of issuing notes and giving it exclusively to a central bank. But nobody has ever argued that because a central bank has a monopoly of issue it cannot therefore over-issue. Similarly, because the Government of India is a monopolist it would be absurd to argue that it cannot therefore over-issue. Indeed, a monopolist can issue as much as private people put together, if not more. Again, from the standpoint of influence of profits on coinage the present plan is much inferior to that of 1878. It is true in both cases profits depend upon the volume of coinage. But in the former the amount of profit was no incentive to coinage, either to the Government, because it had no power to coin, or to the people who determined the volume of coinage, because the regulation of seignorage practically controlled it by making it unprofitable to bring additional bullion to the Mint. In the present case, the coinage being entirely in the hands of the Government, a hankering after profits, generated by the silly notion of the necessity of a "backing" to the currency, might create an impulse to undertake additional coinage, especially if the price of silver fell very low and produced a wide margin between the Mint and the market price of the rupee.*

If it is argued, as it well may be, that the will of the Government of India as a monopolist, i.e. its desire to see that its currency is not depreciated, may bring about a limitation on the

* From this point of view the proposition of Prof. Keynes, that the gold value of the rupee may be fixed irrespective of the cost price of silver, must, having regard to the existing system of currency, be looked upon as a somewhat unsafe position. Cf. his evidence before the Indian Currency Committee of 1919, Q. 2,688.

issue of rupees which could not have been possible had the Mints remained open to the public in general, the reply is that this will to limit could be effective only if the Government had the power to refuse to issue. Central banks limit their currencies so far as will is concerned, because they are not obligated to issue to anyone and every one. But the position of the Government of India is lamentably weak in this respect. It is bound to issue currency when asked for. It is true that every issue does not involve a net addition to the existing volume of currency; for a portion of the new issue is a re-issue of what is returned from circulation. Nonetheless, it cannot be said that the Government by reason of its monopoly has put an effective limit on the volume of rupee currency. On the other hand, having no escape from the liability to issue currency, the exercise of this cherished privilege has recoiled on the Government, so much so that this monopoly of issue, instead of strengthening the position of the Government, has weakened it considerably.* The view of the Chamberlain Commission†

> "that while the Government are very large dealers in the exchange market, they are not monopolists (!) and it seems doubtful if they could successfully stand out for any such [fixed minimum rate] at all times of the year,"

is therefore interesting as a confession that the closing of the Mints has not had the virtue of so limiting the coinage of rupees as to enable the Government to dictate at all times the price of the rupee, which none but it alone can manufacture.

Thus the present standard is different from the standard proposed in 1878 only in name. If this one is characterized by the adoption of the rate of exchange as an index for regulating the volume of currency, the same must be said of the former. But, as Mr. Hawtrey remarks,‡ whatever means are adopted for the manipulation of the currency,

> "the value of the rupee will be determined by the quantity in circulation."

---

* The danger involved in this indefinite liability to issue rupee currency was recognized by the Smith Currency Committee of 1919, which recommended that this obligation should be withdrawn. *See* Report, par. 68. Of course its motive was different.

† Report, par. 182.

‡ *Currency and Credit*, 1919, p. 341.

In other words, what must be said to be essential for the safety of a gold standard is a provision against over-issue of rupees. But, as we saw, neither the plan of 1878 nor the present one can be said to be free from that danger. Consequently we must conclude that, being essentially alike, the arguments that are valid against the former are also valid against the latter.

But the Chamberlain Commission will not allow that the exchange standard is a resuscitation of a condemned plan. On the other hand, it has sought to inspire confidende in that standard by holding out *

> "that the present Indian system has close affinities with other currency systems in some of the great European countries and elsewhere. . . ."

To get an idea as to what these affinities are, or rather were, we must look into Chapter II of Mr. Keynes's interesting teatise on *Indian Currency and Finance*. In that treatise of his, Mr. Keynes has attempted to show that there is a fundamental likeness between the operations of the Indian currency system and the operations as they used to be of the central banks of some of the important countries of Europe. He found that it used to be the practice of these banks to hold foreign bills of exchange for the purpose of making remittances to foreign countries. Between the selling of such foreign bills and selling of reverse councils by the Government of India he observed a close fundamental likeness, inasmuch as both involved

> "the use of a local currency mainly not of gold, some degree of unwillingness to supply gold locally in exchange for the local currency, but a high degree of willingness to sell foreign exchange for payment in local currency at a certain maximum rate." †

But, as Prof. Kemmerer points out,‡ it is difficult to see what likeness there is between the Government of India selling reverse councils and the European banks holding foreign bills. Far from being alike, the two practices must be regarded as the opposite of each other. In selling reverse councils

* Report, par. 46.

† Keynes, *Indian Currency and Finance*, p. 29.

‡ Cf. his review of Keynes in the *Quarterly Journal of Economics*, February, 1914, p. 374.

"the Government sells drafts against its foreign gold credit (i.e. its gold reserve), when money at home is relatively redundant, as evidenced by exchange having reached the gold export point. Thereby it relieves the redundancy through the withdrawing from circulation and locking up the local money received in payment for the drafts. Under the practice of holding foreign bills to protect the money market, the central bank sells its foreign bills, when money at home is relatively scarce, as means of securing gold for importation or preventing its exportation. In the former case, the sale of drafts takes the place of an exportation of gold, and the resulting withdrawal of local money from circulation is in essentials an exportation; in the latter case the sale of the drafts abroad is part of a process for securing gold for importation, or for preventing its exportation."

The Indian currency system therefore bears no analogy to the European currency systems, as Mr. Keynes would have us believe. But if a parallel is needed, then the true parallel to the Indian system of currency is that system which prevailed in England during the Bank Suspension period (1797-1821). The fundamental likeness between the two systems becomes quite unmistakable if we keep aside for the moment the remittance operations of the Government of India and the Secretary of State, which becloud the true features of the Indian currency system. If we tear this veil and take a close view, the following appear to be the prominent features of the Indian system :—

(1) The gold sovereign is full legal tender.

(2) The silver rupee is also full legal tender.

(3) The Government undertakes to give rupees for sovereigns, but does not undertake to give sovereigns for rupees, i.e. the rupee is an inconvertible currency unlimited in issue.

Turning to the English system of currency during the period of the Bank Suspension, we find :—

(1) The gold sovereign was full legal tender.

(2) The paper notes of the Bank of England circulated as money of general acceptability by common custom if not by law.*

(3) The Bank of England undertook to give notes for gold or mercantile bills or any other kind of good equivalent, but did not give gold for notes, i.e. the notes formed an inconvertible currency unlimited in issue.

* Cf. Andreades, *History of Bank of England*, p. 198.

Only in one respect can the analogy be said to be imperfect. The Indian Government has undertaken—not, be it noted, as a statutory obligation, but merely as a matter subject to the will of the executive, to convert the rupee into gold at a fixed rate for foreign remittances if the exchange falls below par. This, it must be allowed, the Bank of England did not do during the suspension period. Everything, therefore, turns upon the question whether this much convertibility is a sufficient distinction to mark off the Indian currency from the English currency of the suspension period into a separate category and invalidate the analogy herein said to exist between the two systems. To be able to decide one way or the other we must firmly grasp what is the true import of convertibility. Prejudice against an inconvertible currency is so strong that people are easily satisfied with a system which provides some kind of convertibility, however small. But to assume this attitude is to trifle with a very crucial question. We must keep clear in our mind what it is that essentially marks off a convertible from an inconvertible currency. The distinction commonly drawn, that the one is an automatic and the other is a managed currency, must be discarded as a gross error. For, if by a managed currency we mean a currency the issue of which depends upon the discretion of the issuer, then a convertible currency is as much a managed currency as an inconvertible currency is. The only point of contrast lies in the fact that in the management of a convertible currency the discretion as to issue is regulated, while in an inconvertible currency it is unregulated. But even if regulated the issue remains discretionary and to that extent a convertible currency is not so safe as to mark it off from an inconvertible currency. The enlargement of its issue being discretionary and the effect of such issues being to drive specie out of circulation, a convertible currency may easily become inconvertible. The difference between a convertible and an inconvertible currency is therefore ultimately a distinction between a prudent and an imprudent management of the right to issue currency. In other words, convertibility is a brake on the power of issue. Bearing this in mind, and also the fact that a convertible currency by reason of mismanagement has the tendency to become inconvertible, it is possible for us to imagine how severe must be the obligations as to convertibility in order to prevent prudent management of currency from degenerating into an imprudent management resulting in over-issue. If, therefore, it is true that in countries having a convertible currency the affairs were so prudently managed that when specie left the country the paper money not only did not increase to take its place, but actually diminished, and that usually by a greater absolute amount than the gold currency, it was because the obligations as to convertibility were those of "effective absolute immediate convertibility."* We can now appreciate why Prof. Sumner said † that

> "convertibility in the currency is like conscientiousness in a man: it has many grades and is valuable in proportion as it is strict and pure."

That being so, it would be foolish to assume that we are immune from the consequences of an inconvertible currency until we know what is the grade of the convertibility that is provided. Now, what is the character of the convertibility of the rupee in India? It is a deferred, delegalized, delocalized, and therefore a devitalized kind of convertibility. Indeed, really speaking it is not a convertibility, but rather it is a moratorium which is a negation of convertibility, for what does the provision for convertibility for foreign remittances mean in practice? It simply means that *until* a fall of exchange takes place there is a moratorium or inconvertibility in respect of the rupee. Not only is there a moratorium as long as exchange does not fall, but there is no guarantee that the moratorium will be lifted when a fall does occur. It may not be lifted, for it is a matter of conscience and not of law. ‡ Is such a grade of convertibility, if one has a predilection for that term, very far removed from the inconvertibility of the bank notes during the suspension period? Let

* "No single word can convey the full meaning," says Prof Nicholson *War Finance*, 2nd ed., 1918, p 36.

† *A History of American Currency*, New York, 1874, p. 116.

‡ The Finance Member of the Viceroy's Council, in his Financial Statement for 1908-09 (p. 23, italics not in the original), observed :— "Had we complied with the demand for issues [of gold] without limit, the whole available supply might have been drawn off in a few weeks.... *For these reasons we decided to stand by our legal rights. We are not bound to give sovereigns in exchange for rupees except at our own convenience.* The currency offices were accordingly

those who will say so. For a person not endowed with high and subtle imagination the distinction between such a convertibility and absolute inconvertibility is too thin to persuade him that the two systems are radically different; indeed, when we come to analyse the problem of prices in India and outside India we shall find another piece of evidence to show that they are not different, and that the analogy between the two is perfect enough for all practical purposes.

It may, however, be said that an inconvertible currency may be so well managed as not to give rise to a premium on gold, so that there may be little to choose between it and a perfectly convertible currency. But whether an inconvertible currency will be so well managed is a question of practical working. Again, whether the absence of premium on gold suffices to place an inconvertible currency on par with a convertible currency, so far as the price problem is concerned, is also a matter depending on circumstances. All these questions will be considered in their proper places.* What we are considering at this stage are the inherent potentialities of an inconvertible currency. Suffice it to say here that the name Gold Exchange Standard cannot conceal the true nature of the Indian Monetary Standard. Its essence consists in the fact that although gold is unlimited legal tender there is alongside an unlimited issue of another form of

---

instructed *not* to issue gold in larger quantities than £10,000 to any individual on any one day." These words were used to explain the attitude of the Government regarding its sense of obligation as to convertibility of the rupee in the exchange crisis of 1907 ! The degree of convertibility being a matter of administrative discretion it is difficult to define the extent to which it is given effect to in practice. Official evidence is inclined to impress upon the public that practically the rupee is convertible. If that is so, why not make it *legally* convertible. For, if convertibility is complete in practice a legal convertibility cannot impose upon the Government greater obligations than what the official evidence suggests the Government to be actually assuming. It is said that Government does not do so because it is afraid that exchange speculators will take advantage of it. But why should they not ? Are they not holders of rupees ? It does not, however, appear to have been adequately realized that this defence implies that the currency is issued so much beyond the point of "saturation" that its value is always on the margin of being affected by an element of speculation.

* For reasons giving rise to a premium on gold in terms of the rupee, *see* Chap. VI. For reasons explaining how there can be a general depreciation of the rupee without there being a specific depreciation of it in terms of gold, *see* end of Chap. VI and beginning of Chap. VII.

fiduciary currency well-nigh inconvertible, and also possessing the quality of unlimited legal tender.

It needs no acute power of penetration to see that, so interpreted, the existing currency system in India is the opposite of the system outlined by the Government in 1898 and passed by the Fowler Committee. The two are opposites of each other for the same reason for which the Bank Charter Act was the opposite of the Bank Suspension Act in England. Under both the Acts the currency in England was a mixed currency, partly gold and partly paper. The difference was that by the Bank Suspension Act the issue of gold became limited and that of paper unlimited, while under the Bank Charter Act the process was reversed, so that the issue of paper became limited and that of gold unlimited. In the same manner, under the original scheme of the Government of India, the issue of rupees was to be limited and that of gold unlimited. Under the existing system the issue of gold has become limited while that of rupee has become unlimited.

Was this an improvement on the plan originally contemplated by the Government of India ? The only objection to that plan was that it made the rupee an inconvertible rupee.* But is convertibility such a necessary condition, and, if so, when ? The idea that convertibility is necessary to maintain the value a currency is, on the face of it, a preposterous idea. No one wants the conversion of bananas into apples to maintain the value of bananas. Bananas maintain their value by reason of the fact that there is a demand for them and their supply is limited. There is no reason to suppose that currency forms an exception to this rule. Only we are more concerned to maintain the value of currency at a stable level than we are of bananas because currency forms a common measure of value. What is wanted to maintain the value of currency, or of any other thing for the matter of that, is an effective limit on its supply. Convertibility is useful, not because it directly maintains the value of a currency, which is nonsense, but because it has the effect of putting a limit on the supply of currency. But con-

* Both Lindsay and Probyn had attacked the plan of the Government of India on this score, and had claimed that their plans were superior because they had at least provided some sort of convertibility.

vertibility is not the only way of achieving that object. A plan which lays down an absolute limit on issue has the same effect—indeed, a far more powerful effect—on the supply of currency. Now, had the Mints remained entirely closed to the coinage of rupees there would have been placed an absolute limit on the issue of currency, and all the purposes of convertibility would have been served by such an inconvertible rupee. Nay, more; such an inconvertible rupee currency would have been infinitely superior to the kind of pseudo-convertible rupee which we have in India to-day.* With an absolute limit there could have been no danger of a fall in the value of the rupee. If anything there would have been a danger of an indefinite appreciation of the rupee, but that was effectually guarded against by gold having been made general legal tender. A second effect of an absolute limit on the currency would have been to free it from management by reason of the fact that all question regarding the volume of issues had been settled once for all.

In these respects, therefore, the gold-exchange standard is an impairment of the original plan of an inconvertible rupee with fixed limit of issue supplemented by gold. Again, from the standpoint of controlling the price-level, the exchange standard cannot be said to have been an improvement on the original plan. Of course, it is possible to say that such a perversion of the original system is no matter for regret. Whether gold is a standard of value, or whether fiduciary money is a standard of value, is a matter of indifference, for neither can be said to have furnished a stable standard of value. A gold standard has proved to be as unstable as a paper standard, because both are susceptible of contraction as well as expansion. All this, no doubt, is true. Nevertheless it is to be noted that in any monetary system there is no danger of indefinite contraction.† What is to be guarded against is the possibility of indefinite expansion. The possibility of indefinite expansion, however, varies with the nature of money. When the standard of value is standard metallic money the expansion cannot be very great, for the cost of production acts

* In his comparison of the Limping Standard with the Exchange Standard, Prof. Fisher seems entirely to overlook these considerations. Cf. his Purchasing Power, etc., 1911, pp. 131-32.

† Cf. Hawtrey, R. G., op. cit, Chap I.

as a sufficient limiting influence. When a standard of value is a convertible paper money the provisions as to reserve act as a check on its expansion. But when a standard of value consists of a money the value of which is greater than its cost and is inconvertible, the currency must be said to be fraught with the fatal facility of indefinite expansion, which is another name for depreciation or rise of prices. It cannot, therefore, be said that the Bank Charter Act made no improvement on the Bank Restriction Act. Indeed, it was a great improvement, for it substituted a currency far more liable to expansion. Now the rupee is a debased coin,* inconvertible, and is unlimited legal tender. As such, it belongs to that order of money which has inherent in it the potentiality of indefinite expansion, i.e. depreciation and rise of prices. As a safeguard against this the better plan was no doubt the one originally designed, namely of putting a limit on the issue of rupees, so as to make the Indian currency system analogous to the English system governed by the Bank Charter Act of 1844.

If there is any force in the line of reasoning adopted above, then it is not easy to agree with the opinion entertained by the Chamberlain Commission of the Exchange Standard. Indeed, it raises a query whether for all that the Commission said there is not somewhere some weakness in the system likely to bring about its breakdown. It therefore becomes incumbent to examine the foundations of that standard from a fresh point of view.

* It is difficult to understand why some writers on Indian currency do not like to admit this fact. Cf. the discussion on Mr. Madan's paper at the annual meeting of the Indian Economic Association (*Indian Journal of Economics*, Vol. III, Part 4, Serial No. 12, p. 560). It is true the debasement of the rupee is not so obvious as it would have been had it taken the form of continuing the weight and making it baser, or of preserving the same fineness and making it lighter. But, as Harris points out in his *Essay upon Money and Coins* (Part II, Chap. I, par. 8), the "altering the denominations of the coins, without making any alteration at the Mint or in the coins themselves," "as supposing ninepence, or as much silver as there is in ninepence, should be called a shilling," is a mode of debasement not different from that of the rupee, and is virtually the same as the other two modes of debasement. So viewed it is difficult to avoid the conclusion that the rupee is a debased coin.

# CHAPTER VI

## STABILITY OF THE EXCHANGE STANDARD

It will be recalled that at the time the Indian Mints were closed to the free coinage of silver there were two parties in the country, one in favour of and the other opposed to the closure. Being placed in an embarrassing position by the fall of the rupee, the Government of the day was anxious to close the Mints and raise its value with a view to obtaining relief from the burden of its gold payments. On the other hand it was urged, on behalf of the producing interest of the country, that a rise in the exchange value of the rupee would cause a disaster to Indian trade and industry. One of the reasons, it was argued, why Indian industry had advanced by such leaps and bounds as it did during the period of 1873-1893 was to be found in the bounty given to the Indian export trade by the falling exchange. If the fall of the rupee was arrested by the Mint closure, it was feared that such an event was bound to cut Indian trade both ways. It would give the silver-using countries a bounty as over against India, and would deprive India of the bounty which it obtained from the falling exchange as over against gold-using countries.

Theory had already scoffed at these fears. It is therefore interesting to see that later history has also confirmed the verdict of theory. Indian trade with a gold-standard country like England or a silver-standard country like China did not suffer a setback, notwithstanding an arrest in the fall of the rupee. The following figures furnish sufficient evidence to support the contrary :—

## TABLE XXV

TRADE OF INDIA WITH UNITED KINGDOM (BEFORE AND AFTER THE MINT CLOSURE)

| Annual Average | Exports to U. K. | | | Imports from U. K. | | |
|---|---|---|---|---|---|---|
| | Merchandise | Bullion and Specie | Total | Merchandise | Bullion and Specie. | Total |
| | £ | £ | £ | £ | £ | £ |
| I 1889-93 | 31,569,891 | 1,180,646 | 32,750,537 | 31,837,482 | 7,694,149 | 39,531,631 |
| II 1894-98 | 26,329,764 | 2,215,049 | 24,544,813 | 28,963,180 | 6,750,736 | 35,713,916 |
| III 1899-1903 | 28,709,819 | 2,089,656 | 30,799,475 | 33,498,480 | 7,301,172 | 40,799,652 |
| IV 1903-8 | 36,784,628 | 2,232,857 | 39,017,485 | 47,294,311 | 9,586,706 | 56,881,017 |
| Percentage of Increase (+) or Decrease (—) in— | | | | | | |
| Period II in comparison with Period I | —16.598 | +87.613 | —25.055 | — 9.028 | —12.261 | — 9.657 |
| Period III in comparison with Period II | + 9.039 | — 5.661 | +25.483 | +15.659 | + 8.154 | +14.240 |
| Period IV in comparison with Period III | +28.126 | + 6.853 | +26.682 | +41.183 | +31.304 | +39.415 |
| Period IV in comparison with Period I | +16.518 | +89.122 | +19.135 | +48.549 | +24.597 | +43.887 |

TABLE XXVI

TRADE OF INDIA WITH CHINA

| Annual Average | Exports to China. | | | Imports from China. | | |
|---|---|---|---|---|---|---|
| | Merchandise | Treasure | Total | Merchandise | Treasure | Total. |
| | £ | £ | £ | £ | £ | £ |
| I 1889-93 | 9,454,014 | 20,223 | 9,474,238 | 1,666,840 | 1,992,914 | 3,659,754 |
| II 1893-98 | 8,509,284 | 112,105 | 8,621,389 | 1,713,529 | 503,357 | 2,216,886 |
| III 1898-1903 | 9,679,830 | 183,647 | 9,863,477 | 1,309,975 | 798,053 | 2,108,028 |
| IV 1903-8 | 12,461,535 | 160,879 | 12,622,414 | 1,248,822 | 919,402 | 2,168,224 |
| Percentage of Increase (+) or Decrease (—) in— | | | | | | |
| Period II in comparison with Period I | — 9.993 | +454.333 | — 9.002 | + 2.801 | —74.743 | —39.425 |
| Period III in comparison with Period II | +13.756 | + 63.817 | +14.407 | —23.551 | +58.546 | — 4.910 |
| Period IV in comparison with Period III | +28.737 | — 12.398 | +27.971 | — 4.668 | +15.206 | + 2.856 |
| Period IV in comparison with Period I | +31.812 | +695.508 | +33.229 | —25.078 | —53.866 | —40.755 |

That the arrest in the fall of the rupee should have lifted the burden from Indian finances was just as was expected to follow from the closure of the Mints. Notwithstanding important reductions in taxation and large expenditure of social utility, the annual budgets since the Mint closure have shown few deficits (*see* p. 171).

Now there is a tendency among some writers to interpret these facts as unmistakable proofs of the soundness of the currency system. It is argued that if the trade of the country has not received a setback,* and if the finances of the country have improved,† then the implication is that the currency of which such results can be predicated must be good. It is not necessary to warn students of currency that such easy views on the soundness of the currency system, however plausible, are devoid of the logic necessary to carry conviction. Trade no doubt is dependent on good money, but the growth of trade is not a conclusive proof that the money is good. It should be noted that during the periods of debased coinages so common at one time the social misery and nuisance arising therefrom were intolerable, yet during the same periods it was possible for countries to make great advance in trade. Speaking of seventeenth-century England, when that country was afflicted with debased and constantly changing coinage and when there was, besides, a long period of civil war and confusion, Lord Liverpool, who was above all statesmen of his day most alive to the evils of a bad currency, remarks :—

> "It is certain, however, that during the whole of this period, when our coins were in so great a state of confusion, the commerce of the kingdom was progressively improving, and the balance of trade almost always in favour of this country." ‡

That commerce can increase even when currency is bad is easily supported from the experience of India herself. In no period did Indian trade make such strides as it did between 1873 and 1893. Was the Indian currency of that period good? On the other hand, it is possible to hold that if trade is

* Keynes, op. cit., p. 3.

† Barbour, D., *The Standard of Value*, p. 224.

‡ *A Treatise on the Coins of the Realm* (reprint of 1880), p. 135.

## TABLE XXVII

FINANCES OF THE GOVERNMENT

| Years | Surplus + Deficit — | Years. | Surplus — Deficit— | Years | Surplus + Deficit — | Years. | Surplus + Deficit — | Years. | Surplus + Deficit — |
|---|---|---|---|---|---|---|---|---|---|
| | Rs. | | £ | | £ | | £ | | £ |
| 1893-94 | —1,546,998 | 1898 9 | +2,640 873 | 1903-4 | +2,996,400 | 1908-9 | —3,737,710 | 1913-14 | +2,312,423 |
| 1894-95 | + 693,110 | 1899-1900 | +2,774,623 | 1904-5 | +3 456,066 | 1909-10 | + 606,641 | 1914-15 | —1,785,270 |
| 1895-96 | +1,533,998 | 1900-1 | +1,670,204 | 1905-6 | +2,091,854 | 1910 11 | +3,936,287 | 1915-16 | —1,188,661 |
| 1896-97 | —1,705,022 | 1901-2 | +4,950,243 | 1906-7 | +1,589,340 | 1911-12 | +3,940,334 | 1916-17 | +7,478,170 |
| 1897-98 | —5,359,211 | 1902-3 | +3,069,549 | 1907-8 | + 300,615 | 1912-13 | +3,107,634 | — | — |

good it may be *because* the currency is bad. The trade of India between 1873 and 1893 flourished because it received a bounty. But the bounty was a mulcting of the Indian labourer, whose wages did not rise as fast as prices, so that the Indian prosperity of that period was founded not upon production, but upon depredation made possible by the inflation of currency.

Similarly it cannot be granted without reserve that the new currency system must be good because it has obviated the burden of the gold payments and given relief to the Indian taxpayer. Such a view involves a misconception of the precise source of the burden of India's gold payments during the period of falling exchange. It has been widely held that the burden of gold payments was caused by the fall in the gold value of silver, a view which carried with it the necessary implication that if India had been a gold-standard country she would have escaped that heavy burden. That it is an erroneous view hardly needs demonstration.* It is not to be denied that India bore an extra burden arising from the increased value of the gold payments. But what is not sufficiently realized is that it was a burden which weighed on all gold debtors irrespective of the question whether their standard was gold or silver. In this respect the position of a gold-standard country like Australia was not different from a silver-standard country like India. In so far as they were gold debtors they suffered each in the same way from the same cause, namely the appreciation of the standard in which their debts were measured. The fact that one discharged her debts in gold and the other in Silver made no difference in their condition, except that the use of silver by India to discharge her debts served as a refractory medium through which it was possible to see the magnitude of the burden she bore. The fall of silver measured and not caused the burden of India's gold payments. The arrest in the fall of the rupee cannot be accepted as a *prima facie* proof of a relief to the taxpayer and therefore an evidence of the soundness of the currency system. It is possible that the benefit may have been too dearly paid for.

---

* Cf. evidence of Prof Marshall before the Gold and Silver Commission, 1886 Q. 10,140-50.

Although favourably impressed by the increase of trade and the buoyancy of Government finances under the exchange standard, the Chamberlain Commission did not care to found its case for it on the basis of such arguments. The chief ground on which it rested was that the currency system was capable of maintaining the exchange value of the rupee at a fixed par with gold.* We must therefore proceed to examine this claim made by the Commission on behalf of the exchange standard. The table on p. 174 presents the requisite data for an elucidation of the question.

Assuming, for the moment, the criterion laid down by the Commission to be correct, can it be said from the data given above that the rupee has maintained its gold value? It would be over-confident if not rash to say that the system, even from the narrow point of view of the Commission, has been an unquestioned success.

Between June, 1893, and January, 1917, the rupee was rated to gold at the rate of 1 rupee equal to 7.53344 troy grs. of fine gold. At that rate the sovereign should be equal to 15 rupees, the mint price of gold should be Rs. 23-14-4 per tola (i.e. 180 grs.) of bar gold 100 touch, and the exchange on London should be 1s. 4d., and should have varied within 1s. 4.125d., the import point, and 1s. 3.906d., the export point, for gold.

Taking a general survey of the stability of the rupee with regard to its value in terms of gold, it will be noticed that from the date of the Mint closure up to 1898 the rupee was far below par. The depreciation of the rupee, measured in terms of exchange or price of gold or sovereign, ranged somewhere between 25 to 30 per cent. So great was the depreciation that it redoubled the difficulties confronting the Government when the rupee was not fixed to gold. The financing the Home Treasury by the usual means of selling Council Bills became well-nigh impossible.† The Secretary of State found himself in an embarrassing position. Offering to sell below par involved the obloquy of having led the way to the defeat of the policy of stabilizing exchange. Refusing to sell at market rates involv-

* Report, pp. 18 and 20.

† *See* Commons Paper 7 of 1894, East India (Currency and Sale of Bills).

## TABLE XXVIII

### Gold Value of the Rupee

| As expressed in Terms of Foreign Exchange Rate on London. Par R. — 1s. 4d. | | | As expressed in Terms of Gold. | | | | |
|---|---|---|---|---|---|---|---|
| | | | Years. | (1) Rupee Price of Sovereigns. Par Rs. 15 — 1 Sovereign. | | (2) Rupee Price of Bar Gold. Par Tola — Rs. 23-14-4. | |
| Years. | Highest. | Lowest | | Highest. | Lowest. | Highest. | Lowest. |
| | s. d | s d. | | Rs A P. | Rs. A. P. | Rs A. P. | Rs. A. P. |
| 1892-93 | 1 3.969 | 1 2.625 | 1893 | 16 10 6 | 15 6 0 | 26 11 0 | 24 14 0 |
| 1893-94 | 1 4.031 | 1 1.500 | 1894 | 19 0 0 | 16 1 0 | 32 4 0 | 25 9 0 |
| 1894-95 | 1 1.906 | 1 0.000 | 1895 | 19 5 0 | 18 2 6 | 30 8 0 | 27 6 0 |
| 1895-96 | 1 2.875 | 1 1.000 | 1896 | 17 7 0 | 16 1 0 | 27 13 6 | 27 2 0 |
| 1896-97 | 1 3.842 | 1 1.781 | 1897 | 16 10 0 | 15 3 0 | 26 12 6 | 25 4 0 |
| 1897-98 | 1 4.125 | 1 2.250 | 1898 | 15 7 0 | 15 1 0 | 24 10 0 | 24 0 0 |
| 1898-99 | 1 4.156 | 1 3.094 | 1899 | 15 4 0 | 15 0 0 | 24 2 0 | 23 4 0 |
| 1899-1900 | 1 4.375 | 1 3.875 | 1900 | 15 1 3 | 15 0 0 | 24 2 0 | 23 15 6 |
| 1900-1901 | 1 4.156 | 1 3.875 | 1901 | 15 0 0 | 15 0 0 | 24 2 0 | 24 0 0 |
| 1901-1902 | 1 4.125 | 1 3.875 | 1902 | 15 4 6 | 15 2 6 | 24 2 6 | 24 0 0 |
| 1902-1903 | 1 4.156 | 1 3.875 | 1903 | 15 3 0 | 15 1 6 | 24 3 0 | 24 0 0 |
| 1903-1904 | 1 4.156 | 1 3.875 | 1904 | 15 5 0 | 15 1 3 | 24 2 0 | 24 0 3 |
| 1904-1905 | 1 4.156 | 1 3.970 | 1905 | 15 4 0 | 15 1 6 | 24 2 0 | 24 0 0 |
| 1905-1906 | 1 4.156 | 1 3.937 | 1906 | 15 1 0 | 15 2 0 | 24 4 6 | 24 0 0 |
| 1906-1907 | 1 4.187 | 1 3.937 | 1907 | 15 4 0 | 15 0 0 | 24 4 0 | 23 15 6 |
| 1907-1908 | 1 4.187 | 1 3.875 | 1908 | 15 1 0 | 15 0 0 | 24 10 0 | 24 2 0 |
| 1908-1909 | 1 4 | 1 3.875 | 1909 | Premium between 12 and 3% | | 24 3 6 | 23 15 0 |
| 1909-1910 | 1 4.156 | 1 3 875 | 1910 | 15 5 0 | 15 0 0 | 24 4 0 | 23 15 0 |
| 1910-1911 | 1 4.156 | 1 3.875 | 1911 | 15 0 0 | 15 0 0 | 24 0 6 | 23 14 0 |
| 1911-1912 | 1 4.156 | 1 3.937 | 1912 | 15 0 0 | 15 0 0 | 24 0 0 | 23 14 0 |
| 1912-1913 | 1 4.156 | 1 3.970 | 1913 | 15 0 0 | 15 0 0 | 24 0 3 | — |
| 1913-1914 | 1 4.156 | 1 3 937 | 1914 | 15 14 0 | 15 2 0 | 26 10 0 | 23 15 6 |
| 1914-1915 | 1 4.094 | 1 3.937 | 1915 | 15 13 6 | 15 5 0 | 25 14 0 | 24 8 0 |

ed the danger of a dry Treasury. The Government of India suggested that the Secretary should lay down a minimum rate for or a maximum amount of the bills that he put upon the market. The Secretary of State agreed to neither, but consented to reduce his drawings so as not to unduly depress the exchange rate. The drawings of the Secretary of State during the first fiscal year since the Mint closure have been the smallest on record :—

TABLE XXIX

COUNCIL DRAWINGS

| Date of Drawing | Amount of Drawings £ 1, 000 omitted | Rate at which drawn (Pence per Rupee). |
|---|---|---|
| 1893. June | 2,478 | 15.039 |
| July | 25 | 15.974 |
| August | 78 | 15.243 |
| September | 7 | 15.350 |
| October | 5 | 15.334 |
| November | 617 | 15.251 |
| December | 14 | 15.242 |
| 1894. January | 98 | 14.408 |
| February | 1,023 | 13.787 |
| March | 1,915 | 13.870 |
| April | 1,368 | 13.626 |

The curtailment of drawings to save the rate of exchange from being lowered was not an unmitigated good, for it imposed the necessity of a resort to the by no means inexpensive method of sterling borrowings to finance the Home Treasury.* The remittances by drawings fell short of the net disbursements of the Home Treasury in 1893-94 by £6,588,000, which deficit was met by permanent sterling borrowings to the extent of £7,430,000, the interest on which added to the already overheavy burden of the gold payments. Rather than incur such a penalty the Secretary of State gave up the attempt to dominate

* Evidence of Sir H. Waterfield before the Fowler Committee, Q. 4,332-39.

the market and preferred to follow it. But this let-go policy was not without its cost. The drop in the exchange below 1s. 4d. added to the burden of remittances to the Home Treasury, and also compelled the Government to grant exchange compensation allowance to its European officers, civil and military—an aid which it had so far withheld. The cost to the Government involved by the fall of the rupee below par was quite a considerable sum.*

## TABLE XXX

### Cost of the Fall of the Rupee

| Years. | Loss on Council Bills being sold below par | Loss by Exchange Compensation Allowance | Loss by Increase of Pay of British Troops | Total on each Account in each Year | Total on all Counts for three Years | |
|---|---|---|---|---|---|---|
| | | | | | In Rupees. | In Sterling at 1s 4d |
| | | | | | Rs. | £ |
| 1894-95 | 3,74,15 000 | 78 02,000 | 37 84 000 | 4 90 01,000 | 11,91 86,000 | 7,945,733 |
| 1895 96 | 3 05 91,000 | 87 18 000 | 49,38,000 | 4 42 47,000 | | |
| 1896 97 | 1,66,48,000 | 48 95,000 | 44,25,000 | 2,59,38 000 | | |

In the midst of such a situation it is no wonder if the faith of the Government in the ultimate stability of the rupee had given way, for we find that in October, 1896, the Financial Member of the Council had personally come to the conclusion that it would be better in the interest of stability to substitute 15d. for 16d. as the par of exchange between the rupee and gold.† But the suggestion was dropped as the rupee showed signs of reaching the gold par, which it did in January, 1898, after a period of full five years of depreciation from the established par.

Between January, 1898, and January, 1917, twice did the rupee fall below its gold par. The year 1907-8 records the second occasion when the parity of the rupee under the exchange standard broke down. The actual rates of exchange prevailing in the market were as follows :—

* Evidence of Hon. A. Arthur before the Fowler Committee. Q 1,806-7.

† Cf. Shirras, *Indian Finance and Banking*, p. 168.

## TABLE XXXI

RATES OF EXCHANGE, LONDON ON INDIA (FROM "THE TIMES")

Par R —1s 4d.

| Date. | On Calcutta | | On Bombay. | |
|---|---|---|---|---|
| | Highest. | Lowest | Highest. | Lowest. |
| 1907. September | 1 $4\frac{1}{32}$ | 1 $3\frac{31}{32}$ | 1 $4\frac{1}{32}$ | 1 $3\frac{31}{32}$ |
| October | 1 $4\frac{1}{32}$ | 1 $3\frac{31}{32}$ | 1 $4\frac{1}{32}$ | 1 $3\frac{31}{32}$ |
| November | 1 4 | 1 $3\frac{15}{16}$ | 1 $3\frac{31}{32}$ | 1 $3\frac{15}{16}$ |
| December | 1 $3\frac{15}{16}$ | 1 $3\frac{27}{32}$ | 1 $3\frac{15}{16}$ | 1 $3\frac{27}{32}$ |
| 1908. January | 1 $3\frac{15}{16}$ | 1 $3\frac{29}{32}$ | 1 $3\frac{15}{16}$ | 1 $3\frac{7}{8}$ |
| February | 1 $3\frac{31}{32}$ | 1 $3\frac{7}{8}$ | 1 $3\frac{31}{32}$ | 1 $3\frac{7}{8}$ |
| March | 1 $3\frac{29}{32}$ | 1 $3\frac{27}{32}$ | 1 $3\frac{29}{32}$ | 1 $3\frac{27}{32}$ |
| April | 1 $3\frac{7}{8}$ | 1 $3\frac{27}{32}$ | 1 $3\frac{27}{32}$ | 1 $3\frac{27}{32}$ |
| May | 1 $3\frac{7}{8}$ | 1 $3\frac{27}{32}$ | 1 $3\frac{15}{16}$ | 1 $3\frac{27}{32}$ |
| June | 1 $3\frac{29}{32}$ | 1 $3\frac{27}{32}$ | 1 $3\frac{7}{8}$ | 1 $3\frac{27}{32}$ |
| July | 1 $3\frac{7}{8}$ | 1 $3\frac{27}{32}$ | 1 $3\frac{7}{8}$ | 1 $3\frac{27}{32}$ |
| August | 1 $3\frac{29}{32}$ | 1 $3\frac{27}{32}$ | 1 $3\frac{29}{32}$ | 1 $3\frac{27}{32}$ |
| September | 1 $3\frac{31}{32}$ | 1 $3\frac{29}{32}$ | 1 $3\frac{31}{32}$ | 1 $3\frac{7}{8}$ |
| October | 1 $3\frac{15}{16}$ | 1 $3\frac{7}{8}$ | 1 $3\frac{29}{32}$ | 1 $3\frac{13}{16}$ |
| November | 1 $3\frac{29}{32}$ | 1 $3\frac{7}{8}$ | 1 $3\frac{7}{8}$ | 1 $3\frac{7}{8}$ |
| December | 1 $3\frac{15}{16}$ | 1 $3\frac{29}{32}$ | 1 $3\frac{31}{32}$ | 1 $3\frac{7}{8}$ |

After a crisis lasting over a year the rupee recovered to its old gold par and remained fixed at it, though by no means firmly, for another seven years, only to suffer another fall from its parity during the year 1914-15 (*see* table, p. 182).

After 1916 the stability of the exchange standard was threatened by a danger arising from quite unsuspected quarters. The Indian exchange standard was based upon the view that the gold value of silver was bound to fall or at least not likely to rise to a level at which the intrinsic value of the rupee became higher than its nominal value. The price of silver at which the intrinsic value of the rupee equalled its nominal value was 43d. per ounce. So long as the intrinsic value of the rupee remained below its nominal value, i.e. the price of silver did not rise above 43d., there was no danger of the rupee circulating as

TABLE XXXII

RATES OF EXCHANGE LONDON ON CALCUTTA (FROM THE NATIONAL BANK OF INDIA)

| Months | 1914. | | 1915. | |
|---|---|---|---|---|
| | Highest | Lowest | Highest. | Lowest |
| January | — | — | 1 3 15/16 | 1 3 15/16 |
| February | — | — | 1 4 1/32 | 1 3 29/32 |
| March | — | — | 1 4 | 1 3 15/16 |
| April | — | — | 1 3 15/16 | 1 3 29/32 |
| May | 1 4 1/4 | 1 3 15/16 | 1 3 15/16 | 1 3 7/8 |
| June | 1 3 31/32 | 1 3 15/16 | 1 3 7/8 | 1 3 27/32 |
| July | 1 3 31/32 | 1 3 13/16 | 1 3 29/32 | 1 3 23/32 |
| August | 1 3 7/8 | 1 3 13/16 | 1 3 15/16 | 1 3 27/32 |
| September | 1 3 15/16 | 1 3 13/16 | 1 4 | 1 3 15/16 |
| October | 1 3 15/16 | 1 3 13/16 | — | — |
| November | 1 3 15/16 | 1 3 15/16 | — | — |
| December | 1 3 15/16 | 1 3 15/16 | — | — |

currency. Once the price of silver rose above that point the danger of the rupee passing from currency to the melting-pot was imminent. Now, with the exception of a brief period from September, 1904, to December, 1907, the gold price of silver had since 1872 showed a marked tendency to fall. The decline in its price was so continuous and so steady as to create the general impression that the low price had come to stay. Indeed, so firm was the impression that the framers of the exchange standard had never taken into account the contingency of a rise in the price of silver above 43d. So little was it anticipated, that the system was not criticized on this ground by any of the witnesses who deposed before the successive Committees and Commission on Indian currency. But the unexpected may happen, and unfortunately did happen after 1916, and happened suddenly. On February 10, 1914, the cash price in London of silver per ounce of standard fineness was 26 5|8d. It fell to 22 11|16d. on February 10, 1915, and though it jumped to 27d. on the same date in 1916, yet it was below the rupee melting-point. After the last-mentioned date its rise was meteoric. On

February 9, 1917, it rose to 37 5|8d.; on February 8, 1918, to 43d.; and on the same date in 1919 to 48 7|16d., thereby quite overshooting the rupee melting-point. But the price of silver broke all record when on February 11, 1920, it reached the colossal figure of 89½d. per standard ounce.

The rise in the intrinsic value of the rupee above the nominal value at once raised a problem as to how the rupee could be preserved in circulation. Two ways seemed open for the solution of the problem. One was to scale down the fineness of the rupee, and the other to raise its gold parity. All other countries which had been confronted by a similar problem adopted the former method of dealing with their silver coinage—a method which was successfully tried in the Philippines and the Straits Settlements and Mexico in 1904-7, when a rise in those years in the price of silver had created a similar problem in those countries.* The Secretary of State for India adopted the second course of action and kept on altering the rupee par with every rise in the price of silver. The alterations of the rupee par following upon the variations in the price of silver are given below :—

TABLE XXXIII

| Date of Alteration of the Rupee Par | Pitch of the Par. |
|---|---|
| | s. d. |
| January 3, 1917 | 1 4¼ |
| August 28, 1917 | 1 5 |
| April 12, 1918 | 1 6 |
| May 13, 1919 | 1 8 |
| August 12, 1919 | 1 10 |
| September 15, 1919 | 2 0 |
| November 22, 1919 | 2 2 |
| December 12, 1919 | 2 4 |

After having played with the rupee par, for two years, in this manner, as though such alterations involved no social con-

* Cf. E. W. Kemmerer, *Modern Currency Reforms*, 1916, pp. 349-354, 445-49, and 535-47.

sequences, the Secretary of State, on May 30, 1919, appointed a new Currency Committee under the chairmanship of Babington Smith, to recommend measures "to ensure a stable gold exchange standard." The majority of the Committee, after half a year of cogitation, reported to the effect* that

> "(i) The object should be to restore stability to the rupee, and to re-establish the automatic working of the currency system at as early a date as practicable.
>
> "(ii) The stable relation to be established should be with gold and not with sterling.
>
> "(iii) The gold equivalent of the rupee should be sufficiently high to give assurance, so far as is practicable, that the rupee, while retaining its present weight and fineness, will remain a token coin, or in other words, that the bullion value of the silver it contains will not exceed its exchange value.
>
> "After most careful consideration" (the Committee said) "we are unanimous (with the exception of one of our members who signs a separate report) in recommending that the stable relation to be established between the rupee and gold should be at the rate of one rupee to 11.30016 grs. of fine gold both for foreign exchange and internal circulation."

i.e. the rupee to be equal to 2s. (gold).

The minority report, which harped on the old cry of a stimulus of low exchange and penalty of high exchange, stood out for the maintenance of the old rate of 15 rupees to the gold sovereign or 113.0016 grs. troy of pure gold, and recommended the issue of a two-rupee silver coin of reduced fineness compared with the old rupee, so long as the price of silver in New York was over 92 cents.†

By the announcements of February 2, 1920, the recommendations of the majority of the Committee were accepted by the Secretary of State and also by the Government of India, which abandoned the old parity of 7.53344 grs. per rupee for the new parity of 11.30016 grs. troy. Now, has the rupee maintained its new parity with gold?

In the matter of ascertaining this fact the exchange quotation on London is no guide, for the value of the rupee was 2s. *gold* and not 2s. sterling. Had gold and sterling been identical the case would have been otherwise. But during the war,

* *See* Report, P.P.Cd. 527 of 1920, par. 59.

† Report, p. 41.

owing to the issue of virtually inconvertible money, the pound sterling had depreciated in terms of gold. We must therefore take as our standard a currency which had kept its par with gold. Such a currency was the American dollar, and the exchange quotation on New York is therefore more directly helpful in measuring the gold value of the rupee than is the sterling quotation on London. We can also employ the actual rupee-sterling quotation as a measure by comparing it with the amount of sterling the rupee should have purchased, as an equivalent of 11.30016 grs. of fine gold, when corrected by the prevailing cross-rate between New York and London*

Compared with the par of exchange, the actual exchange, either on New York or on London, indicates a fall of the rupee which is simply staggering (*see* table, p. 186).

Consider, along with the external gold value of the rupee, its internal value in terms of sovereigns and bar gold (*see* table, p. 187).

The tables need no comment. The rupee is not only far away from 2s. (gold), but is not even 1s. 4d. (sterling).

Do not the facts furnish an incontrovertible proof of the futility of the exchange standard ? How can a system which fails to maintain its value in terms of gold, which it is supposed to do, be regarded as a sound system of currency ? There must be somewhere some weakness in the mechanism of a system which is liable to such occasional breakdowns. The rupee fell or rather was below par in 1893, and did not reach its parity to any real degree of firmness until 1900. After an interval of seven years the rupee again falls below par in 1907. The year 1914 witnesses another fall of the rupee. A meteoric rise since 1917, and again a fall after 1920. This curious phenomenon

* The formula for this computation is as follows:—

If $x$ pence = 1 rupee
= 11·30016 grs. fine gold,
23·22 grs. fine gold = 1 dollar,
D dollars = 1 pound sterling
= 240 pence.

$$\text{Then } x = \frac{11\cdot30016 \times 240}{23\cdot22 \times D} = \frac{11{,}680}{D} \text{ pence.}$$

* Cf. Rushforth, F. V., *The Indian Exchange Problem*, 1921, p. 9.

# TABLE XXXIV

## Actual Gold Value of the Rupee and the new Parity in Terms of Foreign Exchanges

| As in the Middle of the Month of— | New York on Bombay in cents. | | | | | | Bombay on London in s. d. | | | | | |
|---|---|---|---|---|---|---|---|---|---|---|---|---|
| | 1920. | | 1921. | | 1922. | | 1920. | | 1921. | | 1922. | |
| | Par Rate | Actual Rate | Par Rate | Actual Rate. | Par Rate. | Actual Rate | Par Rate. | Actual Rate | Par Rate | Actual Rate | Par Rate. | Actual Rate. |
| January . | 0.4866 | 0.4400 | 0 4866 | 0 2925 | 0.4866 | 0 2800 | 2 $7\frac{1}{2}$ | 2 $3\frac{5}{8}$ | 2 $7\frac{5}{16}$ | 1 $5\frac{5}{8}$ | 2 $3\frac{5}{8}$ | 1 $3\frac{13}{16}$ |
| February . | 0.4866 | 0.4850 | 0.4866 | 0 2800 | 0.4866 | 0.2845 | 2 $10\frac{11}{32}$ | 2 $9\frac{1}{8}$ | 2 $5\frac{13}{16}$ | 1 $4\frac{1}{8}$ | 2 $2\frac{7}{32}$ | 1 $3\frac{9}{16}$ |
| March . | 0.4866 | 0.4850 | 0.4866 | 0 2625 | 0.4866 | 0 2787 | 2 $7\frac{29}{32}$ | 2 $5\frac{3}{4}$ | 2 $5\frac{31}{32}$ | 1 $3\frac{1}{4}$ | 2 $2\frac{29}{32}$ | 1 $3\frac{5}{16}$ |
| April . | 0.4866 | 0.4775 | 0.4866 | 0.2625 | 0.4866 | 0.2785 | 2 $5\frac{7}{16}$ | 2 $3\frac{3}{4}$ | 2 $5\frac{13}{16}$ | 1 $3\frac{5}{8}$ | 2 $2\frac{1}{2}$ | 1 $3\frac{3}{8}$ |
| May . | 0 4866 | 0.4325 | 0.4866 | 0 2765 | 0 4866 | 0 2930 | 2 $6\frac{19}{32}$ | 2 $2\frac{1}{8}$ | 2 $5\frac{27}{32}$ | 1 $3\frac{1}{2}$ | 2 $2\frac{1}{4}$ | 1 $3\frac{9}{16}$ |
| June . | 0.4866 | 0.4125 | 0.4866 | 0 2525 | 0.4866 | 0.2900 | 2 $5\frac{21}{32}$ | 1 $10\frac{13}{16}$ | 2 $6\frac{25}{32}$ | 1 $3\frac{3}{8}$ | 2 $2\frac{1}{8}$ | 1 $3\frac{19}{32}$ |
| July . | 0.4866 | 0.3900 | 0.4866 | 0 2400 | 0.4866 | 0.2900 | 2 $5\frac{21}{32}$ | 1 $8\frac{1}{16}$ | 2 $8\frac{9}{32}$ | 1 $3\frac{1}{4}$ | 2 $2\frac{5}{8}$ | 1 $3\frac{5}{8}$ |
| August . | 0.4866 | 0 3650 | 0.4866 | 0 2475 | 0.4866 | 0 2916 | 2 $8\frac{9}{32}$ | 1 $10\frac{1}{16}$ | 2 $7\frac{19}{32}$ | 1 $4\frac{1}{4}$ | 2 $2\frac{9}{16}$ | 1 $3\frac{19}{32}$ |
| September . | 0.4866 | 0 3325 | 0.4866 | 0 2675 | 0.4866 | 0.2875 | 2 $9\frac{9}{16}$ | 1 $10\frac{1}{16}$ | 2 $7\frac{15}{32}$ | 1 $5\frac{1}{16}$ | 2 $2\frac{5}{16}$ | 1 $3\frac{9}{16}$ |
| October . | 0.4866 | 0.3025 | 0.4866 | 0.2825 | 0 4866 | — | 2 $9\frac{21}{32}$ | 1 $7\frac{3}{8}$ | 2 $6\frac{1}{32}$ | 1 $5\frac{7}{16}$ | — | — |
| November . | 0 4866 | 0.3025 | 0.4866 | 0.2695 | 0.4866 | — | 2 $10\frac{9}{16}$ | 1 $7\frac{1}{8}$ | 2 $5\frac{15}{32}$ | 1 $4\frac{1}{8}$ | — | — |
| December . | 0.4866 | 0.2650 | 0.4866 | 0.2775 | 0 4866 | — | 2 $9\frac{9}{16}$ | 1 $5\frac{1}{4}$ | 2 4 | 1 $3\frac{7}{8}$ | — | — |

## TABLE XXXV

GOLD VALUE OF THE RUPEE AND THE NEW PARITY IN TERMS OF THE PRICE OF SOVEREIGNS AND GOLD

| Months | 1920. | | 1921 | | 1922. | |
|---|---|---|---|---|---|---|
| | Price of British Sovereigns Par 10 Rs = 1 Sov | Price of Bar Gold per Tola 100 touch Par Rs 15-14-10 = 1 Tola | Price of British Sovereigns Par 10 Rs = 1 Sov | Price of Bar Gold per Tola 100 Touch Par Rs 15-14-10 = 1 Tola | Price of British Sovereigns Par 10 Rs 1 Sov. | Price of Bar Gold per Tola 100 touch Par Rs 15-14-10 = 1 Tola. |
| | Rs A. P | Rs A. P | Rs A P | Rs A P | Rs A P | |
| January . . | Nominal | 28 0 0 | Nominal | Official figures not yet published | 17 14 0 | Official figures not yet published |
| February . | ,, | 22 0 0 | ,, | | 17 14 0 | |
| March . . | ,, | 24 0 0 | ,, | | 17 14 0 | |
| April . . | ,, | 24 8 0 | 18 12 0 | | — | |
| May . | ,, | 22 12 0 | 19 0 0 | | — | |
| June . . | ,, | 22 4 0 | 19 12 0 | | — | |
| July . . | ,, | 23 0 0 | 20 9 0 | | — | |
| August . | ,, | 21 8 0 | 20 9 0 | | — | |
| September | ,, | 25 4 0 | 19 2 0 | | — | |
| October . | ,, | 27 6 0 | 18 14 0 | | — | |
| November . | ,, | 28 10 0 | 18 8 0 | | — | |
| December . | ,, | 27 12 0 | 18 6 0 | | — | |

naturally raises the question : Why did the rupee fail to maintain its gold parity on these occasions ? A proper reply to this question will reveal wherein lies the weakness of the exchange standard.

The only scientific explanation sufficient to account for the fall of the rupee would be to say that the rupee had lost its general purchasing power. It is an established proposition that a currency or unit of account will be valued in terms of another currency or unit of account for what it is worth, i.e. for the goods which it will buy. To take a concrete example, Englishmen and others value Indian rupees inasmuch and in so far as those rupees will buy Indian goods. On the other hand, Indians value English pounds (and other units of account, for that matter) inasmuch and in so far as those pounds will buy English goods. If rupees in India rise in purchasing power (i.e. if the Indian price-level falls) while pounds fall in purchasing power or remain stationary or rise less rapidly (i.e. if the English price level rises relative to the Indian price-level), fewer rupees would be worth as much as a pound, i.e. the exchange value of the rupee in terms of the pound will rise. On the other hand, if rupees in India fall in purchasing power (i.e. if the Indian price-level rises) while pounds rise in purchasing power or remain stationary or fall less rapidly (i.e. if the English price-level falls relative to the Indian price-level), it will take more rupees to be worth as much as a pound, i.e. the exchange value of the rupee in terms of the pound will fall.

On the basis of this theory the real explanation for a fall in the Indian exchange should be sought for in the movement of the Indian price-level. Lest there be any doubt regarding the validity of the proposition let us take each of the occasions of the fall and find out whether or not the fall was coincident with the fall in the purchasing power of the rupee.*

TABLE XXXVI

PERIOD I, 1893-98

| Years | Currency in Circulation Rupees + Notes | | Index Number of Prices in India 1890-94=100. | Index Number of Prices in England 1890-94=100. |
|---|---|---|---|---|
| | Amount in Crores of Rs | Index Number 1890-94=100. | | |
| (1) | (2) | (3) | (4) | (5) |
| 1890 | 120 | 92 | 113 | 104 |
| 1891 | 131 | 100 | 106 | 105 |
| 1892 | 141 | 108 | 100 | 99 |
| 1893 | 132 | 101 | 96 | 99 |
| 1894 | 129 | 99 | 85 | 93 |
| 1895 | 132 | 101 | 89 | 90 |
| 1896 | 127 | 97 | 99 | 89 |
| 1897 | 125 | 96 | 120 | 90 |
| 1898 | 122 | 93 | 109 | 91 |
| 1899 | 131 | 100 | 108 | 94 |

* The figures for the following tables are taken, unless otherwise stated, from the Report of the Price Inquiry Committee, Calcutta, 1914.

TABLE XXXVII

PERIOD II, 1900—1908

| Years. | Currency in circulation, Rupees + Notes. | | Index Number of Prices in India 1890-94=100 | Index Number of Prices in England 1890-94=100 |
|---|---|---|---|---|
| | Amount in Crores of Rs. | Index Number 1890 94=100. | | |
| (1) | (2) | (3) | (4) | (5) |
| 1900 | 134 | 103 | 126 | 103 |
| 1901 | 150 | 115 | 120 | 98 |
| 1902 | 143 | 109 | 115 | 96 |
| 1903 | 147 | 113 | 111 | 97 |
| 1904 | 152 | 116 | 110 | 100 |
| 1905 | 164 | 126 | 120 | 100 |
| 1906 | 185 | 142 | 134 | 107 |
| 1907 | 190 | 145 | 138 | 113 |
| 1908 | 181 | 139 | 147 | 104 |

TABLE XXXVIII.

PERIOD III. 1909—14*.

| Years | Currency in Circulation Rupees + Notes | | Index Number of Prices in India 1890-94=100 | Index Numbers of Prices in England 1890 94=100 |
|---|---|---|---|---|
| | Amount in Crores of Rs | Index Number 1890-94=100 | | |
| (1) | (2) | (3) | (4) | (5) |
| 1909 | 198 | 152 | 138 | 105 |
| 1910 | 199 | 152 | 137 | 110 |
| 1911 | 209 | 160 | 139 | 114 |
| 1912 | 214 | 164 | 147 | 117 |
| 1913 | 238 | 182 | 152 | 124 |
| 1914 | 237 | 182 | 156 | 124 |

*Figures for 1913 and 1914 are those of Mr. Shirras given in the Appendix to his Indian Finance and Banking. Figures in column 3 are calculated from his figures.

## TABLE XXXIX

### PERIOD IV, 1915-1921.

| Years. | Currency in Circulation Rupees+Notes | | Index Number of Prices in India 1913=100 | Index Number of Prices in England 1913=100 |
|---|---|---|---|---|
| | Amount in Crores of Rs. | Index Number 1913=100. | | |
| (1) | (2) | (3) | (4) | (5) |
| 1915 | 266 | 104 | 112 | 127·1 |
| 1916 | 297 | 116 | 125 | 159·5 |
| 1917 | 338 | 132 | 142 | 206 1 |
| 1918 | 407 | 156 | 178 | 226 5 |
| 1919 | 463 | 180 | 200 | 241·9 |
| 1920 | 411 | 160 | 209 | 295·3 |
| 1921 | 393 | 114 | 183 | 182·4 |

*Index numbers of prices are taken from the League of Nations *Memorandum on Currency*, 1913-1921, 2nd Ed (1922) Table VIII Figures for Circulation are taken from H S Jevons *The Future of Exchange and Indian Currency*, 1922, P 44, Index numbers of Circulation are Calculated

Now do these tables confirm, or do they not, the argument that the fall in the gold value of the rupee is coincident with a fall in the general purchasing power of the rupee? What was the general purchasing power of the rupee when a fall in its gold value occurred? If we scrutinize the facts given in the above tables in the light of this query there can be no doubt as to the validity of this argument. From the tables it will be seen that the gold value of the rupee improved between 1893-1898 because there was a steady, if not unbroken, improvement in its general purchasing power. Again, on the subsequent occasions when the exchange fell, as it did in 1908, 1914, and 1920, it will be observed that those were the years which marked the peaks in the rising price-level in India; in other words, those were the years in which there was the greatest depreciation in the general purchasing power of the rupee. A further proof, if it be needed, of the argument that the exchange value of the rupee must ultimately be governed by its general purchasing power is afforded by the movements of the rupee-sterling exchange since 1920 (*see Table* XL).

But, although such is the theoretical view confirmed by statistical evidence of the causes which bring about these periodic falls in the gold value of the rupee (otherwise spoken of as the fall of exchange), it is not shared by the Government of India. The official explanation is that a fall in the gold value of the rupee is due to an adverse balance of trade. Such is also the view of eminent supporters of the exchange standard like Mr. Keynes * and Mr. Shirras. †

No doubt, some such line of reasoning is responsible for the currency fiasco of 1920. How is it possible otherwise to explain the policy of raising the exchange value of the rupee ? Both the Smith Committee on Indian Currency‡ and the Government of India § were aware of the fact that the rupee was heavily depreciated, as evidenced by the rise of prices in India.

* Op. cit., p. 16. † Op. cit, p 4 ‡ Cf Report, pp 19-21

§ Memorandum from the Government regarding Indian price movements. App. XXVIII to the Report of the Currency Committee of 1919.

TABLE XL

| Date | Rupee Prices in India 1913=100 | Sterling Prices in England (*Statist*) 1913=100 | Average Rate of Exchange London on Calcutta | Rupee-Sterling Purchasing Power Parity $16d X \frac{Col\ 3}{Col\ 2}$ |
|---|---|---|---|---|
| (1) | (2) | (3) | (4) | (5) |
| | | | d. | d. |
| 1920. January . | 202 | 289 | 27.81 | 22.89 |
| February | 203 | 306 | 32.05 | 24.12 |
| March . | 194 | 301 | 29.66 | 25.40 |
| April . | 193 | 300 | 27.88 | 25.95 |
| May . | 190 | 298 | 25.91 | 25.77 |
| June . | 192 | 293 | 23.63 | 25.08 |
| July . | 196 | 282 | 22.63 | 24.49 |
| August . | 193 | 263 | 22.75 | 24.70 |
| September | 188 | 244 | 22.31 | 24.94 |
| October . | 188 | 232 | 19.88 | 24.00 |
| November | 186 | 215 | 19.69 | 22.62 |
| December | 179 | 209 | 17.44 | 21.81 |
| 1921. January . | 169 | 200 | 17.66 | 21.96 |
| February | 164 | 191 | 16.31 | 20.98 |
| March . | 162 | 183 | 15.53 | 20.40 |
| April . | 163 | 186 | 15.75 | 19.63 |
| May . | 170 | 182 | 15.44 | 17.98 |
| June . | 172 | 176 | 15.53 | 17.14 |
| July . | 171 | 163 | 15.38 | 17.40 |
| August . | 178 | 161 | 16.25 | 16.36 |
| September | 178 | 157 | 17.22 | 15.82 |
| October . | 178 | 156 | 17.02 | 14.65 |
| November | 173 | 161 | 16.25 | 14.89 |
| December | 169 | 157 | 15.94 | 14.86 |
| 1922. January . | 162 | 156 | 15.88 | 15.41 |
| February . | 159 | 156 | 15.59 | 16.70 |
| March . | 160 | 157 | 15.34 | 15.70 |
| April . | 160 | 159 | 15.19 | 15.90 |
| May . | 162 | 159 | 15.59 | 15.70 |
| June . | 169 | 160 | 15.63 | 15.14 |
| July . | 170 | 158 | 15.69 | 14 87 |
| August . | 166 | 153 | 15.66 | 14.74 |

Given this fact, any question of raising the gold value of the rupee to 2s. gold when the rupee had scarcely the power to purchase 1s. 4d. sterling was out of the question. The Committee indulged in loose talk about stabilizing the Indian exchange. But even from this standpoint the Committee's insistence on linking the rupee to gold must be regarded as a little grotesque. Stable exchange, to use Prof. Marshall's language, is something like bringing the railway gauges of the world in unison with the main line. If that is what is expected from a stable exchange, then what was the use of linking the rupee to gold which had ceased to be the "main line" ? What people wanted was a stable exchange in terms of the standard in which prices were measured. Linking to gold involved unlinking to sterling, and it is sterling which mattered and not gold. Given this importance of sterling over gold, was any policy of exchange stabilization called for ? First of all it should have been grasped that such a policy could succeed only if it was possible to make sterling and rupee prices move in unison, for then alone could the ratio of interchange between them be the same. What control had the Government of India over the sterling ? They might have so controlled the rupee as to produce the effect desired, but all that might have been frustrated by an adverse move in the sterling. The success of the policy of linking to sterling would have been highly problematical although highly desirable. But was it called for ?

Now the problem of stabilization is primarily a problem of controlling abnormal deviations from the purchasing-power parity between two currencies. In the case of India there were no abnormal deviations from the rupee-sterling purchasing-power parity. On the other hand, the Indian exchange was moving in a more or less close correspondence with it. There was therefore no ground for originating any policy of exchange stabilization. But, supposing there were abnormal deviations and that, owing to some reasons known to it, the Committee believed that the exchange value of the rupee was not likely to return to the point justified by its general purchasing power, in that case the Committee should have fixed the exchange value well within the range of the purchasing power of the rupee. As it was, the value of the rupee fixed by the Committee the rupee never had. In giving a value to the rupee so much above its purchasing-power parity, it is obvious the Committee originated a solution for the simple problem of stabilizing the rupee which involved the much bigger and quite a different problem of deflation or raising the absolute value of the rupee. How was the object to be attained ? The Committee never considered that problem. And why ? Was it because the price of silver had gone up ? May be. But it is doubtful whether the Committee could have believed firmly that the value of silver was going to be permanently so high as to require a modification of the gold par. Anyone who cared to scrutinize the rise in the price of silver could have found that the rise was largely speculative and could not have been permanent. (*see Table* XLI).

TABLE XLI

PRICE OF SILVER IN STERLING (PENCE) *

| Year. | Highest | Lowest | Average. | Range of Variation |
|---|---|---|---|---|
| 1913 | 29 3/8 | 25 15/16 | 27 9/16 | 3 7/16 |
| 1914 | 27 3/4 | 22 1/8 | 25 5/16 | 5 5/8 |
| 1915 | 27 1/4 | 22 5/16 | 23 11/16 | 4 15/16 |
| 1916 | 37 1/8 | 26 11/16 | 31 5/16 | 10 7/16 |
| 1917 | 55 | 35 11/16 | 40 7/8 | 19 11/16 |
| 1918 | 49 1/2 | 42 1/2 | 47 9/16 | 7 |
| 1919 | 79 1/8 | 47 3/4 | 57 1/16 | 31 3/8 |
| 1920 | 89 1/2 | 38 7/8 | 61 7/16 | 50 5/8 |
| 1921 | 43 3/8 | 30 5/8 | 37 | 12 3/4 |

But supposing that the rise in the price of silver was not speculative, did it follow that the rupee was appreciated ? The diagnosis of the Committee was an egregious blunder. With the facts laid before the Committee it is difficult to understand how anyone with a mere smattering of the knowledge of price movements could have concluded that because silver had appreciated the rupee had therefore appreciated. On the other hand, what had happened was that the rupee had depreciated in terms of general commodities, including gold and silver. Indeed, the appreciation of silver was a depreciation of the rupee. Table XLII is conclusive evidence of that fact:—

* From Kirkaldy's *British War Finance*, 1921, p. 35 Figures for 1921 are added from the Indian Paper Currency Report.

TABLE XLII

DEPRECIATION OF THE RUPEE

| Date | Price of Bar Gold in India (Bombay) per Tola of 180 grs | | Price of Silver in India (Bombay) per 100 Tolas | | Index Number for Prices in India 1913=100. |
|---|---|---|---|---|---|
| | | Rs A | | Rs A. | |
| 1914 . . . . | | 24 10 | | 65 11 | — |
| 1915 . . . . | | 24 14 | | 61 2 | 112 |
| 1916 . . . . | | 27 2 | | 78 10 | 125 |
| 1917 . . . . | | 27 11 | | 94 10 | 142 |
| 1918 . . . . | (July) | 34 0 | (May 16) | 117 2 | 178 |
| ,, . . . . | | | (Nov. 28) | 82 10 | — |
| ,, August . | | 30 0 | | — | — |
| ,, Sept . . | | 32 4 | | — | — |
| 1919, March . | | 32 0 | | 113 0 | 200 |

Thus, the rise in the price of silver was a part of the general rise of prices or the depreciation of the rupee. The Committee desired to raise the gold value of the rupee to 10 rupees per sovereign when it cost twice that number of rupees to purchase a sovereign in the market. So marked was the depreciation of the rupee in terms of gold that a few months before the Committee submitted its report the *Statesman* (a Calcutta paper) wrote :—

> "If you land in the country with a sovereign the Government will take it away from you and give you eleven rupees three annas in return. If you are in the country and happen to have a sovereign and take it to the currency office you will get fifteen rupees for it. On the other hand, if you take it to the bazar you will find purchasers at twenty-one rupees."

These facts were admitted by the Finance Department of the Government of India to be substantially correct,* and yet in the face of them the Committee recommended the 2s. gold parity for the rupee. The Committee confused the rupee with the silver, and thus failed to distinguish the problem of retaining the rupee in circulation and raising its exchange value in terms

* Cf the reply of the Hon Mr Howard to the question of the Hon. Mr. Sinha on September 23, 1919. *S.L.C.P.*, Vol. LVII, p 417

of gold. The latter solution was applicable only if the *rupee* had appreciated. But as it was silver that had appreciated in terms of the rupee, the only feasible solution was to have proposed the reduction of the fineness of the rupee. Had the Committee regarded silver as a commodity distinct from the rupee like any other commodity to be measured in terms of the rupee as a unit of account, probably it might have avoided committing the blunder which it did. But what is more than probable is that the Committee did not think that the general purchasing power of the rupee was a factor of any moment in the consideration of the matter it was asked to report upon. What was of prime importance in its eyes for the maintenance of the exchange value of the rupee was a favourable balance of trade, and that India had at the time the Committee drafted its Report. For the Committee, in the course of its general observations on the exchange standard, remarked:

> "that the system had proved effectual in preventing the fall in the value of the rupee below 1s. 4d., and unless there should have been profound modifications in India's position as an exporting country with a favourable trade balance, there was no reason to apprehend any breakdown in this respect "*

Proceeding on this view of the question it was quite natural for the Committee to have argued that if a favourable balance of trade sustained 1s. 4d. gold exchange, why should a similar balance of trade not sustain 2s. gold exchange ?

Again, it is only on some such hypothesis that one can explain why the recommendations of the Committee were adopted at all when the necessity for their adoption had passed away. Even if the intrinsic value of the rupee exceeded its nominal value, there was no danger of a wholesale disappearance of the rupee from circulation in view of the enormous volume of rupees in India.† What would have taken place was not a wholesale melting of rupees, but a constant dribble of an irregular and illegal character leading to the contravention of the orders then issued by the Government of India against the melting or exportation of the rupee coin. At the time when the Committee reported (December, 1919) the price of

* Report, par. 33.
† Cf evidence of Mr Keynes before the Committee of 1919, Q. 2,665-68.

silver was no doubt high, but it was certainly falling during 1920 when the Government took action on the Report. Indeed, on August 31, 1920, when the Bill to alter the gold value of the rupee was introduced into the Council, gold was selling at 23¼ rupees to the tola, while if the sovereign was to be equal to 10 rupees, the market price of gold should have been Rs. 15-14-0 per tola, so that there was a difference of Rs. 7½ or 33 per cent. between the market ratio of gold to the rupee and the new mint ratio. Moreover, the price of silver had also gone down in the neighbourhood of 44d., so that there was no danger of the rupee being melted out of circulation.* But, nothwithstanding such a disparity, the Government rushed to fix a higher gold parity for the rupee. The financial reason for this rash act was of course obvious. The impending constitutional changes were to bring about a complete separation between provincial and imperial finance in British India. Under the old system of finance it was open for the central Government to levy "benevolences" in the form of contributions on the Provincial Governments to meet such of its imperious wants as remained unsatisfied with the help of its own resources, apart from the lion's share it used to take at every settlement of the provincial finance. Under the new constitution it was to be deprived of this power. The Central Government was therefore in search of some resource to obtain relief without appearing to tax anybody in particular. A high exchange seemed to be just the happy means of doing it, for it was calculated to effect a great saving on the "home charges." But how was this high exchange to be maintained, supposing it was desirable to have a high exchange from the financial point of view ? † Not only had the price and silver gone down and the rupee shown evident marks of depreciation in terms of gold, but the balance of trade had also become adverse to India at the time when the Government proceeded to take action on the Report of the Committee. But

* Cf. the speech of the Hon Mr Tata on the Indian Coinage (Amendment) Bill, *S L C P*, Vol. LIX, p 112

† In the recent discussions on the Indian exchange it has been entirely overlooked that this was the underlying motive of raising the Indian exchange to 2*s*. gold. But it was laid bare by the Finance Member of the Council in his speech on March 10, 1920, in the course of the debate on the resolution *re* Reverse Councils, *S L C P*, Vol. LVIII, p 1292

this enactment, so singular in its rashness, was none the less founded upon the hope that the balance of trade would become favourable in time and thus help to maintain the 2s. gold value of the rupee. That this is a correct interpretation of the Government's calculations is borne out by the following extract from the letter which it addressed to the Bengal Chamber of Commerce in explanation of the currency fiasco.* After speaking of the necessity for granting international credits to revive commerce, the letter goes on to say:—

> "But for the rest they [i.e. the Government of India] can now only rely on the natural course of events and the return of favourable export conditions, combined with the reduction of imports . . . to strengthen the exchange. Experience has demonstrated that in the present condition of the world trade stability is at present unattainable, but the Government of India see no reason why the operation of natural conditions . . . should not allow of the eventual fixation of exchange at the level advocated in the report of the Currency Committee."

Which of the two views is correct? Is it the low purchasing power of the rupee which is responsible for its fall, or is it due to an adverse balance of trade? Now, it must at once be pointed out that an adverse balance of trade, as an explanation of the fall of exchange, is something new in Indian official literature. A fall of exchange was a common occurrence between 1873 and 1893, but no official ever offered the adverse balance of trade as an explanation. Again, can the doctrine of adverse balance of trade furnish an ultimate explanation for the fall that occurred in 1907, 1914, and 1920? First of all, taking into consideration all the items visible and invisible, the balance-sheet of the trade of a country must balance. Indeed, the disquisitions attached to the Indian Paper Currency Reports, wherein this doctrine of adverse balance as a cause of fall in exchange is usually to be found, never fail to insist that there is no such thing as a "drain" from India by showing item by item how the exports of India are paid for by the imports, even in those years in which the exchange has fallen. The queer thing is, the same Reports persist in speaking of an adverse balance of trade. Given the admission that all Indian exports are paid for, it is difficult to see what remains to speak of as a balance.

* The letter was published in the *Times of India*, November 20, 1920, p. 14, col. 6.

Why should that part of trade liquidated by money be spoken of as a "balance"? One might as well speak of a balance of trade in terms of cutlery or any other commodity that enters into the trading operations of the country. The extent to which money enters into the trading transactions of two countries is governed by the same law of relative values as is the case with any other commodity. If more money goes out of a country than did previously, it simply means that relatively to other commodities it has become cheaper. But if there is such a thing as an adverse balance in the sense that commodity imports exceed commodity exports, then there arises the further question: Why do exports fall off and imports mount up? In other words, given a normal equilibrium of trade, what causes an adverse balance of trade? For this there is no official explanation. Indeed, the possibility of such a query is not even anticipated in the official literature. But the question is a fundamental one. An adverse balance of trade in the above sense is only another way of stating that the country has become a market which is good to sell in and bad to buy from. Now a market is good to sell in and bad to buy from when the level of prices ruling in that market is higher than the level of prices ruling outside. Therefore, if an adverse balance of trade is the cause of the fall of exchange, and if the adverse balance of trade is caused by internal prices being higher than external prices, then it follows that the fall of exchange is nothing but the currency's fall in purchasing power, which is the same thing as the rise of prices. The adverse balance of trade is an explanation a step short of the final explanation. Try to circumvent the issue as one may, it is impossible to escape the conclusion that the fall in the exchange value of the rupee is a resultant of the fall in the purchasing power of the rupee.

Now what is the cause of the fall in the purchasing power of the rupee? In that confused, if not absurd, document, the Report of the Price Inquiry Committee,* one cause of the

* This Committee was appointed in 1910 to investigate into the rise of prices in India and was composed of Messrs. Datta, Shirras, and Gupta. The first and the last named commissioners being members of the Finance Department of the Government of India, the Committee may be regarded was more or less an official body. The results of its investigations appeared in 1914 in five volumes, Vol. I of which contained the Report signed by Mr. Datta.

rise of prices in India was assigned, among others,* to the decline in supplies relatively to population. In view of the more or less generally accepted theory of quantity of a currency as the chief determinant of its value, the line of reasoning adopted by the Committee is somewhat surprising. But there is enough reason to imagine why the Committee preferred this particular explanation of the rise of prices. The *position of the Government with regard to the management of the* Indian currency is somewhat delicate. Already the issue of paper currency was in the hands of the Government. By the Mint closure it took over the management of the rupee currency as well. Having the entire control over the issue of currency, rupee and paper, the Government becomes directly responsible for whatever consequences the currency might be said to produce. It must not, also, be forgotten that the Government is constantly under fire from an Opposition by no means over-scrupulous in the selection of its counts. As a result of this situation the Government walks very warily, and is careful as to what it admits. Lord Castlereagh, in the debate on Horner's resolution of 1811 stating that bank notes were depreciated by over-issue, asked the House of Commons to consider what Napoleon would do if he found the House admitting the depreciation even if it was a fact. The Government of India is in the same position, and had to think what the Opposition would do if it admitted this or that principle. The reason why the Government of India adheres to the adverse balance of trade as an explanation of the fall of exchange is the same which led the Committee to ascribe the rise of prices to the shortage of goods. Both the doctrines have the virtue of placing the events beyond the control of the Government and thus materially absolving the Government from any blame that might be otherwise cast upon it. What can the Government do if the balance of trade goes wrong ? Again, is it a fault of the Government if the supply of commodities declines ? The Government can move safely under the cover of such a heavy

* *See* Report, pars. 126-27.

armour !* But does the explanation offered by the Committee invalidate the explanation that the cause of the rise of prices in India was excess of currency ? The value of money is a resultant of an equation between money and goods. To that equation there are obviously two sides, the money side and the commodity side. It is an age-worn dispute among economists as to which of the two is the decisive factor when the result of the equation of exchange undergoes a change, i.e. when the general price-level changes. There are economists who when discussing the value or the general purchasing power of money emphasize the commodity side in preference to the money side of the equation as the chief determinant of it. To them if prices in general fall it may not be due to scarcity of money ; on the other hand, it may be due to an increase in the volume of commodities. Again, if prices in general rise they prefer to ascribe it to a decrease in the volume of commodities rather than to an increase in the quantity of money. It is possible to take this position, as some economists choose to do, but to imagine that the quantity theory of money is thereby overthrown is a mistake. As a matter of fact, in taking that position they are not damaging the quantity theory in the least. They are merely stating it differently. The weakness of the position consists in failing to take note of what the effect on the general price-level would be if in speaking of increase or decrease of commodities they *included* a corresponding increase or decrease of currency. If the volume of commodities increases, including the volume of currency, then there is no reason why general prices should fall. Similarly, if the volume of commodities decreases, including the volume of currency, then there is no reason why general prices should rise. The commodity explanation is but the reverse side of

* It may, however, be noted that this explanation of a shortage of goods, which was apparently offered as most likely to absolve the Government from any blame for having inflated the currency, was repudiated by the Government in its resolution reviewing the Report of the Committee, probably because such an admission on its part was likely to be interpreted as an argument to show that under it India was getting poorer But the Government, in a hurry, did not realize that with the repudiation of this doctrine no other explanation was left except that of an increased issue of money to account for the rise of prices in India.

the quantity explanation of the value of money. Recasting the argument of the Committee in the light of what is said above, we can say without departing from its language that the rise of prices in India was due to the supply of currency not having diminished along with the diminution in the supply of goods. In short, the rupee fell in purchasing power because of currency being issued in excess, and there is scarcely any doubt that there has been a profuse issue of money in India since the closing of the Mints in 1893.

The first period, from 1893-98, was comparatively speaking the only period marked by a rather halting and cautious policy in respect of currency expansion. The reason no doubt was the well-known fact that at the time the Mints were closed the currency was already redundant. Yet the period was not immune from currency expansion.* At the time the Mints were closed the silver bullion then in the hands of the people was depreciated as a result of the fall in its value due to the closure. An agitation was set up by interested parties to compel the Government to make good the loss. Ultimately, the Government was prevailed upon by Sir James Mackay (now Lord Inchcape), the very man who forced Government to close the Mints, to take the silver from the banks. The Government proposed to the Secretary of State that they be allowed to sell the silver even at a loss rather than coin and add to the already redundant volume of currency. The Secretary of State having refused, the silver was coined and added to the currency. The stoppage of Council Bills in 1893-94 had temporarily accumulated a large number of rupees in their Treasuries, a transaction which practically amounted to a contraction of currency. But the Government later decided to spend them on railway construction—a policy tantamount to an addition to currency. The resumption of Council Bills after 1894 had also the same effect, for a sale of bills involves an addition to currency. In view of the heavy cost of financing the Home Treasury by gold borrowings, the resumption of sale was a pardonable act. But what was absolutely unpardonable was the increase in the fiduciary portion of the paper-currency reserve from 8 to 10

* Cf. H. M. Ross, *The Triumph of the Standard*, Calcutta, 1909, pp. 16-17.

crores,* thereby putting 2 crores of coined rupees into circulation, particularly so because the Finance Minister refused to pay any heed to its incidence on the currency policy, arguing :—

> "I am a little doubtful whether, in discussing the question of the investment of the currency reserve, we are at liberty to look at outside considerations of that kind."†

All told, the additions to the currency during the first period were negligible as compared to what took place in the second period, 1900-1908. This period was characterized by a phenomenal increase in the volume of currency poured by the Government into circulation. Speaking of the coinage of rupees during this period, Mr. Keynes, anything but an unfriendly critic of the Government's policy, observed‡:—

> "The coinage of rupees recommended on a significant scale in 1900 a steady annual demand for fresh coinage (low in 1901-2, high in 1903-4, but at no time abnormal), and the Mints were able to meet it with time to spare, though there was some slight difficulty in 1903-4. In 1905-6 the demand quickened, and from July 1905 it quite outstripped the new supplies arising from the mintage of the uncoined silver. . . . This slight scare, however, was more than sufficient to make the Government lose their heads. Having once started on a career of furious coinage, they continued to do so with little regard to considerations of ordinary prudence . . . without waiting to see how the busy seasons of 1906-7 would turn out, they coined heavily throughout the summer months. . . . During the summer of 1907, as in the summer of 1906, they continued to coin without waiting until the prosperity of the season 1907-8 was assured."

Evidently, in this period the Government framed their policy "as though a community consumed currency with the same steady appetite with which some communities consume beer." The period also witnessed a material expansion of the paper currency. Up to 1903 the use of the currency notes was limited by reason of the fact that they were not only legal tender outside their circle of issue, but also because their encashability was restricted to the offices of the circles of their issue. This was a serious limitation on the extension of paper currency in India. By Act VI of 1903 the Rs. 5 was made universal in British India excepting Burma, i.e. was made legal tender in all circles, and also encashable at all offices of issue. Along with this the fiduciary

---

* By Act XV of 1896. † Financial Statement, 1896-97, p. 89.
‡ Op. cit., pp. 131-35

portion of the paper-currency reserve was increased to Rs. 12 crores by Act III of 1905. The first event was only calculated to enlarge the circulation of the notes, but the second event had the direct effect of lowering the value of the rupee currency.

The third period (1909-14) was comparatively a moderate but by no means a slack period from the standpoint of currency expansion in India. The first three years of the period were, so to say, years of subdued emotion with regard to the rupee coinage. With the exception of the year 1910, when there was no net addition to rupee coinage, and 1911, when the addition was a small one, the coinage in the years 1909 and 1912 ranged from 24 to 30 lakhs. But during the last two years of this period there was a sudden burst of rupee coinage, when the total reached 26½ crores. The expansion of paper currency took place also on a great scale during this period. In 1909 the Rs. 5 were universalized in Burma as they had previously been in other parts of India. This process of universalization was carried further during this period, when, under the authority granted by the Paper Currency Act (II of 1910), the Government universalized notes of Rs. 5 and Rs. 50 in 1910, of Rs. 100 in 1911. Along with the stimulus thus given to the increase of paper currency, the Government actually expanded the fiduciary portion of the issue from 12 to 14 crores by Act VII of 1911, thereby throwing into circulation 2 crores of additional rupees.

During the fourth period (1915-1920) all prudential restraints were thrown overboard.* The period coincided with the Great War, which created a great demand for Indian produce and also imposed upon the Government the necessity for meeting large expenditure on behalf of H. M. Government. Both these events necessitated a great increase in the current means of purchase. There were three sources open to the Government to provide for the need: (1) importation of gold; (2) increase of rupee coinage; and (3) increase of paper currency. It must not be supposed that the Government of India had no adequate means to provide the necessary

* For a view of the currency policy of this period the primary source are the Annual Financial Statements, for these years, of the Government of India.

currency. Whatever expenditure the Government of India incurred in India, the Secretary of State was reimbursed in London. So the means were ample. The difficulty was that of converting them to proper account. Ordinarily, the Secretary of State purchases silver out of the gold at his command to be coined in India into rupees. This usual mode was followed for the first two years of the period, and the currency was augmented by that means. But the rise in the price of silver made that resource less available. The Secretary of State had therefore to choose between sending out gold or issuing paper. Of the two, the former was deemed to be too unpatriotic. Indeed, the Secretary of State believed that from an Imperial point of view it was entirely ungracious even to "earmark" the gold he received in London as belonging to India. But how was demand for additional currency in India to be met? As a result of delibera-tion it was agreed that to provide currency in India without employing gold the best plan was for the Secretary of State to invest at one end the gold he received on India's behalf in the purchase of British Treasury bills, and the Indian Government to issue currency notes at the other end on the security of these bills. Such a procedure, it will be observed, involved a profound modification in the basic theory of Indian paper currency. That theory was to increase the fiduciary issue by investing a portion of the metallic reserves only when the proportion of the latter to the total of the notes in active circulation had shown, over a considerable period, a position sufficiently strong to warrant an extension of the invested reserves and a corresponding dimi-nution of the metallic reserves. The main effect of the principle was that the extent of the paper currency was strictly governed by the habits of the people, for whatever the amount of fiduciary issue at any given moment it represented metallic reserves which were once in existence. Under the new scheme the old principle was abandoned and paper currency was issued without any metallic backing, and what is more important is that its magnitude instead of being determined by the habits of the people, was determined by the necessity of the Government and the amount of security it possessed. This fatal and facile procedure was adopted by the

Government of India with such avidity that within four years it passed one after another eight Acts, increasing the volume of notes issuable against securities. The following table gives the changes in the limits fixed by the Acts and the total issues actually made under them :—

TABLE XLIII

ISSUE OF CURRENCY NOTES

| | Acts prescribing the Fiduciary Issue of Currency Notes. | | | | | | |
|---|---|---|---|---|---|---|---|
| I. Limits to fiduciary issues | Act V of 1915 | Act IX of 1916 | Act XI of 1917 | Act XIX of 1917 | Act VI of 1918 | Act II of 1919 | Act XXVI of 1919 |
| | In Lakhs of Rupees | | | | | | |
| (a) Permanent | 14,00 | 14,00 | 14,00 | 14,00 | 14,00 | 84,00 | 14,00 |
| (b) Temporary | 6,00 | 12,00 | 36,00 | 48,00 | 72,00 | 86,00 | 126 00 |
| Total limit | 20,00 | 26,00 | 50,00 | 62,00 | 86,00 | 100,00 | 120,00 |
| II. Total issues of currency notes | 61,63 | 67,73 | 86,38 | | 99,79 | 153,46 | 179,67* |
| III. Reserve — Silver | 32,34 | 23,57 | 19,22 | | 10,79 | 37,39 | 47,44 |
| III. Reserve — Gold | 15,29 | 24,16 | 18,67 | | 27,52 | 17,49 | 32,70 |
| III. Reserve — Securities | 14,00 | 20,00 | 48,49 | | 61,48 | 98,58 | 99,53 |

* On November 30, 1919 The rest of the figures are for March 31.

But this facile procedure could not be carried on *ad infinitum* except by jeopardizing the convertibility of the notes. Consequently the very increase of paper money, added to the increased demand for currency, compelled the Government to go in for the provision of metallic money for providing current means of purchase and also give a backing to the watered paper issues. The rising price of silver naturally made the Government go in for gold. An Ordinance was issued on June 29, 1917, requiring all gold imported into India to be sold to Government at a price based on the sterling exchange, and opened a gold Mint at Bombay for the coinage of it into mohurs.* Frantic efforts were made to acquire

* Act VIX of 1918.

gold from various quarters. The removal of the embargo on the export of gold by the U.S.A. on June 9, 1917, and the freeing of the market for South African and Australian gold, enabled the Government to obtain some supply of that metal. From July 18, 1919, immediate telegraphic transfers on India were offered against deposit at the Ottawa Mint in Canada of gold coin or bullion at a rate corresponding to the prevailing exchange rate, and at New York at competitive tenders from August 22, 1919. Arrangements were also made for the direct purchase of gold in London and U.S.A. Finally, to encourage the private import of gold, the acquisition rate was altered from September 15, 1919, so as to make allowance for the depreciation of the sterling. But the gold thus obtained was a negligible quantity. Besides, the issue of gold did not serve the purpose the Government had in mind—namely its retention in circulation. In the nature of things it was impossible. The rupee was depreciated in terms of gold to an enormous extent, and consequently at the rate of exchange gold passed out of circulation as quickly as it was issued by the Government. What the Government could do was to make the use of gold and silver coins illegal for other than currency purposes and to prevent their exportation, which it did by the Notifications of June 29 and September 3, 1917. Realizing that it could not rely upon gold the Government renewed its efforts to enlarge the rupee coinage. To facilitate the purchase of that metal the import of silver on private account into India was prohibited on September 3, 1917. This measure, however, removed only a few of the smaller competitors for the world's diminished supply of silver, and the world-demand remained so heavy that the Secretary of State was unable to obtain sufficient supply notwithstanding the great conservation effected in the use of silver by substituting nickel coinage for silver coins of subsidiary order,* and by the issue of notes of denominations as low as that of R. 1 † and of R. 2-8.‡ The Government of the United States was therefore approached on the subject of releasing a portion of the silver dollars held in their reserve. The American Government consented and passed the Pittman Act, under which the Government

* Act IV of 1918 and XXI of 1919.

† First issued on December 1, 1917

‡ First put into circulation on January 2, 1918.

of India acquired a substantial volume at 101½ cents per fine ounce. The total silver purchased during this period was as follows :

TABLE XLIV

RUPEE COINAGE, 1915—20

| Year. | Silver purchased in Open Market, Standard Ounces. | Silver purchaced from U. S. A. Standard Ounces | Total Standard Ounces. |
|---|---|---|---|
| 1915-16 . . | 8,636,000 | — | — |
| 1916-17 . . | 124,535,000 | — | — |
| 1917-18 . . | 70,923,000 | — | — |
| 1918-19 . . | 106,410,000 | 152,518,000 | — |
| 1919-20 . . | 14,108,000 | 60,875,000 | — |
| Total . . | 324,612,000 | 213,393 000 | 538,005,000 |

Now, recalling the fact that from 1900 to 1914 the Government had coined about 532 million standard ounces of silver,* it means that the coinage of silver by Government during these five years exceeded the amount coined in the fourteen preceding years by five million ounces.

Thus the fall in the gold value of the rupee is an inevitable consequence of the exercise of the power to issue inconvertible currency in unlimited quantities. This is the fate of all inconvertible currencies known to history. But it is said that an exception must be made in the case of the rupee currency, for if the Government has the liberty of issuing it in unlimited quantities it has also resources to counteract the effects of a fall when it does occur. We must therefore turn to an examination of these resources.

The basis of the reasoning is that the rupee is a token currency, and that if the value of a token currency is maintained at par with

Cf the figures given by L. Abrahms in his evidence to the Currency Committee of 1919—Mit. of Evid, Q. 37—41

gold by applying to it the principle of redemption into gold* it should be possible to maintain the value of the rupee at par with gold by adopting a similar mechanism. What is wanted is an adequate gold fund, and so long as the Government has it, we are assured that we need have no anxiety on the score of a possible fall in the value of the rupee. Such a fund the Government of India has, and on all the three occasions when the gold value of the rupee fell below par that fund was operated upon. The process of redemption is carried on chiefly in three ways: (1) The sale of what are called reverse councils, by which the Government receives rupees in India in return for gold in London; (2) the release of gold internally in receipt for rupees in India; and (3) the stoppage of the Secretary of State's council bills to prevent further rupees from going into circulation. The cumulative effect of these, it is said, is to contract the currency and raise its value to par. Although all the three may be employed, the first is by far the most important means adopted by the Government in carrying through this process of redemption. The extent of the redemption effected on the three occasions when it was employed may be seen from the three following tables: —

* *See* the very interesting discussion by Laughlin of the laws of token money in his *Principles of Money*, Chap XV It may be said in passing that Laughlin is an opponent of the quantity theory of money, but in his discussion of token money he virtually admits it

## I. REDEMPTION OF CURRENCY, 1907-8

### TABLE XLV

| Date. | By the Sale of Reverse Councils | | By Release of Gold Diminution of Govt Stock of Gold during the Month. | Private Exports of Gold Coin during the Month. | Drawings of the Secretary of State. |
|---|---|---|---|---|---|
| | Amount offered. | Amount sold | | | |
| | £ | £ | £ | £ | £ |
| 1907— | | | | | |
| Sept . . | — | — | 152,000 | 14 | 858,896 |
| Oct. . . | — | — | 254,000 | 9,109 | 921,678 |
| Nov. . . | — | — | 532,000 | 3 | 427,344 |
| Dec . . | — | — | 338,000 | 2,501 | 571,905 |
| 1908— | | | | | |
| March 26 | 500,000 | 70,000 | 226,000 | — | 172,669 (for the whole month) |
| April 2 . . | 500,000 | 449,000 | | | |
| ,, 9 . . | 500,000 | 340,000 | | | |
| ,, 16 . . | 500,000 | 441,000 | 461,000 | — | 66,834 |
| ,, 23 . . | 500,000 | 329,000 | | | |
| ,, 30 . . | 500,000 | 205,000 | | | |
| May 7 . . | 500,000 | 81,000 | | | |
| ,, 14 . . | 500,000 | 145,000 | | | |
| ,, 21 . . | 820,000 | 793,000 | 645,000 | — | 62,764 |
| ,, 28 . . | 500,000 | 500,000 | | | |
| June 4 . . | 1,000,000 | 755,000 | | | |
| ,, 11 . . | 1,000,000 | 70,000 | 334,000 | — | 169,810 |
| ,, 18 . . | 500,000 | Nil | | | |
| ,, 25 . . | 500,000 | 50 000 | | | |
| July 2 . . | 500,000 | 470,000 | | | |
| ,, 9 . . | 500,000 | 304,000 | | | |
| ,, 16 . . | 500,000 | 500,000 | 16,000 | — | 186,847 |
| ,, 23 . . | 1,000,000 | 968,000 | | | |
| ,, 30 . . | 1,000,000 | 860 000 | | | |
| Aug 6 . . | 1,000,000 | 418 000 | | | |
| ,, 13 . . | 500,000 | 310,000 | 354,000 | | 262,217 |
| ,, 20 . . | 500,000 | Nil | | | |
| ,, 27 . . | 500,000 | Nil | | | |
| Sept 3 . . | 500,000 | Nil | 502,000 | — | 1,431,012 |
| ,, 10 . . | 500,000 | Nil | | | |
| Total . | 15,320,000 | 8,058,000 | 4,394,000 | 249,942 | |

## II. Redemption in 1914-16

### TABLE XLVI

| Date | Reverse Councils (in £, 000) | Drawings of the S. of S. (in Lakhs) of Rs.). |
|---|---|---|
| 1914. April | Nil | 270 |
| May | ,, | 61 |
| June | ,, | 68 |
| July | ,, | 66 |
| August | 2,778 | 72 |
| September | 1,515 | 25 |
| October | 1,895 | 41 |
| November | 1,044 | 32 |
| December | 1,250 | 30 |
| 1915. January | 225 | 29 |
| February | Nil. | 181 |
| March | ,, | 287 |
| Total | 8,707 | 1,162 |
| 1915. April | Nil. | 1,53 |
| May | ,, | 1,03 |
| June | 651 | 17 |
| July | 3,377 | 8 |
| August | 815 | 23 |
| September | 50 | 2,17 |
| October | Nil | 2,25 |
| November | ,, | 2,02 |
| December | ,, | 3,28 |
| 1916. January | ,, | 5,26 |
| February | ,, | 6,02 |
| March | ,, | 6,33 |
| Total | 4,893 | 30,37 |

## III. Redemption in 1920

### TABLE XLVII

### Sale of Reverse Councils (Figures in Thousands of Pounds)

| Date of Sale | Amount offered at each Sale | Amount applied for at each Sale | Amount sold at each Sale | Progressive Total of Amount sold |
|---|---|---|---|---|
| 1920. January 2 | 1,000 | 770 | 770 | 770 |
| ,, 8 | 1,000 | 8,499 | 990 | 1,760 |
| ,, 15 | 2,000 | 300 | 300 | 2,060 |
| ,, 22 | 2,000 | 4,890 | 2,000 | 4,060 |
| ,, 29 | 2,000 | 1,334 | 5,000 | 5,394 |
| February 5 | 2,000 | 32,390 | 2,000 | 7,394 |
| ,, 12 | 2,000 | 41,312 | 2,000 | 12,394 |
| ,, 19 | 2,000 | 122,335 | 2,000 | 14,394 |
| ,, 26 | 2,000 | 78,417 | 2,000 | 16,394 |
| March 3 | 2,000 | 64,931 | 2,000 | 18,394 |
| ,, 11 | 2 000 | 117,185 | 2,000 | 20,394 |
| ,, 18 | 2,000 | 153,559 | 2,000 | 22,394 |
| ,, 25 | 2,000 | 56,295 | 2,000 | 24,394 |
| ,, 31 } April 1 } | 2,000 | 35,050 | 1,988 | 26,382 |
| ,, 8 | 2,000 | 16,721 | 2,000 | 28,382 |
| ,, 15 | 2,000 | 48,270 | 2,000 | 30,382 |
| ,, 22 | 2,000 | 59,020 | 2,000 | 32,382 |
| ,, 29 | 1,000 | 53,210 | 1,000 | 33,382 |
| May 6 | 1,000 | 89,514 | 1,000 | 34,382 |
| ,, 13 | 1,000 | 101,625 | 1,000 | 35,382 |
| ,, 20 | 1,000 | 122,279 | 1,000 | 36,382 |
| ,, 26 | 1,000 | 85,620 | 1,000 | 37,382 |
| June 3 | 1,000 | 101,821 | 1,000 | 38,382 |
| ,, 10 | 1,000 | 109,245 | 1,000 | 39,382 |
| ,, 15 | 1,000 | 122,991 | 1,000 | 40,382 |
| ,, 24 | 1,000 | 73,391 | 1,000 | 41,382 |
| July 1 | 1,000 | 106,751 | 1,000 | 42,382 |
| ,, 8 | 1,000 | 63,690 | 1,000 | 43,382 |
| ,, 15 | 1,000 | 101,830 | 1,000 | 44,382 |
| ,, 22 | 1,000 | 103,960 | 1,000 | 45,382 |
| ,, 29 | 1,000 | 75,486 | 1,000 | 46,382 |
| August 5 | 1,000 | 101,260 | 1,000 | 47,382 |
| ,, 12 | 1,000 | 112,230 | 1,000 | 48,382 |
| ,, 19 | 1,000 | 114,767 | 1,000 | 49,382 |
| ,, 26 | 1,000 | 117,390 | 1,000 | 50,382 |
| Sept. 2 | 1,000 | 126,425 | 1,000 | 51,382 |
| ,, 7 | 1,000 | 117,200 | 1,000 | 52,382 |
| ,, 13 | 1,000 | 115,095 | 1,000 | 53,382 |
| ,, 21 | 1,000 | 122,590 | 1,000 | 54,382 |
| ,, 28 | 1,000 | 120,050 | 1,000 | 55,382 |

Not only did the Government sell reverse councils on a large scale, but it also sold gold for rupees for internal circulation, a thing which it seldom did before.

### III. Redemption in 1920

TABLE XLVIII

Sale of Gold

| No. of Sale. | Date of Sale. | Minimum Rate of accepted Tenders. | Average Rate of accepted Tenders. | Quantity sold (in Tolas). | Price of Country Bar Gold in the Bombay Bazaar. |
|---|---|---|---|---|---|
| | | Rs A P | Rs. A. P | | Rs. A. P. |
| 1 | 1919, September 3 | 25 8 0 | 26 12 1 | 3,29,130 | 28 10 0 |
| 2 | ,, 17 | 24 8 0 | 24 10 0 | 3,96,640 | 26 1 0 |
| 3 | October 6 | 25 8 0 | 25 9 8 | 3,26,000 | 27 0 0 |
| 4 | ,, 20 | 26 15 3 | 27 0 2 | 3,34,000 | 28 0 0 |
| 5 | November 3 | 27 14 6 | 27 15 6 | 3,25,000 | 28 5 0 |
| 6 | ,, 17 | 26 15 0 | 27 0 11 | 5,18,500 | 28 2 0 |
| 7 | December 8 | 26 0 6 | 26 4 6 | 10,00,650 | 27 10 0 |
| 8 | 1920, January 5 | 26 4 3 | 26 7 9 | 7,63,300 | 27 3 0 |
| 9 | ,, 19 | 26 13 3 | 26 14 7 | 8,00,000 | 27 5 0 |
| 10 | February 5 | 25 2 3 | 25 9 7 | 7,56,450 | 25 6 0 |
| 11 | ,, 19 | 16 2 3 | 21 9 1 | 9,60,590 | 23 4 0 |
| 12 | March 3 | 18 8 0 | 18 12 4 | 12,96,125 | 21 7 0 |
| 13 | ,, 17 | 21 6 0 | 21 7 7 | 12,53,325 | 22 13 0 |
| 14 | April 7 | 22 7 3 | 22 9 4 | 12,46,200 | 24 0 0 |
| 15 | ,, 21 | 23 7 4 | 23 8 6 | 10,68,175 | 24 4 0 |
| 16 | May 5 | 20 13 3 | 21 3 2 | 11,96,750 | 21 8 0 |
| 17 | ,, 19 | 21 0 3 | 21 1 7 | 12,46,050 | 21 12 0 |
| 18 | June 9 | 21 8 9 | 21 9 8 | 11,32,350 | 22 2 6 |
| 19 | ,, 23 | 20 14 10 | 21 0 5 | 12,25,250 | 21 8 0 |
| 20 | July 7 | 21 1 4 | 22 2 2 | 12,81,500 | 21 6 0 |
| 21 | ,, 21 | 22 0 1 | 22 0 11 | 12,42,000 | 22 5 0 |
| 22 | August 4 | 22 5 6 | 22 6 3 | 12,78,950 | 22 7 0 |
| 23 | ,, 19 | 23 9 4 | 23 10 2 | 5,54,500 | 23 7 0 |
| 24 | September 1 | 22 8 3 | 22 10 8 | 8,27,700 | 23 1 6 |
| 25 | ,, 14 | 23 9 4 | 23 12 11 | 2,30,500 | 23 8 0 |
| | | | Total | 2,15,89,635 | |

During 1920 no council bills were drawn by the Secretary of State on the Government of India.

The success of this mechanism on the two previous occasions had strengthened the belief that it had the virtue of restoring the value of the rupee. But the failure of this mechanism in the crisis of 1920 compels one to adopt an attitude of reserve towards its general efficacy. It cannot be said that exchange gave way because this mechanism was not brought into operation. On the other hand, the view of the Government regarding the sale of reverse councils in 1920 had undergone a profound modification as compared with the view it held during the crisis of 1907-8. In that crisis the Government behaved like a miser, sitting tight on its gold reserve and refusing to use it for the very purpose which it was designed to serve. An Accountant-General had "to go on his knees" to persuade the Government of India to release its gold.* It was probably because it was rebuked by the Chamberlain Commission for failing to make use of its gold reserve in 1907 that in the crisis of 1920 the policy of selling reverse councils was so boldly conceived. There was a great deal of ignorant criticism of that policy from the general public that it was an "organized loot." But the Finance Minister was undaunted, and argued†:—

> "It is an essential feature of our exchange policy . . that we should not only provide for remittances from London to India through council bills at approximately gold point, but from India to London in time of exchange weakness also at gold point, through the sale of sterling remittance known as reverse councils. It is simply an alternative to the export of gold. This is no new matter—we have been selling reverse councils for years . . . . and unless we do so the exchange policy does not become effective. . . . This is the reason, and the only reason, why we have sold reverse councils. . . . It is an effort in fact to maintain exchange as near as possible to the gold point. . . What would be the consequence if we yielded to the pressure placed on us and ceased to sell reverse councils at all? I can understand a demand that reverse councils should be sold by some different method, or at rates different from those at present in force, but I must confess that I cannot understand the demand that the facilities for the exchange of rupees into external currency should be entirely withdrawn. I see that in Bombay it is urged that we should let exchange find its 'natural level.' That is a catchword which does not impress me. Used in the sense in which that phrase has been recently used, there is no such thing as a 'natural level' in exchange, for, when one translates the internal currency into another currency, there must be some sort of common denominator to which both currencies can be brought; it may be gold, it may be silver, it may be sterling or it may be Spanish pesetas, which we take as our basis. The rupee must be

* Evidence of Mr. F. C. Harrison before the Chamberlain Commission, Q. 10,209.

† Speech on the resolution *re* "Reverse Councils," March 10, 1920. *S.L.C.P.* Vol. LVIII, p 1291.

> linked on to *something*,* and if it is so linked, then it must be at some definite rate, and this necessarily involves that we must sometimes be prepared to sell reverse councils in order to maintain that rate. If reverse councils be withdrawn entirely, then we should have neither a gold standard, nor a gold-exchange standard, nor any kind of standard at all."

But that only raises the question : If the sale of reverse councils is efficacious in righting the exchange, why was its effect such a disastrous failure ? The Finance Minister answered the point tersely and cogently when he said :—

> "If we have failed in narrowing the gap between the market price and the theoretical gold part of the rupee . . . . it is not because we have sold too many reverse councils; it is because we have sold too few. I put it to any member of the commercial community here, and I put it without fear of contradiction, that if our resources had enabled us .. . . to sell straight away 20, 30, or 40 millions of reverse councils, we should probably have had no gap between the market price of the rupee and the theoretical gold price of the rupee at all. One of our difficulties has been, not that we have sold too many reverse councils, but that we have been obliged to sell too few." †

There would have been some force in this argument if the amount of reverse bills sold were "too few." Not 20, 30, or 40 millions, but 55½ millions of reverse councils were sold, besides the large issue of gold internally, and the complete stoppage of council bills, and yet the rupee did not rise above 1s. 4d. sterling, let alone reaching 2s. gold. Why did not the sale of reverse councils suffice to rectify the exchange ? This leads us to examine the whole question of the efficacy of this redemption.

It is necessary to premise at the outset that redemption may result in mere substitution of one form of currency by another, or it may result in the retirement of currency. In so far as it results in substitution it is of no consequence at all, for substitution of currency is not a shrinkage of currency. To the restoration of the

* By Ordinance III of June 21, 1920, the gold coins referred to in Section 11 of the Indian Coinage Act (III of 1906) ceased to be legal tender in payment or on account, but provision was made for their acceptance by Government at the ratio of Rs. 75 during a moratorium of twenty-one days. This Ordinance continued till September 9, 1920, when by Act XXXVI of 1920 the sovereign was again made legal tender. During this period gold had no legal status in India.

† *Ibid.*, p 1301.

‡ The most notable example is that of American greenbacks. Under the law of 1875 they were by 1879 retired in sufficient numbers to restore parity with gold. But by a counter-law of 1878, 347,000,000 of them have been kept in circulation. As soon as redeemed, they must be reissued; they cannot be retired.

value of a currency what is essential is its shrinkage, i.e. its retirement, cancellation. The important question with regard to this mechanism is not to what extent the currency can be redeemed, but to what extent it can be retired. In the prevalent view of this question it seems to be accepted without question that this extent is determined by the magnitude of the gold resources of the Government of India and the Secretary of State. Let us first make it clear how these gold resources are located and distributed. It will be recalled that these gold resources are distributed between (1) the paper-currency reserve, (2) the gold-standard reserve, and (3) the cash balances of the Secretary of State. It has been the habit to speak of these resources as being three "lines of defence" on which the Government can safely rely when an exchange crisis takes place. But are they ? They can be, for the purposes of retirement, only if they were all "free" resources; in other words, if they were not appropriated resources. To what extent are they unappropriated? Can the Secretary of State take gold from the paper-currency reserve ? He can, but then he must replace it by something else, or must cancel notes to that extent. Can the Secretary of State take gold out of his cash balances? He can, but then he must either borrow to fill his Treasury or draw upon the Government of India if there is anyone to buy his bills, which is tantamount to issuing rupee currency. The gold in the paper-currency reserve and that in the cash balances is of no use at all, for it does not permit of the cancellation of the rupee currency, which is what is wanted in restoring its value when it suffers a fall. It is therefore sheer nonsense to speak of the effectiveness of redemption as being commensurate with the gold resources of the Secretary of State. The matter is important, and an illustration may not be out of place. Suppose A, a holder of rupees, wants to get gold for them. He can go to three counters; (1) that of the controller in charge of cash balances; (2) that of the controller of currency in charge of the paper-currency reserve; or (3) that of the custodian of the gold-standard reserve. If A goes to the first, what is the result? The cash balance is *pro tanto* reduced. On the assumption that the cash balance is at its minimum, as it should be, the controller must reimburse himself immediaitely to maintain his solvency by drawing a bill on India and thereby releasing rupees received for gold again in circulation, so that in this case there is no shrinkage of currency. If A goes to the controller of currency, what happens ? The controller gives him gold, but on the assumption that the paper-currency account is a separate statutory account he must put the rupees received from A in place of the gold issued from his reserve, so that here again what happens is that the composition of the reserve undergoes a change, but the total paper currency remains the same. It must therefore be borne in mind that to the extent the gold in the paper-currency reserve and the cash balances are operated upon the result is not a retirement of currency. To speak of them as "lines of defences," as is so often done, is to overlook the fact that these two are not free resources but are appropriated resources.

What is, then, the resource left to the Government to *retire* the rupee currency? Only the gold-standard reserve. That is the only reserve the amount of which is unappropriated for any particular use. It is free cash, and only to that extent is it possible for the Government to restore the rupee currency when a fall in its gold value eventuates. Of course it is important to bear in mind that this is the extent to which it can retire the currency. Not that it will, for it may not, and there is no want of cases in which it has not. Two instances will suffice. During the first period of the Mint closure, 1893-98, it will be recalled how a large number of rupees had accumulated in the hands of the Government, and in the interest of raising the value of the rupee they should have been locked away. Instead the Government of India released that money in circulation in extending railways and other public works, locked away. As though the spending of rupees by itself produced an effect different to what would have been produced had they been spent by the public Similarly irresponsible conduct marked the sale of reverse councils in 1920. To meet these reverse councils the Secretary of State took the gold from the paper-currency reserve. But instead of cancelling notes to the extent of the gold that was taken out of the reserve, the Government took powers under an Act XXI of 1920 to fill the gap by manufacturing securities *ad hoc*, so that although there was redemption there was no retirement, and so much gold was merely wasted, for it produced no effect on prices or the exchange. This Act, passed in March, 1920, was of temporary duration, and would have obliged the Government to retire the currency by October, 1920, when it was to expire. Rather than do this the Government altered the paper-currency law, not temporarily but permanently (Act XLV of 1920), changing the provisions in such a manner as to require the Government to cancel the currency to the smallest degree possible by retiring their "created securities." Even this was not done, owing to deficits in the Government Budget.

But even if such indiscretions were not repeated the fact remains that Government cannot effect a greater retirement than is permitted by the gold-standard reserve. If that reserve fails Government has only two resources left: (1) to melt down the rupees and sell them as bullion for gold and to go on further contracting the currency, in this way till its value is restored: or (2) to borrow gold. Both these are evidently costly methods. To sell rupees as bullion is bound to result in loss unless the bullion in the rupee fetched more at the time of sale than what it cost when it was purchased for manufacturing it into bullion. The second process, that of borrowing, cannot be lightly resorted to for the purpose of creating a reserve fund to retire the currency. Indeed, so costly are such methods, and so complete would be the proof they would afford of the instability of the exchange standard if they were resorted to, that Government has never contemplated them as possible lines of defence in an exchange crisis. It seems certain, however, that Government does recognise that the gold-standard reserve by itself cannot suffice for the maintenance of exchange. For we find that from the year 1907-8 dates a complete change in the distribution of Government balances between London and India. Up to that period it was the policy of the Secretary of State to draw only as much as necessary to finance his Home Treasury. After that date the practice was originated of drawing as much as the Government of India could provide, and as the Government of India has been supreme in financial matters it provided large sums for council drawings by increased taxation and budgeting for surpluses. The effect of this was to swell the cash balances of the Secretary of State.* No official explanation of a satisfactory character has ever been given for this

*For figures, *see* Chap. VII

novel way of financing the Home Treasury* but we shall not be very far wrong if we say that the object in accumulating these balances is to provide a second gold reserve to supplement the true gold-standard reserve. Whatever strength the Government may derive for the time being from this adventitious resource, it is obvious that it cannot be permanent. Under a more popular control of Government finances the cash balances will have to be kept down to a minimum necessary to work the Treasury, and the gold-standard reserve will be the only reserve on which the Government will have to depend.

The gold-standard reserve is to the rupee what the paper-currency reserve is to the notes. The purport of both is to prevent the respective currencies they support from falling or going to discount. But the treatment accorded by the Government to the rupee and the paper in respect of reserve shows a remarkable degree of contrast. In the case of the paper, as has been previously noted, the reserve is a statutory reserve, and even when the whole basis of Indian paper currency has been changed the provisions as to reserve are none the less strict and cannot be disregarded by the Government without infringing the law. Now, the rupee is nothing but a note printed on silver.† As such, the provisions as to reserve should be analogous to those governing the paper currency. Strange as it may seem, any regulation is conspicuous by its absence in regard to the gold-standard reserve.‡ Not only is it not obligatory on the Government to redeem the rupee, but it does not seem that the Government is even bound to maintain the reserve. And that it has maintained such a reserve is no guarantee that it will replace it supposing that the reserve

* Cf. Memorandum on India Office Balances, Cd. 6619 of 1913.

† "We have virtually relegated our rupee currency to the position of a token currency, and we are now practically in the position of bankers who have issued a certain amount of fiduciary currency (whether paper or metal is immaterial), and to maintain the value of this fiduciary currency we are bound to be in a position to exchange it for gold when presented to meet legitimate trade requirements," said the Financial Statement for 1903—4, p. 14.

‡ The Chamberlain Commission said: "There are disadvantages in restricting the freedom of the Government in a crisis, and it is undesirable that the disposition and amount of the reserve should be stereotyped . . . We therefore do not regard that the gold-standard reserve should be regulated by statute."—Report, Sec. 101.

was dissipated.* Such differences apart, is the gold-standard reserve an adequate reserve? Figures of the magnitude of the gold-standard reserve, as usually given in official publications, are a meaningless array. What is the use of displaying assets without at the same time exhibiting the liabilities? To be able to judge of the adequacy of that reserve we must know what is the total circulation of rupees. When, however, we compare the circulation of the rupees with the reserve, the proportion between the two is not sufficiently large so as to inspire confidence in the stability of the system (*see* Table XLIX.)

How can a reserve so small as this carry through the process of retirement to any sufficient extent? That it will not always do it the crisis of 1920 gives abundant proof. But the supporters of the exchange standard maintain that the smallness of the reserve is a matter of no consequence, for the reserve is kept only for the purposes of foreign remittances. That being the case, it is said the reserve need not be large. Granting that it is so, what must govern the magnitude of the reserve in order that it may prove adequate in any and every case? The only attempt made to enunciate a rule of guidance is that by Prof. Keynes. That rule he finds† in the possible variations in the balance of trade of India. Now, does this make the problem of regulating the reserve more definite? As has been explained previously, the adverse balance of trade would be due to the depreciation of the currency, so that Mr. Keynes's statement amounts to this, that the reserve should vary with the depth of the depreciation. But how is a Government to do this? Only by adverting to the movement of the price level. But in all its currency management the Government of India never pays any attention to the price problem. Indeed, as was pointed out above, its conception of the underlying causes of the

* In the course of his speech on the Indian Paper Currency (Temporary Amendment) Bill, dated March 17, 1920, the Finance Minister observed: " . . . from a practical point of view, it is desirable to leave the gold-standard reserve until the paper-currency reserve has been re-transferred, in case . . . the Secretary of State finds it impossible to keep himself in funds by Councils for his heavy home liabilities. He will then be able to use the gold-standard reserve, and we can credit the gold-standard reserve out here. There is a third point, and I think a conclusive one. When you operate against the paper-Currency reserve you have to operate within the paper-currency reserve; when you operate against the gold-standard reserve it disappears; it melts, and we are under no obligation to replace it; whereas we are under a statutory obligation to replace the paper-currency reserve."—*S.L.C.P* Vol. LVIII, p 1416.

†Op. cit, pp 166—7.

TABLE XLIX

DISTRIBUTION OF THE GOLD-STANDARD RESERVE AND ITS PROPORTION TO RUPEE CIRCULATION (IN THOUSANDS OF POUNDS (STERLING)

| March 31 in each Year. | In England. | | | | | In India. | | | | | Total Reserve, England and India. | Volume of Rs. in Circulation in Crores | Percentage of Reserve to Rs. in Circulation (£ = Rs. 15)* |
|---|---|---|---|---|---|---|---|---|---|---|---|---|---|
| | Purchase Value of Sterling Securities. | Cash at Short Notice. | Temporary Loan to the Home Treasury. | Gold deposited at the Bank of England | Total | Coined Rupees in India | Outstanding Debt from Treasury balances. | Temporary Loan to Treasury Balances. | Gold. | Total. | | | |
| (1) | (2) | (3) | (4) | (5) | (6) | (7) | (8) | (9) | (10) | (11) | (12) | (13) | (14) |
| 1901 | — | — | — | — | — | — | 1,831 | — | 1,200 | 3,031 | 3,031 | 143 | 3.1 |
| 02 | 3,454 | — | — | — | 3,454 | — | — | — | — | — | 3,454 | 138 | 3.7 |
| 03 | 3,810 | — | — | — | 3,810 | — | 1 | — | — | 1 | 3,811 | 136 | 3.4 |
| 04 | 6,377 | — | — | — | 6,377 | — | 167 | — | — | 167 | 6,544 | 144 | 6.8 |
| 05 | 8,377 | — | — | — | 8,377 | — | 152 | — | — | 152 | 8,529 | 152 | 8.4 |
| 06 | 12,165 | — | — | — | 12,165 | — | 287 | — | — | 287 | 12,452 | 164 | 10.7 |
| 07 | 12,519 | — | — | — | 12,519 | 4,000 | 301 | — | 22 | 4,323 | 16,842 | 178 | 10.6 |
| 08 | 13,187 | — | 1,131 | — | 14,318 | 4,000 | — | — | — | 4,000 | 18,318 | 191 | 11.2 |
| 09 | 7,414 | — | 470 | — | 7,884 | 10,587 | — | — | — | 10,587 | 18,471 | 187 | 7.1 |
| 10 | 13,219 | 3,011 | — | — | 16,230 | 2,534 | — | — | — | 2,534 | 18,764 | 186 | 13.8 |
| 11 | 15,849 | 1,477 | — | — | 17,326 | 1,934 | — | — | — | 1,934 | 19,260 | 184 | 14.8 |
| 12 | 16,748 | 1,074 | — | — | 17,822 | 1,934 | — | — | — | 1,934 | 19,956 | 182 | 14.9 |
| 13 | 15,946 | 1,006 | — | 1,620 | 18,572 | 4,000 | 35 | — | — | 4,035 | 22,607 | 191 | 14.8 |
| 14 | 17,165 | 25 | — | 4,320 | 21,510 | 4,000 | 22 | — | — | 4,022 | 25,532 | 187 | 17.2 |
| 15 | 12,149 | 8 | — | 1,250 | 13,407 | — | 70 | 7,000 | 6,238 | 13,308 | 25,715 | 204 | 18.9 |
| 16 | 16,219 | 5,792 | — | — | 22,011 | — | 1 | 4,000 | 239 | 4,240 | 26,251 | 212 | 15.7 |
| 17 | 25,406 | 6,001 | — | — | 31,407 | — | — | — | 103 | 103 | 31,510 | 227 | 20.8 |
| 18 | 28,453 | 6,000 | — | — | 34,453 | — | — | — | — | — | 34,453 | 219 | 23.5 |
| 19 | 29,729 | 6,016 | — | — | 35,745 | — | — | — | — | — | 35,745 | 228 | 23.5 |

* In striking the proportion the rupee portion of the reserve has been omitted.

fall of exchange is totally at variance with the only true conception, nothing but a firm grasp of which can enable it to avert a crisis. Being ignorant of the true conception it blindly goes on issuing currency until there occurs what is called an adverse balance of trade. All it aims at is to maintain a gold reserve, and so long as it has that reserve it does not stop to think how much currency it issues. The proportion of the issues and the reserve not being correlated the stability of the exchange standard, in so far as it depends upon the reserve, must always remain in the region of vagueness, far too problematical to inspire confidence of the system. Nay, the liability of redemption for foreign remittances, small as it appears, may become so indefinite as entirely to jeopardize the restoration of stability to the exchange standard.

But is a gold reserve such an important thing for the maintenance of the value of a currency? All supporters of the exchange standard must be said to be believers in that theory. But the view cannot stand a moment's criticism. To look upon a gold reserve as an efficient cause why all kinds of money remain at par with gold is a gross fallacy.* To take such a view is to invert the casual order. It is not the gold reserve which maintains the value of the circulating medium, but it is the limitation on its volume which not only suffices to maintain its own value, but also makes possible the accumulation and retention of whatever gold reserve there is in the country. Remove the limit on the volume of currency, and not only will it fail to maintain its value, but will prevent the accumulation of any gold reserve whatever. So little indeed is the importance of a gold reserve to the cause of the preservation of the value of currency that provided there is a rigid limit on its issue the gold reserve may be entirely done away with without impairing in the least the value of the currency. The Chamberlain Commission recommended that the Government of India should accumulate a reserve to maintain the value of the rupee because it was by means of their reserves that European banks maintained the value of their currencies. Nothing can be a greater perversion of the truth. What the European banks did was just the

* Cf in this connection the brilliant paper by F A, Fetter, "The Gold Reserve: its Function and its Maintenance," in the *Political Science Quarterly*, 1896, Vol. XI, No. 2.

opposite of what the Commission recommended. Whenever their gold tended to disappear they reduced their currencies not only relatively but absolutely. It was by limitation of their currencies that they protected the value of the currencies and also their gold reserves.

The existence of a reserve, therefore cannot lend any strength to the gold-exchange standard. On the other hand, if we inquire into the genesis of the reserve, its existence is an enormous source of weakness to that standard. For how does the Government obtain its gold-standard reserve? Does it increase its reserve in the same way as the banks do, by reducing their issues? Quite the contrary. So peculiar is the constitution of the Indian gold-standard reserve that in it the assets, i.e., the reserve, and the liabilities, i.e., the rupee, are dangerously concomitant. In other words, the reserve cannot increase without an increase in the rupee currency. This ominous situation arises from the fact that the reserve is built out of the profits of rupee coinage. That being its origin, it is obvious that the fund can grow only as a consequence of increased rupee coinage. What profit the rupee coinage yields depends upon how great is the difference between the cost price of the rupee and its exchange value. Barring the minting charges, which are more or less fixed, the most important factor in the situation is the price of silver. Whether there shall be any profit to be credited to the reserve depends upon the price paid for the silver to be manufactured into rupees *

Not only is the reserve an evil by the nature of its origin, but having regard to its documentary character the reserve cannot be said to be absolutely dependable in a time of crisis. There is no doubt that the intention of the Government in investing the reserve is to promote its increase by adding to it the interest accruing from the securities in which it is invested. The critics of the Government want a *large* and at the same time a *metallic* reserve. But they do not realize that having regard to the origin of the reserve the two demands are incompatible. If the reserve needs to be large then it must be invested. Indeed, if the reserve had not been invested it would have remained distressingly

* See footnote,[1] page 220.

meagre.[*] But is there no danger in a reserve of this kind ?

† In answer to Mr. M. L. Reddi Garu, the following statement was laid on the table:—

*Statement showing the average cost of silver purchased by the—

| Year. | Royal Mint Average Cost for Standard Ounce. | India Office Average Cost for Standard Ounce. | Financial Year |
|---|---|---|---|
| | d. | d. | |
| 1893 . . | $36\frac{4}{16}$ | No purchase | 1893–94 |
| 94 . . | $29\frac{1}{8}$ | ,, | 1894–95 |
| 95 . . | $30\frac{3}{8}$ | ,, | 1895–96 |
| 96 . . | $30\frac{1}{16}$ | ,, | 1896–97 |
| 97 . . | $27\frac{5}{8}$ | ,, | 1897–98 |
| 98 . . | $27\frac{1}{8}$ | ,, | 1898–99 |
| 99 . | $27\frac{3}{8}$ | 28 | 1899–1900 |
| 1900 . | $28\frac{1}{8}$ | 29 | 1900–01 |
| 01 . . | $27\frac{13}{16}$ | No purchase. | 1901–02 |
| 02 . . | $24\frac{1}{16}$ | 22.80 | 1902–03 |
| 03 . . | $23\frac{11}{16}$ | 27 19 | 1903–04 |
| 04 . . | $26\frac{3}{8}$ | 27.14 | 1904–05 |
| 05 . . | $27\frac{7}{16}$ | 29.74 | 1905–06 |
| 06 . . | $31\frac{1}{16}$ | 31.59 | 1906–07 |
| 07 . . | $30\frac{9}{16}$ | 31.27 | 1907–08 |
| 08 . . | $24\frac{7}{16}$ | No purchase | 1908–09 |
| 09 . | $23\frac{11}{16}$ | ,, | 1909–10 |
| 10 . . | $24\frac{5}{8}$ | ,, | 1910–11 |
| 11 . | $24\frac{13}{16}$ | ,, | 1911–12 |
| 12 . . | $27\frac{13}{16}$ | 28 71 | 1912–13 |
| 13 . . | $28\frac{1}{16}$ | 28.71 | 1913–14 |
| 14 . . | $24\frac{5}{16}$ | No purchase | 1914–15 |
| 15 . . | $24\frac{5}{8}$ | 33.96 | 1915–16 |
| 16 . . | $30\frac{3}{8}$ | 33.96 | 1916–17 |
| 17 . | $39\frac{13}{16}$ | 42.78 | 1917–18 |
| 18 . | $47\frac{9}{16}$ | 48.20 | 1918–19 |
| 19 . . | $49\frac{7}{8}$ | 52 04 | 1919–20 |
| 20 . . | $50\frac{7}{8}$ | Silver purchased at special rates from the Baldwin mines and the Perth mint | 1920–21 |

* *Legislative Assembly Debates*, Vol. II, No. 3 September, 10 1920, p. 181.

In the absence of information whether the price is F.O.B. or C.I.F. it is difficult to say that the Secretary of State has had to pay higher prices for silver than were paid by the Master of the Royal Mint.

† From 1900-1 to 1920-21 the profits on coinage credited to the gold-standard reserve amounted to £28,573,606 only; while during the same period Interest and Discount gave £13,306,847 or nearly one half the profits on coinage, Cf. *East India: Accounts and Estimates*, 1921-22. *Cmd*, 1517 of 1921, p. 20.

The source of a danger in a reserve such as this was well pointed out by Jevons when he said* :

> ". . . . good government funds and good bills can always be sold at some price so that a banking firm with a strong reserve of this kind might always maintain their solvency. But the remedy might be worse for the community than the disease, and the forced sale of the reserve might create such a disturbance in the money market as would do more harm than the suspension of payment. . . ."

In the same manner, who can say that all the increase of reserve from interest will not be wiped out by a slump in the value of the securities if put upon the market for conversion into gold at a time when there takes place an exchange crisis? Supposing, however, the full value of the securities is realized, the number of rupees the reserve will "sink" when occasion for redemption arrives depends upon what is the price at which the rupees are bought back. If the fall of the rupee is small, it may help to retire a large volume of currency and thus restore its value. On the other hand, if the fall is great, it will suffice to retire only a small part of the currency and may fail to restore its value as it did in 1920, so that what may appear to be a big reserve may turn out to be very inadequate. But, apart from considerations of the relative magnitude of the reserve that can be built up, the point that seems to have been entirely overlooked is that the process of building up the reserves directly involves the process of augmenting the currency. The Chamberlain Commission was cognizant of the fact that the gold-standard reserve could not be built up except by coining rupees. Indeed, it cautioned those desirous of a gold currency to remember that if gold took the place of "new rupees which it would be necessary otherwise to mint, the effect is to diminish the strength of the gold-standard reserve by the amount of the profit which would have been made from new coinage."† Rather than recommend a policy which "would bring to an end the natural growth of the gold-standard reserve," the Committee permitted the Government to coin rupees. But is there no danger involved in such a reserve? What is the use of a reserve which creates the very evil which it is supposed afterwards to mitigate? Indeed, those who have been agitating

* Money, p. 227.

† Report, par. 63.

for an increase in the Indian gold-standard reserve cannot be said to have been alive to the dangers involved in the existence of such a reserve. The smaller the gold-standard reserve the better it would be, for there would be no inflation, no fall in the purchasing power of the rupee, and no necessity for its retirement.

Having regard to its origin, the gold-standard reserve, instead of acting as a brake upon reckless issue of rupee currency, is the direct cause of it and tends to aggravate the effects of an inconvertible currency rather than counteract them. Perversity cannot go further. If the fact that a mechanism like that of the gold-standard reserve, set up for the purpose of limiting the currency, cannot be made to function without adding to the currency, does not render the system an unsound currency, one begins to wonder what would. Great names have been invoked in support of the exchange standard. After trying hard to find authoritative precedents for his plan,* Mr. Lindsay claimed before the Fowler Committee that it was founded upon the Report of the Parliamentary Committee on Irish Exchange.† There he was on firm ground. Among other things, the Committee did recommend that for stabilizing the exchange between England and Ireland the Bank of Ireland should open credit at the Bank of England and sell drafts on London at a fixed price. In so far as the exchange standard rests on gold reserve in London,

*m In 1876, when Mr. Lindsay first set out his scheme in the pages of his *Calcutta Review*, he mentions no parallel at all. In 1892, in his *Ricardo's Exchange Remedy*, he uttered the name of Ricardo as an authority for his plan, but in 1898 he shifted his ground, so much so that he blamed (*Economic Journal, supra*) Probyn for taking Ricardo's gold-bar plan as a basis. The reason why he disavowed Ricordo as his authority most probably lies in the fact that Ricardo's general views of currency were rather damaging to his position. In view of the fact that there are so many people who assert, no doubt, from the title of his *Proposals for an Economical and Secure Currency*, that Ricardo wrote against a metallic standard, it is worth while recording the following passage from his *Proposals*, in which he says: "During the late discussion on the bullion questions, it was almost justly contended that a currency, to be perfect, should be absolutely invariable in value. But it was said, too, that ours had become such a currency, by the Bank Restriction Bill: for by that bill we had wisely discarded gold and silver as the standard of our money . . . . Those who supported this opinion did not see that such a currency, instead of being variable, was subject to the greatest variations—that the only use of a standard is to regulate the quantity, and by the quantity the value of the currency—and that without a standard it would be exposed to all the fluctuations to which the ignorance or the interests of the issuers might subject it."

† The Report, which is a masterly document, was eclipsed by the Bullion Report, though both contain the same doctrine, by reason of its not being printed till 1826. *See* Lords Paper 48 of 1826.

Lindsay must be said to have faithfully copied the plan of the Irish Committee on exchange. But he totally neglected to give prominence to another and the most vital recommendation of the Committee, in which it is observed:* "*But all the benefits proposed by this Mode of Remedies would be of little Avail and very limited Duration if it* (i.e. Bank of Ireland) *did not promise at the same time to cure the Depreciation of Paper in Ireland by diminishing its over issue.*" Indeed, so great was the stress laid on the limitation of issue that when Parnell, in his resolution in the House of Commons on the reform of the Irish currency, regretted the non-adoption of the recommendations of the Committee,† Thornton in his reply pointed out that nothing would help to stabilize Irish exchange so long as the vital condition laid down by the Committee was disregarded. The recent experience in pegging the exchanges well illustrates the importance of that vital condition. Pegging the exchange is primarily a device to prevent the external value of the currency falling along with its internal value. The way in which pegging effects this divorce is important to note ‡ The primary effect of the peg is to permit the purchases of foreign goods by procuring foreign currency for home currency at a fixed price, which is higher than would be the case if it were determined by the general purchasing power parity of the two currencies. By enabling people to buy foreign goods with foreign currency obtained at a cheaper price the peg virtually raises foreign prices more to the level of the home prices, so that if the exchange is stable it is not because there is a peg, but because the price-levels in the two countries have reached a new equilibrium. Essentially the exchange is stable because it is an artificial purchasing-power parity. Whether it will continue to be so depends upon the movements in the home prices. If the home prices rise more than the rise brought about by the peg in the foreign prices the mechanism must break. It is from this point of view that the condition laid down by the Irish Committee on exchange regarding the limitation on issue must be held as one of vital character. In omitting to advert to that condition the Indian currency contradicts what is best in that Report of the Irish Committee.

* Report, p. 16. Italics not in the original.

Cf. the succinct statement by T. E. Gregory, *Foreign Exchanges*, p. 85

† See *Hansard Parliamentary Debates*, Vol. XIV, pp. 75—91.

The reason why Mr. Lindsay paid no attention to the question of limitation in setting up his exchange standard is largely that, notwithstanding the great reputation he has achieved as an author of a new system, he was profoundly ignorant of the true doctrine regarding the value of a currency. Neither he nor the hosts of currency-mongers who during the nineties exercised their ingenuity to devise plans for remedying Indian exchange troubles,* understood that to stabilize the exchange was essentially a problem of stabilizing the purchasing power of currency by controlling its volume.† The gold-exchange standard ignores the fact that in the long run it is the general purchasing power of a currency that will ultimately govern its exchange value. Its aim is to stabilize exchange and allow the problem of purchasing power to go hang. The true policy should be to stabilize the purchasing power of the currency and let exchange take care of itself. Had the Chamberlain Commission considered the exchange standard from this point of view it could not have called it a sound standard when in its fundamentals it was the very reverse of it.

Now any one who remains unconvinced of this weakness of the exchange standard may say that in examining its stability we have taken only those occasions on which the standard has broken down. Thinking such a treatment to be unfair, he might say: How about the years during which stability was maintained? Is there nothing to be said in favour of a system that maintained the gold value of the rupee from 1901 to 1907, or from 1909 to 1914? The question is a pertinent one, and the position that underlies it is supposed to be so strong that those who hold it have asked the opponents of the exchange standard either to admit that it is a stable standard or to show that under that standard the rupee has *invariably* failed to maintain its gold value.‡

The validity of this position depends upon assumptions so plausible and so widespread that the argument urged so far against the exchange standard will not be of full effect until their futility is fully demonstrated. The first assumption is that there cannot be a depreciation of a currency unless it has depreciated in terms of

---

* *See* Chap. Chap IV.

† Cf. evidence of Mr Lindsay before the Fowler Committee, Q 4,190—95, where he asserted that exchange had nothing to do with the quantity of money in circulation.

‡ Dodwell, "A Gold Currency for India," *Economic Journal*, 1911; *Report on the Enquiry into the Rise of Prices in India*, 1914, p 94

gold. In other words, if the excess has not produced a fall in the value of a currency in terms of a particular commodity such as gold, then there has been no excess at all in terms of commodities in general. Now there was a time, particularly during the discussion on the Bullion Report, when the conception of a change in the value of the currency in relation to things in general was not quite clear even to the most informed minds,* and was even pronounced invalid by high authorities.† In view of the absence of the system of index numbers, this simple faith in the summary method of ascertaining depreciation by some one typical article, gold for instance, as a measure of value, was excusable. But the same view is without any foundation to-day. No one now requires to be shown that the price of each commodity has varied to the same extent and in the same direction as prices of commodities in general before admitting that there has been a change in the value of a currency. Why assume a single commodity like gold as a measure of depreciation? It would be allowable, although it is short-sighted to do so, if the depreciation of gold was an accurate measure of the depreciation of a currency in terms of all other commodities. But such is not the case. Commenting upon the experience of the United States with the greenbacks during the Civil War, Prof. W. C. Mitchell observes ‡ :—

> "The fluctuations in the price of gold which attracted so much attention were much more moderate than the extreme fluctuations in the prices of commodities. The gold quotations lay all the time well within the outer limits of the field covered by the variations of commodity prices. . . . . During the war gold moved up or down in price more quickly than the mass of commodities. . . . . When gold was rising in price the majority of the commodities followed, but more slowly. . . . . When gold was falling in price the majority of commodities stood still or followed more slowly. . . . This more sluggish movement of commodity prices appears still more clearly after the war. Rapid as was the fall of prices it was not so rapid as the fall in gold.. A more curious fact is that the price-level for commodities continued for ten years to be higher than the price-level for gold."

---

* Canning's castigation of Lord Castlereagh's definition of standard as "a sense of value" during the Bullion debates must be attributed to his ignorance on this matter.

† Ricardo, in his *Proposals for an Economical and Secure Currency* says: "It has indeed been said that we might judge of the value of a currency by its relation not to one but to the mass of the commodities. . . . Such a test would be of no use whatever . . . To determine the value of a currency by the test proposed . is evidently impossible."

‡ *Gold Prices and Wages under the Greenback Standard*, 1908, pp. 39—41.

This shows that the test sought to be applied by the adherents of the exchange standard is a false one and gives an inaccurate reading of the value of a currency. There can be no doubt that people who have urged its application to that standard would not have pressed for it so much as they have done if they had taken proper care to distinguish between *specific* depreciation of a currency in terms of gold and its *general* depreciation in terms of commodities.* The experience of the Bank of England during the suspension period is a capital instance of the phenomenon where a currency is generally depreciated, although it showed no sign of specific depreciation :—

TABLE L

DEPRECIATION OF THE NOTES OF THE BANK OF ENGLAND†

| | Percentage Values of Bank Notes in Terms of | |
|---|---|---|
| | (1) Gold | (2) Commodities |
| 1797 | 100.0 | 110 |
| 1798 | 100.0 | 118 |
| 1799 | — | 130 |
| 1800 | 107.0 | 141 |
| 1801 | 109.0 | 153 |
| 1802 | — | 119 |
| 1803 | — | 128 |
| 1804 | 103.0 | 122 |
| 1805 | 103.0 | 136 |
| 1806 | — | 133 |
| 1807 | — | 132 |
| 1808 | — | 149 |
| 1809 | — | 161 |
| 1810 | — | 164 |
| 1811 | 123.9 | 147 |
| 1812 | 130.2 | 148 |
| 1813 | 136.4 | 149 |
| 1814 | 124.4 | 153 |
| 1815 | 118.7 | 132 |
| 1816 | 102.9 | 109 |
| 1817 | 102.2 | 120 |
| 1818 | 104.6 | 135 |

* Cf. Prof. Nicholson's *Principles of Political Economy* (1897), Vol. II, Chap. XV, §4; and Walker, F. A., *Money*, 1878, pp. 387-91.

† From Hawtrey's *Credit and Currency*, p 269 On the values of the notes in terms of gold Prof. Foxwell says: "It is admitted by the severest critics of the bank that there

Which kind of depreciation is the greater evil we will discuss in the next chapter. Dealing for the present with this experience of the Bank of England, we have the fact that there can be a general depreciation without a specific depreciation. In view of this, the upholders of the exchange standard have no reason to be proud of the fact that the rupee has not shown signs of specific depreciation over periods of long duration. That a bank note absolutely inconvertible and unregulated as to issue should have maintained its par for very nearly thirteen years may speak far more in favour of the suspension system than the experience of the rupee can in favour of the exchange standard. There is a greater wonder in the former than there is in the latter, for the value of the rupee is sustained, apart from the fact that gold in terms of which it was measured was itself undergoing a depreciation, as is evident from the foregoing figures of general prices in England, and by a hope in some kind of convertibility, however slight or however remote but which had no place in the case of the Bank of England notes. Yet no one is known to have admired or justified the currency system of the suspension period, although it had not given rise to a specific depreciation for a long time.

This mode of measuring depreciation in terms of gold would be, relatively speaking, a harmless idea if it was not made the basis of another assumption on which the exchange standard is made to rest, that the general and specific depreciations of a currency are unrelated phenomena. As against this it is necessary to urge that the chief lesson to be drawn from this experience of the Bank of England for the benefit of the upholders of the exchange standard consists in demonstrating that although their movements are

---

is no substantial ground for complaint as to its conduct during the restriction until 1808-9. There does not seem, indeed, to have been any real depreciation of its paper until that date. The price of £4 per ounce, which figures monotonously for the years 1803-9, was really an arbitrary price, fixed by the bank itself as one at which it would purchase foreign gold." *Preface to Andreades*, p. xvi. Some people seem to doubt that there was no specific depreciation of the inconvertible notes of the Bank of England till 1810. Unfortunately data are not available to give direct evidence of the fact. But circumstantial evidence there is. It is to be remembered that the premium on gold was the only method then known of measuring depreciation and that Horner, Ricardo and others were open enemies of the Bank of England. That being the case, it does not seem probable that Horner would have waited to introduce his Resolution in the House of Commons till 1810 if the bank notes had shown signs of specific depreciation before that time.

not perfectly harmonious, yet they are essentially inter-related. That lesson may be summed up in the statement that when the general depreciation of currency has taken place the occurrence of a specific depreciation, other things being equal, is only a matter of time, if the general depreciation proceeds beyond a certain limit. What will be the interval before specific depreciation will supervene upon general depreciation depends upon a variety of circumstances. Like the surface of a rising lake, general depreciation touches different commodities at different times according as they are located in the general scheme of things as determined by the relative strength of demand for them. If there is no demand for gold for currency purposes or for industrial purposes, the depreciation of the currency in terms of gold may be delayed. It is only to make foreign remittances that the demand for gold first makes itself felt, and it is there that specific depreciation primarily arises. But there again it need not, for everything depends upon whether other commodities equally good, which the foreigner would take as readily as gold, are forthcoming or not. Now, in the case of India all these three factors tending to postpone specific depreciation are more or less operative. The rupee is a full legal-tender currency and can effectively discharge debts without compelling resort to gold. The industrial demand for gold in a poor country like India cannot be very great.* Consequently, the

[1] The following table regarding the consumption of gold in different countries is interesting :—

*CONSUMPTION OF GOLD (MILLIONS OF POUNDS STERLING AT 85s. PER FINE OUNCE)

| | 1915 | 1916 | 1917 | 1918 | 1919 | 1920 |
|---|---|---|---|---|---|---|
| Industrial Arts (Europe and America) | 17.0 | 18.0 | 16.0 | 17.0 | 22.0 | 22.0 |
| India (Year to March 31 following) | 1.4 | 5.1 | 19.6 | — 3.3 | 27.7 | 5.1 |
| China | — 1.7 | 2 6 | 2.6 | 0 4 | 11 5 | — 3.7 |
| Egypt | — 0.8 | — 0.2 | — 0 1 | — 0.0 | — 0 0 | ? |
| Balance available as money (difference) | 80.5 | 68.0 | 48.2 | 64.9 | 13.8 | 46.6 |
| World | 96 4 | 93.5 | 86 3 | 79 0 | 75.0 | 70.0 |

(*The figures are those of Mr Joseph Kitchin in *The Review of Economic*)

generally depreciated rupee does not show immediate signs of depreciation in the internal trade of the country. As for foreign payments, the position of India is equally strong, not because, as is absurdly supposed, she has a favourable balance of trade, but because she has certain *essential* commodities which a foreigner is obliged to accept* in place of gold. Specific depreciation of the rupee will occur chiefly when the general depreciation has overtaken the commodities that enter into India's foreign trade. That the depreciation should extend to them is inevitable, for, as is well said,

> "in a modern community the prices of different goods constitute a completely organized system, in which the various parts are continually being adjusted to each other by intricate business process. Any marked change in the price of important goods disturbs the equilibrium of this system, and business processes at once set going a series of readjustments in the prices of other goods to restore it."

It is true that in the case of India the interconnection between production for internal trade and production for external trade is not so closely knit as in the case of other countries. The only difference that this can make in the situation is to moderate the pace of general depreciation so that it does not affect foreign trade commodities too soon. But it cannot prevent its effect from ultimately raising their price. And once their price is risen the foreigner will not accept them, however essential. A demand for gold must arise, resulting in the specific depreciation of the currency.

---

*Statistics*, Preliminary volume 3, No 8 for August, 1921, p 257 If figures previous to 1914 are desired, *see* table *ibid.*, p 258)

Omitting the abnormal years of 1917 and 1919 and reducing the figures to *per capita* basis the consumption of gold by India must be said to be remarkably small. Besides, it is to be noted that figures for India include industrial as well as monetary consumption Further, in making comparison account must be taken of the difference in the period taken as unit in the case of India and other countries Of course in these days when gold is so very greatly depreciated in terms of commodities in general, neither is there any necessity to shed tears if its production were to fall off, nor can it be anything but a welcome event if its use were to be extended. It would therefore be unwise to resent an increase, if it were to take place, in the importation and use of gold by India. The greater the use of gold and the less the production of it, the better for the world as it is circumstanced to-day Cf in this connection the remarks of Prof. Cannan on Mr. Shirras's Paper in the *J. R. S. S.* for July, 1920, pp. 623-24

*Evidence of Prof. Marshall, I. C. C. 1898, Q. 11,793.

Mitchell *ibid.*, p. 258

This statement of the case agrees closely with the experience of the Bank of England and that of India as well. In the case of the Bank of England the "great evil," i.e. the specific depreciation of the bank notes, of which Horner complained so much, made its appearance in 1809, some thirteen years after the suspension was declared. Similarly, we find in the case of India specific depreciation tends to appear at different intervals, thereby completely demonstrating that, even for the purpose of avoiding specific depreciation, it is necessary to pay attention to the general depreciation of a currency.

Having regard to these facts, supported as they are by theory as well as history, the incident that the rupee has maintained its gold value over periods of some duration need not frighten anyone into an admission that the exchange standard is therefore a stable standard. Indeed, a recognition of that fact cannot in the least discredit what has been said above. For our position is that in the *long run* general depreciation of a currency will bring about its specific depreciation in terms of gold. That being our position, even if we are confronted with the absence of specific depreciation of the rupee, we are not driven to retract from the opinion that the best currency system is one which provides a brake on the general depreciation of the unit of account. The exchange standard provides no such controlling influence; indeed, its gold reserve, the instrument which controls the depreciation, is the direct cause of such depreciation. The absence of specific depreciation for the time being is not more than a noteworthy and an interesting incident. To read into it an evidence of the security of the exchange standard is to expose oneself, sooner a later, to the consequences that befall all those who choose to live in a fool's paradise.

## CHAPTER VII

# A RETURN TO THE GOLD STANDARD

We have examined the exchange standard in the light of the claim made on behalf of it, that it is capable of maintaining the gold parity of the rupee. This was the criterion laid down by the Chamberlain Commission as a fitting one by which to judge the merits or demerits of that standard. But is the adequacy of that criterion beyond dispute? In other words, supposing the rupee has maintained its gold parity, which it has only as often as not, does it follow that all the purposes of a good monetary system are therefore subserved?

In the exchange standard, "as the system is now operated, the coinage is manipulated to keep it at par with gold"* as though money is only important for the amount of gold it will procure. But what really concerns those who use money is not how much gold that money is worth, but how much of things in general (of which gold is an infinitesimal part) that money is worth. Everywhere, therefore, the attempt is to keep money stable in terms of commodities in general, and that is but proper, for what ministers to the welfare of people is not so much the precious metals as commodities and services of more direct utility. Stability of a currency in terms of gold is of importance only to the dealers in gold, but its stability in terms of commodities in general affects all, including the bullion-dealers. Even Prof. Keynes, in his testimony before the Indian Currency Committee of 1919, observed† :—

> "I should aim always . . . . at keeping Indian prices stable in relation to commodities rather than in relation to any particular metallic or particular foreign currency. That seems to me of far greater importance to India."

---

* Fisher, *Purchasing Power of Money*, 1911, p. 340.
† Q. 2690.

It is, of course, a little difficult to understand how the remedy of high exchange which he supported was calculated to achieve that object. Raising the exchange was a futile project, in so far as it was not in keeping with the purchasing power of the rupee. As an influence governing prices it could hardly be said to possess the virtue he attributed to it. The existing price-level it could affect in no way; nor could a high exchange prevent a future rise of prices. It could only change the base from which to measure prices. Future prices could vary as easily from the new high base-line as prices did in the past from the old base-line. In other words, Mr. Keynes seems to have overlooked the fact that exchange was only an index of the price-level, and to control it, it was necessary to control the price-level, and not merely give it another name which it cannot bear and will not endure, as was proved in 1920 when the rupee was given in law the value of 2s. (gold) when in practice it could not fetch even 1s. 4d. sterling, with the result that the rupee exchange sank to the level determined by its purchasing power. But, apart from this question, we have the admission of the ablest supporter of the exchange standard that the real merit of a currency system lies in maintaining the standard of value stable in terms of commodities in general.

Given that this is the proper criterion by which to judge a currency system, we must ask what has been the course of prices in India since the Mint closure in 1893? This is a fundamental question, and yet not one among the many who have praised the virtues of the exchange standard has paid any attention to it. In vain may one search the pages of Prof. Keynes, Prof. Kemmerer, or Mr. Shirras for what they have to say of the exchange standard from this point of view. The Chamberlain Commission or the Smith Committee on Indian currency never troubled about the problem of prices in India,* and yet without being satisfied on that score it is really difficult to understand how anyone can give an opinion of any value as to the soundness or otherwise of that standard.

In proceeding to consider the exchange standard from the standpoint of prices, it is as well to premise that one of the im-

* Perhaps an exception may be made in the case of the latter Committee; but its object was only to make it a ground for high exchange.

CHART VI

COMPARATIVE PRICE LEVELS, INDIAN AND FOREIGN, 1893–1922

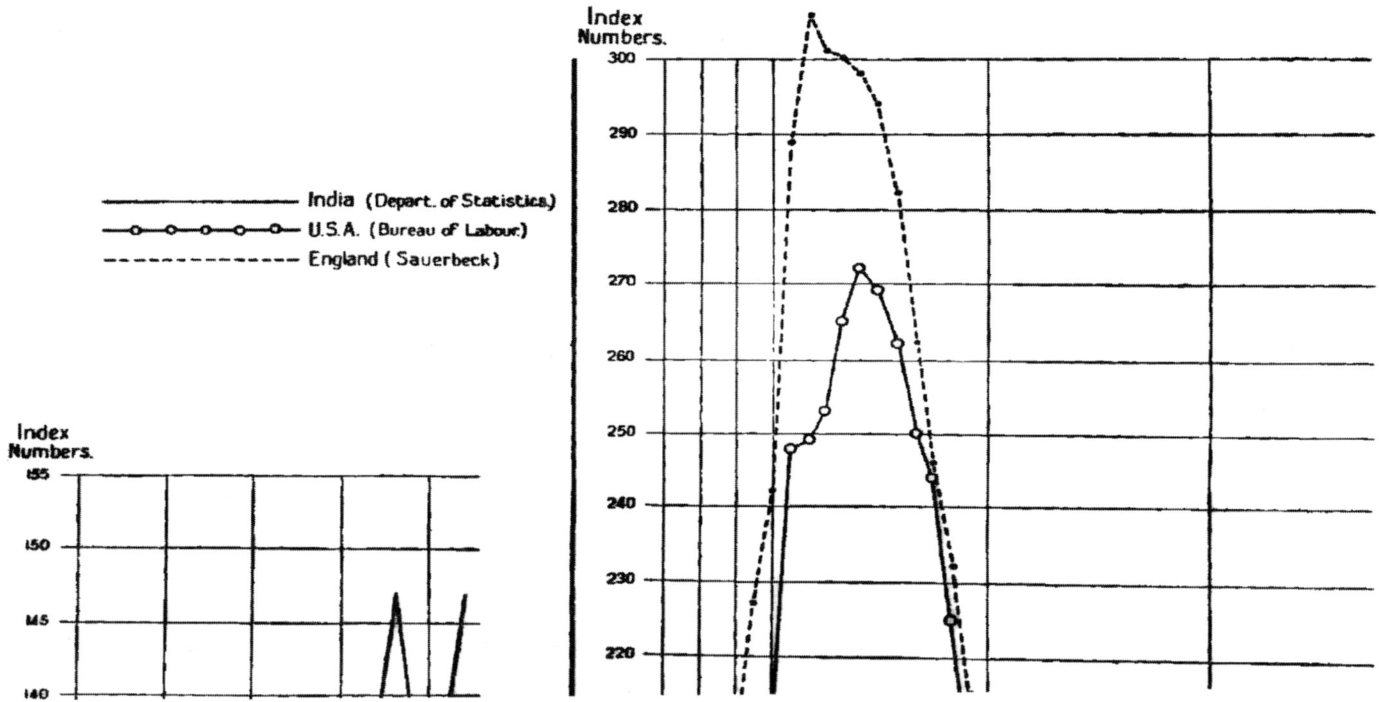

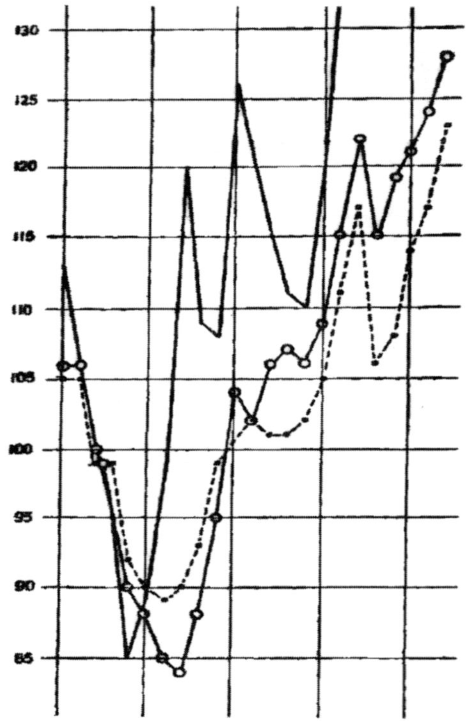
130
125
120
115
110
105
100
95
90
85

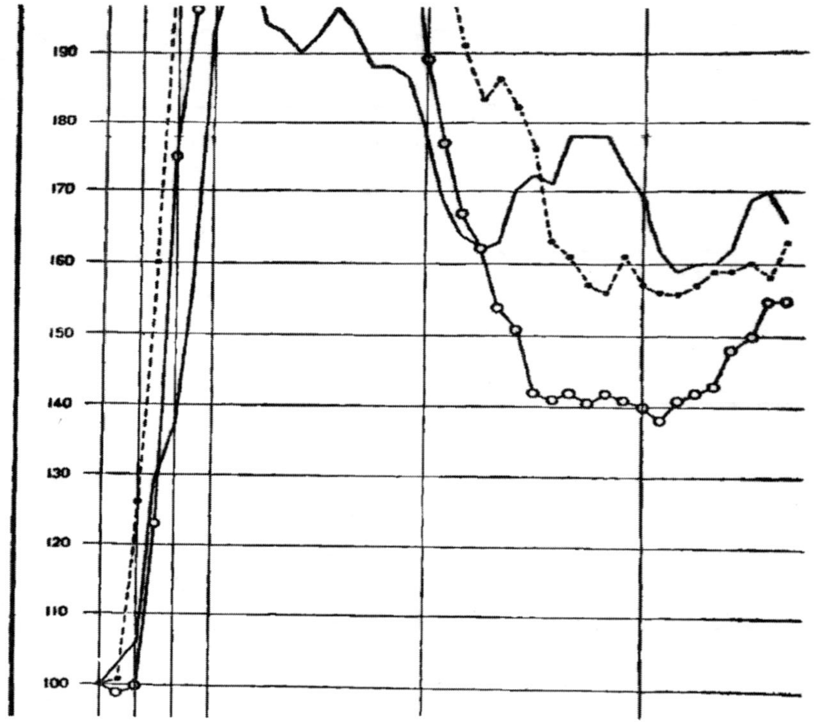
190
180
170
160
150
140
130
120
110
100

portant reasons why the Indian Mints were closed to the free coinage of silver was that the rupee was a depreciating currency resulting in high prices.* The closing of the Mints, therefore, should have been followed by a fall of prices in India; for, to adopt the phraseology of Prof. Fisher,† the pipe-connection between the money reservoir and the silver-bullion reservoir was owing to the Mint closure cut off or stopped, thereby preventing the passage of silver from the bullion reservoir to the money reservoir and the silver-bullion reservoir was owing to the Mint closure cut off or stopped, thereby preventing the passage of silver from the bullion reservoir to the money reservoir. In other words, the newly-mined silver could not become money after the Mint closure and lower the purchasing power of the rupees in circulation. If this is so, then how very disappointing has been the effect of the Mint closure! From the standpoint of prices the rupee has become a problem as it had never been before. The rise of prices in India since the Mint closure (*See* Chart VI) has been quite unprecedented in the history of the country. Indeed, the rise of prices in India before the Mint closure, when the pipe-connection between the silver-bullion reservoir and the rupee-currency reservoir was intact, must be regarded as very trifling compared with the rise of prices after the Mint closure when the pipe-connection was cut off. From the standpoint of prices the Mint closure has therefore turned out to be a curse rather than a blessing, and literally so, for, under an ever-rising price-level, life in India is rendered quite unbearable. No people have undergone so much misery owing to high prices as the Indian people have done. During the war period the price-level reached such a giddy height that the reports of suicide by men and women who were unable to buy food and clothing were in no way few and far between. It may, however, be argued that the rise of prices in India would have been greater if the Mints had not been closed and India had remained a purely silver-standard country. A good deal, no doubt, can be said in favour of this view. It is absolutely true that silver, being universally discarded, has become unfit for functioning as a standard of value. To that extent an exchange standard is better than a pure-silver standard. But is it as good as a gold standard ?

* *Purchasing Power of Money*, 1911, p 128.

† *See supra*, Chap. III.

On the basis of the doctrine of purchasing power parities as an explanation of actual exchange rates, one may be led to answer the question in the affirmative. For it may be argued that if the gold value of the rupee was maintained it is because gold prices and rupee prices were equal.* This, it may be said, is all that the exchange standard aims at doing and can be claimed to have done, for the fact that the gold-standard reserve was seldom depleted is a proof that the general prices inside India were on the same level as those ruling outside India. On *a priori* considerations such as these, the exchange standard may be deemed to be as good as a gold standard.

One may ask as to why Indian prices should have been kept as high, if they were no higher than gold prices, and whether it would not have been better to have kept Indian prices on a lower level. But we shall not raise that question. We shall be satisfied if Indian prices were only as high as gold prices. Now did Indian prices rise only as much as gold prices? A glance at the chart reveals the surprising phenomenon that prices in India not only rose as much as gold prices, but rose more than gold prices. Of course in comparing Indian prices with gold prices to test the efficacy of the exchange standard we must necessarily eliminate the war period, for the reason that gold had been abandoned as a standard of value by most of the countries. And, even if we do take that period into account, it does not materially affect the conclusion, for although India was not a belligerent country, yet prices in India were not very much lower than prices in countries with most inflated currencies during the war, and, barring a short period were certainly higher than gold prices in U.S.A.

It is obvious that the facts do not agree with the *a priori* assumption made in favour of the exchange standard. So noticeable must be said to be the local rise in Indian prices above the general price level in England that even Prof. Keynes, not given to exaggerate the faults of the exchange standard, was, as a result of his own independent investigation, convinced that †

* It is, however, to be noted that neither Prof. Kemmerer nor Prof. Keynes has set up this claim in favour of the exchange standard. If anything, both have argued against the assumption of there being equality of *all* prices.

† "Recent Economic Events in India," in *The Economic Journal*, March, 1909, p. 54. Italic not in the original.

> "A comparison with Sauerbeck's index number for the United Kingdom shows that the change in India is *much greater* than can be accounted for by changes occurring elsewhere."

What is then the explanation of this discrepancy between the *a priori* assumption and the facts of the case. The explanation is that the actual exchange rates correspond to the purchasing power parities of two currencies not with regard to *all* commodities but with regard to *some* only. In this connection it is better to re-state the doctrine of the relation of the purchasing power parities to exchange rates with the necessary qualification. A rigorously strict formulation of the doctrine should require us to state that Englishmen and others value Indian rupees inasmuch as and in so far as those rupees will buy *such Indian goods as Englishmen want*; while Indians value English pounds inasmuch as and in so far as those pounds will buy *such English goods as the Indians want.* So stated it follows that the actual exchange rates are related to purchasing power parities of the two currencies with regard to such commodities only as are internationally traded. To assume that the actual exchange rate is an exact index of the purchasing power parity of the two currencies with regard to *all* the commodities is to suppose that the variations in the purchasing power of a currency over commodities which are traded and which are not traded are the same.* There is certainly a tendency for movements in the prices of these two classes of goods to influence one another *in the long run*; so that it becomes possible to say that the exchange value of a currency will be determined by its internal purchasing power. The doctrine of purchasing power parity as an explanation of exchange rates is valuable as an instrument of practical utility for controlling the foreign exchanges *and* it is as such that the doctrine was employed in an earlier portion of this study to account for the fall in the gold value of the rupee. But to proceed, on the basis of this relationship between the purchasing power of a currency and its exchange value, to

*Prof. Cassel, the modern exponent of this old doctrine of the relation of exchange rates to purchasing power parities, admits that the correspondence between the two depends upon the fulfilment of this assumption, for he says :

"Our calculation of the purchasing power parity rests strictly on the proviso that the rise in prices in the countries concerned has affected all commodities in a like degree. If that proviso is not fulfilled, then the actual exchange rate may deviate from the calculated purchasing power parities"—*Money and Foreign Exchange after* 1914. London, 1922, p. 154.

argue that at any given time the exchange is more or less an exact measure of general purchasing power of the two currencies, is to assume what cannot always be true, namely, that the prices of traded and non-traded goods move in sympathy. This assumption is too large and can only be said to be more or less true according to circumstances. Now as Prof. Kemmerer* points out:

> "While India's exports and imports in the absolute are large, still, in the main, the people of India live on their own products, and a large part of those products run their life history from production to consumption in a very small territory. They have only the remotest connection with foreign trade, gold, and the gold exchanges. In time, of course, any substantial disturbance in the equilibrium of values in the country's import and export trade will make itself felt in these local prices, but allowing for exceptions, it may be said that in a country like India the influences of such disturbances travel very slowly and lose much of their momentum in travelling."

In consequence of the thinness of connection between the two it is obvious that the prices of such Indian goods as do enter into international trade cannot always be said to move in more or less the same proportion as those which do not. Besides this thinness of connection which permits of deviations of the general purchasing power of a currency from the level indicated by the actual exchange rate, it is to be noted that the prices of Indian commodities which largely enter into international trade are not governed by local influences. Such exports of India as wheat, hides, rice and oil seeds are international commodities, not solely amenable to influences originating from changes that may be taking place in the prices of home commodities and services. The combined effect of these two circumstances, except in abnormal events such as the war, is to militate against the prices of traded and non-traded goods moving in quick sympathy.†

If this is true, then, although the maintenance of the exchange standard does imply a purchasing power parity of the rupee with gold, it is not a purchasing power parity of the two currencies

†Op. cit., pp 64.

* This is merely re-stating what has previously been stated to explain why specific depreciation of the rupee does not immediately follow upon its general depreciation.

with respect to *all* the commodities. All that it implies is that the purchasing power of the rupee over such commodities as entered into international trade was on a par with gold, so that there did not often arise the necessity of exhausting the gold reserve. The preservation of the gold reserve only meant that there was equality of prices so far as internationally traded goods were concerned. Thus interpreted, the fact that the rupee maintained its gold value does not preclude the possibility of Indian prices being, on the whole, higher than gold prices, thereby vitiating the *a priori* view that the exchange standard is as good as the gold standard.

It should be pointed out* that all changes of prices affect more or less the welfare of the individual. However, the general flexibility of the modern economic organization, with its mobility of capital and labour, free competition, power of choice, inventive genius and intellectual resources of entrepreneurs and merchants, takes care of the normal and temporary fluctuations of prices. But when a change in the price-level is general and persistent in one direction the case is otherwise. Arrangements based on the expectation that the price movement is only temporary, and that there will be a return to the former normal position, constantly come to naught. Suffering endured in holding on for the turn in the movement cannot be offset by gains in another. In short, such a persistent price movement in one direction is bound to confound ordinary business sagacity and so vitiate all calculations for the future as to result in unlimited dislocation or loss and subject the individual to such powerful and at the same time incalculable influences that his economic welfare cannot but escape entirely from his control, and prudence, fore-thought, and energy become of no avail in the struggle for existence. Perfect stability of value in a monetary standard is as yet only an ideal. But the evil consequences of instability are so great that Prof. Marshall, believing as he did that the general prejudice against tampering with the monetary foundations of economic life was a healthy prejudice, yet observed that much may be done towards safeguarding the economic welfare of communities by lessening its variability.† A

* What follows is condensed from Mayo-Smith's "Price Movements and Individual Welfare," in the *Political Science Quarterly*, Vol. XV, No. 1 (March, 1900). pp. 14—17.

† Cf. "Remedies for Fluctuations of General Prices," in *The Contemporary Review*, March, 1887, *passim*.

depreciating standard of value, as gold has been since 1896, is an evil. But can a standard of value, undergoing a continuous depreciation as has been the case with the exchange standard, and that too of a greater depth than the gold standard—in other words, causing a greater rise of prices—be regarded as a good standard of value?

In the light of this it is strange that Prof. Keynes, in his treatise on *Indian Currency and Finance*, should have maintained that the exchange standard contained an essential element in the ideal standard of the future *—a view subsequently endorsed by the Chamberlain Commission. If stability of purchasing power in terms of commodities in general is the criterion for judging a system of currency, then few students of economics will be found to agree with Prof. Keynes. Perhaps it is not too sanguine to say that even the Prof. Keynes of 1920 will prefer a gold standard to a gold-exchange standard, for under the former prices have varied much less than has been the case under the latter.

In this connection attention may be drawn to the prevalent misconception that India is a gold-standard country. It will be admitted that the best practical test whether any two countries have the same standard of value is to be found in the character of the movements in their price-levels. So sure is the test that Prof. Mitchell, after a very careful and wide survey of the price-level of different countries and the American price-level during the greenback period, was led to observe † that

> "when two countries have a similar monetary system and important business relations with each other, the movements of their price levels as represented by index-numbers are found to agree rather closely This agreement is so strong that similarity of movement is usually found even when comparisons are made with material so crude as index-numbers compiled from unlike lists of commodities and computed on the basis of actual prices in different years."

Now, we know that before the war England was a gold-standard country, and we also know that there was no close correspondence between the contemporary movements of the price-

* Op cit, p 36

† *Gold Prices, and Wages under the Greenback Standard*, 1908, p 27

levels of India and England. In view of this, it is only a delusion to maintain that India has been a gold-standard country. On the other hand, it is better to recognise that India has yet to become a gold-standard country unless we are to fall into the same error that Prof. Fisher * must be said to have committed in attributing the extraordinary rise of prices in India to the existence of a gold standard, when, as a matter of fact, it should have been attributed to the want of a gold standard.

How can she become a gold-standard country? The obvious answer is, by introducing a gold currency. Prof. Keynes scoffs at the view that there cannot be a gold standard without a gold currency as pure nonsense. † He seems to hold that a currency and a standard of value are two different things. Surely there he is wrong. Because a society needs a medium of exchange, a standard of value, and a store of value to sustain its economic life, it is positively erroneous to argue that these three functions can be performed by different instrumentalities. On the other hand, as Professor Davenport insists,‡

> "all the different uses of money are merely different aspects or emphasis of the intermediate function. Deferred payments . . . . are merely deferred payments of the intermediate. So again of the standard aspect; whatever is the general intermediate is by that fact the standard. The functions are not two, but one . . . . . Clearly, also, the intermediate may be a storehouse of purchasing power. The second half of the barter may be deferred. The intermediate is generalized purchasing power. Delay is one of the privileges which especially the intermediate function carries with it."

Thus the rupee by reason of being the currency is also the standard of value. If we wish to make gold the standard of value in India we must introduce it into the currency of India. But it may be asked what difference could it make to the price level in India if gold were made a part of the Indian currency? To answer this question it is necessary to lay bare the nature of the rupee currency. Now it will be granted that a standard of value which is capable of expansion as well as contraction is likely to be more

---

* *Purchasing Power*, etc , 1911, p. 340.

† Op. cit , p 29

‡ Op. cit., pp 255—56; cf. also F A Walker, *Money in its Relation to Trade* p. 27, and C. M. Walsh, *The Fundamental Problem in Monetary Science*, p 304

stable than one which is incapable of easy expansion, but is not capable of easy contraction by reason of the fact that it is neither exportable nor meltable, nor is it convertible at will. The effects of such a currency as compared with those of an exportable currency were well brought out by the late Hon. Mr. Gokhale in a speech in which he observed.*

> "Now, what is the difference if you have an automatic self-adjusting currency, such as we may have with gold or we had with silver before the year 1893, and the kind of artificial currency that we have at present? Situated as India is you will always require, to meet the demands of trade, the coinage of a certain number of gold or silver pieces, as the case may be, during the export season, that is for six months in the year. When the export season is brisk money has to be sent into the interior to purchase commodities. That is a factor common to both situations, whether you have an artificial currency, as now, or a silver currency, as before 1893. But the difference is this. During the remaining six months of the slack season there is undoubtedly experienced a redundancy of currency, and under a self-adjusting automatic system there are three outlets for this redundancy to work itself off. The coins that are superfluous may either come back to the banks and to the coffers of Government, or they may be exported, or they may be melted by people for purposes of consumption for other wants. But where you have no self-adjusting and automatic currency, where the coin is an artificial token currency, such as our rupee is at the present moment, two out of three of these outlets are stopped. You cannot export the rupee without heavy loss, you cannot melt the rupee without heavy loss, and consequently the extra coins must return to the banks and coffers of the Government or they must be absorbed by the people. In the latter case the situation is like that of a soil which is water-logged, which has no efficient drainage, and the moisture from which cannot be removed. In this country the facilities for banking are very inadequate, and therefore our money does not swiftly return back to the banks or Government Treasuries. Consequently, the extra money that is sent into the interior often gathers here and there like pools of water turning the whole soil into a marsh. I believe the fact cannot be gainsaid that the stopping of two outlets out of the three tends to raise prices by making the volume of currency redundant."

* *Supreme Legislative Council Proceedings*, Vol L p 642

Had gold formed a part of the Indian currency it would have not only met the needs for expansion but would have permitted contraction of currency in a degree unknown to the rupee. Gold would be superior to the rupee as a standard of value for the reason that the former is expansible as well as contractible, while the latter is only expansible but not contractible. This is merely to state in different language what has already been said previously, that the Indian monetary standard, instead of being a gold or a gold-exchange standard, is in all essentials an inconvertible rupee standard like the paper pound of the Bank Suspension period, and the extra local rise of prices which, in itself an incontrovertible proof of the identity of the two systems, is characteristic of both, is, to use the language of the Bullion Report.*

> "the effect of an excessive quantity of a circulation medium in a country which has adopted a currency not exportable to other countries, or not convertible at will into a coin which is exportable."

Therefore, if some mitigation of the rise in the Indian price-level is desirable, then the most essential thing to do is to permit some form of "exportable" currency such as gold to be a counterpart of the Indian monetary system.

The Chamberlain Commission expended much ingenuity in making out a case against a gold currency in India. † The arguments it urged were: (1) Indian people will hoard gold and will not make it available in a crisis; (2) that India is too poor a country to maintain such an expensive money material as gold; (3) that the transactions of the Indian people are too small to permit of a gold circulation; and (4) paper convertible into rupees is the best form of currency for the people of India as being the most economical, and that the introduction of a gold currency will militate against the popularity of notes as well as of rupees. The bogy of hoarding is an old one, and would really be an argument of some force if hoarding was something which knew no law. But the case is quite otherwise. Money, being the most saleable

* Prof. Cannan's Reprint, P 17.

† Report, pp. 15—19. The same arguments will be found in Chap. IV of Mr Keynes's treatise.

*commodity and the least likely, in a well-ordered monetary system, to deteriorate in value during short periods,* is hoarded continually by all people, i.e. treated as a store of value. But in treating it as a store of value the possessor of money is comparing the utilities he can get for the money, by disposing of it now, with those he believes he can get for it in the future, and if the highest present utility is not so great as the highest future utility, discounted for risk and time, he will hoard the money. On the other hand, he will not hoard the money if the present use was greater than the future use. That being so, it is difficult to understand why hoarding should be an objection to a gold currency for the Indian people. If they hoard gold that means they do not care to spend it on current purchases or that they have another form of currency which is inferior to gold and which they naturally like to part with first. On the other hand, if they do wish to make current purchases and have no other form of currency they cannot hoard gold. There are instances when precious metals have been exported from India, when occasion had called for it,* showing that the hoarding habit of the Indian peoples is not such an unknown quantity as is often supposed, and if on some occasions † they hoarded an exportable currency when they should have released it, it is not the fault of the people but of the currency system in which the component parts of the total stock of money are not equally good as a store of value. The argument from hoarding, if it is an argument, can be used against any people, and not particularly against the Indian people.

The second argument against a gold currency in India has no greater force than the first. If gold were to disappear from circulation then the cause can be nothing else but the over-issue of another kind of money. In the nineties, when the question of establishing a gold standard in India was being considered, some people used to point to the vain efforts made by Italy and the Austrian Empire to promote the circulation of gold. That their gold used to disappear is a fact, but it was not due to their poverty.

---

* *See* the Memorandum by Mr Dalal to the Chamberlain Commission Appendices, Vol. III, No. XXXIII, pp 673—75, for this and other cognate topics.

† In the crisis of 1907—8 the Indian people were accused of this. Yet it must be noted that in that crisis some gold was exported on private account

It was due to their paper issues. Any country can maintain a gold currency provided it does not issue a cheaper substitute.

Again, if gold will not circulate because transactions are too small the proper conclusion is not that there should be no gold circulation but that the unit of currency should be small enough to meet the situation. The difficulties of circulation raises a problem of coinage. But the considerations in respect of coinage cannot be allowed to rule the question as to what should be the standard of value. If the sovereign does not circulate it cannot follow that India should not have a gold currency. It merely means that the sovereign is too large for circulation. The case, if at all there is one, is against the sovereign as a unit and not against the principle of a gold currency. If the sovereign is not small enough the conclusion is we must find some other coin to make the circulation of gold effective.

The fourth argument against a gold currency is one of fact, and can be neither proved nor disproved except by an appeal to evidence whether or not gold currency has the tendency ascribed to it. But we may ask, is there no danger in a system of currency composed of paper convertible into rupees? Will the paper have no effect on the value of the rupee? The Commission, if it at all considered that question, which is very doubtful, was perhaps persuaded by the view commonly held, that as the paper currency was convertible it could not affect the value or the purchasing power of the rupee. In holding this view it was wrong; for, the convertibility of paper currency to the extent it is uncovered does not prevent it from lowering the value of the unit of account into which it is convertible, because by competition it reduces the demand for the unit of account and thus brings about a fall in its value. Thus the paper, although economical as a currency, is a danger to the value of the rupee. This danger would have been of a limited character if the rupee had been freely convertible into gold. But the danger of a convertible paper currency to the value of a unit of account becomes as great as that of an inconvertible paper currency if that unit is not protected against being driven below the metal of ultimate redemption by free convertibility into that metal.* The rupee is not protected by such convertibility, and as the Commission did not want that it should be so protected

*For an illuminating discussion on this topic, cf. *Money: Its Connection with Rising and Falling Prices*, by Prof. Cannan, 3rd ed., pp. 47-8.

it should have realized that it was as seriously jeopardizing the prospects of the rupee being maintained at par with commodities in general, and therefore with gold, by urging the extension of a paper currency, be it ever so perfectly convertible, as it could have done by making the paper altogether inconvertible. But so obsessed was the Commission with considerations of economy, and so reckless was it with considerations of stability of value, that it actually proposed a change in the basis of the Indian paper currency from a fixed issue system to that of a fixed proportion system.* That, at the dictates of considerations of economy, the Commission should have neglected to take account of this aspect of the question, is only one more evidence of the very perfunctory manner in which it has treated the whole question of stability of purchasing power so far as the Indian currency was concerned.

If there is any force in what has been urged above, then surely a gold currency is not a mere matter of "sentiment" and a "costly luxury," but a necessity dictated by the supreme interest of steadying the Indian standard of value, and thereby to some extent, however slight, safeguarding the welfare of the Indian people from the untoward consequences of a rising price-level.

We now see how very wrong the Chamberlain Commission was from every point of view in upholding the departure from the plan originally outlined by the Government of India and sanctioned by the Fowler Committee. But that raises the question: How did that ideal come to be so ruthlessly defeated? If the Fowler Committee had proposed that gold should be the currency of India, how is it that gold ceased to be the currency? It cannot be said that the door is closed against the entry of gold, for it has been declared legal tender. Speaking in the language of Prof. Fisher, the movement of gold in the money reservoir of India is allowed a much greater freedom so far as law is concerned than can be said of silver. Silver, in the form of rupees, is admitted by a very narrow valve which gives it an inlet into that reservoir, but there is no outlet provided for it. On the other hand, gold is admitted into the same reservoir by a pipe-connection which gives it an inlet as well as an outlet. Why, then, does not gold flow into the currency reservoir of India? A proper understanding on this

* Report, Sec. 112.

question is the first step towards a return to the sound system proposed in 1898.

On an examination of the literature which attempts to deal with this aspect of the question, it will be found that two explanations are usually advanced to account for the non-entry of gold into the currency system of India. One of them is the sale of council bills by the Secretary of State. The effect of the sale of council bills, it is said, is to prevent gold from going to India. Mr. Subhedar, said to be an authority on Indian currency, in his evidence before the Smith Committee (Q. 3,502), observed:—

> "Since 1905 it has been the deliberate attempt of those who control our currency policy to prevent gold going to India and into circulation."

The council bill has a history which goes back to the days of the East India Company.* The peculiar position of the Government of India, arising from the fact that it receives its revenues in India and is obliged to make payments in England, imposes upon it the necessity of making remittances from India to England. Ever since the days of the East India Company the policy has been to arrange for the remittance in such a way as to avoid the transmission of bullion. Three modes of making the remittance were open to the Directors of the East India Company; (1) sending bullion from India to England; (2) receiving money in England in return for bills on the Government of India; and (3) making advances to merchants in India for the purchase of goods consigned to the United Kingdom and repayable in England to the Court of Directors of the Company to whom the goods were hypothecated. Out of these it was on the last two that greater reliance was placed by them. In time the mode of remittance through hypothecation of goods was dropped "as introducing a vicious system of credit, and interfering with the ordinary course of trade." The selling of bills on India survived as the fittest of all the three alternatives,† and was continued by the Secretary of

* Cf. the Memorandum by Sir Henry Waterfield relating to the system of effecting remittances from India, Appendix to the Fowler Committee's Report, p. 24; also Memorandum by F. W Newmarch on the Sale of Council Bills and Telegraphic Transfers. Appendices to the Interim Report of the Royal Commission on Indian Finance and Currency, Vol. I, No. VIII, p. 217.

†There was a fourth one, viz., the Government of India purchasing sterling bills in India on London and sending them to the Secretary of State for collection. It was employed for a short period of time in 1877, but was afterwards dropped.

State in Council—hence the name, council bill—when the Government of India was taken over by the Crown from the Company. In the hands of the Secretary of State the council bill has undergone some modifications. The sales as now effected are weekly sales,* and are managed through the Bank of England, which issues an advertisement on every Wednesday on behalf of the Secretary of State for India, inviting tenders to be submitted on the following Wednesday for bills payable on demand by the Government of India either at Bombay, Madras, or Calcutta The minimum fraction of a penny in the price at which tenders of bills are received has now† been fixed at 1|32nd of a penny. The council bill is no longer of one species as it used to be. On the other hand there are four classes of bills; (1) Ordinary bills of exchange, sold every Wednesday, known as "*Councils*"; (2) telegraphic transfers, sold on Wednesdays, called shortly "*Transfers*"; ‡ (3) ordinary bills of exchange, sold on any day in the week excepting Wednesday, called "*Intermediates*"; and (4) telegraphic transfers, sold on any day excepting Wednesday, named "Specials." Now, in what way does the Secretary of State use his machinery of council bills to prevent gold from going to India? It is said that the price and the magnitude of the sale are so arranged that gold does not go to India. Before we examine to what extent this has defeated the policy of the Fowler Committee, the following figures (Tables LI and LII, pp. 247 and 250) are presented for purposes of elucidation.

From an examination of these tables two facts at once become clear. One is the enormous amount of council bills the Secretary of State sells. Before the closing of the Mints the sales of council bills moved closely with the magnitude of the home charges, and the actual drawings did not materially deviate from the amount estimated in the Budget. Since the closure of the Mints the draw-

* From January 22, 1862, when the Sale of Council Bills under the authority of the Secretary of State first took place, up to November, 1862, the sales were effected monthly. From November, 1862, the sales were effected fortnightly; and in August, 1876, they were made weekly.

† From January to March, 1862, the minimum fraction was a farthing; it was reduced to ⅛th of a penny in March 1862, to 1|16th in January 1875, and to 1|32nd in 1882, at which fraction it has continued since then.

‡First introduced in 1876.

# TABLE LI

## Balance of Trade, Council Drawings and Imports of Gold before 1893

| Years. | Balance of Trade (Merchandise: Private Account). | Net Imports of Treasure. Gold. | Net Imports of Treasure. Silver. | Amount of Council Bills drawn. | Excess (+) or Deficiency (—) of Bills drawn as compared with Budget Estimate. | Home Charges | Cash Balances in the Home Treasury. | Minimum Rate for Council Bills. |
|---|---|---|---|---|---|---|---|---|
| (1) | (2) | (3) | (4) | (5) | (6) | (7) | (8) | (9) |
| | £ | £000,000 | £000,000 | £ | £ | £ | £ | s. d. |
| 1870-71 | 20,863,000 | 2.13 | .9 | — | — | 10,031,261 | 3,305,972 | 1 10[illegible] |
| 1871-72 | 31,094,000 | 3.43 | 6.3 | — | — | 9,703,235 | 2,821,091 | 1 10[illegible] |
| 1872-73 | 23,376,000 | 2.41 | .7 | 13,939,095 | + 939,095 | 10,248,605 | 2,998,444 | 1 10[illegible] |
| 1873-74 | 21,160,000 | 1.29 | 2.3 | 13,285,678 | — 214,322 | 9,310,926 | 2,013,638 | 1 9[illegible] |
| 1874-75 | 20,137,000 | 1.73 | 4.3 | 10,841,615 | + 841,615 | 9,490,391 | 2,796,370 | 1 9[illegible] |
| 1875-76 | 19,204,000 | 1.40 | 1.4 | 12,289,613 | —1,910,387 | 9,155,050 | 919,899 | 1 9 |
| 1876-77 | 23,573,000 | .18 | 6.1 | 12,695,800 | — 964,200 | 13,851,296 | 2,713,967 | 1 8½ |
| 1877-78 | 23,758,000 | .41 | 12.7 | 10,134,455 | —2,115,545 | 14,048,350 | 1,076,657 | 1 $8\frac{1}{16}$ |
| 1878-79 | 23,167,000 | .74 | 3.3 | 13,948,565 | —3,051,345 | 13,851,296 | 1,117,925 | 1 6[illegible] |
| 1879-80 | 26,046,000 | 1.45 | 6.5 | 15,261,810 | + 261,810 | 14,547,684 | 2,270,107 | 1 7 |
| 1880-81 | 21,464,000 | 3.03 | 3.2 | 15,239,677 | —1,660,323 | 14,418,986 | 4,127,749 | 1 7[illegible] |
| 1881-82 | 32,855,000 | 4.02 | 4.5 | 18,412,429 | +1,212,429 | 14,399,083 | 2,620,909 | 1 7[illegible] |
| 1882-83 | 31,389,000 | 4.01 | 6.1 | 15,120,521 | — 221,479 | 14,101,262 | 3,429,874 | 1 7 |
| 1883-84 | 23,611,800 | 4.44 | 5.2 | 17,599,805 | +1,299,805 | 15,030,195 | 4,113,221 | 1 7[illegible] |
| 1884-85 | 20,034,100 | 3.76 | 5.8 | 13,758,909 | —2,741,091 | 14,100,982 | 2,249,378 | 1 6[illegible] |
| 1885-86 | 21,344,200 | 2.10 | 8.8 | 10,292,692 | —3,481,008 | 14,014,733 | 4,726,585 | 1 5[illegible] |
| 1886-87 | 19,844,800 | 1.58 | 5.2 | 12,136,279 | —1,195,121 | 14,409,949 | 5,280,829 | 1 4[illegible] |
| 1887-88 | 18,724,400 | 2.10 | 6.5 | 15,358,577 | — 891,423 | 15,389,065 | 5,900,697 | 1 4[illegible] |
| 1888-89 | 20,271,900 | 1.92 | 6.3 | 14,262,859 | + 262,859 | 14,983,221 | 3,259,933 | 1 4 |
| 1889-90 | 24,557,800 | 3.18 | 7.6 | 15,474,496 | + 784,596 | 14,848,923 | 5,402,873 | 1 4 |
| 1890-91 | 20,733,800 | 4.25 | 10.7 | 15,969,034 | + 980,034 | 15,568,875 | 3,885,050 | 1 4[illegible] |
| 1891-92 | 27,632,400 | 1.68 | 6.3 | 16,093,854 | + 93,854 | 15,874,699 | 4,122,628 | 1 $3\frac{1}{16}$ |
| 1892-93 | 29,287,300 | 1.75 | 8.0 | 16,532,215 | — 467,785 | 16,334,541 | 12,268,388 | 1 2[illegible] |

ings of the Secretary of State have not been governed purely by the needs of the Home Treasury. Since the closure, the Secretary of State has endeavoured*:—

> "(1) To draw from the Treasuries of the Government of India during the financial year the amount that is laid down in the Budget as necessary to carry out the Ways and Means programme of the year.
>
> "(2) To draw such further amounts as may be required to pay for purchases of silver bought for coinage purposes.
>
> "(3) To draw such further amounts as an unexpectedly prosperous season may enable the Government to spare, to be used towards the reduction or avoidance of debt in England.
>
> "(4) To sell additional bills and transfers to meet the convenience of trade.
>
> "(5) To issue telegraphic transfers on India in payment for sovereigns which the Secretary of State has purchased in transit from Australia or from Egypt to India."

The result of such drawings is that the councils are made to play an enormous part in the adjustment of the trade balance of India, and the swelling of balances in the Home Treasury and the locking up of Indian funds in London.

The second point to note in comparing the preceding tables is with regard to the price at which the Secretary of State makes his sales. Before the closure of the Mints the price of the council bills was beyond the control of the Secretary of State, who had therefore to accept the price offered by the highest bidder at the weekly sale of his bills. But it is objected that there is no reason why the Secretary of State should have continued the old practice of auctioning the rupee to the highest bidder when the closing of the Mints had given him the sole right of manufacturing it. Availing himself of his monopoly position, it is insisted, the Secretary of State should not have sold his bills below 1s. 4⅛d or 1s. 4 $\frac{5}{32}$ d., which, under the ratio of 15 rupees to the sovereign, was for India the gold-import point. In practice the Secretary of State has willed away the benefit of his position, and has accepted

* Cf. Memorandum on the Sale of Council Bills, by F. W. Newmarch, to the Chamberlain Commission, App. Vol. I, No. VII. p 222.

tenders at rate below gold-import point, as may be seen from the minimum rates he has accepted for his bills.

It is said that if the council bills were sold in amounts required strictly for the purposes of the Home Treasury, and sold at a price not below gold-import point, gold would tend to be imported into India and would thus become part of the Indian currency media. As it is, the combined effect of the operations of the Secretary of State is said to be to lock up Indian gold in London. With the use or misuse of the Indian gold in London we are not here concerned. But those who are inclined to justify the India Office scandals in the management of Indian funds in London, and have offered their services to place them on a scientific footing, may be reminded that a practice on one side of Downing Street which Bagehot said could not be carried on on the other side of it without raising a storm of criticism, would require more ingenuity than has been displayed in their briefs. This much seems to have been admitted on both sides that the operations of the Secretary of State do prevent the importation of gold into India, not altogether, but to the extent covered by their magnitude. Now, those who have held that the ideal of the Fowler Committee has been defeated are no doubt right in their view that the narrowing of the Secretary of State's operation would lead to the importation of gold into India. But what justification is there for assuming that the imported gold would become a part of the currency of India? The assumption that the abolition of the Secretary of State's financial dealings would automatically make gold the currency of India is simply a gratuitous assumption. Whether the imported gold would become current depends on quite a different circumstances.

The other explanation offered to explain the failure of the ideal of the Fowler Committee is the want of a Mint in India open to the free coinage of gold. The opening of the Mints to the free coinage of gold has been regarded as the most vital recommendation of the Fowler Committee; indeed, so much so that the frustration of its ideal has been attributed to the omission by the Government to carry it out The consent given by the Government in 1900 to drop the proposal under the rather truculent attitude of the Treasury has ever since been resented by the

## TABLE LII

### BALANCE OF TRADE, COUNCIL DRAWINGS AND IMPORTS OF GOLD BEFORE 1893

| Years. | Balance of Trade (Merchandise Private Account) | Net Imports of Treasure. | | Amount of Council Bills drawn. | Excess (+) or Deficiency (—) of bills drawn as compared with Budget Estimate. | Home Charges. | Cash Balances in the Home Treasury. | Minimum Rate for Council Bills. |
|---|---|---|---|---|---|---|---|---|
| | | Gold | Silver. | | | | | |
| (1) | (2) | (3) | (4) | (5) | (6) | (7) | (8) | (9) |
| | £ | £ 000,000 | £ 000,000 | £ | £ | £ | £ | s. d. |
| 1893-94 | 21,660,500 | — .39 | 8.3 | 9,530,235 | — 9,169,765 | 15,826,815 | 1,300,564 | 1 1.500 |
| 1894-95 | 25,765,000 | — 2.7 | 3.4 | 16,905,102 | — 94,898 | 15,707,367 | 1,503,124 | 1 0.000 |
| 1895-96 | 29,963,800 | 1.5 | 3.7 | 17,664,492 | + 664,492 | 15,603,370 | 3,393,798 | 1 1.000 |
| 1896-97 | 21,333,100 | 1.4 | 3.5 | 15,526,547 | — 973,453 | 15,795,836 | 3,832,354 | 1 1.781 |
| 1897-98 | 18,847,000 | 3.2 | 5.4 | 9,506,077 | — 3,493,923 | 16,198,263 | 2,534,244 | 1 2.250 |
| 1898-99 | 29,560,700 | 4.3 | 2.6 | 18,692,377 | + 2,692,377 | 16,303,197 | 2,145,768 | 1 3.094 |
| 1899-1900 | 25,509,600 | 6.3 | 2.4 | 19,067,022 | + 2,067,022 | 16,392,846 | 3,330,943 | 1 3.875 |
| 1900-01 | 20,727,400 | .5 | 6.3 | 13,300,277 | — 3,139,723 | 17,200,957 | 4,091,926 | 1 3.875 |
| 1901-02 | 28,630,600 | 1.3 | 4.8 | 18,539,071 | + 2,039,071 | 17,368,655 | 6,693,137 | 1 3.875 |
| 1902-03 | 33,352,600 | 5.8 | 4.6 | 18,499,946 | + 1,999,946 | 18,361,821 | 5,767,787 | 1 3.875 |
| 1903-04 | 45,424,100 | 6.6 | 9.1 | 23,859,303 | + 6,859,303 | 18,146,474 | 7,294,782 | 1 3.875 |
| 1904-05 | 40,548,200 | 6.5 | 8.9 | 24,425,558 | + 7,925,558 | 19,463,757 | 10,262,581 | 1 3.969 |
| 1905-06 | 39,086,700 | .3 | 10.5 | 32,166,973 | +14,333,973 | 18,617,465 | 8,436,519 | 1 3.938 |
| 1906-07 | 45,506,600 | 9.9 | 16.0 | 33,157,196 | +15,357,196 | 19,208,408 | 5,606,812 | 1 3.969 |
| 1907-08 | 31,640,000 | 11.6 | 13.0 | 16,232,062 | — 1,867,938 | 18,487,267 | 5,738,489 | 1 3.906 |
| 1908-09 | 21,173,300 | 2.9 | 8.0 | 13,915,426 | — 4,584,574 | 18,925,159 | 8,453,715 | 1 3.906 |
| 1909-10 | 47,213,000 | 14.5 | 6.3 | 27,096,586 | +10,896,586 | 19,122,916 | 15,809,618 | 1 3.906 |
| 1910-11 | 53,685,300 | 16.0 | 5.8 | 26,783,303 | +11,283,303 | 19,581,563 | 18,174,349 | 1 3.906 |
| 1911-12 | 59,512,900 | 25.1 | 3.6 | 27,058,550 | + 9,900,250 | 19,957,657 | 19,463,723 | 1 3.937 |
| 1912-13 | 57,020,900 | 22.6 | 11.5 | 25,759,706 | +10,259,706 | 20,279,572 | 9,789,634 | 1 3.969 |
| 1913-14 | 43,753,900 | 15.6 | 8.7 | 31,200,827 | +10,000,827 | 20,311,673 | 3,157,732 | 1 3.937 |
| 1914-15 | 29,108,500 | 5.1 | 5.9 | 7,748,111 | —12,251,889 | 20,208,598 | 7,913,236 | 1 3.937 |
| 1915-16 | 44,026,600 | — .7 | 3.2 | 20,354,517 | +13,354,517 | 20,109,094 | 12,803,348 | 1 3.937 |
| 1916-17 | 60,843,200 | 8.82 | 12.5 | 32,998,095 | +29,093,095 | 21,145,627 | 11,391,993 | 1 4.031 |
| 1917-18 | 61,420,000 | 16.8 | 12.7 | 34,880,682 | +34,880,682 | 26,065,057 | 16,625,416 | 1 4.156 |
| 1918-19 | 56,540,000 | — 3.7 | 45.3 | 20,946,314 | +20,946,314 | 23,629,495 | 14,715,827 | 1 4.906 |

advocates of a gold currency. A resolution was moved in 1911 by Sir V. Thackersay, in the Supreme Legislative Council, urging upon the Government the desirability of opening a gold Mint for the coinage of the sovereign if the Treasury consented, and if not for the coinage of some other gold coin. In deference to the united voice of the Council, the Government of India again asked the Secretary of State to approach the Treasury for its sanction.* The Treasury on this occasion presented the Secretary of State † with two alternatives : (1) That a branch of the Royal Mint be established at Bombay solely for the purpose of coining gold into sovereigns, and exclusively under its control; or (2) that the control of the Mint at Bombay should be entirely transferred to it. Neither of the two alternatives was acceptable to the Government of India; and the Secretary of State, as a concession to Indian sentiment, sanctioned the issue of a ten-rupee gold coin from the Indian Mint. The Government of India preferred this solution to that suggested by the Treasury, but desired that the matter be dealt with afresh by the Chamberlain Commission then sitting. That Commission did not recommend a gold Mint,‡ but saw no objection to its establishment provided the coin issued was a sovereign, and if the coinage of it was desired by Indian sentiment and if the Government did not mind the expense of coinage. § This view of the Commission carried the proposition no further than where it was in 1900, until the war compelled the Government to open the Bombay Mint for the coinage of gold as a branch of the Royal Mint. But it was again closed in 1919. Its reopening was recommended by the Currency Committee of 1919, and so ¶ and so enthusiastically was the project received that an Honourable Member of the Supreme Council took the unique step of tempting the Government into adopting that recommendation by an offer to increase the Budget Estimates under "Mint" to enable the Government to bear the cost of it. The Government, however, declined the offer with

* *See* Commons Paper 495, of 1913; p. 57.

† *Ibid*, p. 64.

‡ Report, secs. 69-71.

§ The Commission recommended that if a gold Mint was not established in India Government should renew the notification withdrawn in 1906 to receive refined gold on suitable terms.—Report, sec. 72.

¶ Report, par. 67.

thanks so we have in India the singular spectacle of a country in which there was a Gold Mint even when Gold was not legal tender, as was the case between 1835-93, while there is no gold Mint, when gold is legal tender, as has been the case since 1893. Just what an open Mint can do in the matter of promoting the ideal of the Fowler Committee it is difficult to imagine; but the following extracts from the evidence of a witness (Mr. Webb), than whom there was no greater advocate of an open gold Mint before the Chamberlain Commission, help to indicate just what is expected from a gold Mint.

> "The principal advantage which you would expect to derive from a gold Mint is that you would increase the amount of gold coin in circulation?—That would be one of the tendencies.
>
> "Is there any other advantage?—The advantage is that the country would be fitted with what I regard as an essential part of its monetary mechanism. I regard it as an essential part of its currency mechanism that it should have a Mint at which money could be coined at the requisition of the public.
>
> "I want to get exactly at your reason why that is essential. Am I right in thinking that you consider it essential to a proper currency system that there should be a gold currency?—Yes.
>
> "And essential to a gold currency that there should be a gold Mint?—Yes, on the spot in India itself It would do away, in a measure, with the management by the Secretary of State of the Foreign Exchanges, in that there would be always the Mint at which the public could convert their gold into legal-tender coins in the event of the Secretary of State taking any action of which the public did not approve. It is a safeguard, so to speak, an additional safeguard, that the people of India can on the spot obtain their own money on presentation of the metal."

Here, again, the assumption that a gold Mint is a guarantee that there will be a gold currency seems to be one as gratuitous as the former assumption that if gold were allowed to be freely imported it would on that account become part of the currency. On the other hand, there are cases where Mints were open, yet there was neither gold coinage nor gold currency. Instances may be cited from the history of the coinage at the Royal Mint in London. The magnitude of gold coinage during the bank suspension period, 1797-1821, or the late war, 1914-18, is instructive from this point of view. The Mint was open in both cases, but what was the total coinage of gold? Throughout the suspension period the gold coined was negligible, and during the years 1807, 1812, and 1814—16 no gold was coined at all at the Royal Mint.* Again, during the late war the coinage of gold fell off from 1915, and from 1917 it ceased altogether.† These instances conclusively show that although a Mint is a useful institution, yet there is no magic in a Mint to attract gold to it. The historical instances adduced above leave no doubt that the circulation of gold is governed by factors quite independent of the existence or non-existence of a Mint open to the coinage thereof.

Now, it is an established proposition of political economy that when two kinds of media are employed for currency purposes the bad one drives out the good one from circulation. Applying this principle to the situation in India, it should be evident that so long as there is an unlimited issue of rupees gold cannot circulate in India. This important principle has been so completely overlooked by those who have insisted on the introduction of a gold currency that they have not raised a finger against the unlimited issue of rupees. Mr. Webb, the fiercest opponent of the India Office malpractices, and the staunchest supporter of the view that if only the Secretary of State could be made to contract his drawings gold would flow and be a part of the currency in India, recommended to the Chamberlain Commission that—

"The sales of Council Drafts should be strictly limited to the sum required to meet the Home Charges, and no allotments should in any circumstances be made below, say, 1s. 4⅛d. to 1s. 4 3/32d. —i.e. about the present equivalent of specie point for gold imports into India. The sum required in London for Home Charges having been realized, *no further sales of Council Drafts should be made except for the express purpose—duly notified to the public—of purchasing metal for the manufacture of further token coinage.* Such special sales of Council Drafts should not be made at anything below specie point for gold imports."‡

Again, Sir V. Thackersay, in the course of his speech on March 22, 1912, moving a resolution in the Legislative Council,

* See G. R Poster, *Progress of the Nation* (Ed. Hirst) p. 568.
† See Report of the Deputy Master of the Royal Mint, 1921.
‡ Italics not in the original.

asking the Government to open the Mint for the coinage of gold in India, observed :—

> "Let me make myself clear on one point. *I do not suggest that Government should give up the right to coin rupees or refuse to give rupees when people demand the same.* I do not propose to touch the gold-standard reserve, which must remain as it is as the ultimate guarantee of our currency policy. My proposal does not interfere with the existing arrangements in any way, but is merely supplementary to them. . . . Let the Government of India accumulate gold to the maximum limit of its capacity, but let the surplus gold which it cannot absorb be coined and circulated if the public chooses to do so. With our expanding trade and the balance in our favour, gold will continue to be imported in ordinary time, and *if the facilities of minting are provided in India, it will go into circulation.*"*

These are surely not the ways of promoting a gold currency. Indeed, they run counter to it. So long as the coinage of rupees goes on gold will not enter into currency. Indeed, to cry out on the one hand against the huge drawings of the Secretary of State and the consequent transfer of Indian funds to London and their mismanagement by the Secretary of State, and on the other hand to permit him to manufacture additional token coinage of rupees, is to display not only a lamentable ignorance of a fundamental principle of currency, but also to show a complete failure to understand the precise source from which the whole trouble arises. It is true that the Government of India cannot bind the Secretary of State to any particular course of action,† and he often does override the provisions of the Annual Budget. But the question remains, How is it that he is able to draw so much more after 1893 than he ever did before? It must be remembered that whatever the Secretary of State does with the funds in London he must pay for his drawings in India. Before 1893 he drew less because his means of payment were less; after 1893 he drew more because his means of payment were greater. And why were his means of payment greater? Simply because he had been able to coin rupees. Indeed, the amount of drawings are limited by the demand for

* *S. L. C. P.*, Vol. L, pp. 637-39. Italics not in the original.

†The legal position of the Secretary of State and the extent to which he can be bound by the provisions of any law passed by the Government of India were well explained by Sir James Westland in his speech on the Indian Paper Currency (Amendment) Bill, which afterwards became Act II of 1898; compare also the peculiar wording of that Act.

them and by his capacity to coin rupees. It is therefore foolish to blame the Secretary of State for betraying the interests of India and at the same time to permit him to coin rupees, the very means by which he is able to betray. If a gold currency is wanted, and it is wanted because the rupee is a bad standard of value, then what is necessary is not to put a limit on the drawings of the Secretary of State or the opening of a gold Mint, but a short enactment stopping the coinage of rupees. Then only gold—made legal tender, at a suitable ratio with the rupee—will become a part of Indian currency.

That the stoppage of rupee coinage is a sufficient remedy is amply corroborated by the now forgotten episode in the history of Indian currency during the years 1898—1902. Within the short space of a year and a half after gold had been made legal tender the Hon. C. E. Dawkins, notwithstanding the fact that there was no gold Mint, was able, in his Budget speech in March, 1901, to observe:—

> "India has at length emerged from a period of transition in her currency, has reached the goal to which she has been struggling for years, has established a gold standard and a gold currency, and has attained that practical fixity in exchange which has brought a relief alike to the private individual and to the Government finances."*

So great was the plethora of gold that Mr. Dawkins further remarked† :—

". . . . We have been nearly swamped . . . . by gold. . . . "

The transformation in the currency position which then took place was graphically describers by Lord Curzon, the then Viceroy, in the following words ‡:—

> "Mr Dawkins . . . . has successfully inaugurated the new era under which the sovereign has become legal tender in India, and stability in exchange has assumed what we hope may be a stereotyped form. This great change has been introduced in defiance of the vaticinations of all the prophets of evil, and more especially of the particular prophecy that we could not get gold to come to India, that we could not keep it in our hands if we got it here, but that it would slip so quickly through our fingers that we should have even to borrow to maintain the necessary supply. As a matter of fact, we are almost in the position of the mythological king, who prayed

* *Financial Statement*, 1900—1, p. 14

‡ *Ibid.*, p 167.

that all he touched might be turned into gold, and was then rather painfully surprised when he found that his food had been converted into the same somewhat indigestible material. So much gold, indeed, have we got, that we are now giving gold for rupees as well as rupees for gold, i.e. we are really in the enjoyment of complete convertibility—a state of affairs which would have been derided as impossible by the experts a year ago."

Compare this state of affairs in 1900-1 with that found to exist in 1910-11, for instance. Speaking of the currency situation as it was in that year, the Hon. Sir James (now Lord) Meston, observed *:—

"We have passed through many changes in currency policy and made not a few mistakes. But the broad lines of our action and our objects are clear and unmistakable, and there has been no great or fundamental sacrifice of consistency in progress towards our ideal. Since the Fowler Committee that progress has been real and unbroken. There is still one great step forward before the ideal can be reached. We have linked India with the gold countries of the world, we have reached a gold-exchange standard, which we are steadily developing and improving. The next and final step is a true gold currency. That, I have every hope, will come in time. . . . ."

Leaving aside for the moment the extenuatory remarks of the speaker, the fact remains that in 1900 India had a gold currency. But, taking stock of the position at the end of 1910, it had ceased to have it. What is it that made this difference? Nothing but the fact that between 1893-1900 no rupees were coined, but between 1900-1910 the number of rupees coined was enormous. During the first period the inducement to coin rupees was very great indeed. The exchange was not quite stable, and the Government had still to find an increasing number of rupees to pay for the "Home Charges." And an Honourable Member† of the Supreme Legislative Council actually asked:—

"Is there any objection to the Government working the Mints on their own account? Considering the low value of silver and the great margin between the respective prices of bullion and the rupee, would not Government by manufacturing rupees for itself make sufficient profit to meet at least a substantial portion of the present deficit? It seems to me to be a legitimate source of revenue and one capable of materially easing our finances."

* *Financial Statement,* 1910–11, p. 346.

† This was no other than the Hon. Fazulbhai Vishram, the well-known financier of Bombay. Cf. his speech in the *Financial Statement,* 1894—95, p. 96.

But Sir James Westland, who was then in charge of the finances of India, replied*:—

> "I must confess to a little surprise in finding the proposal put forward by one of the commercial members of your Excellency's Council that we should buy silver at its present low price, and coin it for issue at the appreciated value of the rupee . . . . . I shall certainly refuse myself to fall into this temptation."

Again, in 1898, when some of the followers of Mr. Lindsay desired that Government should coin rupees to relieve the monetary stringency, Sir James Westland remarked†:—

> " . . . . in our opinion the silver standard is now a question of the past. It is a case of *vestigia nulla retrorsum*. The only question before us is how best to attain the gold standard. We cannot go back to the position of the open Mints. There are only two ways in which we can go back to that position. We can either open the Mints to the public generally, or we can open them to coinage by ourselves. In either case what it means, is that the value of the rupee will go down to something approaching the value of silver. If the case is that of opening the Mints to the public, the descent of the rupee will be rapid. If it is that of opening only to coinage by the Government, the descent of the rupee may be slow but it will be no less inevitable."

The Hon. C. E. Dawkins was equally emphatic in his denunciation of the project of Government coining rupees. When he was tempted to acquiesce in the proposal by holding out the prospects of a profit from coinage, he replied*:—

> "I think I ought . . . . to beg my hon. friend not to dangle the profits on silver too conspicuously before the eyes even of a most virtuous Government. Once let these profits become a determining factor in your action, then good-bye stability."

Another instance of the Government's determination not to coin rupees is furnished by inquiring into the reasons as to why it is that the Government has never assumed the responsibility of selling council bills in indefinite amount and at a fixed rate. The Chamberlain Commission argued that the Government cannot undertake such a responsibility because it cannot hold out for a fixed rate, and may have to sell at any rate even lower than par. This is true so far as it is a confession of a position weakened by

*Ibid., p. 123.

† *Financial Statement*, 1989—9, p. 169.

* *Financial Statement*, 1900—1, p. 163.

the Government's folly of indulging in excessive rupee coinage. But this was certainly not the explanation which the Government gave in 1900 when it was first asked to assume that responsibility. The Government know perfectly well that to keep on selling bills indefinitely was to keep on coining rupees indefinitely. They refused to assume that responsibility because they did not want to coin rupees. That this was the original reason was made quite plain by the Hon. Mr. Dawkins,* who reminded those who asked Government to undertake such a responsibility that

> "the silver coin reserve of Government in consequence rapidly neared a point at which it was impossible to continue to meet unlimited transfers [i.e. council bills]. Therefore the Secretary of State decided to limit the demands by gradually raising the rate, thus meeting the most urgent demands, and weeding out the less urgent, while warning those whose demands were not so urgent to ship gold to India. No other course was practicable. The liability of the Secretary of State to keep the tap turned on indefinitely at 1s. 4 5|32d. has been asserted. But I cannot see that any positive liability exists, and I wonder if those who assert its existence would have preferred that the stability of our currency (whose situation they are well able to appreciate and follow) should have been affected by the reserve of rupees being dangerously reduced?" [and which could not be augmented except by coining more rupees].

Just at the nick of time, when the ideal of a gold standard with a gold currency was about to be realized, there came on the scene Sir Edward Law as the Finance Minister of India and tore the whole structure of the new currency to pieces with a piratical nonchalance that was as stupid as it was wanton. His was the Minute of June 28, 1900, which changed the whole course of events.† In that Minute occurs the following important passage:—

> "15. As a result of these considerations it must, I think, be admitted that the amount of gold which can safely be held in the currency reserve must for the present be regulated by the same rules as would guide the consideration of the amount by which the proportion invested in Government securities could be safely increased. Pending an increase in the note circulation . . . . . or some other change in existing conditions, I am of opinion that a maximum sum of approximately £7,000,000 in gold may now be

* Cf. his Budget speech, *Financial Statement*, 1900—1, p. 27.

† For a copy of the Minute and the correspondence thereon, *see* Appendix V to the Interim Report of the Chamberlain Commission, Cd. 7070 of 1913.

> safely held in the currency reserve. I should not, however, wish to be bound absolutely to this figure, which is necessarily an arbitrary one, and particularly I should not wish any public announcement to be made which might seem to tie the hands of the Government in the event of circumstances, at present unforeseen, rendering its reduction hereafter desirable."

In outlining this Minute, which with modifications in the maximum gold to be held in the currency reserve, remains the foundation of the currency system in India, the author of it never seems to have asked for one moment what was to happen to the ideal of a gold standard and a gold currency? Was he assisting the consummation of the gold standard or was he projecting the abandonment of the gold standard in thus putting a limit on the holding of gold? Before the policy of this Minute was put into execution the Indian currency system was approximating to that of the Bank Charter Act of 1844, in which the issue of rupees was limited and that of gold unlimited. This Minute proposed that the issue of gold should be limited and that of rupees unlimited —an exact reversal to the system of the Bank Suspension period. In this lies the great significance of the Minute, which deliberately outlined a policy of substituting rupees for gold in Indian currency and thereby defeating the ideal held out since 1893 and well-nigh accomplished in 1900.

If Sir Edward Law had realized that this meant an abandonment of the gold standard, perhaps he would not have recorded the Minute. But what were the considerations alluded to in the Minute which led him thus to subvert the policy of a gold standard and a gold currency and put a limit on the gold part of the currency rather than on the rupee part of the currency? They are to be found in a despatch, No. 302, dated September 6, 1900, from the Government of India, which says:—

> "2. . . . . the receipts of gold continued and increased after December last. For more than eight months the gold in the currency reserve has exceeded, and the silver has been less, than the limits suggested in the despatch of June 18. By the middle of January the stock of gold in the currency reserve in India reached £5,000,000. The proposal made in that despatch was at once brought into operation; later on we sent supplies of sovereigns to the larger District Treasuries, with instructions that they should be issued to anyone who desired to receive them in payments due or in exchange for rupees; and in March we directed the Post Office

to make in sovereigns all payments of money orders in the Presidency towns and Rangoon, and we requested the Presidency Banks to make in the Presidency towns and Rangoon payments on Government account as far as possible in sovereigns. These measures were taken, not so much in the expectation that they would in the early future relieve us of any large part of our surplus gold, but in the hope that they would accustom the people to gold, would hasten the time when it will pass into general circulation in considerable quantities, and by so doing would mitigate in future years the difficulties that we were experiencing from the magnitude of our stock of gold and the depletion of our stock of rupees.

"3. In order to meet these difficulties and to secure, if possible, that we should have enough rupees for payment to presenters of currency notes and tenderers of gold, we began to coin additional rupees. . . . .

* * * * *

"14. We may mention that we have closely watched the result of the measures described in paragraph 2. The issues of gold have been considerable; but much has come back to us through the Currency Department and the Presidency banks. The Comptroller-General estimated the amount remaining in circulation at the end of June at over a million and a quarter out of nearly two millions issued up to that time; but there are many uncertain data in the calculation. We are not yet able to say that gold has passed into use as money to any appreciable extent.

"15. It is very desirable that we should feel assured of being able to meet the public demand for rupees, as indicated by the presentation of currency notes and gold. We therefore strongly press on your Lordship the expediency of sanctioning the above proposal for further coinage [of rupees]. . . . .

* * * * *

"17. But we do not wish our proposal to be considered as dependent on such arguments as those just stated. We make it primarily on the practical ground that we consider it necessary in order to enable us to fulfil an obligation which, though we are not, and do not propose to be, legally committed thereto, we think it desirable to undertake so long as we can do it without excessive inconvenience; namely, to pay rupees to all tenderers of gold and to give rupees in encashment of currency notes to all who prefer rupees to sovereigns."

The arguments advanced in this statement of the case for coining rupees are a motley lot. At the outset it is something unheard of that a Government which was proceeding to establish a gold standard and a gold currency should have been so very alarmed at the sight of increased gold when it should have thanked its stars for such an early consummation of its ideal. Leaving aside the psychological aspect of the question, the Government, according to its own statement, undertook to coin rupees for two reasons: (1) because it felt itself obliged to give rupees whenever asked for, and (2) because people did not want gold. What force is there in these arguments? Respecting the first argument it is difficult to undrstand why Government should feel itself obliged to give rupees. The obligation of a debtor is to pay the legal-tender money of the country. Gold had been made legal tender, and the Government could have discharged its obligations by paying out without shame or apology. Secondly, what is the proof that people did not want gold? It is said that the fact that the gold paid out by Government returned to it is evidence enough that people did not want it. But this is a fallacy. In a country like India Government dues form a large part of the people's expenditure, and if people used that gold to meet those dues—this is what is meant by the return of gold to Government—then it is an evidence in support of the contention that people were prepared to use gold as currency. But if it is true that people do not want gold, how does it accord with the fact that Government refuses to give gold when people make a demand for it? Does not the standing refusal imply that there is a standing demand? There is no consistency in this mode of reasoning. The fact is, all this confused advocacy is employed to divert attention from the truth that the Government was anxious to coin rupees not because people did no want gold, but because Government was anxious to build a gold reserve out of the profits of additional coinage of rupees. That this was the underlying motive is manifest from the minute of Sir Edward Law. That the argument about people disliking gold, and so forth, and so forth, was only a cover for the true motive comes out prominently from that part of the Minute in which its author had argued that:—

> "16. If it be accepted that £7,000,000 is the maximum sum which, under existing conditions, can be held in gold in the currency reserve, in addition to the 10 crores already invested, it is evident that such assistance as can be obtained from manipulating the reserve will fail to provide the sum in gold which it is con-

sidered advisable to hold in connection with the maintenance of a steady exchange. So far no authority has ventured to name a definite sum which should suffice for this purpose, but there is a general consensus of opinion, in which I fully concur, that a very considerable sum is required. The most ready way of obtaining such a large sum is by gold borrowings, but the opinion of the Currency Commission was strongly hostile to such a course, and the question therefore remains unanswered· How is the necessary stock of gold to be obtained?

"17. I do not presume to offer any cut-and-dried solution of this difficult problem, but I venture to offer certain suggestions which, if adopted, would, I believe, go a considerable way towards meeting the difficulty. I propose to create a special 'Gold Exchange Fund,' independent of, but in case of extraordinary requirements for exchange purposes to be used in conjunction with, the gold resources of the currency reserve. The foundation of this fund would be the profit to be realized by converting into rupees the excess above £7,000,000 now held in gold in the currency reserve"

Can there be any doubt now as to the true cause for coining rupees? Writers who have broadcasted that rupees were coined because people did not want gold cannot be said to have read correctly the history of the genesis of the exchange standard in India.

But was Sir Edward Law the evil genius who turned a sound system of currency into an unsound one by his disastrous policy of coining rupees? Opponents of the Government as well as its supporters are all agreed* that this was a departure from the ideal of the Fowler Committee. In what precise respect the Government has departed from the recommendations of the Fowler Committee has, however, never been made clear anywhere in the official or non-official literature on the subject of Indian currency. What were the recommendations of the Fowler Committee? It is usually pointed out, to the shame of the Government of India, that the Fowler Committee had said (it is as well to repeat it):—

"We are in favour of making the British sovereign a legal tender and a current coin in India We also consider that, at the same time, the Indian Mints should be thrown open to the unrestricted coinage of gold. . . . . Looking forward as we do the

* Even the Chamberlain Commission said that the Government had departed from the ideal of the Fowler Committee

effective establishment of a gold standard and currency based on the principles of the free inflow and outflow of gold, we recommend these measures for adoption."

That is true. But those who have blamed the Government have forgotten that same Committee also recommended that—

"The exclusive right to coin fresh rupees must remain vested in the Government of India; and though the existing stock of rupees may suffice for some time, regulations will ultimately be needed for providing such additions to the silver currency as may prove necessary. The Government should continue to give rupees for gold, but fresh rupees should not be coined until the proportion of gold in the currency is found to exceed the requirements of the public. We also recommend that any profit on the coinage of rupees should not be credited to the revenue or held as a portion of the ordinary balance of the Government of India, but should be kept in gold as a special reserve, entirely apart from the paper-currency reserve and the ordinary Treasury balances" [and be made freely available for foreign remittances whenever the exchange falls below specie point.]

Taking the two recommendations of the Committee together, where is the departure? What the Government has done is precisely what the Committee had recommended. That the Government of India or the Chamberlain Commission should have admitted for a moment that there was a departure is not a little odd, for the very despatch which conveyed the Minute of Sir Edward Law to the Secretary of State opens with remarks which show that Government was earnestly following the recommendations of the Fowler Committee. It runs :—

"In our despatch No. 301 of August 24, 1899, we wrote with reference to paragraph 60 of the Report of the Indian Currency Committee [i.e. the Fowler Committee], that any profit made on rupee coinage should be held in gold as a special reserve, has not escaped our attention; but the need for the coinage of additional rupees is not likely to occur for some time, and a decision on this point may be conveniently deferred."

What Sir Edward Law did was to carry that recommendation into effect when the occasion arrived. In view of this it is useless to belabour the Government of India if the ideal of a gold standard with a gold currency was defeated by the coinage of rupees. But, even though the Government has in ignorance taken the blame on itself, it cannot be rightly thrown at its door. If the project has been defeated by the coinage of rupees, the question must be referred to the Fowler Committee. Why did the Committee permit the coinage of rupees? There is no direct answer, but it may be guessed. It seems the Committee first decided that there should be a gold standard and a gold currency as desired by the Government of India. But then they seemed to have been worried by the question whether in the ideal they had sketched they had made enough provision for the maintenance of the gold value of the rupee. In the view of the opponents of the Government of India the rupee ought to have been made either convertible as a bank note or a limited legal tender as a shilling. The Committee rejected both these demands as being unnecessary. Stating their ground for refusing to reduce the rupee to the status of a shilling, the Committee argued*:—

> "It is true that in the United Kingdom the silver currency has a fixed limit of 40s., beyond which it cannot be used to pay a debt. . . . While it cannot be denied that 40s. limitation tends to emphasize and maintain the subsidiary character of our silver coinage, yet the essential factor in maintaining those tokens at their representative nominal value is not the statutory limit on the amount for which they are a legal tender in any one payment, but the limitation of their total issue. Provided the latter restriction is adequate, there is no essential reason why there need be any limit on the amount for which tokens are a tender by law."

Regarding the necessity for convertibility the Committee observed †:—

> "Outside the United Kingdom there are two principal instances of countries with a gold standard and currency, which admit silver coins to unlimited tender. These countries are France and the United States of America. In France the five-franc piece is an unlimited tender and for all internal purposes is equivalent to gold. The same remark applies in the United States to the silver dollar. . . . Both in France and the United States the Mints are now closed to the coinage of silver coins convertible by law into gold; in both countries alike they are equivalent to gold for all internal purposes. For international payments, so far as specie is concerned, France and the United States depend ultimately on the international medium of exchange, which is gold. In the last resort, it is their gold which, acting through the foreign exchanges, maintains the whole mass of their currency at its nominal value for internal purposes.

* Report, par. 56.

† Report, pars. 57—60.

> "The position of the currency question in India being such as we have explained in the preceding paragraph, we do not consider it necessary to recommend a different policy in the case of that country from that which is found sufficient in France and the United States, by imposing a legal obligation on the Government of India to give gold for rupees, or, in other words, to substitute the former for the latter on the demand of the holders. This obligation would impose on the Government of India a liability to find gold at a moment's notice to an amount which cannot be defined beforehand, and the liability is one which, in our opinion, ought not to be accepted."

Although confident of its opinions, the Committee was considerably impressed by those who, owing to the large quantity of rupees in circulation, entertained doubts

> "whether the mere closing of the Indian Mints to silver would in practice be attended with such a restriction of the rupee currency as would make the rupee permanently exchangeable for gold at a fixed rate."

So much was the Committee shaken by these doubts that it admitted that*

> "the forces which affect the gold value of the rupee are complicated and obscure in their mode of operation, and we are unable, therefore, to say positively that the mere closing of the Mints to silver will, in practice, lead to such a limitation of the rupee currency, relatively to the demands for it, as will make the rupee permanently exchangeable for gold at a fixed rate."

As a remedy against such a contingency the Committee thought that the Government of India should accept the obligation of convertibility of the rupee into gold for foreign remittances whenever the rupee fell below specie point. Having hit upon such a simple solution the next question was how was the Government to get its gold reserve? Borrowing for the purposes of such a gold reserve was one way of doing it. But that project was somehow unpalatable to the Committee. Perhaps because it had admonished the Goverment, in another part of its Report,† to

> "husband the resources at their command, exercise a resolute economy, and restrict the growth of their gold obligations,"

or because it was a vicious principle to borrow

> "for the establishment or the maintenance of a gold standard,"‡

the Committee was averse to the proposal for gold borrowing. But if a gold reserve was not to be built up by borrowing, how

* Report, par. 58. †Report, par. 70.

‡ *See* the Reservations to the Report by Compbell Holland and Muir Report, p. 27.

could it be built up otherwise ? The Committee seems to have been considerably troubled over the problem of finding an alternative mode of raising a reserve until some member of it, probably at a moment when his intellect was rather weak, proposed 'Well, why not allow the Government to coin rupees? If that were allowed it could easily build up a gold reserve without having to borrow, and can then discharge the obligation of convertibility for foreign remittances.' So innocuous seemed the proposal that the Committee wholeheartedly adopted and incorporated it into its Report with a certain sigh of relief that is unmistakable from the firm language in which it was expressed.

This may or may not be a correct interpretation of the reasoning employed by the Committee in permitting the Government to coin rupees. But the fact remains that the Committee did not realize what was involved in that recommendation. First of all, what was to happen to the gold standard and currency if the coinage of rupees was to go on? In this regard is it possible to have more respect for a Committee which lays down on the one hand the ideal of a gold standard and currency, and permits on the other hand the coinage of rupees, than Bagehot felt for the Directors of the Bank of England, who on March 25, 1819, passed that notorious resolution :—

> "That the Court cannot refrain from advertising to an opinion, strongly insisted upon by some, that the Bank has only to reduce its issues to obtain a favourable turn in the Exchanges, and a consequent influx of the precious metals; the Court conceives it to be its duty to declare that it is unable to discover any solid foundation for such a sentiment"?

If the opinions of the Directors were classical for their nonsense, are those of the Fowler Committee less so? Is there any difference between them? Bagehot, in commenting upon the sentiments embodied in the resolution, not dissimilar to the recommendations of the Fowler Committee, urged some extenuating circumstances which compel us to forgive the Bank Directors their nonsense. The Directors lived in an age when economic reasoning was in a confused state; nor were they anxious for the "influx of gold," being perfectly satisfied with paper. None of these circumstances can excuse the nonsense of the Fowler Committee. They framed their recommendations at a time when the contrary of what the Bank Directors had held was an established axiom. Besides, it cannot be said that they were not anxious for the influx of gold into the Indian currency. On the other hand, that was just the thing they were looking forward to. Consequently, they should have carefully weighed their words and allowed nothing that was inconsistent with their main object. In not paying sufficient heed to that elementary principle known as Gresham's Law, the Committee not only made a fool of itself but defeated the principal object it had set forth in the earlier part of its Report.

Secondly, was it necessary to endow the Government with a power to coin rupees? What was the nature of the problem the Committee was called upon to decide? Let us re-state it. The Herschell Committee,* by way of modifying the proposals of the Government of India, submitted to it in 1892, had introduced a proviso by which the Mints, although closed to the public, were to remain open to the Government for the coinage of rupees—a proviso which, by the way, reveals that after all that imposing survey the Committee remained supremely ignorant of the secret why, in the monetary systems it investigated, the currency maintained its parity with gold with little or no gold. If it had understood that it was limitation of issue which maintained this parity it would not have introduced the proviso which it did. However pernicious the proviso, the Committee must be excused for that indiscretion, for it was afraid that owing to the Mint closure there might be a sudden contraction of currency, and as it had not made gold general legal tender it had to provide for the necessary addition to the currency, and this it thought could best be done by Government having the power to coin rupees. Fortunately for the Government the occasion for an addition did not arise for some time, till 1898, and there was therefore no necessity to exercise, that power. But when such an occasion did arise the Government, as was pointed out before, refused to exercise that power—and held to the view that the additions to Indian currency, instead of being made by further coinage of rupees, should be made by an influx of gold. The Government was the strongest opponent of Mr. Lindsay, who was then agitating that it was safe and econo-

* *See* Chap. IV, *supra*, p. 147.

mical to compel it to make the necessary additions by undertaking to coin rupees. It was to adjudicate in the dispute between the Government of India on the one hand and Mr. Lindsay on the other, the former desiring additions by gold coinage and the latter by rupee coinage, that the Fowler Committee was called into being. If the Government was anxious to add to the currency by coining more rupees rather than by the influx of gold, there was no necessity to appoint the Fowler Committee. Such a power had already been given to it by the Herschell Committee. It was because the Government did not want to exercise that ill-charged power that an appeal to a new Committee became necessary. Faced with this immediate problem of how best to expand the currency in relief of monetary stringency, the Committee had solved it in one part of its Report by prescribing that gold should be made legal tender, so that any debtor who was unable to find rupees could have the option of paying his creditors in gold. If gold was allowed to be the general medium of exchange, was not the proposal to coin rupees a superfluous one, quite uncalled for?

Thirdly, could the proposal to coin rupees as a means of building up a gold reserve be justified as calculated to maintain the value of the rupee? The one thing essential to the maintenance of the value of the rupee was a limitation on its issue. The Committee talked in a very learned manner about the shilling as being maintained in value in consequence of a limitation in its issue. But did it understand how the shilling was maintained limited in quantity? If it is true that it is not the limit on legal tender, but the limit on the total volume, that maintains the value of the shilling, why is not the shilling issued in unlimited quantities? The manufacture of the shilling is profitable in the same way as is the manufacture of the rupee. Why does not the British Government coin it in unlimited quantities? Only because shillings cannot be paid out in unlimited quantities? If the Government could pay its Chancellors of Exchequer, Cabinet Ministers, and the hosts of officials and clerks, and if they in turn could pay their grocers, milkmen, brewers, and butchers in shillings, there could be nothing to prevent the over-issue of shillings. But it is because nobody can pay out shillings in unlimited quantities that nobody will have them in unlimited quantities. It is the absence of a wholesale market, so to say, due to a limit on legal tender, that stops the Government from indulging in the over-issue of shillings. The Committee was therefore wrong in arguing that the limit on legal tender had nothing to do with the maintenance of the value of the shilling. On the other hand, if limitation of issue is the prime condition which maintains the value of a token coin, one means of making such a limit effective is to put a limit on its legal tender.

With regard to its views on convertibility, its reasoning was equally confused. To say what was sufficient for France and America should be sufficient for India, was like the blind leading the blind. It was entirely erroneous to argue that it was not convertibility but their gold

> "which, acting through the foreign exchanges, maintains the whole mass of their currency at its nominal value for internal purposes."

Quite the contrary. France and America did not need convertibility to protect their currency because the silver franc and the silver dollar were absolutely limited in quantity. Indeed, far from being protected by the influx of gold, the limitation of issue not only maintained their value, but permitted the retention of whatever gold there was in those countries. Now, the Committee, instead of venturing into long-winded and pointless disquisitions, should have insisted that there was no necessity either to prescribe a limit of tender or convertibility with regard to the rupee, so long as there were other ways of restricting its over-issue. Limitation of legal tender or convertibility can be said to be essential only because they are the means of bringing about a limitation of issue, and if the requisite limitation of issue was provided for in other ways, the purpose for which convertibility or limitation of legal tender were asked for was accomplished. Now, was not the closing of the Mints a sufficient limitation on the volume of rupees? Indeed, if the closing of the Mints was not an effective limitation on the issue of rupees, what else could have been? Was not the closing of the Mints the same thing as regulating the currency on the principle of a fixed-issue system so well known in the matter of regulating paper currencies? That it was, could hardly be denied. That being so, the only question was whether the volume of rupees already in circulation was distinctly less than the minimum amount of legal-tender money ever necessary for the internal circulation of the country. The Government of India had forseen the volume of rupees in circulation becoming in excess of such a minimum and had accordingly provided against it. In their despatch of March 3, 1898, outlining their plans, the Government observed :—

"9. . . . . We know now that one of the main reasons of this failure [to maintain the exchange value of the rupee] is that our rupee circulation had before the closing of the Mints been increased to such an extent that it fully, and more than fully, supplied all the demands of trade, and allowed no room for any further addition in the form of gold. . . . . The necessary condition of a fixed rate of exchange between two countries is that, when the currency of one of them becomes redundant as compared with that of the other, the redundancy may be relieved by the withdrawal, for a time, of the excess coin, and we wish, therefore, to reach the condition in which our circulating medium . . . . is not composed wholly of silver coin which has no equal value outside the country, but contains also a margin of gold which is capable of being used elsewhere as coin, and will therefore in natural course flow to where it is most wanted. Our total rupee currency is estimated to be at present somewhere about 120 crores, to which we have to add 10 crores of fiduciary circulation of currency notes.

"10. It is impossible with any exactness to say, and it can only be ascertained by actual experience, by how much this rupee circulation has to be decreased in order to remove its redundancy. . . . . But some considerations point to the amount being within quite manageable limits. For example, there are twenty-four crores, more or less, of currency notes in circulation, including the amounts held in our Treasuries. If we could imagine that amount of circulation at present existing in the form of currency notes suddenly converted into £16,000,000 in gold, it seems impossible that Indian trade should be able to get on without having part at least of that amount held in actual circulation, in other words, it would not be possible for that amount of gold coin to be remitted out of the country without the value of the rupee being forced up to a point which would arrest the stream of export. If this is the case, twenty-four crores of rupees is the outside limit of the amount it might be necessary to convert into gold coin in order to introduce a stable exchange of 16d., accompanied by an actual (active or inactive) circulation of gold at that comparative value; and it is more than probable that the amount required may really fall far short of this.

"11. The mere reduction of circulation might be carried out in the same way in which it was effected in 1893, namely, by abstaining from withdrawing council bills, until we have an accumulation of, say, twenty crores in excess of our ordinary balances. But this procedure would be both costly and, as we believe, ineffective; in the first place the permanent locking up of twenty crores would cost us the interest on that amount, or on the amount of gold borrowed in England during the suspension of drawings, and in the second place the existence of this accumulation of silver coin would be a perpetual menace to the exchange market, and would entirely prevent any confidence in the future of the rupee. We must not only withdraw the amount from circulation, but we must show by the method we adopt that our intention is that it should cease to exist in the form of coin, and that its place, as coin, is to be taken by gold. Our proposal is therefore to melt down existing rupees, having first provided a reserve of gold [by borrowing] both for the practical purpose of taking the place of the silver, and in order to establish confidence in the issue of our measures."

At the time the Committee reported the volume of rupees in circulation was not redundant, as was proved by the fact that exchange was rising and gold was flowing in. That the closing of the Mints had therefore brought about an effective limit is beyond dispute, and was even admitted by the Committee.* But supposing that the closing of the Mints did not constitute an effective limitation on the volume of rupees in circulation, what was the remedy? Was the plan of a gold reserve to assure convertibility for foreign remittances calculated to promote that object if the gold reserve was to be got by coining more rupees? If the limitation of rupees was going to maintain their value, as it did the value of the shilling, was the permission to add to the volume of rupees which the Committee feared was over-abundant if not redundant, for the sake of a gold reserve, designed to limit their volume?

It is difficult to read the report of the Fowler Committee without exasperation. The permission to coin rupees was mischievous in every way. It was destructive of a true gold standard; it was not wanted as a relief against monetary stringency, and was calculated to lower the value of the rupee. If it was anxious for a gold standard and currency, as it undoubtedly was, it should have absolutely stopped the coinage of rupees and suppressed the notification holding the Government ready to give rupees for gold. In failing to do that it not only deprived the country of a sound system, but actually, albeit unwittingly, helped to place the entire Indian currency, including paper currency, on the basis of an inconvertible rupee. Few people seem to be alive to the precise significance of that pernicious proviso introduced by the Herschell Committee, and remorselessly upheld by the Fowler Committee, that the Government shall always be ready

* Report, p 17.

to give rupees for gold, but there can be no doubt that in the absence of a counter-proviso, requiring Government to give gold for rupees, the proviso is simply a cover for an authority to the Indian Government to issue inconvertible rupee currency of unlimited legal tender in the same way as the bank restriction was for an authority to the Bank of England to issue inconvertible notes in unlimited quantities. The first step in the right direction would be to scrap that Report and make a speedy return to the safe and sound proposals of the Government of India as outlined in the despatch referred to above. The primary condition is to stop the coinage of rupees and not merely close the Mints to the public. Whether it would be necessary to melt a portion of the rupees depends upon what gold value it is desired the rupee should have. Once the total contraction of the rupee is settled upon and all further coinage is stopped, India will be in a position to have an effective gold standard based on a free inflow and outflow of gold. There will be no necessity to reduce the rupee in legal tender and provide for its convertibility. Its value would be maintained intact by sheer force of its quantity being limited, provided the quantity in circulation has been reduced so far as to be always below the minimum demand.

Supporters of the existing system of rupee currency have ever since its inauguration held out that the currency is economical and secure. Its claim for security, both in terms of gold and commodities, has been tested, and the grounds of it have been analysed in the course of this and previous chapters, wherein is demonstrated how very much wanting it is in the essentials that go to make up a secure currency. We must now endeavour to assess whether it is economical, for if it were really so, then that might be a point of some value against its opponents. We must therefore scrutinize the economy effected by the rupee currency.

Kemmerer says.*

> "A convertible money finds its *raison d'etre* largely in the fact that it economizes the precious metals, and makes possible a saving to the community. If paper money or token money are substituted for primary money, their substitution reduces the demand for the precious metals by the difference between the amount of metal used in the token money introduced plus that

* Money and Credit Instruments in Relation to Prices, p. 63.

> contained in the primary money required for the redemption fund. This economy of the precious metals results in an increased supply being thrown upon the market" [which supply goes abroad and into the arts and increases the non-monetary wealth of the country by an equivalent amount: the gold obtained for the metal economized represents a net gain to the community].

The same kind of gain, says Kemmerer, attaches to the use of inconvertible money, and even on a larger scale, because there is no necessity to use primary money even for a redemption fund, as there is when the money is convertible. Such views as these haved led Prof. Keynes to opine that the Indian currency system is a marvel of economy, and that other more advanced countries might usefully follow the lead. We will not draw from this the uncharitable conclusion that either Prof. Kemmerer or Prof. Keynes would recommend that because an inconvertible paper currency is the most economical currency a country should adopt it without remorse. What we are concerned with is to find out whether the rupee currency is really economical. When the process by which the rupee comes into being is carefully analysed it becomes impossible to take seriously the plea that the Indian currency is economical. First of all, gold is tendered to the Secretary of State in London for his council bills, or gold is tendered to the Government of India in India in payment of taxes or otherwise. Out of this gold the Secretary of State buys silver and coins rupees. As the price of silver is below the ratio, there arises a difference between the cost price of the rupee and its selling price in gold. To the extent of this difference there is, of course, a gain. But this gain or profit on coinage, as it is called, is no benefit to society. It is a hoard, and to that extent represents a useless abstraction of wealth. If the profit is not to be used for any current purposes of society it is as well not to coin rupees. It is therefore obvious that so long as the profits are merely held apart from the revenue resources of India there is no economy in the rupee currency worth naming. From another standpoint the currency of India is a wasteful asset to society. Metallic currency is primarily a capital good representing a form of social investment. Consequently it is necessary to see that the capital value of the currency is maintained. It is a happy circumstance to note that the Government of India is not dead to this aspect of the question with regard to its paper-currency reserve, and has very recently instituted a depreciation fund for the preservation of its capital value.* Now, the considerations that apply to the paper currency should apply also to the rupee currency. Has the rupee currency maintained its capital value? The gold part of it, called the gold-standard reserve, is invested in interest-bearing securities. Interest is no doubt an additional source of gain, but have the securities maintained their capital value ? Far from it. Turn to the rupee half of the currency. Has the bullion in the rupee maintained its capital value? There have been endless charts and diagrams drawn by playful economists in which the black line, showing the nominal value of the rupee, has remained up while the red line, showing the bullion value of the rupee, has gone down with the falling gold value of silver. But what does that mean? Simply that the rupee is a wasting asset and is not worth at a later date what it cost to society when it was manufactured. Surely there was more economy in the project of the mad Chinaman who burnt his house to roast his pig than there is in the Indian rupee currency. The Chinaman's house must have been very old and uninhabitable. The same cannot, however, be said of this converting of gold money into silver money, because we know that silver is an inferior kind of investment to gold. Thus viewed, the currency is not in the least economical. It appears to be so because people look only to the rupee. But, adding the cost of the rupee currency to that of the gold-standard reserve, can it be said that India would have required more gold if she had a gold currency in place of a rupee currency? Bearing in mind that with a fixed limit on the issue of rupees there can be no reason for a gold reserve, the only result of a stoppage of rupee coinage would be that gold, instead of being, as now, part reserved as a sinking fund and part transmuted into a rupee currency, would enter into circulation without being subjected to this baneful and wasteful process.

No more gold would be required in the one case than in the other. We can therefore conclude without fear of challenge that with a complete stoppage of rupee coinage Indian currency would be truly economical, prices would be more stable, and exchange

* Cf. the Speech of the Finance Minister, Mr. Hailey, on the Indian Paper Currency (Amendment) Bill, dated September 16, 1920, *S.L.C.P.*, Vol. LIX, pp. 308—9.

secure, in the only way in which it can really be said to be secure, and the rupee, although inconvertible, will cease to be a problem, which it has been ever since 1873.

But will that be all the advantage to the country? By no means. In drawing a moral from his comparison of the paper pound of 1797 with the paper pound of 1914, Prof. Cannan* points out that

> "there can in these days be no doubt that the experiment of entrusting what no community should entrust to any institution, the power of creating money without limit, to the Bank of England, compares very favourably with the modern plan of entrusting it to the Government itself or to a State bank completely under the control of the Government. In the comparatively short war of 1914-18 currencies 'not convertible at will into a coin which is exportable' were issued by Governments and Government banks in amounts compared with which the 100 per cent. increase in thirteen years, which made the Bullion Committee complain so vigorously in 1810, look absolutely trifling."

There was a time when it could have been said that this indictment did not apply to the Government of India. Few Governments could be said to have been so very anxious to wash their hands of the responsibilities involved in the management of a currency as the Government of India once was. In 1861, when the Government first undertook the issue of paper money in India, the anxiety it displayed was laudable. An impecunious Government, made prostrate by the heavy burdens of the Mutiny, should have welcomed the project of a paper currency as a source of profit. But so great was its sense of responsibility that the Government refused to be content with convertibility as a check on over-issue. One of the principal reasons why the desperate paper-currency scheme, which that straitened financier Mr. Wilson had devised in 1860 to find ways and means for improving the finances of India, was rejected was so well stated by his successor, Mr. Laing, that in these days of frenzied finance his remarks may as well be reproduced in full. He said†:—

> "There was another important reason why he (Mr. Laing) thought that Sir Charles Wood's principle was the soundest. All

* *The Paper Pound of* 1797—1821, Introduction, p. xxxix.

† His speech on the Paper Currency Bill dated February 16, 1861, *S.L.C.P.*, Vol. VII, pp. 66—7.

parties were agreed that a paper currency ought to be identical with the metallic currency which it displaced. But the system of issuing against two-thirds of securities and one-third of specie, as was proposed by Mr. Wilson, would not always ensure this identity, and there was considerable risk that in times of buoyancy and speculation the circulation would be unduly extended. He thought that that was a point of considerable importance, because if we looked at what had taken place in India during the last three years, we should find a great increase in the wages of labour and the prices of commodities, which should warn us as to what the consequences might be if we were to accelerate the process already going on so rapidly by any artificial inflation of the currency. If you unnaturally stimulated the rise of prices by an over-issue of paper circulation you ran considerable risk of changing the healthy action of commerce into a feverish excitement which was sure to bring about a reaction. If we continued to go on as we had done for the last two or three years, the result would be that many articles of Indian produce might be driven out of the market by the competition of other countries, and he therefore thought that the Government ought to be exceedingly cautious how it took any step that might unduly accelerate the tendency to a general advance, as might be the case under the system of paper currency which to any considerable extent represented securities and not bullion. Such an advance might even reach a point seriously embarrassing to the Government if the general rise in the rate of wages and cost of living made the present scale of salaries and the pay of troops no longer adequate.* For these reasons he thought it by far the wisest course to adhere to the principle of paper currency adopted in England as laid down in Sir Charles Wood's despatch."

Not only was the Government anxious to put a limit on the issue over and above making it convertible, but it did not want to be vested with the legal authority to issue notes. In a despatch dated April 27, 1859,† to the Secretary of State, the Government of the day observed :—

"We believe that the convertibility of the notes on demand would not be a sufficient guarantee against over-issue. When once the paper currency is established in public confidence, the temptation to take dangerous advantage of this confidence will be very great in a time of difficulty, if the power of doing so is left in the hands of the Government of India alone. Restriction by law, either to a certain amount of issue absolutely, or to any amount relative to the balances in India, will, in our opinion, be necessary.

* During the bank suspension period in England it is to be noted that the Army and the Navy were paid in gold, for fear of causing discontent.

†For a copy of it, *see* Commons Paper 183, of 1860, p. 1.

> We think that such a law ought to be passed by Parliament, and not by the Legislative Council of India."

Equally sane was the view of the Government in 1876 with regard to the rupee currency. The Bengal Chamber of Commerce, it will be recalled, had urged upon the Government of India to close the Mints to the free coinage of silver, without opening them to the free coinage of gold—a project which practically meant that the Government should undertake the management of the rupee currency. The reply of the Government of India was a sharp rebuke. It declared *:—

> "8. . .. the Chamber invite the Government to take a measure calculated to enhance indefinitely the value of the rupee by suspending the long-established legal right of all comers to have silver bullion manufactured upon uniform conditions under State supervision into legal-tender coin, and temporarily substituting a system of coinage at the discretion of the State. . . .
>
> * * * * *
>
> "11. It is essential to a sound system of currency that it be automatic. No man or body of men can ascertain whether at any particular moment the interests of the community as a whole require an increase or diminution of the currency; still less, how much increase or how much decrease is, at any moment, exactly needed. No Government which aspires to keep its currency in a sound condition would be justified in attempting that impossible task, or in leaving the community, even for a short interval, without a fixed metallic standard of value. Under an 'open coinage system' these things regulate themselves without official interference." . .

Now, compare with this the later pronouncements of the Government with regard to the principles governing the paper and rupee currency respectively. During the war, when the Government of India resorted to the enlargement of paper issues, Honourable Members of the Supreme Legislative Council pointed out the effects it would produce on prices in India. But the late Hon. Sir Wm. Meyer, who as a Finance Minister piloted the Indian finances during the last war, in the course of a speech on the Indian Paper Currency (Amendment) Bill, dated September 5, 1917, replied †:—

> "The note circulation was sixty crores before the war and is now about a hundred crores. But the Hon. Mr. Sarma shivered

* Resolution of the Government of India, relating to the Depreciation in the Value of Silver, dated September 22, 1870, Commons Paper 449 of 1893.

† *S.L.C.P*, Vol. LVI, p. 35.

> at the idea of inflation. I may remind him that one of the accepted(!) doctrines of economists is that artificial inflation of paper currency only exists when the note circulation is not fully covered. Now we have covered every rupee of our note circulation . . . . in securities. . . ." [How could there be an inflation ?]

The change in the Government's view with regard to the rupee currency is equally noteworthy. In 1908, when the exchange value of the rupee fell below par, the Government was reminded that it was the result of the excessive coinage of rupees. But although in 1876 the Government did not think it was possible for it to so increase and decrease the currency to suit the needs of commerce, yet in 1908 the Government advanced the opposite view. The Finance Minister, the Hon. Mr. Baker, in his reply, went on to argue*:—

> "In the first place the whole of the new coinage, that we have undertaken during this period has been undertaken solely to meet the demands of trade. Not one single rupee has been added to the circulation except to enable us to meet these demands. . . ."

Now, if it is dangerous to entrust a Government with the power to manage currency, how very dangerous is it to entrust it to the Government of India, which professes to carry out its trust on the basis of doctrines such as these! No one is so ill-instructed in these days as to suppose that these are sound maxims. If security is enough, what need is there for convertibility? If currency is issued only in response to trade demand, what fear is there of over-issue? A Government acting on such a principle may well go on indefinitely increasing the currency without remorse. History abounds with instances of ruin caused by the management of currencies on such naive principles as these.† Happily for the country, the paper currency profoundly altered in its basis—one might almost say, tampered with—in 1920 by the Government is yet far away from currencies regulated on the theory enunciated by the Finance Minister. It is the rupee currency which has been, ever since the Mint closure, the chief source of danger to the welfare of the Indian people, particularly because of the principle governing its issue. Because that principle has the support, in

* Cf. Financial Statement for 1908—9, p. 229

† Cf. E. R. A. Seligman, *Currency Inflation and Public Debts* New York, 1922, *passim*.

itself a surprising thing, of such eminent authorities as Prof. Keynes,* Mr. Shirras,† and the Chamberlain Commission,‡ it cannot alter the case for depriving the Government of this power of managing the rupee currency, for the principle is essentially unsound. The reason why the fallacy in the reasoning, that there could be no excess of rupees because of their being issued in response to trade demand, does not appear on the surface is due to the peculiar nature of money. Money is said to be wanted only because money has a purchasing power. That is no doubt true, but that does not quite explain why people so incessantly want money, even when they know that the value of money is so unstable. Indeed, if purchasing power was the only consideration we should not find such a desire for the current means of purchase. That desire can only be accounted for by the fact that money has a differential advantage over other goods, in that it has in the highest degree what Menger called the quality of saleability. That one can more often buy at a bargain than sell at a bargain is simply another way of stating that every one desires to hold his resources in the most saleable form of money. In this sense it is absolutely true that no more money can be issued than there is demand for. But from that it does not follow that there can be no over-issue of money purely for the currency needs at any given time. All money is acquired in response to trade or services, but all money is not retained in currency. Indeed, all commodities are exchanged for money, because money is supposed to bear the option of being used for non-monetary purposes. In the case of the rupee the option-of-use quality is non-existent. Consequently, although issued in response to trade demand, it remains in currency whether it is wanted or not, and thus tends to bring about its depreciation. That such a depreciation is possible cannot be denied even by those who maintain that rupees are issued only in response to trade demand, otherwise why should they be so very anxious for an increase of the gold reserves of the country. But the danger to the rupee currency does not merely arise from the possibility of indiscretion on the part of the Government. Besides the Government there have been statesmen in India so interested in the welfare of their fellow-subjects that

* Of. Cit., p 111. † Of cit., p. 39. ‡ Report, par. 66

they have rebuked the Government on several occasions for not making the profits on rupee coinage available for the advancement of the moral and material progress of the country,* and in 1907 the profits on rupees were actually emlpoyed in the extension of railways. It must fill every one with horror and despair to contemplate the consequences sure to emanate from the manipulation of currency for such ends. Is it not time this source of danger and temptation be removed by depriving the Government of this power to manage the rupee currency? But what is the means of bringing this about? If it is desirable to do away with the management then convertibility is an insufficient measure: for with convertibility the rupee will still remain a managed rupee. Only the complete stoppage of rupee coinage will remove the governmental interference in the management of Indian currency; and it is this that we must therefore ask for.

Queer as it may seem, SAFETY LIES IN AN INCONVERTIBLE *Rupee with a fixed limit of Issue.*

* Such a sober politician as the late Mr Gokhale took the lead in this matter Cf. his speech in the *Financial Statement* for 1907-8, pp. 203-4; and the same indiscretion is repeated by Prof. V. G. Kale in his *Currency Reform in India*, 1919, p. 65.

# INDEX

# INDEX

# INDEX

# INDEX

# INDEX